Securing Windows Server 2003

Other Microsoft Windows resources from O'Reilly

Related titles
DNS on Windows Server 2003

Windows Server 2003 in a Nutshell

Windows Server Hacks

Windows 2000 Administration in a Nutshell

Windows 2000 Commands Pocket Reference

Windows Books Resource Center
windows.oreilly.com is a complete catalog of O'Reilly's Windows and Office books, including sample chapters and code examples.

oreillynet.com is the essential portal for developers interested in open and emerging technologies, including new platforms, programming languages, and operating systems.

Conferences
O'Reilly brings diverse innovators together to nurture the ideas that spark revolutionary industries. We specialize in documenting the latest tools and systems, translating the innovator's knowledge into useful skills for those in the trenches. Visit *conferences.oreilly.com* for our upcoming events.

Safari Bookshelf (*safari.oreilly.com*) is the premier online reference library for programmers and IT professionals. Conduct searches across more than 1,000 books. Subscribers can zero in on answers to time-critical questions in a matter of seconds. Read the books on your Bookshelf from cover to cover or simply flip to the page you need. Try it today with a free trial.

Securing Windows Server 2003

Mike Danseglio

O'REILLY®

Beijing · Cambridge · Farnham · Köln · Paris · Sebastopol · Taipei · Tokyo

Securing Windows Server 2003
by Mike Danseglio

Copyright © 2005 O'Reilly Media, Inc. All rights reserved.
Printed in the United States of America.

Published by O'Reilly Media, Inc., 1005 Gravenstein Highway North, Sebastopol, CA 95472.

O'Reilly books may be purchased for educational, business, or sales promotional use. Online editions are also available for most titles (*safari.oreilly.com*). For more information, contact our corporate/institutional sales department: (800) 998-9938 or *corporate@oreilly.com*.

Editors:	Robbie Allen and John Osborn
Production Editor:	Claire Cloutier
Cover Designer:	Emma Colby
Interior Designer:	Melanie Wang

Printing History:

November 2004:   First Edition.

 This book uses RepKover™, a durable and flexible lay-flat binding.

ISBN: 0-596-00685-3
[M]

For my Kleo. I miss you every day, little one.
Your strength was my inspiration for this book.

Table of Contents

Preface

As the title implies, this book is about security in the Windows Server 2003 operating system and how to put it to work on behalf of your organization and your users.

Windows Server 2003 has quite a number of uses. It can serve in a network support role, supplying services such as DHCP and DNS. It can take a more active part in object management, such as when used as an Active Directory domain controller. It can also serve as a personal operating system, since it is so closely tied with its brother, Windows XP. In this role, it might provide security of local data and host-based network communications.

I've broken down the book by technology. Each chapter covers one or more of the technologies that Windows Server 2003 provides. Most of these—such as IPSec—are primarily security-focused. However, some—such as DHCP—are not.

Each chapter answers three questions about the technology it covers:

What the technology is and how it's used
> Each chapter begins with a brief introduction to the technology. If you have no idea what this technology does, this is a quick way to learn about it. I don't bore you with marketing spin or polished terms. I just tell you what the technology does and what a few of the most likely uses might be.

How the technology works
> To understand a technology's security implications, you usually need to know how it works. This section is kept deliberately brief and sometimes excludes details that you don't need to know. I do this, not to keep you in the dark, but to make sure that you're focused on how the thing works and that you don't bog down in minutia that, in your job and scope, would be useless and distracting.

How to use the technology properly to serve your system
> Through lots of research and direct interaction, the book's contributors and I have come up with a set of common uses for the technologies detailed in this book. All of these are based on real experience, not theoretical environments or

marketing-based blue sky scenarios. I take you through these examples and show you exactly how to get the desired results. In most cases, I provide a keystroke level of detail to ensure you don't miss a thing.

Of course, all possible scenarios can't be covered in this book. Because the different Windows components can be configured so many ways, it would be impossible to present all approaches to all possible scenarios. But the content of this book should provide more than enough information for you to make decisions on the technologies as well as test and understand them.

One thing you'll see in this book that you may not have seen before is Security Showdown sections. This is a point-counterpoint debate between myself and a semifictional coworker, Don. I use it several times throughout the book to show that some debates about security methodologies and techniques are not easily answered. Some of them are so contentious that they seem like religious debates at times. You should understand that security-focused individuals tend to have opinions about security and that they like to argue with people who hold different values. These are good-natured and often help explain both positions. So please read these sections as I've intended, as an open discussion of the merits and hazards of multiple tactics to achieve the same goal.

What's in This Book?

This book consists of 15 chapters and an appendix. Here is a brief overview of each chapter:

Chapter 1, *Introduction to Windows Server 2003 Security*
    This chapter sets the stage for the book by providing an introduction to Windows Server 2003.

Chapter 2, *Basics of Computer Security*
    This chapter covers basic computer security concepts, including cryptography and fundamental practices for security administrators.

Chapter 3, *Physical Security*
    This chapter covers various aspects of physical security, which is essential for any data security to succeed.

Chapter 4, *File System Security*
    This chapter is all about securing files with Encrypting File System and other file-oriented technologies.

Chapter 5, *Group Policy and Security Templates*
    This chapter focuses on using Group Policy as a security tool and utilizing Security Templates.

Chapter 6, *Running Secure Code*
    This chapter discusses ways you can protect against running bad applications.

Chapter 7, *Authentication*

This chapter covers the various authentication protocols supported by Windows Server 2003, including Kerberos.

Chapter 8, *IP Security*

This chapter examines IP Security and its proper deployment to secure network communication.

Chapter 9, *Certificates and Public Key Infrastructure*

This chapter is an exhaustive examination of PKI and certificate-based cryptography.

Chapter 10, *Smart Card Technology*

This chapter covers smart card technologies and their proper deployment.

Chapter 11, *DHCP and DNS Security*

This chapter focuses on the grotesque lack of security in DHCP and DNS technologies and how you can try to shore them up.

Chapter 12, *Internet Information Services Security*

This chapter covers Internet Information Services security, or the lack thereof.

Chapter 13, *Active Directory Security*

This chapter examines Active Directory design and operation from a security standpoint, including proper planning and deployment, as well as securing data between domain controllers.

Chapter 14, *Remote Access Security*

This chapter covers the security features of Remote Access, including dial-up and VPN connectivity.

Chapter 15, *Auditing and Ongoing Security*

This chapter covers additional topics such as administrative security, patch management, and auditing.

Appendix, *Sending Secure Email*

This appendix covers topics relating to secure email.

Audience

I've written this book for the folks who actually use Windows Server 2003. If you use Windows Server 2003 in any environment, you most likely already have a basic knowledge of the operating system and how it works. So that fundamental knowledge is assumed in this book.

I jump straight into the topics of interest in the security area. However, I don't assume you have a deep architectural knowledge of every Windows component and subsystem. So, when appropriate, I use diagrams and flowcharts to help illustrate security-specific features and components that you may not have encountered.

About This Book

This book covers Windows Server 2003 and some amount of Windows XP security. It is almost entirely focused on Windows-based security, but has several sections on non-Windows security topics that must be understood. These include physical security, security policy, and risk management.

Now that you know what this book is about, I should explain what this book is not about. This book is not a compendious reference of every possible setting or feature in Windows. It's not intended to be a sit-on-the-shelf book. I've written it so that you can actually use the content to do things. As such, it's direct and brief. I've included links to resources when appropriate so you can access the reference-style material you might need without having to slog through it here.

Assumptions This Book Makes

You should have a fundamental understanding of Windows server operating systems to use this book. If you have experience installing and running Windows Server 2003 and Windows XP, you will get a lot out of this book.

To an extent, I assume you're running Windows Server 2003 in a business of some significant size. Many of the examples in the book assume a network infrastructure that is most often seen in mid- to large-size businesses, such as a distributed Active Directory forest. However, I do attempt to frame each example with the assumptions I make for it. In most cases, these examples will scale up or down to fit your specific environment.

You do not need an in-depth understanding of security topics or a Ph.D. in mathematics to read this book. Who would use a book like that anyway? Those people already know everything.

Conventions Used in This Book

The following typographical conventions are used in this book:

Plain text
> Indicates menu titles, menu options, menu buttons, and keyboard accelerators (such as Alt and Ctrl).

Italic
> Indicates new terms, URLs, email addresses, filenames, file extensions, pathnames, directories, and Unix utilities.

`Constant width`
> Indicates commands, options, switches, parameters, the contents of files, or the output from commands.

Constant width bold
Shows commands or other text that should be typed literally by the user.

Constant width italic
Shows text that should be replaced with user-supplied values.

 This icon signifies a tip, suggestion, or general note.

 This icon indicates a warning or caution.

Comments and Questions

Please address comments and questions concerning this book to the publisher:

O'Reilly Media, Inc.
1005 Gravenstein Highway North
Sebastopol, CA 95472
(800) 998-9938 (in the United States or Canada)
(707) 829-0515 (international or local)
(707) 829-0104 (fax)

We have a web page for this book, where we list errata, examples, and any additional information. You can access this page at:

http://www.oreilly.com/catalog/securews

To comment or ask technical questions about this book, send email to:

bookquestions@oreilly.com

For more information about our books, conferences, Resource Centers, and the O'Reilly Network, see our web site at:

http://www.oreilly.com

Acknowledgments

This book would not be possible without the gracious help of the following individuals, who are listed in no particular order.

Content
Derek Melber wrote the Active Directory chapter of this book. Without that content, there would have been a huge hole in coverage of Active Directory. Well done, Derek.

Technical input

No single person could possibly know everything about Windows security. I was happy to receive technical input from all of these people, without whom the book would have been a series of errors and overstatements:

Darren Canavor, Drew Cooper, Michael Cretzman, David Cross, William Dixon, Eric Fitzgerald, Trevor Freeman, Robert Gu, Cliff Hall, Vic Heller, Pat Hoffer, Don Jones, Connie LaChasse, Derek Melber, James McIllece, Jeremy Moskowitz, Radia Perlman, Xiaohong Su, Laudon Williams, and Helle Vu and her Microsoft PKI Test Team (whom I paid in beer and toys for their services).

Writing input

Knowing how to say something is often more important than saying it. I received great advice on this front from Vince "Kahuna" Abella, Jen Bayer, John Coates, Jason Garms, Ken Klavonic, Jason Rush, Michiko Short, Dionysia Sofos, and Jim Wickham. We worked (and argued) through many ideas together and were able to turn them into useful information in this book.

Technical editing

I feel lucky in that I had great technical editing feedback from Rick Kingslan, Joe Richards, Paul Robichaux, Mitch Tulloch, and Bob Williams. My thanks to them for catching all the errors and omissions before the readers did.

Editing

Robbie Allen did a phenomenal job of putting up with my crap and still getting the book out. He made me look good by fixing so many errors. Most importantly, Robbie ran interference when he knew I couldn't deal with situations. For that, I'll be eternally grateful. I could never have shipped this book without him.

Norma Emory did a very thorough copyedit, and Brian MacDonald supplied a valuable developmental edit at just the right time that helped streamline the content, especially in the PKI chapter. Rob Romano of O'Reilly did a bang-up job of the book's art. John Osborn of O'Reilly was a great support when Robbie and I needed help but spared the rod more often than not.

Special thanks

Special thanks go to Jeremy Eisenman of nCipher for the use of an HSM, Brian Valentine for the WIM, and my students for helping me think in new ways during every class.

Deepest thanks go to my wife Heide, who supported me all through the process of this book's creation. This book took precedence over so many other things, and she always understood and made it OK. She also made sure I got the work done!

CHAPTER 1

Introduction to Windows Server 2003 Security

Security is one of the primary functions of any server-based operating system. Without security, any user or program could do anything to your servers—and wreak havoc on your ability to effectively manage the environment. As a security administrator, you want to provide functionality and security to your users without burdening them or restricting them in a way that hinders their work. This is the mark of a great security administrator: the ability to successfully balance the security of proprietary and personal data and the usability of your systems in a way that maximizes the productivity of your organization. This book will show you how to do exactly that.

What Is Security?

To have a meaningful discussion of security in Windows Server 2003, we should first establish what security is. A dictionary definition might refer to security as "measures adopted to provide safety." For the purposes of this book, that definition will work very well.

Computer security is not normally defined as a state of safety. Rather, it is defined as the collection of protective measures (including technology-based and non-technology-based measures) that provide a defined level of safety. When security is mentioned throughout the book, you should keep this definition in mind. Security is neither a single protective measure nor a complete protection against all attacks. It is a set of measures that provide the desired level of protection.

Many readers may say "I want *complete security* for my data against all attacks. Tell me how to do that." The only solution that provides complete security is to put that data on a hard drive, incinerate the drive until it is completely turned to vapor, and then randomly mix the hard drive vapor with outside air until completely dissipated. Anything less is a compromise of security in the interest of another business factor such as usability or cost. The need for such compromises is a common theme throughout all computer security topics and is discussed in every chapter of this book.

What Is Windows Server 2003?

Windows Server 2003 in its several editions is the latest generation of the Microsoft family of server operating systems, incorporating the advances achieved by the earlier Windows NT and Windows 2000 Server families of products. These operating systems have been tested and proven since 1993 to be a solid platform for applications and server-based functions.

Windows XP is also derived from the same code base as Windows Server 2003. This common base ensures that the core functionality of the two operating systems remains identical. The numerous benefits this approach provides include the following:

Common device drivers
If you've ever gone searching for a device driver for a specific operating system, you can immediately recognize this benefit. Hardware vendors need to write only one device driver that will work on both operating systems.

Software compatibility
If software works on Windows XP, it'll work on Windows Server 2003.

More stable core
All the work done to make Windows XP a solid and stable operating system benefits Windows Server 2003, as it's simply an extension of that work. Windows Server 2003 benefits from having had an additional year of bulletproofing done on top of the enormous work already done on Windows XP. In addition, many flaws discovered in Windows XP were fixed in Windows Server 2003 before it even shipped.

Unified user interface and experience
Although some of the "pretty" features have been removed from Windows Server 2003 to gain performance benefits, an administrator who is comfortable working with Windows XP will immediately feel at home with the server version. Almost all user interface objects are in the same place, which decreases the time needed to master the differences.

Windows Server 2003 is the operating system platform that is used by Microsoft and other companies to run server-based software such as Microsoft SQL Server and Microsoft Exchange Server. This requires Windows Server 2003 to be scalable while achieving the stability needed to provide critical business services and the necessary uptime. Windows Server 2003 delivers in all these areas. This is in contrast to other server operating systems that usually focus on only one of the following areas: raw horsepower, usability, security, and the like. Windows provides strength in all these areas without significantly detracting from any others. In this book, I'll focus on security and show how the built-in features of Windows can help provide very secure solutions without sacrificing the other benefits of the operating system.

Security Design in Windows Server 2003

The Windows NT and Windows 2000 operating systems were designed from inception to be secure. Both enforce user logon and ensure that all software runs within the context of an account, which can be restricted or permitted appropriately. Windows security is not limited to user logon–based security, but extends to all objects within the operating system. Files on the hard drive, entries in the registry, software components—all these elements have a security aspect. Operating system components can access objects only with the appropriate permissions and credentials. This can be both a benefit and a detriment.

Enforcing security restrictions on every component of the operating system can seem daunting. Access checks must occur when one Windows component talks to another. These include programs, device drivers, core operating system components, and so on—in short, everything. Setting appropriate security permissions is a task that requires detailed knowledge of the subject and the interaction between the components being configured. Misconfiguration of these permissions could cause undesirable behavior ranging in severity from a minor and easily fixed problem to a complete and irreversible loss of functionality.

The fact that this daunting security environment is part of the fundamental design of Windows Server 2003 is a big advantage. If strong and pervasive security is not designed into the core of an operating system (for example, Windows 95), it is nearly impossible to add it later. Developers and testers may find holes or make compromises when they patch security into an operating system. Legitimate components may already be designed to take advantage of the lack of security. The environment would necessarily be less secure than one designed for security from the beginning.

Security Features in the Windows Server 2003 Family

Compared to their predecessors, Windows NT and Windows 2000 provided numerous security features. In fact, since the inception of Windows NT Advanced Server 3.1 in 1993, the Windows NT family has always provided a suite of security-focused features. Over the years, subsequent releases have added new security features and expanded existing ones.

Just as with earlier releases, Windows Server 2003 improves on previous operating system releases by enhancing existing security features and adding new ones. Some of the security features that are carried forward from previous versions include:

Kerberos authentication
> Kerberos is a standardized and widely used network authentication protocol. Originally incorporated into Windows 2000, Kerberos provides proof of identity for users, computers, and services running on Windows 2000, Windows XP

Professional, and Windows Server 2003. Prior to the use of Kerberos in Windows 2000, NTLM was used as the authentication protocol. While NTLM is still a useful protocol for maintaining compatibility with older operating systems, it is not as efficient or interoperable as Kerberos. NTLM also has some security shortfalls that Kerberos does not. Kerberos and NTLM are described in depth in Chapter 7.

IP Security

TCP/IP's use has become widespread. While TCP/IP provides enormous benefits over other network protocols, it is not desirable from a security standpoint. Data sent over a network with this suite of protocols is not designed to be secure and can be easily intercepted and decoded. IP Security (IPSec) is a set of RFC-based standards that defines how data can be sent securely via TCP/IP. Data can be encrypted, digitally signed, or both using IPSec. Many hardware devices, such as routers and firewalls, support IPSec communications. IPSec is available in Windows 2000, Windows XP Professional, and Windows Server 2003 family products. It's incorporated right into the networking drivers, which allows it to integrate smoothly with the existing TCP/IP software. The implementation is compliant with established standards, which allows Windows Server 2003 to communicate with other properly equipped network devices via IPSec. IPSec is described in depth in Chapter 8.

Encrypting File System

Files on a hard drive may be compromised when the physical security of a computer is compromised. Because physical security cannot always be guaranteed, an additional measure of safety can be taken to safeguard against data stolen from a hard drive. The Encrypting File System (EFS) can be used to encrypt the data written to the hard drive. This ensures that only the user holding the appropriate decryption key can retrieve the data. If the hard drive is compromised and the decryption key is not stored on that hard drive, the data is not readable. EFS is described in depth in Chapter 4.

Group Policy

When you create a security infrastructure, you want the ability to make configuration settings for all objects within that infrastructure. These settings often include minimum password requirements, user session restrictions, and so on. Group Policy provides a mechanism to transparently configure computers within an enterprise with all desired security settings. You, as an administrator, can force users and computers to use the settings you want. This allows you to keep your users more secure and protect them against a multitude of attacks. Users do not know how they receive the security settings, and the settings cannot be overridden without the appropriate privilege. Group Policy is described in depth in Chapter 5.

Certificate Services

Use of public key cryptography has become common across a wide variety of applications and services. Public key certificates are essential to providing and trusting these keys across organizations and around the world. Certificate Services provides a software application that receives, approves, issues, and stores public key certificates. This book examines both the cryptography behind the certificates and exactly how to plan and deploy a public key infrastructure (PKI). Public key cryptography is discussed in depth in Chapter 2. Because of the complexity and importance of Certificate Services, it is covered in depth in Chapter 9.

Smart card support

All security in Windows is based on the concept of a user context. This user context is usually proven to the local and remote computers with the use of a username and password supplied by the user or software component. Because the username and password are bits of information a user enters, they can be replicated or stolen in a variety of ways. Requiring some physical component in addition to the username and password data adds a great deal of security to that user context. Smart cards are devices that are designed to store information that, in conjunction with a personal identification number (PIN), takes the place of the username and password. If you require the use of smart cards, a user cannot prove his identity without both the physical card and the corresponding PIN. Smart cards are discussed in depth in Chapter 10.

Security Enhancements in Windows XP and the Windows Server 2003 Family

During the development of Windows XP and Windows Server 2003, Microsoft gave close scrutiny to all security components. This scrutiny culminated in a months-long halt to the development of Windows so that Microsoft could take the time it needed to examine existing code, processes, and features for vulnerabilities and weaknesses. These were analyzed and addressed in a methodical fashion. Occasionally this review bordered on the brutal in its results, with entire features being removed from the operating system when they could not be made reasonably secure. Some less frequently used or more vulnerable features were not removed, although their configuration was changed to make them disabled or not installed by default. Although this effort did delay the production of Windows Server 2003, it was certainly a valuable investment of time and resources.

Because Windows XP and Windows Server 2003 share many common software components, some of the security improvements affect both versions in the same way. Besides the strong underlying security architecture, you can directly observe and configure several improvements. A few of the big ones include:

Encrypting File System (EFS) improvements
> In Windows 2000, EFS provided encryption for files with the DESX encryption algorithm (a stronger variant of the Data Encryption Standard—DES). This algorithm provides better data protection than the generic DES algorithm, but several stronger options are available. In Windows XP and Windows Server 2003, EFS can now encrypt files using the triple-DES (3DES) encryption algorithm. This improvement provides 168-bit encryption for data, which is reasonably resistant to most current attacks. Another improvement to EFS is the removal of the requirement for a data recovery agent. This allows you to configure EFS with fewer options for recovering data but increases the level of data security. In addition, you can add more than one user to an EFS file to allow multiple users to decrypt the contents. This enables more secure file sharing both locally and over the network.

Smart card support
> Windows 2000 provided a foundation for smart card support. However, its use was somewhat restricted to logon operations within an Active Directory domain. A common administrative scenario that was not addressed by Windows 2000 smart card support was using smart card credentials to run specific applications while remaining logged in as a different user. This scenario is addressed in Windows XP and Windows Server 2003 and allows an administrator to remain logged in as a standard user while providing specific, isolated administrative functions using credentials from the smart card.

IP Security
> While the underlying components of IPSec remain largely the same as Windows 2000, a significant improvement is introduced for its monitoring and troubleshooting. In Windows 2000, a standalone tool called IPSecMon was the only way to discover what IPSec was doing. In Windows XP and Windows Server 2003, a new Microsoft Management Console tool is available to monitor IPSec. Called IP Security Monitor, it provides detail about the operation of IPSec and can help assess misconfigurations. IP Security Monitor works well as a complement to other tools such as Resultant Set of Policy (RSoP), Netdiag, Network Monitor, and the IPSec logs to help ensure that your IPSec communications are indeed secure.

Security Enhancements in Windows Server 2003, Standard Server Edition

Windows Server 2003 Standard Server is the foundation of the Windows Server 2003 server architecture. This version of Windows Server 2003 is suitable for a wide range of applications in a server environment, providing services from file storage to user account management to HTTP. Because it is likely to be used for many different tasks, numerous security improvements were made to Windows Server 2003 Standard Server, including:

Even stronger encryption for EFS

Because EFS is a strong method of protection against physical compromise of a computer, you want to use the strongest possible encryption available. The recently finalized Advanced Encryption Standard (AES) algorithm was designed as a replacement for the DES suite of algorithms. EFS supports file encryption with this new AES algorithm, which uses a 256-bit key.

Enhanced Group Policy

Group Policy remains the easiest and most powerful way to restrict and configure a user's experience. Because numerous features have been added to Windows XP and Windows Server 2003, new group policy settings were added to configure them. This allows these new features to be used exactly as you want across the organization or disabled entirely when appropriate. And proper configuration of all features through rich Group Policy is essential to deploying and configuring more secure client and server environments.

Software Restriction Policy

Users running arbitrary software from unsafe sources are some of the biggest security risks you will face as an administrator. Ensuring they are protected from email attachments and software sent on CD-ROM or other removable media is critical. Virus scanners are often effective in combating this issue, but new virus variants and methods appear almost daily. To help stop the problem at its source, Windows Server 2003 Standard Server provides a specific type of group policy restriction called the software restriction policy (SRP). This allows you to describe what programs users can or cannot run. Users who try to run software disallowed by this policy will not be successful, and their computers will remain safe. Although SRP was made available in Windows XP, the management and control of those policies are greatly enhanced with Windows Server 2003. Configuring SRP is discussed in depth in Chapter 6.

Improved certification authority

The certification authority available on Windows 2000 provided a simple way to configure and issue certificates to users and computers in an enterprise. It did not provide a great deal of flexibility for customization or newly developed PKI-aware applications. Windows Server 2003 Standard Server further improves the certification authority by offering new features such as client autoenrollment to automatically deploy and manage client certificates, configurable application and issuance policies to give the administrator deep configuration control of issued certificates, and certificate authority administrative roles to help prevent any single administrator from holding too much power within a certification authority.

IIS Lockdown

Internet Information Services (IIS) provides web-based services for Windows and is in widespread use. It is frequently used on computers that are accessed anonymously from the Internet. Its security must often be more relaxed than other computers within an organization to allow some of its primary functions to run correctly. In addition, many administrators never configure IIS on their servers, especially if it is not intended to be used on that computer or if the computer is not exposed directly to the Internet.

Because IIS is, by its nature, frequently exposed to the Internet, its relaxed security requirements and its frequent misconfiguration make it one of the biggest areas of security exposure for Windows 2000. This is addressed by Windows Server 2003 in a straightforward manner: IIS is not installed by default. When IIS is explicitly installed, most of its features are disabled and must be enabled manually. For previous versions of IIS and Windows, a tool called IIS Lockdown was provided. The functionality of that tool is now integrated with Windows Server 2003 and IIS 6.0. For more information on IIS and its new security options, see Chapter 12.

Security Enhancements in Windows Server 2003, Enterprise Server Edition

Windows Server 2003 Enterprise Server is the most feature-rich version of Windows Server 2003 available. It has the ability to scale to meet the needs of most deployments.

There are several differences in the security features between Windows Server 2003 Standard Server and Windows Server 2003 Enterprise Server. Windows Server 2003 Enterprise Server provides all the functionality of Windows Server 2003 Standard Server plus several enhancements:

Configurable certificate templates

All public key certificate requests are issued based on configuration settings. Some of these settings are configured for each certification authority, while others are configured based on the type of certificate requested. Certificate templates contain the settings for each type of certificate that can be issued. In Windows Server 2003 Enterprise Server, certificate templates can be created, deleted, and customized to provide the exact functionality desired.

Separation of certification authority roles

A number of standards define how a certification authority must be administered. Most of them require different users to perform different tasks, such as requiring an administrator to configure the certification authority and a separate auditor to monitor the activity on that certification authority. Role separation is a new feature that requires a user to have no more than one certification authority management role. This is to ensure that there are no "superusers" who can perform all tasks and potentially mask their own manipulation of the system.

Key recovery

When a certification authority receives a certificate request, the request normally contains the public key, the requester's identification, and other information that is configured in the certificate template. The associated private key is generated on the requester's computer and does not leave that computer, assuring its secrecy. When key recovery is configured on Windows Server 2003, the certificate request process will also securely provide the requester's private key to the certification authority. The certification authority will then encrypt and store that key until the requester needs to recover it. At that time, a designated recovery agent will decrypt the private key and provide it to the requester. The requester need not lose all data encrypted with that private key if it is stored on the certification authority.

There are many other differences between Windows Server 2003 Standard and Enterprise, including a significant price difference. Any decision to deploy one version in preference to the other should be made only after carefully planning the server's business roles and determining the needs it must meet. Once you define the functionality you need, you should carefully review each product's features and from that determine which one best suits your needs. Both servers provide the same level of core security—it's not easier to compromise Standard Server than the Enterprise Edition. The difference lies in the additional security features that Enterprise Edition provides and the higher cost of its license.

Summary

The Windows Server 2003 family of servers is the latest generation of operating systems to be built on the Windows NT code base. It provides numerous security advantages over its predecessors, but ultimately the level of security it provides depends on the level of security you want to deploy.

Throughout this book, I will examine the various security technologies that are a part of Windows Server 2003. Typically, I'll provide a detailed explanation of how each works and how it can be used within a comprehensive security plan. Then I'll examine common scenarios and show you, in detail, how to employ the technology correctly. I'll also cross-reference complementary security technologies that should be used together to provide a complete solution.

CHAPTER 2
Basics of Computer Security

Computer security is becoming more and more important to Windows administrators. This trend is a result of several conditions in today's world, including the increase of computer competence among evildoers, the worldwide terror threat that was clearly illustrated on September 11, 2001, and the proliferation of computers and the Internet. Many companies are retraining their IT staffs to be more security-aware. Threat modeling in the data center has become commonplace. There are even vendor-independent security certifications, such as Certified Information Systems Security Professional (CISSP), which have become widely known and sought after. But before the security of your Windows Server 2003 computers can be addressed, you need to understand some of the basic concepts and terms of computer security. In this chapter, I'll introduce you to computer security fundamentals such as encryption and show you the difference between technology-based security and administration-based security. I'll also discuss other fundamental concepts like password strength and the idea of authorization versus authentication. If you are new to computer security or would like a refresher of the concepts and terms that will be used in the rest of the book, this chapter is for you.

Why Computer Security Is Important

It's almost impossible not to recognize the importance of computer security in today's economic and political climate. The national news media devotes ample coverage to computer security issues, often sensationalizing the latest computer virus or so-called hacker attack. In fact, that very sensationalism can distract you from day-to-day security threats. Computer security encompasses a wide range of potential threats and basic concepts, and you can never underestimate the real business costs of security failures. Consider the following:

- Most companies store proprietary information regarding their products or services both online and in hardcopy documents. If competitors obtain a company's product specifications and plans, they may be able to drive it out of business.

- Companies have a legal obligation to protect the sensitive employee information they collect for payroll and other purposes. If the security of that information is compromised, the company may be subject to lawsuits and legal fines.

- Some companies, such as banks, are subject to laws regarding the security of the information they use. For example, if a bank's customer records are accessed by unauthorized personnel, the bank can be subject to hundreds of thousands of dollars in fines, not to mention lawsuits by their customers.

Sixty years ago, companies kept sensitive information in locked filing cabinets. The cabinets made the information difficult to share throughout the company, but they helped keep the information secure. Today, almost every important piece of company information is kept on a computer. Computers make it very easy for employees to share information with one another—even if that information is sensitive and shouldn't be shared. As more and more information is stored on computers, computer security will play a more important role in protecting that information. And because some of that information is more sensitive than others, you should consider defining the security criteria for that information. See the "How Secure Is 'Secure Enough'?" sidebar and Chapter 15 for more information.

How Secure Is "Secure Enough"?

How do your company's employees know when the workday is over? Generally, a written policy establishes regular working hours. So how do you know what corporate information is sensitive and how strongly it should be protected? Again, a written policy should tell you. The primary focus of this book is to tell you how to implement security measures, but only your company's written security policies can tell you *what* security measures are required.

If your company doesn't have a written security policy, it needs one. A security policy provides you with guidelines that tell you how much security is necessary in your environment. The policy also provides you, as a Windows administrator, with the authority to implement actual security mechanisms to protect corporate information. Security policy is discussed in depth in Chapter 15.

Creating a Security Policy Is a Political Problem

Too often, administrators are asked to create and enforce the security policies for their companies. Often, the assignment is implied in a simple question like "Hey, are our files secure?" But administrators are rarely in a position to create and enforce corporate security policies. For example, do you consider yourself an expert on intellectual property law? What about trade secret law? Do you know what damage a competitor could do if they obtained information from your company's files? Can you quantify the risk of such damage in financial terms? Do you know exactly what information each and every person in your company needs to do her job? Most likely, the answer to one or more of these questions is "no." That's why security needs to be much more than a technical concern; it needs to be a *political* concern first. Throughout most of this book, I'll show you *how* to use Windows technologies to implement security, but the political powers at your company—management and executive—need to define the need for security and tell you *what* needs to be implemented or protected.

For security to be effective, you need to have a clear, written policy. That policy needs to be written—or at least approved—by the people in your company with the power to make it stick. Generally, that group should include the president of your company or perhaps a chief operating officer or a group of managers. Without full management support, a security policy may not be implemented correctly and will almost certainly be circumvented or discarded in the future.

Think of security policy as a form of law and you and your fellow administrators as police officers. Your company's management represents Congress or some other legislative body. Your job as a police officer is to *enforce* the law. You don't get to decide what's legal and what isn't; that's Congress' role. Without clearly written laws from Congress, you won't be able to enforce anything. As a police officer, you know that all laws you enforce have passed through Congress, and you can be reasonably sure that these laws represent the best interest of the people they govern. You cannot distinguish between good and bad laws; you enforce them all evenhandedly.

Sometimes a good police officer sees a law that should be struck down or modified. As a security administrator, you will periodically see security policies or procedures that are flawed. This does not entitle you to deviate from the job; the policy in question may be crucial for another element of the business that's outside your scope of awareness. However, as a good employee and administrator, you should be alert for such flaws and bring them to the attention of the policy makers. In this way, your expertise flows back into the policy-making process, and the system is improved.

What's in a Good Security Policy?

So what constitutes a good security policy? Policies will differ widely from company to company and may differ widely even between departments within the same company. But all good security policies will have a number of common characteristics. Every good security policy:

Is written
> Written security policies can be easily communicated without loss or distortion of information.

Focuses on rules, not implementation
> In other words, the policy shouldn't worry about *how* the policy is enforced, it should just state what will be enforced. For example, "Documents pertaining to

company projects must never be accessible to nonemployees" is a good policy statement. "Documents must be protected by NTFS security" is a poor policy statement, because it focuses on the implementation of the policy.

Covers both printed and online information

A policy that says "Information pertaining to company projects must never be accessible to nonemployees" works because it can apply both to physical paper documents as well as electronic documents. This broader coverage ensures that the security policy is comprehensive. Simply requiring password protection for electronic documents, for example, won't protect those documents once they are printed and left lying on someone's desk.

Defines information-handling roles within the organization

One role might be "document owner," applied to the person or group of people responsible for the security and contents of a particular group of documents. Another role might be "document reviewer," applied to anyone who needs to read documents but doesn't need to modify them and isn't responsible for the documents' security. These roles can be used to determine what people can do with documents. For example, your policy might state that "Document reviewers may access only electronic documents and may not create hardcopies of the documents they review." This type of policy gives you, the policy enforcer, clear directions on how to configure your computer systems to comply with the policy.

Ensures that separate roles are held by different people

The person who submits a document for classification, for example, should not be the same person that assigns the classification. This could lead to a single person owning the entire security process, thus negating the benefit of having multiple people involved in a security audit trail of the secured information. A general rule is that, within reason, the more individually implemented roles that are required to implement a security process, the less likely it is that a single compromised or untrustworthy employee can compromise the data. This practice is often called *role separation* and is discussed throughout the rest of this book.

Requires and specifies the implementation of audit procedures or policies

Perhaps a quarterly audit of the security mechanisms is appropriate in your company, allowing an independent person to verify that you've implemented measures to enforce and comply with the written policy. Other companies might need more frequent or less frequent audits, depending upon their needs.

As you can see, security policies can be quite detailed. They don't have to start that way; simply starting with a basic written policy is better than having no policy at all. As your company grows more comfortable with the policy and begins to better identify potential security risks, the policy can be revised and expanded accordingly. For more information on security policies, see Chapter 15.

Security Enforcement Mechanisms

Operating systems like Windows Server 2003 provide powerful tools to protect data, including the Encrypting File System (EFS), file permissions, user accounts and passwords, and much more. As powerful as those tools are, though, they can't provide a completely secure environment by themselves. For example, Windows can ensure that only authorized users have access to a particular file, but Windows can't stop users from leaving hardcopies of the document lying on their desks. All the computer security in the world is useless if information that is protected on your computers can be compromised in other ways. Similarly, suppose you implement a complete security plan includes computer-based file protection and locked filing cabinets. Without a well-thought-out physical security plan, there might not be anything stopping someone from carrying away a computer or filing cabinet, which would completely defeat your security measures.

Any useful computer security plan has to provide a complete security solution: one that addresses both technological solutions and administration solutions to security threats. If you find that your company is unwilling or unable to implement a complete security plan, you probably don't need to spend a lot of time worrying about the computer-specific aspects of security. Again, you don't need to spend weeks locking down your servers against intruders if your company won't keep sensitive computers in a locked room where they can't be easily carried away by a physical intruder.

That said, security is not an all-or-nothing game. While locking your file cabinet may not be a complete security solution, it is one element of that solution. Locking the front door, arming the burglar alarm, and hiring a security guard may be other elements that contribute to an overall security solution for the data in that filing cabinet. The same works for data security. While IPSec, for example, may be a great security solution, it should never be considered the only data security mechanism in a whole solution. Other components such as Internet Connection Firewall (ICF), EFS, NTFS, or access control lists (ACLs) may be incorporated with IPSec to provide a complete security solution. Each is valuable by itself; together, they provide the desired level of protection.

All security described in this book can be broken down as a combination of two security approaches: technology-based and administration-based. The primary focus of this book is technology-based security, that is, the security controls that you can implement with Windows-based technologies. However, administration-based security is equally important in any security implementation. Moreover, some controls are entirely administration-based. Attention should always be paid to both approaches.

Technology-Based Security

Technology-based .security mechanisms are the ones that you, as a Windows administrator, will implement and work with most closely. You probably bought this book to learn about them. These mechanisms include:

Strong, hard-to-guess passwords for user accounts
Generally, passwords should be at least eight characters long and contain uppercase letters, lowercase letters, symbols, and numbers. Symbols and numbers should appear in the middle of the password, ensuring that users can't make up easy-to-guess passwords like "DonJones1234." Although this password technically qualifies as a complex password, it's obviously a pretty simple and easily guessed one if used for a user named Don Jones. Generally, the longer and more complex a password, the harder it is to obtain by an attacker. Password considerations are detailed later in this chapter.

Carefully applied permissions on files and folders to help keep unauthorized users out
These permissions should comply with your written security policies. You should never rely on the default NTFS permissions as described in Chapter 4; instead, always apply specific permissions to your files to ensure that they're completely secure. While Windows Server 2003 does offer a more secure set of default NTFS permissions, it still includes the Everyone group with Read permissions by default, which is all most intruders will need to gain access to proprietary information.

The use of encryption to protect sensitive data
Data contained on portable computers is especially at risk, since portable computers are so easy to steal. Encrypting data using Windows' Encrypting File System (EFS) or other encryption mechanisms helps ensure that data is useless even if physically stolen. Encryption (through other technologies) can also be used to protect data in transit across the network, as I'll explain in Chapter 8.

Mechanisms like smart cards that allow you to positively identify users
Passwords can be easy to guess, and users may write them down (despite policies to the contrary). Smart cards are more secure because they don't require users to remember anything but a short personal identification number (PIN). Also, users won't know that someone has stolen their password, if that happens; users are immediately aware that a smart card has been stolen, if it happens, and can immediately report it to an administrator. The administrator can then issue a new card and disable the old one, eliminating the security breach. Another benefit to the smart card is its hiding of private key data from attackers who do not have physical access to the card, which provides a huge boundary for an attacker to overcome. The benefits of smart cards are discussed in great detail in Chapter 10.

Techniques to prevent unauthorized code from running on company computers

I'll discuss these techniques throughout this book, including software restrictions and code signing, and how you can administer them to provide the best security possible to your users. These techniques ensure that viruses and other unauthorized code aren't allowed to execute on your computers. Viruses are a favored way for attackers to gain confidential information, and preventing them from running is a great start to a more secure computing environment.

Disabling unnecessary network services

This is done to help prevent them from becoming security vulnerabilities. For example, versions of Windows prior to Windows Server 2003 often installed Internet Information Services (IIS) by default. IIS was used in several well-publicized instances to propagate viruses throughout large organizations, such as the well-known Code Red virus. Had administrators at the time been more security-conscious, they would have disabled IIS on computers where it wasn't being used, drastically reducing the number of potential entry points for these viruses.

Technology-based security provides powerful tools for protecting information. Unfortunately, too many companies rely solely on technology-based solutions and forget about the necessity of administrative security.

Administration-Based Security

Administration-based security consists of carefully written security policies, day-to-day practices, and other concepts that aren't implemented by a computer or an operating system. Administration-based security mechanisms include:

A written security policy

I've already discussed some of the characteristics of a good security policy. In addition to previously mentioned components, a good security policy identifies role holders and responsibilities. It should tell employees what information they may access and outline penalties for employees who break or circumvent security policies. Everyone has a stake in corporate security, from the bottom-rung employee to the CEO. Each role must be clearly defined.

Policies that require users to physically secure hardcopies of data

Policies should address security of information in all its forms: electronic and physical. The policies should also address the destruction of data (i.e., shredding versus recycling). This point is discussed throughout the book.

Physically protected assets

For example, your servers should be kept in locked data centers, and your doors should have some type of access control mechanism. I'll discuss physical security in more detail in Chapter 3.

Minimized access
>You must ensure both procedurally and practically that employees log on with user accounts that have only the access required to complete the employees' job tasks. This is known as the *principle of least access*, which I'll discuss later in this chapter and throughout the rest of this book.

Regular audits of access and configuration
>The only way to know that the data you carefully secured is still secure is to periodically check. Audits should be scheduled to verify the security defined by policy is still in force. Audits are discussed in Chapter 15.

You'd be surprised at the number of companies that spend hundreds of thousands of dollars a year to secure their computer-based data and then allow authorized employees to print that data and leave the hardcopies lying around on their desks for passers-by to read. Technology-enforced security is *useless* without administrative security; in fact, administrative security should be the driving force behind security in any company, and technology-based security should be used only to implement those administrative policies.

It's not up to you to enforce administrative security, unless you happen to be the president of your company as well as its network administrator. Administrative security has to come from the top down and be enforced by all levels of company management. Your company should have an education program, perhaps administered by human resources personnel, to educate users on their rights and responsibilities with regard to company security. Many companies are forming new information security departments to deal exclusively with the administrative side of security, user education, and auditing.

POLA: The Principle of Least Access

One of the most common (and commonsense) concepts in computer security is POLA, the principle of least access. It simply states that employees should have access to only the resources they need to perform their day-to-day tasks. POLA applies to noncomputer security, although most people don't think of it that way very often.

 You may also hear POLA referred to as the principle of least privilege.

For example, suppose you work for a bank. As in most banks, your customers' data is kept in computer files, but you still have to maintain paper records for many documents, such as signature cards. Those cards might be kept in locked cabinets in your bank's headquarters. Tellers don't need to access the signature cards very often, so they aren't given keys to the cabinets. When a teller needs to access a signature card, he asks a manager to unlock the cabinet and retrieve the card. That's POLA in action. It's not that the bank doesn't want the tellers to see the cards; the bank just doesn't want tellers to have casual access to the cards. The tellers have the least amount of access possible for the day-to-day needs, and when they need to go beyond those needs on occasion, they have a means to do so.

In the world of computer security, POLA is most often applied to administrators. Although administrators have job tasks that require a great deal of privilege over computer systems, they're also regular users who check email, work with Microsoft Word, and surf the Internet. POLA means that administrators should have a regular user account that doesn't have administrative privileges and that they should use that account when they're performing regular, day-to-day tasks. A second computer account might belong to the Domain Admins group, and administrators would log on with that account to perform administrative tasks.

POLA offers real security benefits in any environment. Because of the job tasks they must complete, administrators (when logged on with an administrative user account) have an incredible amount of control over a company's computer systems. Programs like viruses can take advantage of that control and wreak havoc on a company's network. When administrators use a regular user account, though, they can perform only actions that a regular user could perform—limiting the scope of damage a malicious virus can cause.

This book describes numerous technology-specific ways to implement POLA. These methods often restrict users or force role separation between user accounts. However, POLA doesn't come from these software enforcements. POLA must be a direct result of a strong security policy and good administrative practices. Security policy is discussed in Chapter 15, and good administrative practices are discussed throughout this book.

 Remember that Windows Server 2003 supports the RUNAS command, which allows an administrator to log on to her client computer using a regular user account and then launch administrative utilities under the authority of an administrative user account. RUNAS helps maintain the security principle and protection of POLA.

Key-Based Cryptography

Cryptography is perhaps one of the most important fundamental concepts in computer security today. Cryptography has played a role in every version of Windows to date, and it plays an even larger role in Windows Server 2003 than ever before. Many of the technologies and techniques I discuss in this book rely heavily on cryptography, including smart cards, data encryption, digital signatures, and email security. For that reason, it's important that you understand what cryptography is and how it works.

At its heart, cryptography is about scrambling data so that only the sender and the recipient can read it. Modern cryptography serves the same purpose as the secret decoder ring you had as a kid, although it's vastly more complex and powerful than that ring. Modern cryptography uses complicated mathematical processes called *algorithms* to scramble and unscramble data. And I mean *complicated*. In fact, some of the world's most popular cryptography algorithms are so complex and unique that they've received worldwide patents.

There are three basic kinds of cryptography: keyed hashing, shared secret keys, and public keys. Each provides a slightly different technique for encrypting data, and each is used for a specific set of purposes.

Hashing

A *hash* is a form of encryption in which a computer uses a well-known algorithm to scramble data and return a fixed-length result that is reasonably unique to the data. Theoretically, hashes aren't really that secure, because the algorithm is often *very* well known. The most common use of a hash, however, cannot be decrypted by anyone. Such *one-way hashes* are "lossy" and do not contain a full representation of all the original data, making it impossible to ever decrypt the result and retrieve the original data. As an analogy, one-way hashes are similar to your fingerprint. I can't make a complete copy of you out of your fingerprint, but I can statistically rely on the fact that your thumbprint is unique to you.

One-way hashes are similar to long division. For example, five divided by six equals one, with a remainder of one. Think of the five as the original data, the six as part of the hash algorithm, and the answer (one with a remainder of one) as the encrypted result. So long as you have the complete answer and the original algorithm, you can work the math backward to arrive at the original data. A one-way hash might discard the remainder and keep only part of the answer: one. Even if you have the original algorithm, you can't determine what the original data was with only part of the answer.

Windows Server 2003 uses a one-way cryptographic hash to store local user passwords within its Security Accounts Manager (SAM) and within Active Directory. Once a password is hashed and stored, Windows Server 2003 has absolutely no way of retrieving the original password. When Windows Server 2003 needs to check the password, it takes the password that the user types in, runs it through the same hash, and compares the result to the stored, hashed password. If the two match, the user must have typed the correct password.

 The description of password checking here is an oversimplification, because Windows Server 2003 actually uses a more complicated means of validating user passwords, as you'll learn in Chapter 7.

The hashed password makes it impossible to easily retrieve the original password, even for an administrator. If a user forgets his password, an administrator's only option is to reset the password, create a new one, and communicate it to the user, because the original password is hashed.

Hashing Isn't Totally Secure

I do need to note that hashed passwords aren't completely unbreakable. The algorithm that Windows uses to create its hashes is fairly well known, especially to security specialists and programmers. This fact allows attackers to conduct *dictionary attacks* to try and discover the original unhashed passwords. For example, suppose a user named Kevin uses "Doggie" as his password. Hashed, that password might be "34$_h7G5Sjka$87*jdjN#lSlnjFnl@ln#ln$#lk4nln" or something similar. Now suppose that an attacker is able to obtain the hashed password. Since the hash algorithm is well known, the attacker simply has to run lots of words through the algorithm until a matching hash is produced. When the attacker runs "Doggie" through the algorithm, and it produces the matching hash "34$_h7G5Sjka$87*jdjN#lSln-jFnl@ln#ln$#lk4nln," the attacker knows that the original password is "Doggie" and can use that password to gain access to network resources.

Dictionary attacks can be quite sophisticated, although they can obviously take a long time to run. Attackers know that users commonly substitute the number 1 for the letter I, commonly capitalize the first character of a password, use the number 3 for the letter E, or the symbol @ for the letter O. Attackers take these common substitutions into account when conducting dictionary attacks.

The best defense against dictionary attacks is to ensure passwords can't be recognized as words and that passwords are as long as possible. "mY5#CoMp_teR" is a decent password, because it isn't based on a single English word and it's littered with numbers and symbols. It's also quite long, meaning a dictionary attack—which generally focuses on English words with common letter substitutions—won't likely guess it.

Enforcing this type of password requirement is discussed later in this chapter.

Shared Secret Key Cryptography

Shared secrets are one of the oldest forms of cryptography. A shared secret is simply an encryption key that is known to two or more parties. The same key is used to encrypt and decrypt data. Because the same key is used to encrypt and decrypt data, shared secrets are sometimes referred to as *symmetric keys*, meaning both cryptographic operations—encryption and decryption—are performed with the same key. Similarly, shared secret key cryptographic algorithms (such as AES and DES) are known as *symmetric algorithms*, because the keys are the same for encryption and decryption.

The problem with shared secrets lies in securely communicating the secret to the other parties. Until each party has a copy of the key, they won't be able to encrypt or decrypt data with it. And because the key itself is usually transmitted over the network, the key can theoretically be intercepted by unauthorized users, compromising the security of any data encrypted with the key. There are ways to combat this key interception, such as using a specific cryptographic technique called the Diffie-Hellman Key Exchange algorithm to publicly exchange private key material.

As you'll learn in Chapter 7, Windows Server 2003 makes use of shared secrets for Kerberos authentication and many other types of data protection. The operating system takes special steps to secure the shared secret from interception, which is also discussed in Chapter 7.

Public Key Cryptography

Public key cryptography, also referred to as public/private key cryptography, is perhaps the most secure form of cryptography available today. Encryption and decryption is performed with a pair of keys, rather than just one. One key, the *private key*, is held only by an individual person or computer. That key can be used to either encrypt or decrypt data (but not both).

The other half of the equation is a *public key*. Public keys are easily accessible by almost anyone. The public half of a key pair can be used to decrypt anything that was encrypted with the private half or, more frequently, to encrypt things that will be decrypted with the private half. Simply put, when one key encrypts data, only the other key can decrypt that data. Which key encrypts and which decrypts is important and depends entirely on the type of protection desired.

Because the two keys work together, they are sometimes referred to as *asymmetric keys*, and the corresponding algorithms are known as *asymmetric algorithms*. RSA is an example of a popular asymmetric algorithm.

Public key cryptography has hundreds of uses in today's business environments. If someone wants to send you sensitive data, they obtain your public key and use it to encrypt the data. Once encrypted, only your private key can be used to decrypt the data. Public key cryptography can also be used to verify the contents of less-sensitive data. For example, suppose you want to send an email to someone and you want her to be able to verify that the contents of the email didn't change in transit. You could send the email in clear (unencrypted) text, along with a second copy that you encrypted with your private key. Anyone receiving the email could use your public key to decrypt the attachment and ensure that the now-decrypted version of the email matches the original. Since only your private key could have been used to create the encrypted version, recipients can be sure that the email came from you and wasn't altered in transit.

Public key cryptography's single point of weakness is the private key. If your private key is obtained by anyone else, everything you use the key for is compromised. As you'll learn in Chapter 9, most public key implementations include a means for publishing revocation lists. Revocation lists contain a list of keys that should no longer be used because they have been compromised, similar to the "bad credit card lists" distributed to retail merchants.

Windows Server 2003 allows you to use public key cryptography in a number of ways, although it doesn't require you to use public key cryptography at all. Public keys can be used instead of shared secrets in Kerberos authentication (Chapter 7), for example. They are also used in several optional security components within Windows Server 2003 including EFS, IIS, and IPSec. The most common uses for public key cryptography are for tasks performed by third-party software, such as accessing applications or validating user identity on the Internet. Windows Server 2003 provides a complete public key cryptography infrastructure, which I'll cover in Chapter 9.

You've Probably Already Used Public Key Encryption

If you've ever purchased something on the Internet, you've probably used public key encryption without knowing it. Whenever the little lock icon appears on your web browser's status bar, public key encryption is in use.

Secure web servers—servers capable of using the HTTPS (Hypertext Transport Protocol Secure) protocol—are configured with digital encryption certificates. When your web browser requests a secure connection, the server transmits a copy of its certificate to your web browser. The certificate contains the server's public encryption key, which your web browser is able to read. Your browser uses the server's public key to encrypt a randomly generated session key, which the browser transmits to the server. The server uses its public key to decrypt the session key, providing a shared key that the browser and server can use to encrypt further communications between them. There are several standards for this exchange and the resultant secure communication, including Secure Sockets Layer (SSL) and Transport Layer Security (TLS).

The server's certificate ensures that your browser is communicating with the server you intended, because only the intended server possesses the private key necessary to decrypt that initial session key. Public key encryption has been making Internet shopping safer for millions of users who don't even realize that they're using it!

Authorization and Authentication

Two additional security concepts you need to be familiar with are authorization and authentication.

Authentication is the process of validating a user's identity, ensuring he is who he says he is. Passwords are a common component in the authentication process, although the use of biometric components like smart cards and fingerprint readers are becoming more common.

Authorization is the process of determining what an authenticated user has access to. Windows Server 2003 uses a variety of mechanisms to accomplish authorization on files and folders, for remote access, and so forth, which you'll learn about throughout this book.

Password Basics

Passwords are the basis of most security schemes, including Windows Server 2003. Passwords are used by client computers to log on to a domain, and they're also used by users to log on to a domain or to a computer's local user accounts.

In a default Windows Server 2003 environment, passwords are the keys to the entire kingdom. For example, the only difference between an unauthorized intruder and a domain administrator is that the domain administrator knows the password to a powerful user account. For that reason, it's important that you implement procedures and policies that require strong passwords of your users.

What's a Strong Password?

Strong passwords are passwords that are difficult for intruders to guess or successfully duplicate. So, before you can accurately define *strong*, you need to understand the techniques that an intruder might use to compromise a password.

As I mentioned earlier in this chapter, Windows Server 2003 stores passwords after running them through a one-way hash. That means attackers have no possibility of successfully decrypting a stored password, even if they somehow come into possession of a stored password. If an attacker does manage to obtain a hashed password and knows the hash algorithm (which she will), she must run combinations of passwords through the hash algorithm until she gets a hash result that matches the stored password. Then she'll know the clear-text version of the password. The most common form of this attack is called a *dictionary attack*, which I described earlier.

Another way attackers can compromise a password is to try and log on to the domain, guessing a new password until the domain lets them in. There are readily available tools that can do this for the attacker rapidly. This technique is often called a *brute force attack*, because the attacker is simply trying every possible password in a brute attempt to obtain the right one. This technique isn't really that different than the first technique, although an administrator can implement account policies to limit the effectiveness of this attack. If you've also implemented a strong password requirement, the odds that the attacker can guess the right password before being caught or locked out are slim.

 Always consider implementing strict account lockout policies within your domain and on the local accounts of individual computers. Account lockout causes the computer (or domain) to disable a user account after a specific number of bad passwords are tried (say, 10 attempts). An attacker attempting to log on by guessing passwords won't get very many guesses before the account is disabled—and useless. You can also configure Windows to leave the account locked out until an administrator takes action, giving you the opportunity to discover why the account was locked out and take protective measures if necessary. For more on account lockout policies, see Chapter 13.

Enforcing Strong Passwords

Strong passwords, therefore, are ones that are especially hard to guess. Words that wouldn't ever appear in a dictionary are good choices, too. The common definition of a strong password is:

- At least eight characters in length. Fifteen characters or more is best because of the cryptography Windows uses behind the scenes. With passwords, longer is *always* better.
- Contains characters from at least three of the following categories:
  - Uppercase letters
  - Lowercase letters
  - Numbers
  - Symbols, punctuation marks, and nonkeyboard characters
- Changed on a regular basis.
- Never shared.

So while "doggie" would be a poor password choice, "My:-)Doggie" would be considered a much stronger password, and "ih8!myy0At3m3eL$0" would be very resistant to attacks. Requiring users to change their passwords on a regular basis—every 30 to 60 days—also makes attacks more difficult. I'll further discuss how Windows Server 2003 stores passwords later in this book.

Of course, changing passwords frequently makes it more difficult for users to remember their passwords, making it more likely that they will write them down. Encourage users to use passwords that combine two or more words to form a "pass phrase." Here are some good examples, but please never use these actual passwords (attackers read this book too!):

---

bIrth@dAy

Notice that the second character of each word is capitalized, making the change in case easier to remember.

k130iz@N1C3ki7Ty

This is a good example of letter replacement and "dewd speak"—replacing letters with numbers that look similar and mixing upper- and lowercase. Pronounced out loud (at least by me) it says "Kleo is a nice kitty," which is easy to remember. Also, this scheme might help the crazy cat lady type who has numerous pets, as she could simply replace Kleo's name at the beginning of the string with another one at the next password change. Another benefit of this password is that it's large enough to present any attacker with a difficult task to decrypt while still remaining relatively easy for the crazy cat lady to memorize.

Ti@@eR!p3Twe3zil

The first and last letters are capitalized, and two letters (lowercase *g*) are replaced with @ symbols, a less common substitution. If you have a pet weasel named Tigger, this is a reasonably easy one to remember while being cryptographically difficult to attack.

R456!rtS

For a user with the last name of Roberts, this isn't bad. It substitutes meaningless numbers for three of the characters and throws punctuation in the middle. Although a bit short, this is a strong password.

My cat, Lucy, likes to bathe in my presence.

This is a true pass phrase. It's quite long with 44 total characters, which makes it exceedingly difficult to attack with current brute force password attacks. It's also easy for me to remember—in fact, my cat Lucy reminds me of it nightly. And while it seems a bit longish, it's pretty easy to type because it's a sentence. I'm used to typing English sentences with spaces, capitalization, and punctuation. So the length is offset by the natural feel of it.

The trick is to come up with passwords that have some meaning or follow some private pattern, while keeping them nice and complex. The best password in the world is the longest and most complex one that you won't forget.

The strongest password is no good if users divulge them or write them down. Make sure your security policy helps your users understand the necessity of keeping their passwords secret from everyone, including administrators and managers. For rarely used accounts with high privilege, such as Enterprise Admins or Schema Admins, consider generating a complex pseudorandom password and locking it in a safe or perhaps giving portions of the password to multiple administrators for safekeeping.

Windows Server 2003 lets you configure the password policies on your computers' local accounts and in Active Directory. As shown in Figure 2-1, you can configure account lockout policies as well as set a minimum password length, maximum password age, and so on. To configure these policies on a standalone or member server, use the Microsoft Management Console (MMC) Local Security Policy snap-in. A complete example, including portions of a security policy, appears in Chapter 5.

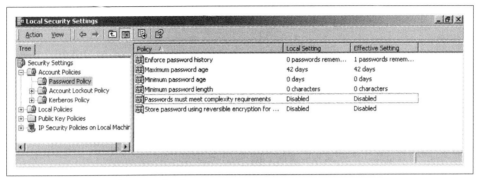

Figure 2-1. Account and password policies

 The Local Security Policy snap-in allows you to modify policy for a computer's local accounts. On a domain controller, the Local Security Policy snap-in is unavailable due to the computer's role in the domain.

Network Security

The first step most companies take for their physical security is simple: locked doors to keep out potential intruders. Network security plays a similar role in computer security, by simply keeping unauthorized personnel away from your sensitive data. Network security also needs to address the times when data must be transmitted outside of your company's secure network and should address the possibility of your network's outer security being compromised. I'll discuss two kinds of network security in this book: *boundary security*, which is a technique that protects your network from outside attack and is intended to protect your network from intrusion, and *data encryption*, which protects data that travels outside your network and provides data protection within your secure network.

Boundary Security

Network security, like physical security, starts with strong walls. Typically, those walls are provided by *firewalls*, which prevent unauthorized data from traveling to and from your network. Windows Server 2003 doesn't provide the functionality required of a firewall, although it does provide an excellent platform for firewall products, such as Microsoft's Internet Security and Acceleration Server.

There are a wide variety of firewall products on the market, including some that are built into or run on various Microsoft operating systems. Other firewalls are implemented as standalone devices. All networks should have one or more firewalls, period. Exactly which firewall product you should use, where you should place it, and how you should configure it, is beyond the scope of this book. However, you'll find dedicated books available for most major firewall products that can help you make those decisions.

Windows Server 2003 does provide one feature that firewalls can take advantage of: *port blocking*. Port blocking allows Windows Server 2003 to accept or reject specific types of data sent to or from specific IP addresses or ports. Firewalls use this capability to prevent unauthorized data from entering or leaving your network. Firewalls usually expand on this capability by analyzing data and allowing only authorized users to send or receive data outside your network. You can read more about Windows Server 2003's basic port blocking capabilities in Chapter 14.

Another feature provided by Windows Server 2003 that can effectively block some communications is IP Security (IPSec). IPSec is normally used to secure or digitally sign TCP/IP traffic. However, it can very effectively block network traffic as well. IPSec is covered in depth in Chapter 8.

Windows Server 2003 has a firewall feature—called the Internet Connection Firewall, or ICF—that's designed to provide basic protection for computers on the Internet. You may be familiar with ICF from Windows XP Professional and Windows XP Home. However, don't mistake ICF for a dedicated firewall product. ICF doesn't contain the broad features, scalability, or functionality of a dedicated firewall solution, and you shouldn't rely on ICF alone to protect a corporate network from Internet-based attacks. Because I don't consider ICF an appropriate solution for network administrators, I won't cover it in detail. If you'd like to learn more about ICF for use on a home network, check out Windows' Help and Support Center.

It is worth noting that many of today's attacks come from inside the network. Certainly a huge number of attackers are trying to gain access to your network through your firewalls, web servers, and so forth. But an increasing number of attacks are coming from trusted users, vendors, and guests who have direct access to your network. In these cases, boundary security that consists of a single boundary between your network and the Internet is useless. Only layered security will help mitigate this attack. Layering security is discussed throughout this book.

Data Encryption

When data must leave your network, it should be protected from electronic eavesdropping. Data encryption can provide that protection. Windows Server 2003 supports IP Security, or IPSec, which includes built-in data encryption capabilities.

Windows Server 2003 also supports the use of Virtual Private Networks, which provide an easy means for encrypting data transmitted between two points. You'll learn about IPSec in Chapter 8, and Virtual Private Networks are covered in Chapter 14. IPSec is most useful within your network, while Virtual Private Networks are designed for data traveling between networks over the Internet. IPSec, in fact, provides the encryption technology for one type of Virtual Private Network, as you'll learn in Chapter 14.

Even if your network has powerful firewalls to keep intruders out, you must plan for the possibility that those firewalls will fail or that an intruder will find a way around them. The example of the Trojan horse from classical mythology teaches us that intruders can sneak inside your perimeter, and if you don't provide security at an internal layer, your enterprise (or Troy) will be compromised. By routinely encrypting sensitive data on your network and taking the other important security measures I'll discuss throughout this book, you'll protect your network even if intruders manage to break through your "outer walls." Data encryption is also useful for those who need to access sensitive corporate data from across the public Internet.

Keeping Your Eyes Open

The key to successful security is constant vigilance. While you can configure your servers with strong passwords, restrictive security policies, and powerful network protection, attackers can almost always find a way to get through if they're determined enough. The only way to catch them is to constantly be on your guard. This includes watching for security intrusion signs, patching security vulnerabilities immediately, and remaining alert for new conditions that could expose your enterprise to attack.

Windows Server 2003 provides a number of tools for monitoring security. The Windows Event Log has an entire Security Log in it, and Windows supports complete security auditing for file and object access, user logons, and so forth. You'll learn more about auditing in Chapter 15, where I'll also discuss the Security Log in more detail and show several types of security events that you can look for in your environment. Web sites, DNS services, and many other network services maintain their own logs, which you can review for possible security problems. You'll learn about those services and their security implications throughout this book.

Of course, you'll want to establish a regular pattern of security checks in your environment. That way, you'll be sure to check each and every facet of your organization that is open to security breaches. The exact contents of a security checklist will depend on your organization's security needs, but might include:

Checking the Security Event Log for any unusual messages
> If you've enabled auditing, watch for events that indicate a user is being repeatedly denied access to a file. That behavior may indicate an in-progress attack.

Watching the Security Event Log for logon failures
>These are often a first pointer to attackers performing a dictionary attack, both successful and not.

Inventorying servers' software regularly
>Regular inventories of software installed on all servers should be conducted to be sure unauthorized software hasn't been installed. Use the Task Manager to view running processes and make sure each process is approved within your organization.

Reviewing firewall and intrusion detection system logs to look for attacks
>Some firewall products can even scan their own logs for common attacks and alert you automatically; check your firewall product to see if it has this or other intrusion detection features.

Chapter 15 contains a more complete guide to ongoing auditing and security maintenance.

Summary

Computer security is a lot more complicated than just making your users change their passwords every so often. Computer security involves powerful cryptography, a variety of security mechanisms, and principles designed to prevent security breaches. But computer security does not stand alone. It requires strong administrative security policies that define security within your organization and policies that protect data even after it leaves the computers.

All companies need to have a written security policy that describes what resources require protection. Such a policy must come from company management, not from network administrators. Several characteristics of a good policy were shown in this chapter.

The encryption technologies used within Windows Server 2003 (hashing, shared secret encryption, and public key encryption) are important to understand. These technologies play a key role in Windows authentication, the Encrypting File System, and other security technologies. You'll see them come up again and again in the following chapters.

Strong passwords are extremely important in all environments. Attackers use many techniques to compromise passwords. But there are ways that you can help users (and other administrators!) create memorable, strong passwords on your network.

In the next chapters, I'll build on the basics that I covered here. You'll find that encryption plays a strong role throughout Windows Server 2003, for example. Also, much of the rest of this book focuses on *how* to implement security, meaning you should already have a written policy that tells you *what* needs to be secured.

CHAPTER 3

Physical Security

You might think it strange for a book on Windows Server 2003 security to discuss physical security. After all, Windows Server 2003 itself doesn't make any significant contribution to physical security. Yet without physical security, Windows Server 2003's own powerful security mechanisms can be easily defeated. As you learned in Chapter 2, administrative security mechanisms—including physical security—are just as important as the technology-based security provided by Windows Server 2003.

In this chapter, I'm going to start by identifying physical security vulnerabilities. Try to get into a paranoid frame of mind for this discussion and think of every little thing that could represent a weak point in your company's physical security. After we've gotten a plate full of potential vulnerabilities, I'll show you some strategies for addressing these vulnerabilities. By the end of the chapter, you'll automatically scrutinize the physical security of virtually every building you enter—a good behavior for a security administrator.

Identifying Physical Security Vulnerabilities

No matter how secure your server operating systems are, physical security vulnerabilities can allow intruders—or even misguided employees—to compromise your company's information security. Learning to identify physical security vulnerabilities requires you to look at your entire network from a whole new point of view. It's time to get paranoid and think about all the ways in which your network's security could be compromised.

 Even if your company's security plans don't require you to provide a solution for every physical security vulnerability you find, you should make yourself aware of them all anyway. You never know when your company might need to provide extra security for some collection of information, and understanding your vulnerabilities up front will make that task easier.

As an example, let's consider a typical corporate office with typical physical security measures. The office contains any number of client computers, which connect to network jacks installed in the walls. Those jacks, in turn, are wired back to a cable plant, where they're all connected to switches or hubs. Larger offices might have several cable plants, or wiring closets, which are connected to one another. The office probably has a data center of some size. Access to the data center might be restricted to individuals with an authorized card key, or the data center's door might have a combination lock. Within the data center, servers are installed in racks. Especially security-aware companies might even keep a log of who goes in and out of the computer room. Card key systems make that easier, since the systems can usually keep track of who uses the door in a master log file.

Your company's offices are probably similar to that theoretical office. And that means your network is positively *full* of security vulnerabilities.

Your People

Tommy Lee Jones said it best in the movie *Men in Black*: people are stupid. They're often the biggest security vulnerability in any company. From a two-person office to a multinational conglomerate, you can expect some significant percentage of people will have no idea about security. These people are a bigger risk than the failure of a firewall, the opening of a port, or the receipt of an email virus.

For example, my mother works at a law firm that forecloses on homes. Not a wonderful thing, but she tries really hard to keep people in their homes. This firm sometimes has clients who bring checks or cash physically to the firm to keep from having their houses sold. At the front of the firm is a huge bulletproof glass window, and all the doors are equipped with proximity card readers that allow only authorized employees to open them. However, the receptionist allows anyone who shows up to enter the unprotected waiting room. In addition, the doors are often propped open to allow vendors easy access during their visits. So the security is in place but is being circumvented by people who are oblivious to the security implications—that is, until something bad happens.

Physical attack isn't the only avenue that's opened by people that don't think about security. Social engineering, or the practice of manipulating people to do what you want them to do, has gained popularity. This is partially fueled by Kevin Mitnick's book *The Art of Deception* from Wiley. In it, Mitnick shows numerous examples of situations in which users are simply asked for information such as passwords, domain names, and sensitive files. Naïve users and administrators provide this information far more often than you might expect. In fact, a recent study conducted by Infosecurity Europe 2004 found that 71 percent of users were willing to provide their password to a stranger on the street in exchange for a bar of chocolate.

Although I said people are stupid, I also believe that almost all people can be educated. A strong security awareness and employee education program can help mitigate people-based attacks. This should be required for all new employees and followed up periodically with refreshers, leaflets, posters, and so on. Maintaining even a minimal amount of security awareness greatly improves the security of most organizations.

What do people need to know about security? This is very role-dependent. A DNS administrator, for example, needs to know more specialized security information than a janitor. However, they both have common security responsibilities and should both be aware of a minimum set of security concepts and practices. Some of the more common security concepts that all employees should be made aware of include:

- Do not open email attachments that are sent from unknown individuals. In fact, never open executable email attachments at all, no matter who they come from.
- Leave the security on your computer alone. Don't disable virus scanners, firewalls, content filters, or anything else without permission.
- Report suspicious activities to corporate security. This can include activities such as an unknown individual trying to log onto a coworker's computer, folks wandering the halls without ID, or a phone call from "Joe in IT" asking for your password.
- Be especially careful with laptop or home computers. Any computer that you use on any network is potentially part of the corporate network.

Of course any security awareness and education program should be developed based on a risk analysis so that you're delivering the shortest and most effective message to your users. You should also ensure that your human resources and executive management groups approve and support any lessons you intend to teach users. After all, what good is security barking without some bite behind it?

Your Office

Who's plugging into your network? With network jacks liberally scattered throughout your office, how can you be sure that a visiting salesperson, or even the custodial staff, isn't plugging a laptop in, receiving a TCP/IP address via DHCP (Dynamic Host Configuration Protocol), and launching an automated attack against the data on your servers? Some intruders would think nothing of sneaking into your company's office dressed as a janitor and plugging a laptop into your network to see what data could be accessed from there.

Your office probably includes phone lines, and some of those phone lines are probably connected to computers. Are you sure those phone lines and computers are secured? That phone line connected to your sales manager's client computer is a security vulnerability that could be exploited to provide complete access to your entire network—bypassing your firewalls and other security measures.

What about the floppy disks and other removable media in your users' computers such as CD-ROMs and portable USB "thumb" drives? How many users actually use floppy disks for business purposes any more? Very few. But floppy disks are the number-two source of viruses on corporate networks (email is number one). If a malicious intruder were able to sneak ninja-like into your office, he could pop a floppy disk into any computer he found. That floppy disk could easily contain a trojan that collected sensitive data and transmitted it back to a home base across the Internet, all without your knowledge.

Floppy disks and other removable media are also a great way for disgruntled employees to make off with sensitive data. Some government facilities, for example, completely prohibit the use of removable media for this exact reason. Many have even gone as far as physically removing the removable drives from computers and installing hardware devices to prevent their reinstallation.

Your Laptops

Some percentage of the workforce of almost all companies uses laptops. These users may have a variety of requirements for using laptops such as travel, executives who need data access in meetings, and trainers who need laptops for presentations. In virtually all cases, these users will store data on the laptops that should not be disclosed to anyone outside the organization. This is often where the true cost of a loss occurs: not with the physical replacement of the laptop, but with the lost data.

Protecting the data on the laptop, as well as the laptop itself, is an administrator's nightmare. Essentially you need to secure something that cannot be completely secured and is often lightly managed or unmanaged. Measures can be taken, however, to help ensure that the loss of a laptop has a reduced impact on the security of the data it contains and your network as a whole.

Your Data Center

How secure is your data center? Combination door locks are easily defeated, since a careful observer can determine the door combination. Card keys are much better, but too often a company's card keys are managed by the company's facilities personnel, who aren't always fully aware of the implications of granting access to a data center.

And what about tailgating, the polite practice of holding the door open for the person coming in behind you? Although our society stresses being polite to our fellow humans, this practice is an enormous security vulnerability. Tailgating defeats card key logging, since someone enters the room without using her card key. Similarly, authorized personnel often take visitors into data centers, partially defeating the security of the data center by allowing an unauthorized person to carefully observe the security precautions that are in place. Company employees tend to assume that only authorized personnel are in the office, but it's usually pretty easy for a determined intruder to get into an office without anyone knowing. Always assume your office's first lines of defense—your receptionist, security guard, and locked doors—will fail and that your network and data center security will need to provide a second line of defense. This is one example of defense in depth.

Your Servers

How secure are your servers? Imagine a scenario in which an unauthorized person gained access to your data center. Could he restart servers with an MS-DOS floppy disk? Could he unplug key network connections? Although most companies use racks in their data centers, those racks are usually left unlocked. Few companies install the rear doors of the racks, making the servers within completely vulnerable to tampering. Some companies even leave the sidewalls off the racks in a misguided attempt to improve ventilation (which it doesn't), leaving the servers within vulnerable to tampering.

An intruder would have a field day in a data center with unlocked server cabinets. She could place network taps that capture every byte of data transmitted from a server or reboot servers with floppy disks and access their file systems. She could easily install keyboard monitor devices, which would quickly provide her with your most sensitive passwords. Making your servers physically inaccessible would prevent these types of security breaches, with the trade-off of reducing ease of access for administrators.

Your Wiring Closets

Do your wiring closets make security administration easier? Messy wiring closets are easy for an intruder to tap into, since the additional cables will never be noticed. Hubs and switches installed on open shelving or in unlocked racks are also easy targets, since intruders can connect to the devices' serial management ports and alter the way your network operates to conceal a security breach.

Many organizations keep their network cabling, switches, and hubs in easily accessible closets. If someone gained access to the office—usually not too difficult a task—she could plant equipment that transmitted a copy of your network's sensitive data to her home base. Failing to protect your network's cabling and infrastructure devices makes it easy for intruders to implement long-term schemes to compromise your company's sensitive data.

The Reality of Stolen Computers

Computer theft isn't rare. Once computers became reasonably small (smaller than a refrigerator), they became the target of thieves. Their high resale value and relative mystery (could they contain financial info, network maps, and the like?) contributed to this. So when I was recently asked to help assess the impact of a computer theft, I thought nothing of it. Generally speaking, the value of a computer is the hardware plus any difficult- or impossible-to-replace data it contains. I quickly found out that I was wrong. This stolen computer wasn't really a stolen computer.

Imagine a small data warehousing and consulting company with its headquarters in a light industrial park. I pass dozens of these every day when I go to work, and I hope you can form the picture in your mind. Most of these buildings are huge, with very high roofs, and many companies coexist within one larger structure. This is where the consulting company is.

The thief didn't, as you might expect, crash through the plate glass in the lobby and dash off with the receptionist's desktop. He had followed this rough procedure (based on physical evidence):

1. Identify the target computer. This is usually done by social engineering—posing as a worker, bribing an employee or contractor, or some other trick.
2. Bring a ladder, cutting tools, a dead hard drive, and small computer tools back to this business late at night.
3. Extend the ladder on the side of the building, and climb to the roof.
4. Cut a hole in the roof above the neighboring business (in this case, a luncheonette).
5. Drop down into the luncheonette.
6. Identify the point in the adjoining wall where the target hardware is.
7. Carefully cut a hole in the drywall about the size of the target computer.
8. Unplug the target computer.
9. Remove its hard drive and replace it with the damaged one he brought.
10. Plug it in and power it back up.
11. Roughly patch up wall and ceiling, remove all material, and leave.

This attack, as you can see, is a bit more sophisticated than a "bash and dash." And the thief obviously didn't go to all this trouble to steal a useless file or print server hard drive. No, he stole a domain controller's hard drive. And he did it on a Friday night when the office would be closed until Monday. Because the burglar alarm didn't go off and because the machine seemed to just have a failed hard drive, the IT staff pushed it to the bottom of the priority list. Only when they discovered the evidence of a physical break-in and the replaced hard drive did they raise the alarm.

—continued—

So what was the value of the lost hard drive? The hardware itself was no more than $200. But the cost to the corporation was enormous and probably hasn't been fully realized yet. Since the burglar stole a domain controller, every user's password had to be changed, and that's just the beginning. Having to rebuild much of the IT infrastructure securely to prevent any compromised information from being leveraged is the real cost. So this seemingly minor theft actually cost more than the consulting firm could imagine.

Your Network Cables

Even if every other aspect of your network is physically secure, your data is still vulnerable as it is transmitted across the network cables in your office. Typical Ethernet networks use electrical signals to transmit data, and those signals can be intercepted from many feet away, with the right equipment. These cables can also be physically tapped without interfering with their operation, allowing transparent monitoring of network data.

Fiber-optic cables, such as those used in high-speed backbone networks, aren't susceptible to electronic eavesdropping, because the light signals used in fiber-optic networks don't create any electromagnetic radiation for intruders to capture. But fiber-optic cables can still be spliced and tapped, presenting a security vulnerability. Although this type of attack is complex and costly to execute, it happens often in corporate environments where industrial espionage payoffs can be high.

 With the proliferation of wireless networks, the network cable defense changes. Essentially, anyone within a few hundred feet of your office has the potential to gain access to your network "cables" through wireless access.

Protecting Physical Assets

So how paranoid do you have to be to protect your company's information? That depends entirely on your company, the potential cost of losing data, and the security policies your company adopts. Typical American businesses might not need to worry about intruders tapping into their network cables, but many government organizations worry about precisely that. Most companies might not need to worry about someone reprogramming hubs and switches to eavesdrop on network traffic, although large financial institutions, with their increased liability for compromised information, take extra steps to protect their hubs and switches. Some organizations, such as companies in the health care industry, are required by law to provide security measures for certain types of data. Physical security can be expensive; the level of physical security you implement will depend upon your organization's needs and requirements.

As I mentioned earlier, simply knowing about your security vulnerabilities—even if you choose to do nothing about them—is half the battle. Once you know what your vulnerabilities are, you and your company's managers can look at the cost of fixing those vulnerabilities and decide what's right for your company.

As with all security implementations, the measures you take to mitigate vulnerabilities depend on your particular situation. There is no one-size-fits-all security strategy. For example, an airline may value its reservations database above all other assets, and any compromise of that database would cause irreparable harm to the company. On the other hand, a law firm may care little about its databases but place immense value on its file shares that contain client communications and legal research. These two companies will eventually need to assign values to the importance and expected cost of compromise of their assets and implement appropriate security based on these values. This type of analysis and cost factoring is discussed in Chapter 15.

In the next few sections, I'll give you some tips for securing specific vulnerabilities.

Securing the Office

Most companies use DHCP to make IP address management easier. Unfortunately, DHCP makes it easy for unauthorized users as well, allowing them to obtain a valid IP address on your network and the address of your name resolution server, and from there, the IP address of every important server on your network. You may as well pass out maps to everyone who comes into your office. Without DHCP, the intruder would have to spend more time figuring out this information.

DHCP can be controlled, and I talk about that more in Chapter 11. If you're concerned about unauthorized users accessing the network, configure your DHCP server with reservations. Those reservations would allow computers with known physical addresses (also known as MAC addresses) to obtain an IP address and other information via DHCP. Computers with unknown MAC addresses would be unable to obtain any addressing information, rendering your network useless to them. Although this method requires a significant amount of administration to implement and maintain, you will defeat all but the most determined network intruders. Using DHCP to secure your network in this fashion is often easier and more efficient than trying to maintain physical control over every network jack in your building. Essentially, you're not worrying so much about the network jacks because you're tightly controlling the IP addresses issued to the computers plugged into those jacks. And although those IP addresses can be spoofed by an attacker, it's a bit harder for them.

Several other solutions to this problem have been gaining attention lately. They mainly culminate into two distinct solutions:

Routers as network filters

In this solution, the network must be heavily routed. Network segments must be small and often segregated by the type of data used or the classification of users on that segment. This solution identifies all legal MAC addresses and instructs the router to block traffic from any unauthorized MAC address. While this solution could work, it's mostly theoretical. The expense of implementing the solution is two-fold: the initial infrastructure is costly, as is the daily maintenance of the MAC address lists. For these reasons, this solution remains mostly unimplemented.

802.1x for wired clients

This solution has the administrator create a public key infrastructure (PKI) and issue certificates to all users. Routers are configured to require 802.1x authentication for all network clients. Although 802.1x is primarily a wireless security solution, it is an open standard and can be used to restrict network port access to authorized entities. This solution is similar to the other solution in that the routers do the security work, which can be considered a fundamental flaw in the theory. Also, the initial setup of client computers requires a complex enrollment process before they can communicate normally on the network.

 If you want to prevent visitors from accessing your network resources but still allow them to use your network to reach the Internet, you can configure your DHCP server with a separate scope of IP addresses that don't overlap your existing IP addresses. Company users will still get a valid IP address through their reservation; visitors will receive an address from the other scope. The addresses used by the "visitor scope" should work with your routers and firewalls but not with your corporate servers. You can also segment your network so that visitor data ports are filtered on routers to allow only specific, untrusted network access.

Phone lines present a potential security vulnerability that is easily controlled. Have your local phone company provide you with a list of phone numbers that are supplied to your location. Cancel any phone numbers that aren't authorized and instruct the phone company to disregard requests for new lines unless they are approved by a specific group or individual within your company who is responsible for information security. Ensure that any computer attached to a phone line is secured in such a way that outsiders can't use the phone line to access your network. For example, computers with attached phone lines shouldn't run software like pcAnywhere, which would allow anyone with a phone line and relatively unsophisticated password-guessing software to gain full remote access to them. Phone lines also present a way for employees to transmit information off your network without using centrally controlled resources such as an email server. Organizations that need to tightly control the transmission of information should view phone lines as a major vulnerability.

Floppy drives (and other removable media drives, like CD-ROM and ZIP drives) on most office computers can be disabled or completely removed. Users who require access to removable media can use external floppy drives or other forms of removable media, connected to their computers via USB. In addition, you can enforce security on USB devices so only authorized users have access. By restricting the users with access to a removable media drive, you can significantly reduce the threat of computer virus incursions on your network. Organizations desiring an especially high level of security will prohibit the use of removable media drives on client computers, and instead require users to submit removable media to an administrator. The administrator can then scan the media for viruses and mount the media in a network-accessible drive for the user to access.

Securing Laptops

Chapter 4 has detailed descriptions of several technologies that help protect against data compromise on a stolen laptop. In addition, the prevention of physical theft of the laptop is important. Laptop locks should be distributed with all laptops, and the users should be educated on their proper use in theft prevention. Users should further be educated on how to prevent theft via awareness of their surroundings, proper storage of laptops when not in use, and so forth. An administrative policy that requires laptop owners to attend training before taking possession of their laptops is a great way to ensure this occurs.

Securing the Data Center

Use card key access systems instead of combination locks, because card keys are much more secure. Make sure you have a proactive system that detects when employees have lost a card key. For example, requiring employees to use their card keys to reach their offices will allow you to spot any missing cards first thing in the morning.

Make sure that the folks managing your card key system understand the need to keep the data center secure. If necessary, implement a separate card key system to protect the data center and place it under the control of your company's information technology or information security staff.

Use cameras in the data center to spot tailgating and unauthorized visitors. Make sure employees are aware that they must use their card keys even if someone holds the door open for them, and make sure your policy on data center visitors is clearly displayed on the door. High-end security companies can install detection systems that will sound an alarm if someone attempts to tailgate, helping ensure that employees use their card keys. If you experience repeated tailgating incidents, you may consider entry access devices that allow exactly one person entry at a time (think of the older subway entry gates). Although primitive, they are effective at ensuring that each card key use admits just one person.

Card key systems can also be used to log employees out of the data center, not just in. These exit-based systems allow you to keep a complete log of who entered the data center and how long they stayed. Due to fire regulations, these systems usually cannot be mechanically enforced and are based on the diligence of your employees. You should always consult with an experienced physical security expert before employing any physical security control.

Securing Servers

Never assume that your company's data center safeguards are enough. Keep servers in locked racks with secure rear doors and sidewall panels. The keys for these racks might be stored in a locked cabinet in the data center, requiring a combination or, even better, a card key to open the cabinet and obtain a rack key.

Every Windows Server 2003 includes Remote Desktop, which allows up to two different administrators to remotely administer the computer at the same time. Locking your servers in racks shouldn't present a significant burden, because most administrative tasks can be performed without even entering the data center. As a rule of thumb, once a server is installed in a rack, the only time you should need to physically touch it is to manually power it down—for example, to replace or upgrade hardware.

Consider disabling or removing the floppy drives and even the CD or DVD drives in your servers. They are rarely needed for business purposes and present a significant security threat, since they can be used to start the computer or introduce viruses. You can always keep a USB floppy drive or CD drive handy in case you need to use removable media with a server. Ensuring that the server racks' rear doors are locked will prevent anyone from plugging in the USB drive without a key to the rack.

In Windows XP and Windows Server 2003, you must have administrative rights on the computer to install new device drivers. This is to help combat the security issue presented when a user installs a removable media drive on a computer. Using the principle of least privilege, very few users should have administrative rights on their computer. This should help ensure that unauthorized individuals cannot just insert a convenient storage device and have it work.

Securing the Wiring Closet

Few companies bother to lock their cable plants or wiring closets. Given the large number of vulnerabilities that network wiring presents, locking the cable plant definitely seems a bit futile. But remember that the cable plant often includes hubs and switches, and those devices can be accessed by intruders and turned into powerful network eavesdropping tools. If you don't lock your cable plant (which you should definitely do), at least keep your hubs, switches, routers, and other connectivity devices in locked cabinets.

Keeping your cable plant neat and tidy is another intruder deterrent. Neat, orderly cabling makes it easier to notice additional cables that an intruder may have added or to spot changes that an intruder may have made. If you have standardized a color for your network and patch cords, leave no extra cables unlocked. This forces intruders to either cannibalize existing cable, which will alert you in the form of a network disconnection, or use the wrong color cable. The only purple cable in a cabinet full of pink cables can be spotted quickly and easily.

Securing Network Transmissions

Network cabling is practically impossible to protect. It's snaked throughout the walls, ceilings, and sometimes even floors of your office. Copper-based cabling emits electromagnetic waves that can be detected and used to eavesdrop without even touching the cabling. Fiber-optic cabling is not only more secure, but also significantly more expensive.

You have to work under the assumption that your network cables aren't secure and that they are instead broadcasting every byte they carry into the air for anyone to receive. In fact, that's pretty much exactly what they do. With all your data being transmitted into the air, if you've based your security solution on the fact that wires are secure, your other security precautions are potentially meaningless.

You need to make those transmissions useless to an intruder. Technologies like IP Security (IPSec), which you'll learn about in Chapter 8, allow you to encrypt sensitive data before it is transmitted across your network cabling. Encrypted traffic is useless to an intruder without the private key, which is well protected in these configurations.

Wireless networks in particular seem like a huge security problem because they literally transmit network data for hundreds of feet. Most wireless networking products include built-in encryption capabilities, but those encryption capabilities are not foolproof, and several security schemes have been compromised by attackers. Wireless networks should be considered a major security concern, especially since they allow intruders to tap into your network without entering your building. While wireless networks can be convenient in certain situations, they should never be allowed to carry sensitive data without heavy-duty encryption using something like IPSec.

Wireless Security?

Can you actually implement some type of wireless network that's "secure"? No. There's no such thing as absolute security and doubly so for something you have little control over such as the airwaves. Unless your building is shielded in copper and lead and has a one-mile guarded perimeter, someone from outside your property will try to attack your wireless network.

How do you prevent an attack from succeeding? That's a bit easier to address. You must make it difficult for the attacker. Numerous layers of security are required here. MAC filtering, service set identifier (SSID) broadcast restriction, 802.1x certificates, and encryption keys are all elements that can help protect against attack. In addition, a strong security policy that states that certain classes of data cannot be passed through the wireless network is required. This can be enforced by careful routing and addressing (i.e., all sensitive servers are within a specific IP address range and your wireless routers are configured to disallow communications with hosts in that range).

Holistic Security: Best Practices

Although you have to think about security vulnerabilities individually, you should plan your security solutions as a system of complementary techniques and technologies. Each level of the security solution should take into account preceding layers, but never assume that those preceding layers will stop an intruder. The following tips are best practices that most companies can use to significantly enhance their physical security:

- Your network's physical cabling is almost impossible to completely secure. Do the best you can by locking up wiring closets, hubs, switches, and so on, and assume that intruders will find a way to access transmitted data anyway.

- Use technology-based solutions like IPSec to protect network transmissions against eavesdroppers.

- Buy a laptop chain lock whenever a new laptop is purchased, and instruct the new laptop owner on its proper use. These simple $20 devices deter many thieves. You should also implement policy that requires their use at all times and specifically states that anyone whose laptop is stolen without the cable connected will repay the company for the laptop and the cost of the security administration (i.e., revoking certificates on the laptop).

- Keep unauthorized computers off your network completely by not issuing IP addresses to unknown MAC addresses. You can also use nonstandard network plugs and jacks, which make it more difficult for outsiders to physically connect to your network (although expensive, this is a popular technique in high-security government facilities and some technology companies).

- Secure your data center with electronic locks and, if possible, recording cameras. Require anyone exiting the data center to use his card key and you'll have a complete electronic in-and-out log.

- Lock servers in cabinets with secure cabinet rear doors and sidewalls. Keep the cabinet keys in a secure location, and require administrators to check keys out using a card key or some other system.

- Use high-quality locks. You would be surprised how often security consultants find a data center protected by a $15 deadbolt installed in a hollow core door purchased from a building supply store. If you're going to protect the data center, protect it with effective hardware from a qualified locksmith. Many high-end locks have keys that can be duplicated only at the factory or by a factory-authorized locksmith. If you're using a card key system, consider using a multiperimeter approach, with one perimeter secured by lock and the other secured by card key.

- Physically examine your data center for security vulnerabilities. Does the data center share a common wall with an unsecured portion of your building? If so, the only tool an intruder will need is a screwdriver to get through some drywall. Extra wall studs or rebar in the walls is inexpensive and can shore up those security holes easily. If you've got an elevated data center on a hollow floor, remember to check down there too.

- Use Remote Desktop to manage servers remotely, reducing the number of administrators who need authority to physically enter the data center.

- Implement policies that help further protect your physical assets. For example, screensavers that kick in after a few minutes and require a password to disable can help defend a server whose cabinet was left unlocked.

- Use multiple layers of security. For example, use NTFS to secure files, but don't assume that only authorized users will get to them. Secure your physical network jacks, and also issue IP addresses only to authorized MAC addresses, assuming that the security on the jacks will be bypassed. For every security measure you implement, imagine that it *will* be broken or circumvented, and take additional steps to protect your resources. This technique is called *layered* security, because it relies on multiple layers of security techniques to protect assets.

When You're Strapped for Cash

Physical security can, by its very nature, be very expensive. Card-keyed doors, cameras, and lockable server racks are pricey items, and smaller organizations might not be able to afford every precaution. When your budget doesn't include much money for physical security, try and maximize your investment to get the most security you can for your money. Here are some tips:

- Get some kind of locks for your data center. Even if all you can afford is an off-the-shelf combination lock on the door, get it. Keeping unauthorized users away from your servers is critical.

- Most data center budgets include server racks, simply because racks provide a space-efficient means of storing servers. Most server racks include lockable doors, or at least the option to add door locks for very little additional money. Get those locks and use them. While an attacker can break a lock, it's one more hurdle between her and a successful attack. Plus, a broken lock leaves evidence for later forensic investigation and possible prosecution.

- Implement security policies that require users to use password protected screen-savers and other basic security measures. These measures don't cost extra, and they can significantly enhance security. Use group policies to centrally configure security on your client computers.

- Provide all laptop users with locking cables. Establish a security policy that users must always have their laptops locked to something when not in use, and instruct them on what items are better to attach their laptops to. These locking cables are cheap, simple, and very effective.

You can implement good physical security with very little extra cash, and the extra peace of mind and corporate security are well worth it. You may also be able to increase your budget for physical security measures by helping your company's management understand the risks that a physically insecure environment presents. For example, a bank spends tens of thousands of dollars protecting the bank's cash vaults, but a single compromised server could result in the bank's customer accounts being compromised, making the cash itself useless. Helping the bank's management understand that the data center's physical security is just as important as the cash vault's will help them create a more reasonable budget for physical security.

Summary

All the technological security marvels in the world are useless without proper accompanying physical security. While most companies implement some form of physical security, few take into account the many security vulnerabilities that exist in their environment. Take the time to think about physical security, document the vulnerabilities in your environment, and make business decisions about how to prevent those vulnerabilities from compromising the security of your company's information systems.

CHAPTER 4

File System Security

Whenever data is stored on physical media, it has the potential to become compromised. For example, secret notes between Napoleon and his generals were compromised and led, in part, to his defeat. Napoleon's secret notes were written on leather or paper and sent by fast riders. In a computer context, those secret notes are stored on a hard drive and either used locally or transmitted across a network to a friend, coworker, Internet site, or other location beyond your server or organization. In this chapter, you'll see who can access those secret notes on the local hard drive and how to ensure only the desired people and groups can access them. Techniques for ensuring that your data remains secret when transmitted on a network will be covered in subsequent chapters.

The use of long-term computer data storage, whose benefits are numerous, raises special security consideration for the system administrator: how do you protect data so that only the intended user has access while ensuring some level of recoverability over time? In this chapter, you'll learn how to use file permissions and EFS—the two main file protection mechanisms provided by Windows Server 2003—to control user access to files. You'll see how to use these mechanisms appropriately and how they are often misconfigured in ways that prevent desired access. You'll also learn how to plan for a number of special security concerns specific to the use of portable computers. These plans may include Syskey, a special tool for protecting the account database, which I show you how to use properly.

Protecting Files with NTFS File Permissions

The primary technique for protecting data on a hard drive is to use the built-in NTFS file permissions to allow or restrict specific users and groups. A user could allow his user account to access his personal research data while restricting other users. He could also designate some files as readable by all users but writable by only his coworkers and manager. At home, he could restrict certain folders so that only he could read their contents, while allowing only himself and his wife to read others.

You may want to share files on Windows Server 2003 and allow only the HR group access. File permissions are configurable and flexible enough to work in many different scenarios.

How File Permissions Work

When a user logs into a Windows system, as described in Chapter 7, an access token is granted to the user's session, which the operating system uses to prove her identity to local and network resources. Every access token contains the security identifier (SID) of the user as its key component and the SIDs of the groups she belongs to. This information allows operating system components that are concerned about security to simply check to see whether any of the SIDs provided in the access token have been granted or denied access to their data or services.

File permissions simply attach a list of SIDs and the access rights granted or denied for each SID to a file or directory. This list of SIDs is known as an access control list (ACL), and each entry in the list is an access control entry (ACE). An ACL is composed of one or more ACEs. Whenever a user or process makes a request to access a file or directory, NTFS retrieves the corresponding ACL for that object. It then runs down the list of ACEs on the object, comparing each to every SID in the access token of the requesting entity (usually a user). NTFS accumulates the permissions it finds and determines whether the permissions are enough to meet the requested needs of the requester. If the permissions are sufficient, the process succeeds and the requester accesses the object. When all the requested permissions are not granted, the request fails.

 Permissions can be set on individual files or on the folders that contain them. When permissions are set on files, there is no effect on the other files in the same folder. Setting permissions on folders allows NTFS to configure all subfolders and files with the same permissions. This also ensures that new files within that folder inherit the same permissions. This can be beneficial when setting up secure file shares and when one wants to ensure that both existing and new files have appropriate permissions configured.

Consider our user David Loudon. David has an account in an Active Directory domain that he logs into daily to perform his work. David is a member of several security groups, as shown in Figure 4-1.

David wants to open a file on the local hard drive called *Super Secret Info.txt*. Because David is concerned with security, he sets permissions on it. He doesn't want any other users, including domain administrators, to access the file. He configures the file with the permissions shown in Figure 4-2.

File Security and NTFS

It is worth noting at this point that all Windows operating systems rely on the NT File System (NTFS) for providing file system security. Windows XP and the Windows Server 2003 family also support older versions of the File Allocation Table (FAT) file system in its many variations, including FAT12, FAT16, and FAT32. These file systems were not designed to incorporate access control and security mechanisms in their data storage. They provide no data security whatsoever. You should always use NTFS unless you have a strong need for one of the older file systems, such as a need to boot multiple operating systems on a single computer. Because this configuration is unwise and unsupported, you should avoid it.

Using NTFS also helps to prevent another insecure computer configuration—the dual-boot configuration. Having more than one operating system on a computer at any given time allows an attacker a far greater attack surface. Often one operating system can bypass or ignore security measures implemented by another. Though there are some technical means that you can employ to prevent this configuration, a strong administrative policy and an educated IT staff will most likely prevent such configurations.

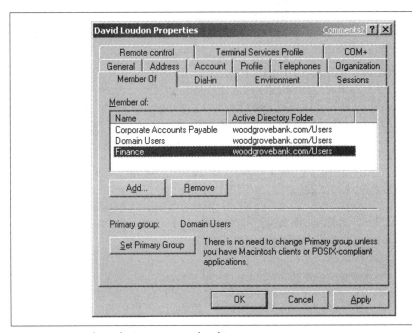

Figure 4-1. David Loudon's group memberships

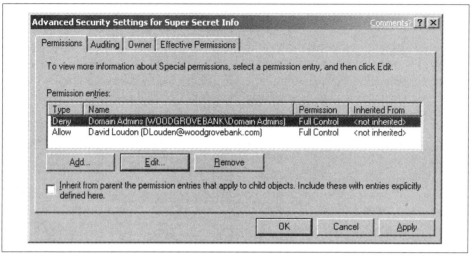

Figure 4-2. David has restricted the file permissions so that he is the only user with access

David now has full control of the file, and members of the Domain Admins group are explicitly denied access. Notice that there are no other entries in the ACL. Because the default behavior of Windows Server 2003 is to deny permission unless granted, any user that is not on the list will be denied access to *Super Secret Info.txt*. David doesn't need to add a Deny ACE for every user or group in the domain. He simply needs to ensure that no unintended users or groups are granted permission.

Let's assume that at some point David is promoted or transferred into a job that requires him to have different permission on the domain. Don, our security administrator, adds David to the Domain Admins group to ensure he has the proper permissions. David thinks nothing of this change, as he is being granted additional permissions that should allow him to perform any task on any computer within the domain. However, when David attempts to open *Super Secret Info.txt*, he gets an "Access denied" error message. This is because NTFS considers the Deny permission to be most important. Whenever an ACL is interpreted, an explicitly denied permission takes precedence over all other permissions. If David or any group he is a member of is explicitly denied permission, he is denied permission to access the file, even in the case of conflicting levels of permission.

> A good administrative practice is to add groups, not individual users, to permissions for file and folder objects. Then you can rely on proper group maintenance to ensure that access is maintained.

A quick way to verify David's access to the file is the Effective Permissions tab of the Advanced Security Settings dialog box shown in Figure 4-2. This tab allows an administrator to type a username and view the effective permissions that the user will receive. In this case, providing David's name would show that he has no access. This tab is currently available only in Windows Server 2003.

To allow David to access his file again, Don temporarily removes him from the Domain Admins group.

 Even though David is getting an access denied message, security is working properly. This concept will be detailed later in this chapter.

David may have another file that he wants to share among his peers. He wants to ensure that only his group has access. He also wants to avoid ongoing maintenance of the ACL on this file, allowing users who enter and leave his workgroup to be automatically added and removed from the file permissions. He sets security on the file as shown in Figure 4-3. This security has no permissions for individual users, only the Corporate Accounts Payable group. So as long as the group membership is maintained, the file will be accessible by the appropriate users.

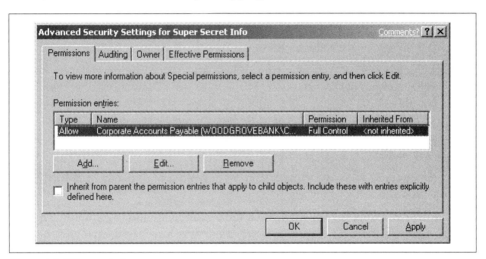

Figure 4-3. File permissions

This configuration works well for David. Because only the Corporate Accounts Payable group is given access to the file, only members of that group can access the file. All other users receive the default permission, which is no access. As users join and leave the corporate accounts payable staff, the group is updated by human resources and the IT department's Domain Admins groups. David needs to take no action to maintain access on the file now that it is configured correctly.

How to Configure File Permissions

You learned in the previous section that setting appropriate file permissions is not terribly difficult when some basic guidelines are considered. These guidelines can be summarized as follows:

- Apply only granted permissions whenever possible. Avoid Deny permissions, as they override all other permissions and can be difficult to implement when many permissions are assigned to one file.

- Use the Deny—Full Control permission sparingly for the same reason. This is especially true when you think about assigning Deny to Everyone. At that point, you've essentially rendered the data inaccessible to anyone except administrators, who can manually take ownership and reestablish the proper permissions on the object.

- Permit groups of users instead of individual users when possible. This permits you to allow and deny user access to files by simply modifying a group's membership, rather than having to reapply permissions to all files and folders.

- Permit access to folders instead of individual files.

Example: setting up a secure file share

Imagine an employee of your company, David, asks you to set up a place where he can share files within his branch office. He plans to store a few spreadsheets and documents on this share, consuming a minimum of space. He wants the files to remain confidential to only the employees at his branch. While he is not the least-savvy computer user in the organization, you do not want him to have to maintain any of this security manually.

To set up the file share and configure it for the appropriate level of security, you would perform these tasks:

1. Create a folder on the appropriate hard drive using Windows Explorer. This can be right off the root directory or in a subdirectory based on organizational boundaries, geographical region of the user, and so on. The location of the directory does not matter.

2. Right-click the folder, click Properties, and then click Security. The default ACL for folders on this drive is displayed as shown in Figure 4-4.

3. Click Advanced to display the advanced folder permissions dialog as shown in Figure 4-5.

4. Deselect the option of "Inherit from parent the permission entries that apply to child objects. Include these with entries explicitly defined here." Deselecting this option allows explicit ACLs to be set on this folder without inheriting other ACLs from the parent folder. This is not required but allows Don, the administrator, to ensure that even administrators do not have access to this folder.

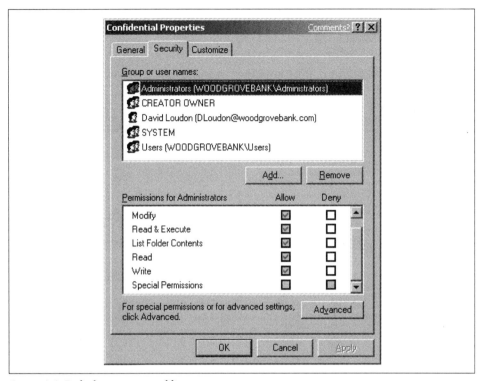

Figure 4-4. Default access control list

5. Click Remove on the dialog box that appears for all the existing ACEs. The ACL will now be blank.

6. Add the desired groups and users as shown in Figure 4-6. In our example, David Loudon's branch users in Valdosta are the only users with access permission. Because this group is administered by the IT and HR departments, we can configure the folder so that it will not require maintenance every time an employee joins or leaves the branch.

7. Click OK to finish configuring the file permissions. Click Sharing to share this folder on the network. Select Share This Folder and click OK.

You will notice that permissions can also be set on the share. These permissions are similar to the permissions you just set on the folder, although folder permissions are more granular. The difference is that you configured the folder permissions so that access is restricted both locally and on the network. Although share permissions can be set to be similar to the file and folder permissions, it is not required to meet the goal of securing the files.

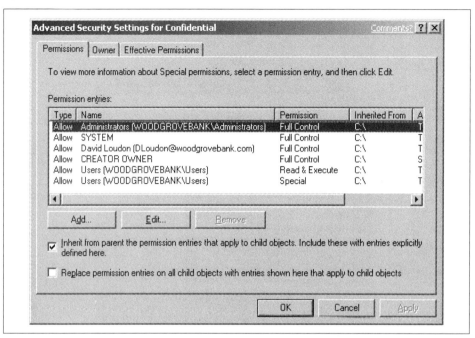

Figure 4-5. The advanced folder permissions list

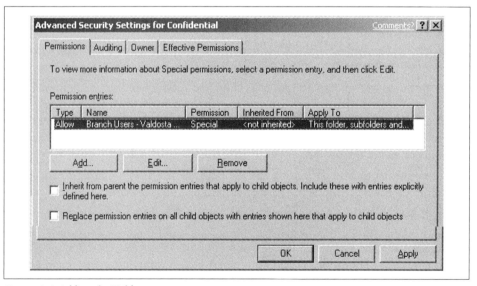

Figure 4-6. Adding the Valdosta users

Deciding whether to use NTFS or share permissions is a bit like deciding which hair color is best. There's no perfect answer, and whichever option suits you and meets the security goal should be used. The most important thing to remember is that NTFS permissions apply both locally and over the network, while share permissions affect only network access. While many argue that this means NTFS permissions are universally a better practice than share permissions, I leave it to you to decide. Personally, I apply both just to be sure.

Now the folder is secure. David's group can access the folder and all its files and subfolders. No other users can access the contents, as they are not explicitly granted permissions. The permissions will dynamically change as David's group grows or shrinks, because the group membership is managed separately. No further security maintenance on this folder is needed to ensure its security.

Example: implementing local file security for a shared computer

Frequently, computers are shared by two or more users. This is often the case in manufacturing departments with multiple shifts when it makes no sense to provide individual computers for each shift worker.

Consider a fictional company, Woodgrove Bank. In Woodgrove Bank, two or three receptionists share one computer during the day. One receptionist, Brian Valentine, wants to keep personal data on the local computer but protect it from being accessed by the other receptionists. Because the data is of a personal nature, he wants to ensure that the most security possible is applied to these files.

Brian can use the following procedure to apply strong security to his local folder and its contents:

1. Create a folder on a local hard drive or choose an existing folder with the files already in place. The location of the directory does not matter.
2. Right-click the folder, click Properties, and then click Security. The default ACL for folders on this drive is displayed.
3. Click Advanced to display the advanced folder permissions dialog.
4. Deselect the option to "Inherit from parent the permission entries that apply to child objects. Include these with entries explicitly defined here." Deselecting this option allows explicit ACLs to be set on this folder without inheriting other ACLs from the parent folder.
5. Select the option to "Replace permission entries on all child objects with entries shown here that apply to child objects." This ensures that all existing files and subfolders receive the new ACL.
6. Click Remove on the dialog box that appears for all the existing ACEs. The ACL will now be blank.

7. Add only Brian's account with Full Control configured as Allow. Because Brian is a bit paranoid, also add Domain Admins with Full Control configured as Deny. This is shown in Figure 4-7.

8. Click OK to finish configuring the permissions.

 I said earlier that setting Deny permissions on files and folders is a bad idea. If Brian is ever added to the Domain Admins group, he will be denied access to the files in this folder. Because this is highly unlikely, Brian will probably never encounter problems with this permission.

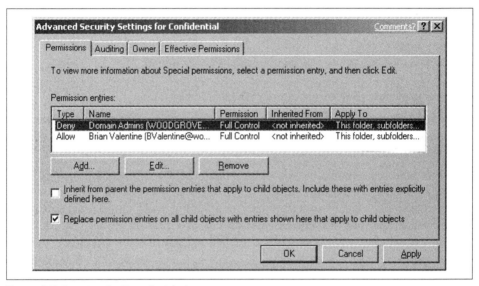

Figure 4-7. Denying the Domain Admins group access

The result of this procedure is that Brian is the only user who has access to his folder and its contents. Any other user attempting to view his data will receive an "Access denied" message. However, an administrator could still gain access by simply adding himself to the ACL list. Because Brian is not a local administrator, he cannot prevent this possibility.

Protecting Data with the Encrypting File System

As I discussed in the previous section, NTFS checks the ACL for each file and folder a user accesses and compares it against her access token. Access is granted only when the appropriate permissions are held by the the requester. However, this architecture has the potential to be circumvented. If NTFS isn't used to access the hard disk, the data can be read just like any other data. Because Windows Server 2003 and Windows XP allow only NTFS to access its own partitions, this security is effective. If another operating system is used, or if special disk-reading equipment is connected to the hard disk, the data is completely unprotected.

The only way to ensure that data on the hard disk is not susceptible to this type of attack is to protect it with encryption. Storing the data on the hard drive in an encrypted state means that the requester must provide the decryption key for the data to be usable. Without the decryption key, the data is useless to the requester—regardless of the operating system making the request. Windows XP and Windows Server 2003 allow files on the hard disk to be encrypted using the Encrypting File System, or EFS.

How EFS Works

To discuss the concepts and processes of EFS, I must first dispel a myth. EFS is not really a file system at all. It is a set of functions that work in conjunction with NTFS to encrypt and decrypt files that are stored on the hard drive. NTFS provides the core mechanics of fetching data from the hard drive, writing to the hard drive, checking ACLs, and so on. EFS does the added work of determining when a file must be encrypted or decrypted and performing that action.

Specifically, EFS works by generating a random symmetric key for a file, called the file encryption key (FEK), and encrypting the data portion of the file with that key. It then takes the requester's public key from the local key store and encrypts the FEK with that public key. This chunk of encrypted data that allows the requester to decrypt the file is called the data decryption field (DDF). There is always at least one DDF for an encrypted file.

EFS then checks to see if any data recovery agents (DRAs) have been defined in a recovery policy. A recovery agent is an optional user who holds a specific type of certificate private key that, when configured properly, allows him to decrypt EFS files. If recovery agents have been defined, their public key is also used to encrypt a copy of the FEK. This chunk of encrypted data that allows a recovery agent to decrypt a file is called a data recovery field (DRF). Because more than one recovery agent can be defined through a recovery policy, there may be more than one DRF per encrypted file.

In Windows 2000, EFS required at least one recovery agent to operate. When no recovery agents were available, EFS would refuse to encrypt files. In Windows XP and Windows Server 2003, EFS allows full functionality without a recovery agent in place. This allows configurations in which only one unique key can decrypt data. To disable EFS in Windows XP and Windows Server 2003, a Group Policy Object must be defined or a group of registry settings must be made.

The result of all these operations is encrypted data, one or more DDFs, and zero or more DRFs. This data is then handed back to NTFS. NTFS writes all this data as provided to the hard drive and additionally marks the file as being encrypted with EFS. This process of encrypting files with EFS is shown in Figure 4-8.

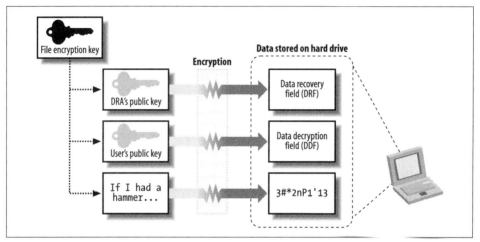

Figure 4-8. The EFS encryption process

 Another common myth about EFS is that folders can be encrypted. While folders can be flagged to encrypt their contents, the folders themselves are not encrypted. Rather, new files within those folders will be automatically encrypted when they are created in that folder, and optionally, any existing files in the folder will be encrypted. This is a desired configuration for EFS, as it will ensure that new datafiles or temporary copies of encrypted files in the same directory will be protected. When individual files are marked for encryption and not the parent directory, data may unwittingly be written to the hard drive unencrypted.

When an application requests data from an encrypted file, EFS has to decrypt it. To do so, NTFS retrieves the entire file and passes the information to EFS. EFS examines the public and private keys of the requester to determine whether any of these keys can be used to decrypt a DDF or DRF associated with the file. When such a key is found, the FEK is decrypted and used to decrypt the file data. This decrypted data is then passed back to NTFS, which provides it to the original requester. Because all this is handled by NTFS and EFS, applications do not need to be aware of EFS files or take any special actions to handle them. This process of decrypting files with EFS is shown in Figure 4-9.

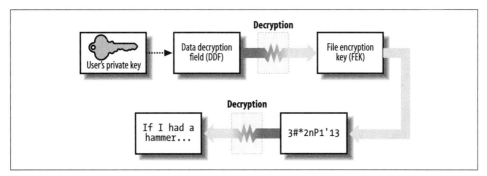

Figure 4-9. EFS decryption

The process of decryption with a data recovery agent's private key is the same as with the user's private key, except that the DRF is decrypted instead of the DDF.

A new feature of EFS in Windows XP and Windows Server 2003 is the ability to have more than one DDF per file. This allows a user to add users to a file and give those users the ability to decrypt the file without being recovery agents. This EFS file sharing provides a highly secure way to share data between users when the data is located either on a local hard drive or on a network file share. The ability to have more than one DRF recovery agent per file has existed since EFS was first implemented in Windows 2000; it is only the ability to have multiple DDFs that's new.

This new ability of EFS has one roadblock. The public keys of all additional users must be available to the file's owner to add them as potential decryptors of the data. There are a few mechanisms to aid in locating public key certificates, such as Active Directory, but this is still largely a manual process. In most cases, the file owner must ask the desired user to identify, export, and then transfer a public key certificate. This can be time-consuming and is not a simple operation to perform for the majority of users. For more information on certificate stores and operations, see Chapter 9.

Benefits of the Encrypting File System

The true benefit of EFS is that the encrypted files are stored in a secure manner. Physical compromise of the computer does not necessarily compromise the data.

Consider our IT manager, Don Fink. Don uses a laptop as his primary work computer. He stores all his data on it, whether sensitive or not. He carries it to work and back home every day. When the laptop is at work, he keeps it chained to his desk there, and when at home, he chains it to his home desk. Don also happens to travel frequently by air and is no stranger to airports.

Karen Shaughnnessy, a would-be corporate espionage operative, has been hired by a rival to learn key information about Woodgrove Bank. Karen has targeted Don as a potential wealth of information. She feels Don will have enough information stored on his laptop to make overt theft worthwhile. Although Don doesn't know it yet, he's about to become a victim.

Through a process of careful observation and intelligence gathering, Karen knows what type of laptop Don has, as well as the briefcase he uses when traveling. She also learns when Don's next trip is scheduled. Karen obtains a duplicate of the briefcase and ensures she is in line directly behind Don when going through the airport security checkpoint. This allows Karen to switch briefcases and leave with Don's laptop. Don may not notice for a few minutes or even until he's on his airplane. Either way, once the laptop is out of Don's possession it's too late.

Karen knows that there may be security safeguards on the computer. To work around any potential traps or protections, she removes the laptop's hard drive. She then connects it to a computer already running another operating system, one that recognizes NTFS but doesn't interpret ACLs (there are many of them). From there, it's a simple matter for Karen to copy the contents of Don's hard drive to her computer and begin sifting through the data.

This scenario happens more often than people realize. I periodically see news articles about laptops being stolen from corporate employees during transport. Unfortunately, there is no supplemental data to cite which laptops are business-oriented versus personal, but common sense says that a majority of laptops carried while traveling are corporate laptops. In all likelihood, a majority of these laptops contained at least a small amount of sensitive data. However, most corporations simply refuse to publicly admit that this happens to them. They may put procedures in place to try to avoid future repeats of the same incident, but often these attempts fail. If you use EFS to protect the data correctly, however, the problem can be solved.

Let's assume Karen stole Don's laptop as mentioned earlier. If Don has encrypted his sensitive data with EFS, Karen must obtain Don's private key to decrypt the data. As long as Don's password is sufficiently complex, this will take Karen a very long time. If Don were carrying particularly sensitive data, he may have removed the private key entirely from the computer and stored it on a floppy that he kept separate from his laptop. In that case, Karen must use a brute force attack to try to decrypt the data. Assuming Don is using AES encryption for his file (Don can configure the encryption EFS uses, though it's not advisable), there are 2^{256}, or about 1.158×10^{77}, possible keys. Considering current technology, this type of attack would take so long to break that the data would be useless long before the attack succeeded. Also, remember that each EFS file has its own unique FEK. This means that the number of possible keys applies to each encrypted file individually.

Laptop Lost and Found at Seattle-Tacoma International Airport

I read about the most alarming cases—laptops and hard drives with secret data being lost—in the news periodically. But the reality of data compromise due to lost laptops exists every day. Because of the frequency of business travel, the loss of laptops at major airports is far more common than you might think. Monique Reed-Jones, operations manager of lost and found at Seattle-Tacoma International Airport, was kind enough to furnish us with statistics and current trends.

Monique is not a computer person by trade. In fact, she works for the subcontractor that holds the lost and found contract—the YWCA. She receives all items lost at the airport and is responsible for reuniting these items with their rightful owners. She speaks with a certain pride in her work: "In virtually all cases involving laptops, we're able to return them to their owners quickly." This is great news from a capital standpoint, as the individual or company won't have to purchase a new laptop to replace the loss. However, it's the frequency with which Monique has to do this task and her investigative methods that should alarm security professionals.

During 2002, Monique had 697 laptops come through her lost and found department. Of those laptops, every single one was reunited with its owner. Monique has developed a very basic flow for identifying the owner of each laptop. First, she visually scans the outside of the laptop and any containers it came in for identification. Wise business travelers, Monique says, keep some basic contact information outside the computer, such as a laminated business card. She also looks for any corporate property tags.

Next, she boots the computer. "Very few computers need a password," says Monique. Once she reaches the desktop, she looks for recently used documents or scans the My Documents folder. More often than not she can find a document with identifying information there and quickly make contact with the owner. The most common document found? A resume.

If she fails to locate a resume or other suitable document, Monique starts the laptop's email program and scans the inbox and address book. She's looking for easily identified parties such as correspondence with family members or coworkers.

Monique's last resort is to call the laptop manufacturer and provide the serial number of the laptop. Some manufacturers are able to associate registered laptops with their owners and either provide contact information or initiate the contact themselves.

The fact that Monique gets information from computer manufacturers shouldn't alarm you. Neither should the fact that one of her investigative tools is to attempt to boot the operating system. What should make your jaw drop open is the fact that this is her most successful method. The vast majority of the laptops Monique sees are completely unprotected—both the operating system and the data on the hard drive. If there is any sensitive data on the computer, she now has unfettered access to it. She could easily sell this information on the black market, snipe patent filings, or commit insider trading depending on the laptop. Although this behavior is illegal (and Monique certainly never does it), it's quite profitable and happens frequently.

—continued—

There is some good news. Monique says lost laptop instances have signifigantly dropped off since the Transportation Security Administration (TSA) took over airport security screening procedures. This is primarily due to the TSA's security screening procedures. They now ensure that at least one TSA employee is responsible for ensuring that each screened passenger leaves the area with exactly what she arrived with. When individuals are screened with greater scrutiny or taken aside, the employee ensures her items follow. In the long run, this may reduce the number of all items left in the screening area and help prevent data compromise.

And that would be fine by Monique.

Karen might use an attack commonly referred to as the Nordahl attack to gain access to Don's files. In this attack, Karen installs another operating system or boots to another operating system with the compromised hard drive attached. Karen then uses tools to reset or overwrite the security information in Don's SAM database. Very often, the attacker can overwrite the administrator password with her own. It's then a simple matter of booting to the target OS and logging in. The two mitigations to this type of attack—removing the DRA's key from the local computer and using Syskey to protect the operating system's account database integrity—are both discussed in this chapter.

Drawbacks of the Encrypting File System

As you can see, EFS is a strong and effective way to protect data. Although it has enormous benefits, it does have some drawbacks. For example, encrypting a large amount of data with a strong key can take a noticeable amount of time. With the computing power available today to most users, this isn't usually a problem. However, when used inappropriately, EFS can degrade a system's performance. Consider the suggestions in the next section to ensure that it is used to maximum benefit while avoiding potential performance pitfalls.

Another feature that's often considered a drawback is EFS' reliance on private keys. Now that you know how EFS works, you can see that it requires the private key of a configured user or DRA to decrypt the data in a file. Without an appropriate private key, the data is lost. This makes the private key very valuable—without it, your data is lost! Sadly, most users and administrators do not realize this and reformat or reinstall their computers without backing up their private key stores. This often results in lost data.

You can avoid lost data in many ways. Simply backing up the private key is a very effective preventative measure. You can also configure a DRA in your domain and ensure that the DRA's private key is kept safe. Both of these measures prevent EFS data loss, and both are discussed in this book.

Using the Encrypting File System Correctly

EFS is simple to use and is only slightly more difficult to use correctly. Remember these few basic guidelines when using and deploying EFS:

- Encrypt at the folder level instead of at the file level. This marks the folder so that new files created in the folder are encrypted at creation and continue to be encrypted.

- Remove the private key of both the user and recovery agent when not in use. If a valid private key exists on the hard drive when it is compromised, it may be easier to attack that private key storage than to attack the EFS-protected files. Although this is cumbersome and temporarily prevents authorized users from reading files, it's necessary to separate the key from the data to maximize the effectiveness of any encrypted data. For detailed guidance on this, see Chapter 9.

- Encrypt only data that must be protected. Judicious use of EFS helps ensure system performace remains as high as possible.

- Wipe the hard drive free of unencrypted data remnants after encrypting sensitive data. The process for doing this is covered later in this chapter.

- Ensure an appropriate data recovery strategy is deployed throughout your organization before EFS is used. Clients lose their private keys more often than you might think. If there's no way for you or a designated recovery agent to decrypt the files, the protected data may be lost. Either back up each user's private key or establish a DRA to prevent against data loss.

Example: Ensuring New Files are Encrypted

Don Fink knows that his laptop is susceptible to theft. Unfortunately, he cannot avoid storing sensitive and proprietary data on it when traveling between offices. Don wants to store data securely so that, no matter what the situation, his data will remain confidential and only he can retrieve it. He would rather lose the data entirely than have the data fall into the hands of his competitors.

Don's Windows Server 2003 infrastructure does not yet include a centralized certification authority (CA). He knows very little about public key cryptography and certificates. He only knows that he must keep his data confidential. Here are the steps that Don would take to create a new directory and ensure that its contents are encrypted:

1. Create a new folder on the hard drive to store his sensitive files. The path to Don's folder is *C:\Secrets*, although this name could be anything.
2. Right-click on the folder and choose Properties.
3. Click Advanced.
4. Select the Encrypt Contents to Protect Data checkbox.
5. Click OK, then click OK. If the Confirm Attribute Changes dialog box appears, choose "Apply changes to this folder, subfolders and files."

Security Showdown: EFS Data Recovery Strategies

Most security policies recognize that recovery of protected data is important. EFS has two distinct approaches to providing that data recovery. In this segment of Security Showdown, Don and Mike will debate the benefits of each.

Mike: My preference in this technology is to implement a PKI-based key recovery agent and provide for centralized key distribution and archival. The EFS recovery agent configuration is more work than it's worth. Every time any of my users encrypts a file, he must use that RA's certificate to create the DRF. When you add up the number of files and users in an enterprise, it adds up to an unacceptable level of waste.

This does require that a PKI is established. But even creating a single certification authority (CA) in its own hierarchy will allow you to provide for this type of certificate issuance. Then you get the benefits of an enterprise CA—including autoenrollment, customizable templates, and so on—as well as a single private key repository. How can you go wrong? And if you already have a PKI, you need do nothing more than issue EFS certificates from that existing hierarchy.

In addition, if I'm already archiving keys in my PKI, I can leverage that for EFS. I don't have to establish a new set of recovery agents, establish trust in them, obtain senior-level buyoff on the configuration, and so forth. I can simply tack on the EFS-specific needs and hit the ground running.

Finally, the Windows Server 2003 enterprise CAs provide a highly functional key recovery technology. The CA database stores the private keys, which are cryptographically protected. You can even configure it to require more than one party to recover a key—which is great for accountability and auditing. EFS RAs have no such requirement, as any RA can recover the files single-handedly and without scrutiny.

Don: Good points, but a centralized recovery isn't always the right answer. In smaller organizations, for example, implementing the PKI necessary to support a key recovery agent is overkill—something like building a dedicated highway from your house to the convenience store. Might be nice, but it's expensive and a lot of work.

On the other hand, you could just distribute the RA's certificate via Group Policy. Group Policy is definitely the thousand-pound gorilla of centralized control, so you can't argue that it's too much work—even in a large organization. Instead of distributing certificates to each and every user manually, you just have Group Policy configure their client computers to have the certificate. It's automatic and transparent and requires very little effort. At the same time, you don't have to fuss with a PKI, worry about revocation lists, and so forth. Heck, with PKI, you'll still have to use Group Policy to configure client computers to trust your CA; why not use Group Policy to solve the problem directly by distributing the RA certificate?

Mike: I've got to admit you have a point. A full PKI solution just for EFS is a bit of overkill. Using Group Policy to distribute the RA's certificate is elegant and well distributed. I still prefer a full PKI, because I think most organizations could benefit from deploying PKI. But in some cases, an EFS RA might be acceptable.

The folder and all its contents, including files and subfolders, are now encrypted. Because Don did not already have a certificate and private key that EFS could use, EFS generated one before encrypting the contents.

 A public key certificate and associated private key may already exist for Don. This depends on whether a certification authority has been installed and configured within Woodgrove Bank and, if so, whether it is configured to issue EFS-usable certificates. In many cases, Don will have such a certificate and not know he has one. The only way Don can determine what certificate is used for EFS is to use the Certificates MMC snap-in as described later to identify the certificate with the Encrypting File System listed as its Intended Purpose.

Example: Managing the Private Key to Ensure Maximum Protection

Don knows that retaining the private key on the hard disk is inadvisable and that he must export the certificate and private key to a floppy disk for safekeeping. He can do this by completing the following steps whenever he is finished working with his encrypted data:

1. Click Start, click Run, type **mmc.exe**, then press Enter.
2. Click File, then click Add/Remove Snap-in.
3. Click Add.
4. Click Certificates, then click Add.
5. Select My User Account and then click Finish.
6. Click Close, then click OK.
7. Expand the Certificates—Current User container, expand the Personal container, then click Certificates.
8. Click the certificate that lists Encrypting File System under the Intended Purposes column. This is shown in Figure 4-10.
9. Click Action, click All tasks, then click Export.
10. Within the Certificate Export Wizard:
    a. Select "Yes, export the private key."
    b. Select "Delete the private key if the export is successful."
    c. Enter a strong password that is difficult to guess.
    d. Enter a save path to a floppy disk and click OK.

Now the private key is removed from Don's saved private keys. EFS can continue to operate using the private key it has cached, but once Don logs off the computer, this cache will be erased. Don must import the private key from the floppy disk before he

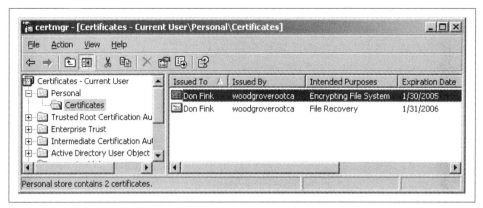

Figure 4-10. Selecting the EFS certificate based on the Intended Purposes field

can decrypt any files encrypted with that private key. Importing a private key from a saved file is extremely simple:

1. Insert the floppy disk in the disk drive.
2. Click Start, click My Computer, then double-click the floppy drive.
3. Double-click the file saved earlier to import the private key.
4. Enter the password when prompted.

 I frequently refer to the use of a floppy disk throughout the book. This is because the floppy drive is the most universal removable media device available and has been installed in computers as standard equipment for decades. However, floppy disks can go bad over time or with minimal abuse. Many other portable storage solutions—such as USB key drives, memory cards, and rewritable CDs—are available. In many cases, these removable solutions will work exactly the same as a floppy disk. When a floppy disk is specifically required, a note will be added to indicate that fact.

Example: Using cipher.exe to Remove Old Unencrypted Data

In our example, Don creates the folder for his encrypted data and marks it for encryption before any data is actually created. However, this may not always be possible. He may want the same level of protection for the data that he has already saved on his hard disk. He can follow the previous steps to mark a folder as encrypted and remove the private key. He would then drag files into the folder and they would become encrypted. However, because the files were previously stored as unencrypted on the hard disk, portions of those files may still exist unencrypted on the disk. Those file portions are often called *data remnants*. And although this data would not be easy to retrieve, a dedicated attacker with sophisticated equipment could do so.

To avoid data remnants on the disk for an indeterminant period, the disk should be wiped clean of unused data. This process, while fairly lengthy, can ensure that current technology cannot recover the old unencrypted data remnants. The procedure can be done by following these steps:

1. Click Start → All Programs → Accessories → Command Prompt.
2. Type **cipher.exe** **/w:***directory* where *directory* is a directory on the desired hard drive.

cipher.exe then identifies any portions of the hard drive that are not currently in use and may contain old unencrypted portions of protected files. It completely eradicates the data from these portions, one at a time, across the entire hard disk. Because of its thoroughness and the size of most current hard drives, this process can take a very long time to complete. Use the `cipher` `/w` command only occasionally when the above circumstances exist.

Identifying the EFS recovery agent

In Don's scenario, I assume that there is either no EFS recovery agent or that the recovery agent is configured by Group Policy. Don knows that the recovery agent can decrypt any files on the hard drive. He must identify the recovery agents, if any, and if their private key is located on his computer, it must be removed. This is to ensure that an unintended private key stored on the local hard drive cannot be compromised by an intruder and used to decrypt the files. To identify the EFS recovery agent(s) in use, Don will:

1. Right-click on an encrypted file in his encrypted folder and choose Properties.
2. Click Advanced.
3. Click Details.
4. The data recovery agents are identified in the list labeled "Data recovery agents for this file as defined by recovery policy," as shown in Figure 4-11.

If any of the private keys for the listed recovery agent(s) are on the local computer, they should be removed using the procedure described earlier in this chapter.

Example: Storing Shared Encrypted Files on a Windows Server 2003 File Server

EFS is primarily designed to encrypt local files. However, files stored on a file server can also be encrypted. Windows Server 2003 supports two methods of file sharing that can be used with EFS—the classic SMB file sharing and WebDAV file sharing. This complements file permissions on the remotely stored files and ensures that even with server compromise, only individuals with the appropriate private key can decrypt the files.

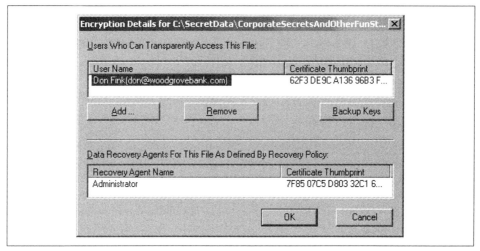

Figure 4-11. Administrator is the data recovery agent for this file

 Remember that EFS works in conjunction with NTFS. When using a normal file share to save or open files, the NTFS operations are done at the file server. This means that all encryption and decryption of EFS files is done by the file server. The data on the network between your computer and the file server is not protected by EFS. To ensure true end-to-end security of your data, you must protect the data as it travels on the network. IP Security (IPSec) is a great way to do that and is the topic of discussion in Chapter 8.

David wants to save some files in a place where both he and Don can access them. He applies NTFS file permissions to these files and their parent directory. However, David is aware that many administrators have access to the file server. Because the data is extremely sensitive, David wants to ensure that even in the event of compromise of the file server, only he and Don can access the files. David also wants to ensure the availability and redundancy of the data, both of which are provided by a well-managed and -maintained file server.

To configure EFS to allow only himself and Don to access the files on a file share, David can take the following steps:

1. Contact the file server administrator and request access to a file share.

2. Map a drive letter to the file share.

3. Create a new subfolder on the file share or identify an existing folder to contain the protected data.

4. Apply file permissions to the folder as described earlier in this chapter. Ensure that only he and Don have access to the folder and files.

5. Right-click on each file and choose Properties.

How cipher /w Works

The cipher /w command, also known as the *wipe* command, is one of the most powerful security features in Windows Server 2003. In many cases, it can mean the difference between an unsuccessful attack and having otherwise–well-protected data compromised.

When the wipe command is called, *cipher* obtains a list of unused hard drive sectors from NTFS. It then goes to the first sector in the list and performs the following actions:

1. Writes all zeros
2. Writes all ones
3. Requests a pseudorandom number from the Cryptographic API (CAPI)
4. Writes the pseudorandom number

cipher then moves to the next sector in the list and repeats the set of wipe actions. Once all sectors on the list are written in such a fashion, *cipher* requests a list of unused NTFS metadata sectors (*metadata* is the set of files that NTFS uses internally to manage the file system). The wipe operation is then performed on each unused NTFS metadata sector.

Because of the extensive amount of work done by the wipe operation, it takes a very long time to complete. Unfortunately, NTFS is operating the entire time the wipe operation is being performed. During this time, sectors can be used or released by NTFS, thereby changing the list without informing *cipher*. In addition, some small files may reside entirely within NTFS metadata sectors and therefore may not be entirely eradicated by the wipe operation.

The best solution to this situation is to ensure that files are created in an encrypted state and are never written to the hard drive as plain text. Wiping the hard drive will almost certainly remove plain text slack from previously encrypted files, but it is not guaranteed.

6. Click Advanced.
7. Click Details.
8. Because David is the creator of the folder and file, he already exists as a valid user. To add Don to the list of users able to decrypt this file, click Add.
9. Select Don's EFS certificate from the list, or click Find User to browse Active Directory for Don's certificate. The former requires that Don's certificate was imported to this computer, and the latter requires a CA configured to publish issued certificates to Active Directory.

Because of the way EFS encrypts the FEK with the user's public key, Don does not share his private key with David. David can add any user whose public key certificate he can access, as long as that public key is configured to support EFS. When a user attempts to access the file, she must provide her private key, securely, to the file server. This is because the decryption occurs at the file server. Because this obviously assumes a high level of trust for the file server, any file server that will work with EFS must be configured within Active Directory as trusted for delegation. For more information about trusting a computer for delegation, see Chapter 7.

Configuring EFS with Group Policy

As discussed earlier, EFS works well without any administrative control. EFS can request a self-signed certificate and private key and is configured to work well with default settings. However, to provide centralized management and configuration, a number of settings can be configured. These settings determine whether EFS is enabled on the computer as well as identify the EFS recovery agent and the encryption algorithm used by EFS. All these settings are configured by Group Policy.

Don wants to ensure that a specific certificate is used as the recovery agent and that EFS uses the AES algorithm for file encryption. He also requires that users in the Interns organizational unit be unable to use EFS to encrypt their data. To stop the Interns users from using EFS, he configures a Group Policy Object (GPO) on the Interns OU, using the following steps:

1. Log on to a domain controller or a computer that has the Windows Server 2003 Administration Tools Pack installed as a Domain Admin.
2. Click Start → All Programs → Administration Tools → Active Directory Users and Computers.
3. Right-click the Interns OU and click Properties.
4. Click the Group Policy tab.
5. Click New and name the new policy EFS Lockout.
6. Click Edit to edit the EFS Lockout GPO.
7. Expand Computer Configuration → Windows Settings → Security Settings → Public Key Policies → Encrypting File System.
8. Right-click Encrypting File System and choose Properties.
9. Clear the checkbox for "Allow users to encrypt files using Encrypting File System (EFS)."

This policy will be applied to all interns and ensure that they do not encrypt files on their local hard drive. Because it is applied at the OU that contains the actual user and computer accounts, these policies will be enforced. For more information on how Group Policy applies to users and computers, see Chapter 5.

For the rest of the users in the domain, Don wants to configure them to use EFS properly as discussed earlier. He modifies the Default Domain Policy to correctly configure EFS using the following steps:

1. Log on to a domain controller or a computer that has the Administrative Tools Pack installed as a Domain Admin.
2. Click Start → All Programs → Administrative Tools → Active Directory Users and Computers.
3. Right-click the domain name and click Properties.
4. Click the Group Policy tab.
5. Click New and name the new policy EFS Configuration.
6. Click Edit to edit the EFS Configuration GPO.
7. Expand Computer Configuration → Windows Settings → Security Settings → Public Key Policies → Encrypting File System.
8. Right-click Encrypting File System and choose Add Data Recovery Agent.
9. Provide the public key certificate of the desired recovery agent.
10. Expand Computer Configuration → Windows Settings → Security Settings → Local Policies → Security Options.
11. Double-click the policy object labeled System Cryptography: Use FIPS-compliant algorithms for encryption, hashing, and signing.
12. Check Define This Policy Setting and choose Disabled.

These two policy settings will configure EFS with the desired recovery agent and configure it to use the AES encryption algorithm. Note that the algorithm policy setting may seem a bit backward in that you disable FIPS-compliant algorithms. In this case, the FIPS-compliant algorithm included with Windows XP and Windows Server 2003 is triple-DES. When the non-FIPS algorithm is selected, the strongest algorithm EFS supports is used. In Windows Server 2003 and Windows XP Service Pack 1 or later, that is the AES algorithm.

Don has now configured EFS for proper use within Woodgrove Bank. For some users, EFS is disabled entirely. For others, EFS is configured to use the strong AES algorithm and use a specific certificate as a recovery agent. This allows Don to be confident that EFS is being used consistently and securely, and that he can recover sensitive files when required.

Protecting System Information with Syskey

EFS protects files on the hard disk against attack, but the storage location of the private keys for the EFS-protected files presents unique challenges for the system administrator.

As previously discussed, EFS files are encrypted with a FEK that is itself encrypted with the user's public key. The user must possess the corresponding private key to decrypt that data. During normal operation, that private key must obviously be stored somewhere on the hard drive—if it were stored only in protected volatile memory, EFS files would not be accessible once a computer was restarted.

The location of a user's private keys is not a big secret, although it is obfuscated to keep casual attackers away. The keys are stored in a protected key store database. These keys are all protected by a single key called a *master key*. Other keys used by the system for various cryptographic operations, called *protection keys*, are also stored in a similar fashion.

Because an attacker who is able to obtain the master key for that account can decrypt the stored private keys, it must be protected. To counter this type of attack, Microsoft provides a utility called Syskey.

How Syskey Works

When activated as shown later, the Syskey utility simply encrypts the private key store and the SAM using a 128-bit symmetric key called the system key, or *syskey*. The syskey must be read into system memory during boot to decrypt the SAM and private key store to allow the operating system to start. Without this information, the operating system itself cannot start and will fail. This is a minor benefit, as failure to boot may thwart lightweight attackers. Syskey also prevents offline attackers from copying the SAM and using brute force attacks against stored passwords.

 One other very important piece of information protected by Syskey is the administrator's safe mode password. If you are unable to provide the information necessary for Syskey to start the operating system (in mode 2 or 3, described in this section), safe mode will not be available. This is done to ensure that data is not compromised by a specific attack against the safe mode password.

The syskey must be stored somewhere, just as the master and protection keys are stored somewhere. Syskey allows you to choose one of three methods, or modes, of protection. These modes correspond to different locations and protection levels for the 128-bit syskey. These modes are:

Mode 1
> The syskey is stored on the local computer in the registry. It is hidden from casual access, but a dedicated attacker can quickly access the key. This mode is the most insecure, as the key is stored with the data it is protecting. However, it is the simplest from a user's perspective. There is no additional interaction or change of functionality from the user's perspective when Syskey mode 1 is enabled.

Mode 2
> The syskey is generated from a user-supplied password. This password and its derivitave key are never stored on the hard disk. The user must supply the pass-

word during system startup. This provides a huge benefit over mode 1, because the cryptographic key is never stored with the data—in fact, it's never stored on disk at all. The downside is that if the user forgets the password, all data protected by the syskey, including the master key and all protection keys, is lost forever. In addition, someone must type the password onto the local console whenever the computer is restarted This can be problematic if the computer is in a remote data center.

 Syskey mode 2 allows you to specify any password. There are no minimum criteria applied, even if you have applied password policy on your domain user accounts. This does not mean that Syskey passwords should be any shorter or less complex than your domain user accounts. Passwords should be as long and complex as possible while remaining easily remembered. Because this password is supplied only once per operating system boot, a more aggressive Syskey password shouldn't present usability issues.

Mode 3

A pseudorandom syskey is generated and stored on a floppy disk. The mechanism behind this is very simple: a file is created on the disk that contains only the syskey. During system startup, the user inserts the disk and the syskey is read into memory to decrypt the data. This mode provides the same benefits as mode 2 and also eliminates the need for a user to memorize a static password. However, the user must be very careful with the floppy disk. The disk should never be stored in or near the computer, as this would reduce the security to the same as mode 1 (by storing the key and data together). Also, floppy disks have a tendency to fail over time. A backup of the disk should be made and stored securely in case it's needed.

 Syskey mode 3 requires a floppy disk. No other type of removable media is supported for syskey storage.

Syskey does not take the place of other data protection mechanisms such as EFS or NTFS permissions. It is a complementary technology that protects the operating system against a different type of attack. Syskey primarily prevents an attacker from conducting an offline brute force attack against its password database. Other data, such as confidential documents and email, must be protected using the other security mechanisms described earlier in this chapter.

Rather than showing you how to use Syskey as a standalone utility, it's much more useful to look at it as a part of a complete security solution. The following example shows how Syskey is used as part of an end-to-end procedure for protecting the information on a portable computer.

Protecting a Portable Computer

A number of techniques should be used to stop theft of data from laptop computers. I described in great detail earlier how vulnerable these objects are. But one single solution will never be enough to stop a motivated attacker. You need to provide multiple complementary layers of security. One of the most important, Syskey, is described in the previous section. I've summarized many of the other important ones later.

Consider a user, David, who has had a company-owned laptop running Windows XP Professional for a year. David hasn't traveled as part of his job; he uses a portable computer because that's what he was allocated. His manager has determined that he'll be going on a series of short business trips over the following months. He'd like your help to ensure that the data on his laptop is secure. David does keep some confidential files on his laptop. His laptop is joined to your company's domain and he logs in using a domain account. He does not share this laptop with other users.

Configure Syskey mode 2

The first step in securing David's computer is to run Syskey to prevent any offline attacks against his SAM and private key information. You determine that Syskey mode 2 or 3 would be best, as mode 1 is not secure enough for a portable computer. You also determine that traveling with a floppy disk is not a preferred option, as David may either lose or damage the disk or potentially leave it in the laptop at all times. Therefore, you decide to implement Syskey mode 2. You take the following steps:

1. Back up all important data and store it in a secure location.
2. Run a command prompt.
3. Type **Syskey.exe** and then press Enter. The Syskey dialog box, as shown in Figure 4-12, appears.
4. Click Encryption Enabled to activate Syskey, then click OK. The account database key dialog box, as shown in Figure 4-13, appears.
5. Click Password Startup, then provide the password used for Syskey mode 2. This can be up to 128 characters.
6. Reboot the computer to begin Syskey protection and ensure that the password is working correctly.

The user should select the Syskey password. It should be a strong password but one that the user remembers easily. In some cases, IT departments keep a secure log of Syskey passwords for recoverability. Since domain membership and other security policies do not give the network administrators the ability to recover Syskey passwords, this may be a good strategy. Extreme caution should be exercised in the employment of such a database to ensure that only authorized security personnel are able to access the passwords.

Figure 4-12. The initial Syskey dialog allows you to enable Syskey; however, once enabled, it can never be disabled

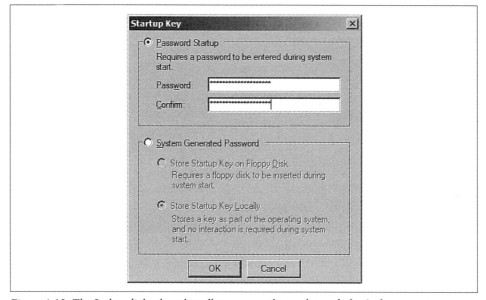

Figure 4-13. The Syskey dialog box that allows you to choose the mode for Syskey protection

Encrypt data directories

Although you could encrypt all data on the hard drive, this would be an enormous waste of resources. Instead, all datafiles that David uses should be kept in a specific directory or set of directories. Those directories should be protected using EFS. For simplicity (which is beneficial in providing security), one directory with multiple sub-directories is the desired configuration.

Why not use both NTFS and EFS? David is the only user of this laptop. David will normally be the only user attempting to access the data. The only time another user will open the files is when the computer is compromised and an attacker is seeking access. In that case, NTFS permissions are not going to stop the attacker. Although NTFS permissions might provide some protection against some attacks, only the encryption provided by EFS will protect the data against this type of physical attack. So although EFS is more effective against different types of offline attacks, using both NTFS and EFS may hinder the attacker more than using one or the other.

You protect the datafiles by completing the following process:

1. Create a new directory.
2. Move all files from their current locations to the new directory or a subdirectory.
3. Ensure David has received the domain policy that contains your designated EFS recovery agents.
4. Have David mark the new directory for encryption and apply the encryption to existing files within the directory.

The procedures for the preceding steps are all documented earlier in this chapter. Once the files are centrally stored and encrypted, they can be accessed only by David or a designated EFS recovery agent.

Run cipher /w

Because David has been using the laptop for some time without using EFS, a large amount of unencrypted data almost certainly resides on his hard drive. Although you've encrypted his files, the remnants of the unencrypted files could reside on the disk for a long time. You can ensure that an attacker cannot make use of these unencrypted remnants by running `cipher /w`. You take the following steps:

1. Run a command prompt.
2. Type `cipher.exe /w:c:\`, then press Enter.

This process will take a very long time, depending on the size of the hard drive and the amount of free space. I recommend you do this in the evening, lock the computer, and go home. The process should be completed by morning.

Summary

Security settings on files and folders can prevent unauthorized users from accessing data. Setting file security is appropriate for most files on the hard drive, as it adds no discernible overhead and works with little or no additional configuration. EFS protects files from intruders who have physical access to the hard drive (such as when it's stolen). Syskey provides strong protection against compromised computers, because it encrypts a great deal of the registry and helps stop an attacker from using the existing operating system. When configured correctly, the combination of file security, Syskey, and EFS helps to ensure that only authorized users may access data.

Educate Users About Traveling with a Laptop

The most important tool in securing a laptop is educating the user. Though this book isn't about user education, it should be part of any security implementation. This education can be brief or even simply printed on a quick reference card for later review.

Of importance when educating the user on safe laptop practices are the following:

- Never leave your laptop anywhere insecure. This includes placing your briefcase on an airport seat while you get a latte or leaving it in a cab while you get money from an ATM. It should be kept under lock and key at all times.

- Require a password when resuming from hibernation on laptops configured to hibernate. Allowing an attacker to resume a logon session with the current user's credentials essentially provides unlimited access to that user's assets.

- Memorize passwords, don't write them down. It's great if users have strong passwords for Syskey and their user accounts. However, if they write the passwords down and keep them with a laptop, the benefit of those strong passwords is lost.

- Never leave your computer unlocked. Pressing Ctrl-Alt-Delete and clicking Lock Computer, or Windows-L, is a simple and effective way to avoid computer intrusion. Many domains deploy Group Policy that configures a screensaver to lock the computer after a short interval. If such a policy is not implemented, the user should be shown how to do this and taught that, with the cable lock, they are providing both physical and logical security.

- Keep all data in the EFS-protected directory structure. Saving secure documents in random unprotected locations is a very simple thing for the user to do. It also discards the EFS protection that we worked hard to provide.

- Report any security compromise to the IT group, and law enforcement, as quickly as possible. Obviously, a stolen laptop should be reported to the authorities. The IT group should also be made aware so that they can disable user accounts, closely audit dial-up links, and so on. Even a small infraction such as someone trying to unlock the user's desktop could be an indication of a larger problem such as targeted corporate espionage. Users may not be in a position to recognize this, so they should report all occurrences.

- Look around in public places periodically. A very common attack is "shoulder surfing," where an attacker simply watches the user type in a password or reads valuable information right from the screen. Cheap devices are available to help counter these attacks; one is a polarizing filter that, when placed over a laptop screen, allows only a user directly in front of the display to see it.

CHAPTER 5

Group Policy and Security Templates

Group Policy is one of the best features of Microsoft Active Directory. Introduced in Windows 2000, Group Policy provides a way for administrators to apply consistent configurations to groups of users and computers. Group policies can help you enforce your organization's written policies. For example, your company's security manual might require that all computers in the research department display a message when users log on, informing them of increased security monitoring in that department. Group Policy allows you to centrally configure, implement, and manage such a warning message, and apply it to the necessary computers.

One of the greatest security-related features of Group Policy is the ability to deploy *security templates* across an enterprise. Security templates, which I'll discuss throughout this chapter, make it possible to bundle an entire security configuration into a single file (the template). For example, you might create a security template for client computers in your organization and then use Group Policy to deploy the security template to the client computers. In this manner, you can centrally configure computers to have a consistent security configuration. You're assured that the configuration will be enforced, thus protecting your computers. Because templates can be centrally managed, you can update, revise, and improve your security configuration over time as required by your organization.

Group Policy has many other important benefits. These include its ability to configure logon and logoff scripts for users and computers, which allows you to run code on target computers that can perform any management or configuration operations you desire. Also, Group Policy has a useful though somewhat limited software distribution feature. While not nearly as robust as Microsoft's Systems Management Server (SMS), this feature can prove useful in deploying necessary software to your end users and servers.

In this chapter, I'll introduce you to Group Policy and show you how Group Policy can be used to enhance the security in your organization. I'll also introduce you to security templates and to the tools Windows Server 2003 provides to create and manage security templates. Keep in mind that Group Policy offers much broader functionality than just security, which is what I focus on in this chapter. If you'd like to learn more about Group Policy and its many other uses, refer to *Group Policy, Profiles, and IntelliMirror* from Sybex.

What Is Group Policy?

Group Policy is a collection of configuration settings and instructions that can apply to user accounts or to computers. Group Policy allows you to manipulate an almost unlimited array of configuration settings and provides a flexible model for applying those configuration settings to specific users or computers within your organization. Many of those settings are completely unrelated to security. For example, you can use Group Policy to deploy a single, corporate-approved desktop wallpaper bitmap to all client computers or to force all users in your organization to use a particular screensaver. Group Policy does contain security-related settings and as I mentioned previously can be used to deploy security templates for comprehensive security control of an entire enterprise. Group Policy also contains instructions to computers that can perform tasks such as installing software or running a script. Although these are technically just one-time settings, they are a bit different in their functionality.

Every Windows 2000, Windows XP, and Windows Server 2003 computer has its own Group Policy, referred to as *Local Group Policy*, or just *local policy*. Active Directory domains allow policies to be stored on and applied by the domain. These policies are collectively called *domain policy*. Both local and domain policies allow you to configure many of the same settings as Group Policy. The difference is that local and domain policies are configured on individual computers and domain controllers. If you change your mind about a configuration setting, you have to modify it on every computer, which can be an administrative nightmare. Figure 5-1 shows the Local Security Policy console, which you can find in the Administrative Tools section of the Start menu. You use this tool to configure the local policy of a single computer.

Group Policy provides a solution to the nightmare of managing distributed computers by allowing you to centrally configure settings in Active Directory. When computers and users log on to an Active Directory domain, the computers download and apply the appropriate Group Policy. Group Policy settings always override any local policy settings, allowing you to centrally manage the policy settings that affect each computer and user in your domain. As a result, Group Policy provides a perfect way to centrally configure security settings for all the computers in your organization. Any administrator with a need to centrally configure security on an organization's computers should be using Group Policy to do so.

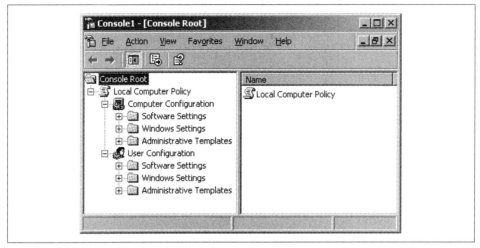

Figure 5-1. The Local Security Policy console

How Group Policy Works

Unfortunately, Group Policy isn't something you can just jump in and start using. Group Policy is heavily integrated with Active Directory and requires a good bit of planning before it can be used effectively. Most of that planning simply involves understanding how Group Policy works.

Because Group Policy works within Active Directory, you have a lot of flexibility in applying Group Policy settings to your users and computers. Active Directory allows you to create any number of different *Group Policy Objects*, or GPOs, which are a collection of settings. You can link a GPO to an *organizational unit* (OU), site, or domain within Active Directory. When a computer starts up or a user logs on to the domain, any GPOs that are linked to the domain, site, or OU the computer or user resides in are automatically applied.

 Group Policy applies to both computers and users; however, some settings may apply only to computers or to certain users of a computer. Computer policies are always applied before user policies.

GPOs are applied in a specific order:

1. Settings from the local policy are applied first, if they've been configured.
2. If a GPO is linked to the computer's site, it applies next. Because users don't belong to sites, this is applicable only to computers.

3. If a GPO is linked to the user's (or computer's) domain, it applies next.

4. Any GPOs linked to the OUs that contain the user's (or computer's) account are applied next, in order. For example, suppose a user account is contained in an OU named Sales, which in turn is contained in an OU named NorthAmerica. Any GPO linked to NorthAmerica will apply first, and any GPO linked to Sales will apply next.

The memory aid for this application is LSDOU—*local, site, domain, organizational unit*. This is the order in which policies are always applied. As you can see, if a user configures local policy, it is overwritten by any domain-based GPO that configures the same setting. This is one way that Group Policy forces companywide settings to take effect on all computers. It's important to note that GPOs don't "merge" in some way. For example, if you link a GPO to a domain and a different GPO to a subordinate OU, those two GPOs don't get magically added together by the operating system. Instead, they both apply in order—any settings configured in the domain's GPO will apply, and then any settings configured in the OU's GPO will apply. If the domain's GPO, for example, specifies a companywide standard wallpaper bitmap and the OU's GPO specifies a different bitmap, then the OU's GPO will "win" simply because it applies last. On the other hand, if the OU's GPO didn't contain any settings for the wallpaper bitmap, the domain's setting would take effect, because it applied first, and nothing in the OU's GPO contradicted it.

Because you can have multiple layers of GPOs, you need to be especially careful about where you place them. For example, you might use domain-level GPOs to enforce broad corporate security guidelines, while using more specific, OU-level GPOs to enforce security settings that are specific to a particular department or office. Site-level GPOs can be used to apply settings that are specific to a particular office or other geographic location. For example, you might use a domainwide GPO to specify a standardized wallpaper bitmap and then use a site-specific GPO to configure foreign-language versions of the bitmap for your company's international offices.

GPO configuration can become quite complex. Administrators can configure OUs to block any higher-level GPOs and also configure specific GPOs so that they cannot be blocked by an OU's configuration. While complex GPO configuration is beyond the scope of this book, you should definitely become familiar with the capabilities of Group Policy before you begin using them in your production domain. Try to avoid using the blocking and overriding capabilities of GPOs until you're completely at ease with how they work and how they will complicate your domain's GPO management. For more information on GPO blocking and overriding, see *http://www.microsoft.com/technet/prodtechnol/windowsserver2003/proddocs/entserver/Block.asp*.

Security Showdown: Group Policy Philosophy

Safety in numbers or all your eggs in one basket? Windows Server 2003 allows you to manage GPOs any way you like, whether you prefer to create many smaller GPOs, each implementing a small number of policies, or create a few giant GPOs that include all your settings. Which is better?

Mike: My philosophy on Group Policy is simple: the fewer the better. The primary benefit for this is simplicity. As we know, complexity is the enemy of security. Having numerous tiny policies scattered through your sites, domains, and organizational units is as complex as you can make it. It's an open invitation to unintended policy application—whether it's too much or too little policy applying. Then the nightmare of unwinding which policy applied to which computer and why begins to unfold.

Creating one policy for domain controllers, one at the top level of the domain, and perhaps the occasional one at OU level is more than sufficient. You can immediately identify where a policy is coming from, as policy is applied in a very specific location. This policy can be as detailed as you like, containing numerous settings. It also speeds up client logon, as one larger policy is far easier to apply than hundreds of small ones.

The single-GPO method also has a benefit specific to security. Having one policy ensures that all computers receive the same set of policies. This is extremely important when you have documented security policies that are mandated across the organization. With one well-configured policy, you can ensure complete compliance with these policies. If you have numerous little policies, you might never know that at some obscure OU buried in your tree, there's a policy that was misconfigured and blocks a required policy setting. Or you might not know about it until it's too late.

If you can apply the intended settings with one or two GPOs in an organization, do it.

Don: Perhaps, Mike, but I prefer many, smaller GPOs to the big monolithic ones you're prescribing. True, it takes more time and effort to manage many GPOs, but I find that they can be used more effectively. For example, a single GPO that implements a root certification authority trust can be widely applied across multiple domains if it doesn't contain a billion other settings that might not be so globally applicable.

Smaller GPOs also make it easier to apply GPOs in just the right place for the perfect effect. Larger GPOs tend to get deployed at the domain and site levels, ignoring the flexibility of deploying more customized settings to specific OUs when the situation calls for it. Larger GPOs also make it harder to use the Block Policy Inheritance and No Override features to control GPO application. Granted, those features can make it tough to figure out what policies a user will actually receive, but Windows Server 2003's new RSoP feature in Active Directory Users and Computers provides an easy way to get a resultant set of policies.

For flexibility, precision application of settings, and more fine-tuned control, many, smaller GPOs are the way to go.

Mike: I'll buy that, but for pure ease of management and troubleshooting, I'll continue to advocate fewer, larger GPOs. Of course, in the real world, the right answer is somewhere in the middle, right? As few GPOs as you can have but as many as you need.

How Does Group Policy Actually Configure a Computer?

Modern Windows operating systems—Windows 2000, Windows XP, and Windows Server 2003—obtain most of their configuration settings from the registry. Group Policy works by modifying the registry on a computer, thereby modifying the computer's behavior.

The registry contains two main hives that are affected by Group Policy. The first hive, HKEY_LOCAL_MACHINE, contains settings that apply to a computer and all the users of that computer. The other main hive, HKEY_CURRENT_USER, contains settings that are specific to the user that is currently logged on to the computer. Group Policy also contains a computer configuration section and a user configuration section, which correspond to the two registry hives. Group policy settings in the user configurations section, for example, are applied to HKEY_CURRENT_USER when the user logs on to the domain.

Group Policy works with only Windows operating systems that include native Active Directory support: Windows 2000 Professional, the Windows 2000 Server family, Windows XP Professional, and the Windows Server 2003 family.

How Do Security Templates Work?

Security templates are INF files that contain security settings. These settings can include certain local policies but can also include things like file auditing settings, file permissions, IPSec configurations, registry permissions, and so forth—pretty much any security-related settings, in fact.

You can use a number of different tools to apply a security template to a computer. For example, Windows 2000 and higher includes *Secedit.exe*, a command-line tool that can be used to (among other things) apply a security template to a computer, effectively copying the settings in the template into the computer's active configuration. Group Policy can also be used to deploy security templates.

Security templates work a bit like Group Policy, in that you can apply multiple templates to a computer. As with Group Policy, the last template applied to a computer "wins." It's as if several different individuals walked up to a computer, one at a time, and made configuration changes. If the first person set up very restrictive file permissions on a folder, but the second person walked up and configured much more lenient permissions, the effective permissions would be whatever the second person configured. If neither person configured a specific setting, that setting remains unchanged—the default setting for the operating system.

Security templates and Group Policy may seem like two different ways to accomplish the same tasks. They aren't. Security templates configure a wide range of security settings that aren't available directly in a GPO, such as file system ACL settings and direct registry settings. A GPO can, however, *contain* a security template, making it possible to use Group Policy as a security configuration tool.

Some important security technologies that can be implemented, configured, and enforced with Group Policy include:

- IP Security
- Encrypting File System
- Software Restriction Policy
- Certificate autoenrollment
- User rights
- Auditing
- Password policy
- Any registry changes, whether they apply to an existing Group Policy setting or not
- Local group membership requirements

Security templates can also contain configuration information such as:

- File permissions
- User desktop settings (some of which are configured with Group Policy settings)
- User access to various Windows components such as Control Panel or Command Prompt

Together, these two configuration options allow you to control virtually every aspect of a user's Windows environment. However, all this control can be a bad thing. It's important to understand when to use this solution and when not to. Careful planning and risk assessment must be performed before implementing any of these solutions. You can easily destroy a network by implementing the wrong group policy or security template. More information on planning is provided in Chapter 15.

 When I say *destroy*, I mean *destroy*. As in having to reinstall or restore from backup all computers on the network. Group Policy is very powerful stuff.

Using Group Policy to Enforce Security

Some basic steps are involved in using Group Policy to enforce security.

First, you need to identify exactly what security settings you need to deploy. Do you simply need to ensure that all users are forced to use a password-protected screensaver? If so, a simple GPO will probably provide the necessary functionality. How-

When Can't I Use Group Policy or Security Templates?

Group Policy and security templates are available only on Windows 2000, Windows XP, and Windows Server 2003 computers. As a result, you won't be able to secure computers that run an older operating system by using Group Policy or security templates. That's an important consideration for enterprisewide security planning. For example, simply deploying Windows Server 2003 on all your organization's domain controllers won't provide you with any special client security configuration capabilities if all your client computers run Windows 98 or Windows NT Workstation 4.0. Windows Server 2003's centralized security management technologies work only in conjunction with Microsoft's newer Windows operating systems.

ever, if you need to deploy complex security settings, including file permissions and network security settings, you'll need to configure a security template and add that template to a GPO.

The next step requires you to determine the scope for your security deployment. Do you need to deploy all your security settings domainwide or to particular OUs? It's actually quite rare to deploy one all-encompassing set of security settings across an entire domain, because those settings would affect *every* user and computer in the domain, including domain controllers and servers. Instead, you'll typically deploy security settings to specific OUs. In fact, once you start thinking about where you want to deploy your security settings, you may find that you need to restructure your Active Directory OU hierarchy a bit to accommodate your security deployment needs.

Of course, you'll need to thoroughly test your security settings before deploying them companywide. Create a test OU (or even an entire test network) that you can use to deploy your security settings to a small number of computers for evaluation. It's very easy to create security templates that make client computers essentially unusable or even prevent communications between server and client computers. Careful testing is a must, especially as you start configuring more complex security settings.

 A very important component of Group Policy that provides security is not covered in this chapter. Software Restriction Policy (SRP) allows an administrator to determine what programs a user can and cannot run on his computer. This goes beyond not installing software and actively polices a user's computer to ensure that unauthorized software is not run. SRP is so powerful and effective that an entire chapter (Chapter 6) is devoted to it.

Controlling Password Policies with Group Policy

Password and account lockout policies are certainly the most commonly implemented security policies. They provide enforcement of basic security mechanisms across your enterprise. If you do not currently employ these types of safeguards in your environment, you should examine your need for this type of security. Weak passwords are one of the most commonly compromised system vulnerabilities. If users are not forced to use difficult passwords, an intruder can easily guess or determine passwords and gain access to corporate resources.

All accounts in your domains should be protected by these policies. Local user accounts on member servers and client computers should also be protected, because they represent a potential security hole that attackers love to exploit. Keep in mind that an attacker can use *any* account to gain access into your environment (yes, even an unprivileged local account). Compromise of even the most restricted account in your enterprise will allow an attacker to gain valuable knowledge of your environment, and that knowledge can be used to launch a more sophisticated attack against more powerful accounts. Additionally, consistency is your friend. If all accounts are protected to the same level, you are assured of an enterprisewide minimum level of security. If you allow exceptions and inconsistencies, a user could claim that her account was compromised because she was an exception to the policy. That's no way to maintain corporate security! Service accounts are often a major exception to security policies, because they are more difficult to change on a regular basis. Although service accounts are more difficult to manage to the same level as user accounts in this regard, service accounts are critical resources and should also receive the same level of security.

 Windows Server 2003 recognizes only one password and account lockout policy configuration per domain. Setting the desired password policy at the domain level works properly. Although you can make these Group Policy changes at the OU or site level, they will not apply.

Example problem: Woodgrove Bank password policy

Don Fink, our security administrator, has noticed a recent anomaly in the security audit logs. He's noticed an increase in failed logon attempts. The failed attempts apparently affect the account of one user, David Loudon, who is on paternity leave for a month. These failed attempts began shortly after David began his leave. No other accounts are showing this type of behavior, only David's. The most disturbing fact is that after four days of consistently failing logon attempts, no more such events are recorded. Unfortunately, Don doesn't audit logon success activity, as it generates too many events.

Don calls David to try to learn what's happening. David says he does not have a computer at home nor has he been in to work. Don is concerned that David's account may be compromised and that an attacker is attempting to use David's account to access the network. Don immediately disables David's account. Don has no idea what resources, if any, David's account may have accessed without a detailed query of his audit logs, which he begins immediately. He also notifies his manager, who convenes a series of meetings to address the implementation of preventive measures to secure against future attacks of this nature.

The meeting results in a new password policy being created. Woodgrove Bank has had no formal password policy, relying on the default Windows Server 2003 policy. This default policy is examined and found to not be strong enough for the bank. The behavior of account lockout is also examined during the meeting and also found to not be strong enough for current security needs. The following new policy is specified and approved:

- A user's password can be no shorter than six characters and must contain letters in both upper- and lowercase and either numbers or nonalphanumeric characters.
- Each user must reset his password every 28 days.
- A user cannot reuse the same password until the password has changed at least 10 times since last use.
- A user can change her password no more frequently than once every seven days. This is to ensure users do not manually or programmatically change passwords back to original values through several quick, successive changes.
- An account can make only five unsuccessful logon attempts within 30 minutes before that account is disabled. The account must remain disabled until the corporate helpdesk is contacted by both the affected employee and his manager, and the identity of the user is verified. At that time, the helpdesk will reset the account's password to a new value and provide it via voicemail on the manager's phone, then reenable the account.

Most of these settings can be enforced through a well-planned and properly deployed group policy, specifically through the security settings portion of Group Policy. However, no group policy is fully effective unless it is supported by corporate administrative policy. For more information on this interaction, see Chapter 15.

Example implementation: controlling password policy

Don must implement the approved security policy for all users in the woodgrovebank.com domain. This example implements the policy discussed in the previous section, but more policies may be required.

Implementing the specified policy is easily accomplished with Windows Server 2003 by taking the following steps:

1. Open Active Directory Users and Computers.

2. Right-click on woodgrovebank.com and click Properties.

3. Click the Group Policy tab, click the Default Domain Policy, and choose Edit to edit the default GPO. The Default Domain Policy applies to all objects in the domain, including domain controllers. Since domain controllers are responsible for storing user passwords, applying the policy to the domain controllers will ensure that all user passwords comply with the policy.

4. Navigate to Computer Configuration → Windows Settings → Security Settings → Account Policies, then click on Password Policy. All password policies are displayed in the righthand pane as shown in Figure 5-2.

5. Double-click the Password Must Meet Complexity Requirements setting and choose Enabled, then click OK.

6. Double-click the Maximum Password Age setting and change the Password Will Expire In value to 28 days, then click OK.

7. Double-click the Minimum Password Age setting and change the value to 7 days.

8. Double-click the Enforce Password History setting and change the Keep Password History For value to 10, then click OK. This setting will also meet the requirement to disallow users from reusing a password within 60 days, as 10 password history × 7-day minimum password duration = 70 days. This exceeds the minimum required value.

9. Double-click the Minimum Password Length setting and change the value to 6. This is redundant with the Password Must Meet Complexity Requirements setting but is important for completeness.

10. In the left pane, click Account Lockout Policy.

11. Double-click the Account Lockout Duration setting, check the Define This Policy Setting checkbox and change the value to 0. The description will change to "Account is locked out until administrator unlocks it." Click OK. The Suggested Value Changes dialog box will offer to change the other account lockout settings to the values that you were already planning to use. Click OK to accept these values.

12. Confirm that all three account lockout policy settings are configured correctly as shown in Figure 5-3.

13. Close all open windows.

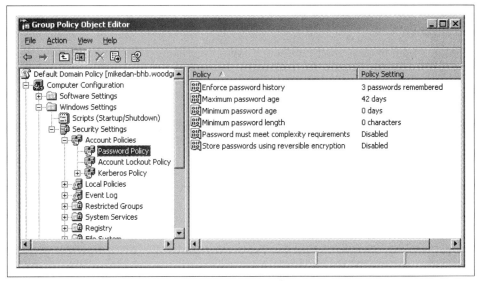

Figure 5-2. The default account policies within the Default Domain Policy at woodgrovebank.com

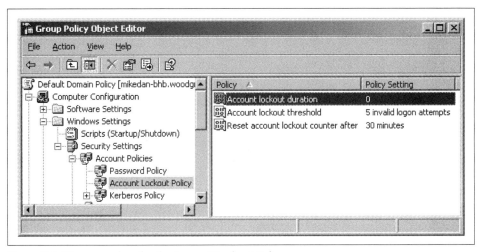

Figure 5-3. The new values for the Account Lockout Policy

Once the Group Policy changes are saved, Active Directory will replicate these changes to all domain controllers within the woodgrovebank.com domain.

Users with weak passwords will not be challenged to change to a stronger password until their current passwords expire, since Windows Server 2003 checks for password complexity and length only when a password is changed. Also, users who infrequently log on or are on extended leave may not be forced to change their passwords for quite some time, leaving these accounts open to an interval of potential attack You can mitigate this temporary weak password threat by forcing all users to change their passwords at next logon. This can be done through the Active Directory Users and Computers console or by running a script. One such script is provided in Chapter 6 of *Active Directory Cookbook* (O'Reilly).

Configuring the Desktop with Group Policy

Group Policy can be used to great effect to control users' capabilities on their own computers. This can limit users' opportunities to get themselves into trouble or limit their access to potentially sensitive features, such as mapping network drives or modifying their computers' networking configuration.

Example problem: Woodgrove tellers

Tellers at Woodgrove Bank get little computer training before they are sent to the branches to do their job. This has always been somewhat of a problem, so Don has provided as much ongoing assistance as possible. Don has created short and straightforward procedural checklists for performing all the common teller tasks. He has also provided new tellers with a list of common questions and answers to both procedural and troubleshooting questions. The IT group has also staffed a special technical support queue to specifically help tellers with their computer tasks.

Recently, there has been a very high turnover of tellers. Because of the rapid personnel turnover, most new tellers are given virtually no computer training. These new tellers are mostly unfamiliar with computers. This has resulted in a surge in IT workload from two factors: the new tellers are calling technical support for help, and they are experimenting with ways to complete their tasks. Unfortunately, the experimentation has caused numerous computer problems requiring the dispatch of technicians to various branches to repair damage to the operating system. This is causing loss of productivity for all parties involved and is getting worse by the day.

Don's boss wants him to help find a solution. Don believes that applying Group Policy correctly can help. He can restrict the actions these tellers can take and ensure that they can perform only the tasks required by their job. He also wants to make the computers more intruder-resistant, as he is concerned that employees, even trusted tellers, may attempt to attack computer systems over the course of the years. Finally, he wants to remove temptation from these tellers by reducing the number of Start menu items available to them.

When locking down the user's environment, Windows Server 2003 offers an extensive selection of policies that enable the administrator to have very specific control of a user's environment. There are so many options that using the editor without an advance plan is overwhelming and may result in an incomplete or undesired policy being deployed. To determine what options are available and would be appropriate to meet his needs, Don should consult Windows Server 2003's Help and Support Center. There is a complete list of all Group Policy settings and their results available within Help in the Security and Administration topic. This will make planning more effective and allow Don to model various solutions as well as implement the right policy the first time. Also, as stated earlier, these Group Policy deployments must be tested in a lab environment before being rolled out to users. Deploying untested Group Policy is a recipe for disaster—stopping the tellers from doing their job could stop Woodgrove Bank from doing business entirely, effectively shutting down the company.

 Microsoft provides a complete list of available Group Policy settings and defaults that covers several operating systems, including Windows XP and Windows Server 2003. This list is updated frequently and can be found at *http://www.microsoft.com/downloads/details.aspx?FamilyID=7821c32f-da15-438d-8e48-45915cd2bc14.*

Example implementation: controlling desktop resources

Don starts by ensuring that all teller user and computer accounts are in an OU called Tellers. This will allow him to create group policies that will apply only to the tellers' environments, as these new group policies will be more restrictive than the policies for users in other roles within the bank. Although separate Group Policy is often deployed to user and computer OU containers, in this case we can simplify by deploying one set of group policies to the tellers' computer and user accounts.

Before Don makes any changes, he should carefully plan out the policies he is going to change. This can be done through a variety of processes. For most security planning, a risk analysis process is normally used. In this process, the administrator examines the risks that are presented, and the solution provides appropriate mitigations for those risks. This type of process is discussed further in Chapter 15. For the purpose of this example, I'll assume Don has developed a list of desired settings based on a risk analysis.

Don can configure Group Policy with the following steps:

1. Open Active Directory Users and Computers.
2. Double-click on woodgrovebank.com, right-click on the Tellers OU, and click Properties.

3. Click the Group Policy tab and click New to create a new GPO called Teller Restrictions.

4. Click Edit to edit this GPO.

5. Navigate to User Configuration → Administrative Templates. This section of the Group Policy Object Editor lists numerous Group Policy settings, some of which are shown in Figure 5-4.

6. Make the policy changes that were determined to be appropriate for the Tellers group. The bulk of user environment restriction policies are in this section. If the changes have not been planned, you can browse through this portion of the editor to learn what options are available. However, you should not change any options until you have a complete list of desired changes and have tested those changes in an isolated test environment.

7. If restriction of the user's access to Internet Explorer is desired, locate those settings under Windows Settings → Internet Explorer Maintenance.

8. Close all open windows and wait for Active Directory to replicate the new Group Policy information to all domain controllers.

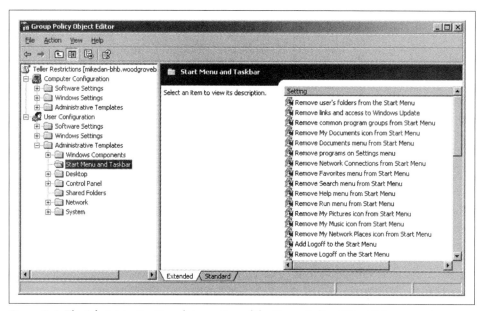

Figure 5-4. The Administrative Templates section of the Group Policy Object Editor contains more options for restricting the user's environment than you might expect

To ensure that the changes were properly made, Don could install a computer and place its account in the Tellers OU and then create a user account in the Tellers OU. Logging in using this test account on the computer would simulate the environment the tellers will receive with the same policies. If the environment allows Don to complete the tasks the tellers must accomplish while still restricting their other activities, the Group Policy is effective. If any undesired results are obtained (e.g., Don forgot to lock down a specific component), the policy can be modified before the tellers receive it.

In addition to the steps provided, Don should consider deploying software restriction policies to limit the programs that the tellers can run. This is discussed in detail in Chapter 6.

Configuring Auditing with Group Policy

The previous section demonstrated a relatively simple application of Group Policy, locking down the desktop options of a group of users. But you can do much more with Group Policy. Virtually any configuration you want to make on a computer can be done with Group Policy.

The example in this section details configuring security auditing. *Auditing* records events as they happen and stores them in logs. Administrators and automated systems can then access these records to determine the cause of an intrusion that has already happened, search them for suspicious patterns that may indicate an intruder trying to break in, or best of all, review them to determine potential vulnerabilities and fix them before an attacker finds them. Security and system logs may also provide forensic evidence in the case of legal proceedings against attackers. More information on auditing is provided in Chapter 15.

Example problem: security auditing for servers

Assume for this scenario (and it's a big assumption!) that Woodgrove Bank has a history of carefully protecting its servers from attack. However, they realize that protection is not enough. If a successful attack occurs, it may not have obvious and immediate symptoms such as a service outage or data loss. Instead, an attacker may copy information and disconnect without disrupting service. An intruder might also plant some malicious software that continuously monitors the server and forwards desired information to the attacker. This is obviously something that needs to be prevented, but if prevention fails, the bank will need evidence that the events took place. Auditing can help provide that evidence.

Don is required by company policy to implement security auditing on all human resources computers within woodgrovebank.com. Important security events must be logged by Windows Server 2003 and stored until Don reviews and saves the log to a file for archival. The log must not clear itself automatically, as that could result in a loss of evidentiary data. He also wants to audit logon activity for domain accounts to determine if any users are displaying unusual account behavior that might indicate a potential account compromise—multiple logons within a short period of time, logons at odd hours, and so on. Finally, Don must ensure that any attempt to add users to groups is logged for later auditing to verify that the user is authorized to be a member of that group. This will help unveil any attempts by rogue administrators to place innocent-looking user accounts in highly privileged groups for later unauthorized use.

Example implementation: controlling auditing

Don begins this implementation by ensuring that all the desired human resources computers are in an OU called HR Servers. User accounts do not matter, as the auditing is configured for the computer and not for the user. All domain controllers are automatically placed in their own OU called Domain Controllers, so Don does not need to move them.

Don can configure Group Policy with the following steps:

1. Open Active Directory Users and Computers.
2. Double-click on woodgrovebank.com, right-click on the Domain Controllers OU, and click Properties. This OU is selected because domain controllers are the desired computers for auditing in this scenario.
3. Click the Group Policy tab, click Default Domain Controllers Policy, then click Edit to edit the GPO.
4. Navigate to Computer Configuration → Windows Settings → Security Settings → Local Policies → Audit Policy. This section of the Group Policy Object Editor controls what events are audited on the target computers. The default settings of Windows Server 2003 are shown in Figure 5-5. Don verifies that the current settings already meet his planned requirements for auditing account management and logon events.
5. Navigate to the Security Options node. Double-click the "Audit: shut down system immediately if unable to log security audits" setting, check the Define This Policy Setting checkbox and set the value to Enabled.
6. Navigate to the Event Log node.
7. Double-click the Maximum Security Log Size setting, check the Define This Policy Setting checkbox and set the value to a sufficiently large number such as 32768. This will vary depending on the number of audit events created and the frequency of the logs being archived and cleared.
8. Double-click the Retention Method for Security Log setting, check the Define This Policy Setting checkbox and select the "Do not overwrite events (clear log manually)" value.

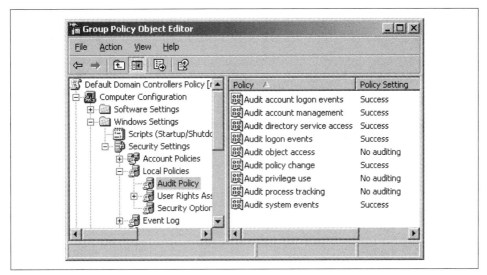

Figure 5-5. The default domain controller audit policies

The changes to the way security audit events are stored and retained are shown in Figure 5-6. These settings directly control how many audit events are stored and what the operating system will do if the log becomes full. In the configuration shown, 32 megabytes of security log entries will be stored before the security log is full. When the security log is full, the system will automatically shut down and be unavailable until the log is manually cleared.

 How do you clear a security log on a computer that will not boot because of a full security log? This is a complex issue that must be addressed by following the instructions provided at *http://support. microsoft.com/default.aspx?scid=kb;en-us;829082.*

Because the audit events will eventually fill the system, Don must simultaneously (or previously) implement a system for archiving and clearing the event logs for all domain controllers. This has to be done before the event logs fill up. Many software products are available to automate this process and roll all events up into one single database that can be queried and analyzed. Don could also do this manually or delegate the task to a worker within the organization. Because so many selections are available, Don should carefully weigh all factors when determining how to handle the audit logs. As long as they are regularly cleared, the domain controllers will remain available. And as long as they are reviewed for nefarious activity on a regular basis, the security information that the logs provide will prove useful.

More information on configuring event logs properly is provided in Chapter 15.

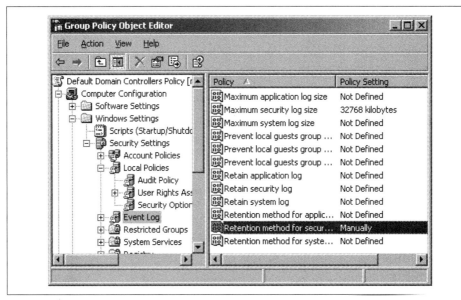

Figure 5-6. This properly configured Group Policy will retain 32 megabytes of security audit events and never overwrite a previous audit event to store a new one

Verifying Group Policy Application with RSoP

Deploying Group Policy is great, but as a security administrator, how do you verify that the configured policies are being applied and enforced on computers in your enterprise? One way is to conduct periodic audits and tests to verify these settings.

Microsoft provides a very useful tool called Group Policy Resultant Set of Policy (RSoP) to help you perform these audits. RSoP is an immensely useful tool when it comes to verifying Group Policy. Some of its features include:

- Verifying Group Policy application against a user, a computer, or both
- Verifying Group Policy application against a site, a domain, or an organizational unit
- Simulating policy application without actually implementing the policy through planning mode
- Verifying Group Policy application against the local or a remote computer

There is a great deal of documentation on RSoP available from Microsoft. It is also discussed in Chapter 15 of this book.

Using Security Templates to Deploy Secure Configurations

You've now seen several examples of how you can configure Group Policy to implement your company's specific security policies, and you've seen how you can apply different settings to large or small groups of users and computers. With such a large number of settings available, though, you may find yourself in a record-keeping nightmare trying to keep track of which settings are applied to which groups. To help solve this problem, Windows provides a number of templates that contain common security and configuration settings for a variety of purposes, from domain controllers to workstations. Of course, you may find that the built-in templates don't provide exactly what you need for your situation, and for that purpose, you can create your own templates. You'll learn about both kinds of templates in this section, and how to deploy them effectively.

Using Built-in Templates

Windows Server 2003 comes with several built-in security templates located in *%SystemRoot%\Security\Templates*, which you can use to configure specific security behaviors within your environment. For example, the Highly Secure template is designed to be applied to server computers and configures them to accept only encrypted connections from clients and from other servers. The Highly Secure template can be used to configure client computers (running Windows 2000 Professional or Windows XP) to make encrypted connections to other computers.

Here is a list of the built-in security templates:

Setup Security (setup security.inf)
> This template is created during installation on each Windows Server 2003 computer and contains the default security settings for that computer. This template will differ from computer to computer. It can be used to restore the default permissions on the computer, if necessary, but should not be used on domain controllers. Domain controllers do not use their default security settings; the act of promoting a server to a domain controller changes its security settings to be different than those contained in *setup security.inf*.

Domain Controller Security (DC security.inf)
> This template contains the default permissions for a domain controller.

Compatible Workstation Security (compatws.inf)
> This template lowers system security to help improve compatibility with older applications that expect the local Users group to have slightly more powerful capabilities.

Secure Workstation and Secure Domain Controller Security (securews.inf and securedc.inf)
These templates limit the use of older NTLM authentication and prevent anonymous users from enumerating account names and shared folders. They also configure SMB packet signing for file sharing, which is disabled by default on servers. *securews.inf* can be applied to anything but a domain controller; *securedc.inf* can be applied to domain controllers.

High Security Workstation and Domain Controller Security (hisecws.inf and hisecdc.inf)
These templates improve upon *securews.inf* and *securedc.inf* by requiring SMB packet signing and strong encryption and signing for interdomain communications.

Root Directory Security (rootsec.inf)
This template contains directory permissions for the root directory of the system drive. While not completely useful on its own, it can be copied and used as a template, enabling you to apply desired ACLs to directories.

Internet Explorer Security ACLs (iesacls.inf)
The new, stronger security settings for Internet Explorer in Windows Server 2003 are stored in *iesacls.inf*. This template may not prove useful unless you plan to reapply the original Internet Explorer security settings through Group Policy.

 You need to be exceedingly cautious when applying any security template—built-in or customized—and you need to thoroughly test it in your environment. For example, suppose you have one or two lingering Windows 98 computers that access a Windows Server 2003 file server and you apply the Highly Secure template to that file server and to your client computers. Because Windows 98 doesn't support some required security features, those computers will no longer be able to communicate with the file server, which is now configured to accept only encrypted communications. This may also be true for some network-attached storage devices and other devices that cannot provide the advanced security that's now required.

Example problem: the human resources department

Woodgrove Bank's human resources department handles a large number of sensitive files. The department maintains its own file server to store these files and employs a Windows administrator exclusively for the department's needs. However, the department is still connected to the same network as all other corporate users, and the department's managers have concerns that sensitive data could be intercepted and modified as it passes from the server to client computers in the department.

Don is called in to advise the department's administrator on possible solutions. After discussing the business needs of the department, they decide to configure the department's file server and client computers to require SMB packet signing, which will ensure data is not modified during transmission. The administrator manually applies the Highly Secure security template, *hisecws.inf*, which is located in the *%SystemRoot%\Security\Templates* folder of all Windows Server 2003 computers, to the server. Don sets out to apply the template to the department's client computers, which are all located in an Active Directory OU named HRDept.

Example implementation: controlling network communications security

Don needs to use Group Policy to deploy *hisecws.inf* to each client computer in the HRDept OU. He'll follow these steps:

1. Open Active Directory Users and Computers and navigate to the HRDept OU.
2. Right-click the OU and select Properties from the context menu.
3. Select the Group Policy tab and click New to create a new GPO.
4. Type a name for the GPO: `Hisec Template`, and press Enter.
5. Select the new GPO and click Edit. The Group Policy Object Editor window appears.
6. Expand the Computer Configuration portion of the GPO.
7. Expand the Windows Settings folder.
8. Right-click Security Settings and select Import from the context menu. You'll see the Import Policy From dialog box, shown in Figure 5-7.
9. Double-click *hisecws.inf*.
10. Exit the Group Policy Object Editor and click OK to close the OU's Properties dialog box.

The computers in the HRDept OU will receive the new GPO within an hour or so, depending upon how the domain is configured.

Analyzing Your Security Configuration

The security templates included with Windows Server 2003 are great for the specific behaviors that they configure, but they really just scratch the surface of what security templates are capable of doing. Fortunately, Windows Server 2003 provides the Security Configuration and Analysis (SCA) toolset, which you can use to analyze the security templates and then create new ones of your own, as you'll see in the following section.

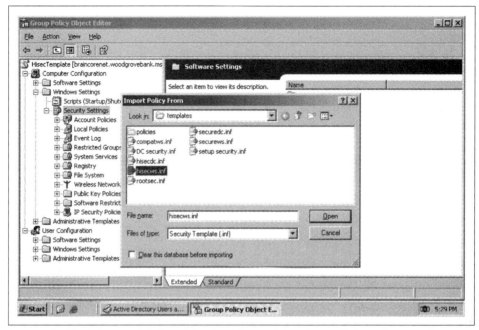

Figure 5-7. The dialog box defaults to \Windows\Security\Templates, which is where Windows Server 2003's bundled security templates reside

Creating a Security Configuration and Analysis console

The main Security Configuration and Analysis console is a Microsoft Management Console (MMC) snap-in. Typically, you won't find the SCA console preinstalled on the Administrative Tools program group on the Start menu. Instead, you'll need to configure a customized console that contains the snap-in:

1. From the Start menu, select Run.
2. Type **mmc.exe** and click OK or press Enter. A blank MMC console will appear.
3. From the File menu, select Add/Remove Snap-ins.
4. Click Add.
5. Locate Security Configuration and Analysis, as shown in Figure 5-8, and double-click it.
6. Click Close and then click OK.
7. You should see a blank SCA console, as shown in Figure 5-9.

Creating a new security database

The SCA snap-in is designed to work with *security databases*. These databases represent the active configuration of your computer and allow you to apply and analyze security templates without actually affecting your computer. The databases allow

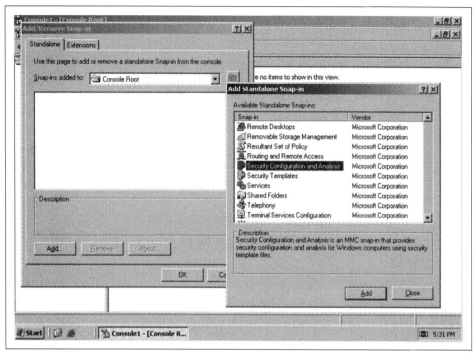

Figure 5-8. You can add other snap-ins, such as Security Templates, to create a comprehensive security management console

you to layer multiple security templates on top of one another and analyze the resulting final security configuration. You can then deploy the final configuration through Group Policy or simply configure your local computer to use the final configuration.

To start working with the SCA, you'll need to create a fresh security database:

1. In the SCA console, right-click Security Configuration and Analysis, and select Open Database from the context menu.
2. Type a name, such as **MyDatabase**, for the new database, and click Open.
3. Select a template to import into the new database. If there's an existing template that you want to start with, select it and click Open.

The SCA console won't do anything with your new database by default. At this point, you can continue to import templates or perform an analysis of the template you've already imported.

Importing security templates

If you already have a security template (or several templates) that you want to use as the basis for your new security database, you can import them into the SCA. Keep in mind that security templates layer on top of one another, so the order in which you

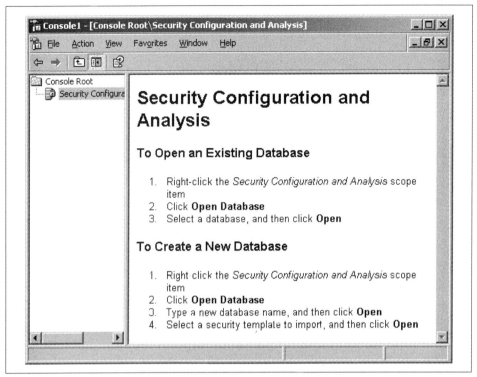

Figure 5-9. The SCA console isn't ready to use until you open a database or create a new one

import them is significant. Suppose your company is already using the Secure Workstation template, which I used in an earlier example, and that you want to deploy those security settings plus some new ones to your client computers. You start by importing the Secure Workstation template into the SCA snap-in:

1. Right-click Security Configuration and Analysis and select Import Template from the context menu.

2. Select the *securews.inf* template and click Open.

3. Repeat these steps until you've imported all the templates that you want to include in your database.

When you're finished, the SCA still won't look very exciting, as shown in Figure 5-10. It's waiting for you to perform an analysis.

 Always work with a fresh-from-the-factory installation of the operating system when you're testing security templates. That way, the base computer settings will be at their defaults, and you can analyze the differences made by the security templates.

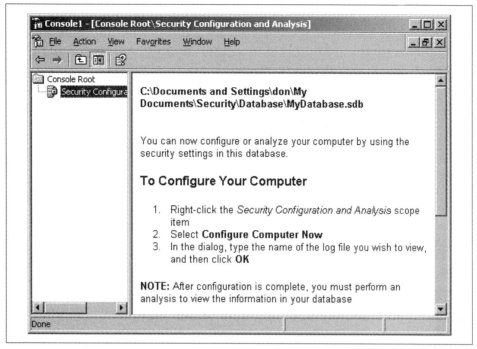

Figure 5-10. You can continue to import templates while the SCA is in this mode

Analyzing the security settings

With your base template imported, use the SCA to perform an *analysis* operation. This will compare the computer's current, active configuration with the configuration specified in the security template (or templates) you've imported. Every single setting will be analyzed and reported with a status indicator. Several possible statuses may exist:

- Settings may be specified in the template but not present on the computer.
- Settings may be specified in the template, and present on the computer, but configured differently than in the template.
- Settings may be present on the computer but not specified in the template.

You can use these status indicators to see what changes would be made if the template were applied to the computer. You can see why it would be more valuable to run the analysis against a computer that's using the default settings; if you ran the analysis against a computer that had already had the template (or templates) applied, the analysis would be empty, because applying the templates again wouldn't have any effect.

To run an analysis in the SCA console:

1. Right-click Security Configuration and Analysis and select Analyze Computer Now from the context menu.

2. Provide a path and filename for a log file, which will contain any errors that occur during the analysis.

While the analysis is running, you'll see a status screen like the one in Figure 5-11.

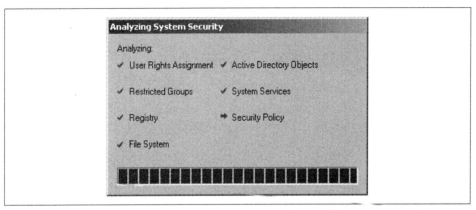

Figure 5-11. Larger security databases will take longer to analyze, and this status screen lets you know how the analysis is proceeding

When the analysis is complete, you can browse the security database. Figure 5-12 shows the initial screen, which has categories for the various security settings that can be configured within a template.

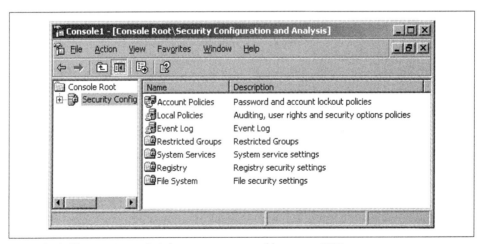

Figure 5-12. The security analysis bears a strong resemblance to a GPO

The icons within the console provide a visual cue as to the status of the various policies. For example, look at Figure 5-13. The Maximum Security Log Size policy includes a red *X*, indicating that the computer isn't configured to have the same setting as the database. In this case, the database sets the log size to 19,456KB, while the local computer is configured to have a maximum log size of 131,072KB. Were you to apply this database to the computer, this setting would change. A green check mark indicates that the database and the computer configurations match.

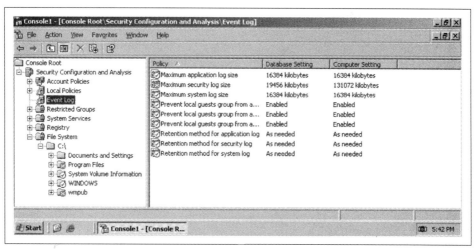

Figure 5-13. Icons make it easy to spot the settings that don't match

File system icons are also used in the lefthand tree view. Notice how the *Program Files* folder contains a red *X* icon. This indicates that *C:\Program Files* doesn't match the security settings in the database. You can expand the tree view to locate the noncompliant folder or file.

Creating Your Own Security Template

Once you've used the SCA to create a security analysis, you can modify the analysis to include your own security settings and then use the database to create a new template. For example, you might want to change the default file permissions on a particular folder that exists on your company's computers. To do so:

1. Double-click a policy or right-click one and select Properties from the context menu. For example, right-click the *Program Files* folder and select Properties.

2. You'll see a dialog box like the one shown in Figure 5-14. The dialog box will be different depending on the type of policy you opened; in this example, you can configure the folder's security settings. All policies have a "Define this policy in the database" checkbox, which effectively turns the policy "on" in the database.

3. Click OK to close the dialog box.

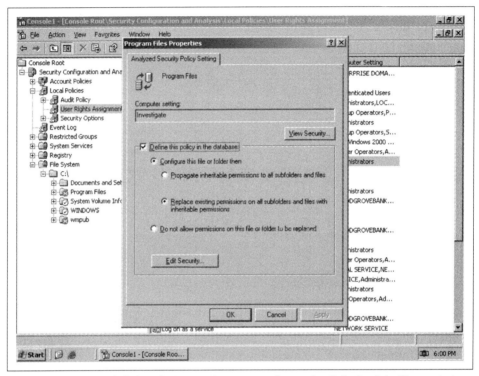

Figure 5-14. You can click the Edit Security button to perform a detailed edit of the file permissions contained in the database for this folder

Make all the security changes you like. When you export the database to a security template, any policies that are defined in the database will be included in the template; any policies left undefined in the database (meaning the "Define this policy in the database" checkbox is cleared) will be left out of the template.

Once you've configured your security database to have the settings that you intend to deploy throughout your organization, you can create a security template. The template will contain *each and every setting that is different from the computer's active configuration*. Any setting that is the same in the database as on the computer won't be included in the template and so won't be applied to any computers that receive the template.

To create a template from a database:

1. Right-click Security Configuration and Analysis and select Export Template from the context menu.

2. As shown in Figure 5-15, provide a filename for your new template, and click Save.

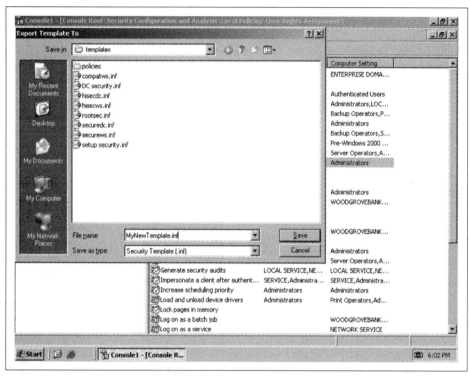

Figure 5-15. Large databases will take several minutes to export into a template

Once your database is exported to a template, you're ready to deploy it. You can use the Secedit command-line tool to apply a template to a single computer, but it's far more efficient to use Group Policy to deploy templates to multiple computers.

 It's possible to configure these settings directly within a GPO, so why bother using templates? Security templates provide an easy way to store batches of security settings for future use. Security templates are simple INF files, so they can be easily transported by floppy disk or sent to other administrators via email to deploy elsewhere. You can also use them to compare INF-stored settings against actual settings on a computer to audit security policy application. All in all, they represent a great way to manage and organize security settings.

Deploying the Security Template with Group Policy

With a security template in hand, you can use Group Policy to deploy the template to the proper computers. Keep in mind that normal Group Policy deployment planning applies: You'll need to be aware of conflicts between GPOs at the domain, site, and various OU levels, and you'll need to be fully aware of the computers or users that will be affected by the new GPO that you create.

To deploy a security template in a GPO:

1. Open Active Directory Users and Computers and navigate to the OU or domain where you want to link the security template. Or, to link the template to a site, open Active Directory Sites and Services.
2. Right-click the OU (or domain or site) and select Properties from the context menu.
3. Select the Group Policy tab and click New to create a new GPO.
4. Type a name for the GPO and press Enter.
5. Select the new GPO and click Edit. The Group Policy Object Editor window appears.
6. Expand the Computer Configuration portion of the GPO.
7. Expand the Windows Settings folder.
8. Right-click Security Settings and select Import from the context menu. You'll see the Import Policy From dialog box, which allows you to select your template.
9. Double-click your template.
10. Exit the Group Policy Object Editor and click OK to close the OU's Properties dialog box.

Using Security Templates Effectively

Security templates work best, and are easiest to manage, if a single template contains just the security settings to achieve a particular goal, such as configuring file security on a particular folder or configuring user password settings. Keep in mind that you can apply as many templates as you like through one or more GPOs; keeping each template small and discrete makes it easier to apply just the right settings to the correct users and computers.

Example problem: Woodgrove server file security

While performing routine maintenance on a Windows Server 2003 server, Don discovered that the server's NTFS file permissions weren't correct. Although the default permissions provide the special Everyone group with Read and Execute permissions, this server was configured to allow the Everyone group Full Control over all files.

The problem was the permissions applied to the root of the D: drive, which contained all shared files. An erroneous access control list entry was granting permission, and that permission was being inherited by all other folders on the drive.

Fixing the one server was easy enough, but Woodgrove Bank has more than 300 file servers in various offices. Don's manager couldn't give Don the time to manually investigate and repair every server. In addition, having Don fix each server couldn't guarantee that another administrator wouldn't incorrectly configure the permissions again at some point in the future.

Don decided to create a security template that contained the proper NTFS file permissions and to apply that template to all file servers in the company. Fortunately, all of the company's file servers were contained in dedicated OUs within Active Directory. Don would simply need to create the proper security template, import it into a GPO, and link that GPO to the OUs containing the file servers—after testing the GPO, of course.

Example implementation: controlling security settings

Don opens his custom SCA console on a Windows Server 2003 file server that contains the incorrect file permissions. Don isn't starting with a predefined template, but rather making his own from scratch, so he'll follow these steps:

1. Right-click Security Configuration and Analysis and select Open Database from the context menu.
2. Type **DonsDatabase** in the dialog box and click Open to create a new database.
3. Select a relatively empty security template as the first one to import. For example, Don selects *rootsec.inf*, which is the root security template that has already been applied to his servers.
4. Right-click Security Configuration and Analysis and select Analyze Computer from the context menu.
5. Expand the File System folder and right-click D:\. Select Properties from the context menu.
6. Select the "Define this policy in the database" checkbox to enable the policy in the database.
7. Ensure that the "Configure this file or folder then" radio button is selected, and select the "Propagate inheritable permissions to all subfolders and files" radio button.
8. Click the Edit Security button.
9. As shown in Figure 5-16, modify the file system security settings as desired. Then, click OK.
10. Click OK to close the properties dialog for the D:\ policy.

11. Right-click Security Configuration and Analysis and select Export Template from the context menu.

12. Provide a name for the new template and click Save.

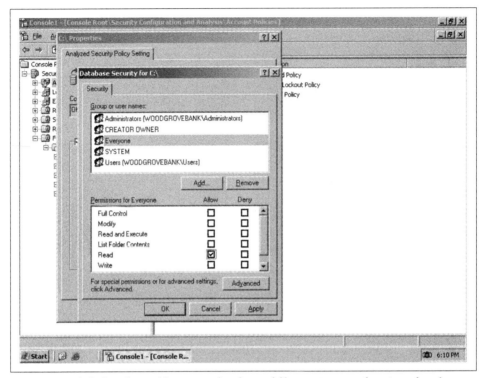

Figure 5-16. Click the Advanced button to edit advanced file permissions; otherwise, select the appropriate permissions for this folder and click OK

Once saved into a template, the security settings can be imported into a GPO and linked to the appropriate OU to apply to the servers.

Summary

Group Policy is an invaluable tool for applying consistent security settings to the users and computers in your organization. In combination with security templates, another key technology for configuring the client, you can centrally configure and manage almost every security setting that is applied to the client computers, servers, and users in an Active Directory domain. In addition, you have almost complete control over a user's experience. However, Group Policy and security templates are very powerful and complex technologies. Poor planning or inappropriate configuration can cause far more damage than expected. Planned, tested, and carefully deployed Group Policy can help secure your network and simplify security for everyone.

CHAPTER 6

Running Secure Code

Malicious and poorly written software costs businesses millions of dollars every year. Whether the software is a virus deliberately written to wreak havoc or simply a poorly written game that causes computers to crash, unauthorized or insecure software is a clear and present security threat. Each version of the Windows operating system has added features to help protect against unsecured code. Over the years, technologies such as code signing and signed driver verification have been added. Windows Server 2003 takes the biggest leap yet, allowing you to completely control the ability of your users to run unsecured software on your company's computers.

This chapter describes two of the newest features in this area: software restriction policies and unsigned driver behavior. *Software restriction policies* (SRP) is a powerful configuration option that can allow or deny software to run based on a number of different rules. These rules are set up by an administrator and reflect the desired level of security established by policy or driven by known threats. *Unsigned driver behavior* is similar in that it uses an administrator-defined setting whenever an unsigned or untrusted hardware driver is installed. The administrator can define whether to allow these potentially dangerous drivers to operate. Together, these two features dramatically increase the ability of Windows to reject untrusted code.

Identifying Secure Code

Secure code is software that doesn't create security vulnerabilities on your computer. Previous versions of IIS, for example, included a number of vulnerabilities that attackers could use to gain unauthorized access to your servers, and so could be considered insecure code.

So how can you tell if code is secure? There's no easy way, because modern software is very complex, and you as an administrator don't have much input into how it's created. In fact, you can make the point that no code can ever be considered completely secure. However, you can decide which software authors—both individuals and companies—you trust to do a good job of writing secure code. As long as you can guarantee that your software comes from them with no alterations, you can trust the code to be as secure as possible.

Windows Server 2003 includes the ability to run *signed code*, which is software that carries a digital signature. The signature gives you two guarantees:

- The software definitely comes from that particular author or manufacturer.
- The software has not been altered since it was signed.

 Not all code is signed. If you determine that running only signed code is a good idea, you need to ensure that your corporate policy reflects that. As a result, part of both your code purchasing and developing processes would need to include a requirement that the code be signed and that the signature chain belong to a trusted CA.

How Code Is Signed

Code signing uses public key encryption to produce a digital signature (see Chapter 9 for more details on this process). The software author uses code signing software, along with a private encryption key issued for the purpose of signing code. The signing software examines the author's software code and produces a *checksum*. The checksum is a reasonably unique number produced by a mathematical algorithm, and any given software code will always produce the same checksum. If so much as a single byte of the code is altered, the checksum will be significantly different.

The signing software encrypts the checksum using the author's private encryption key. The encrypted checksum, known as a digital signature, is attached as part of the software code file, making it available to anyone who receives the software. The signing software also attaches the digital certificate that contains the software publisher's public key.

When a user installs or downloads the software, Windows automatically retrieves the author's public encryption key from the certificate that is distributed in the file. This certificate is first validated to ensure that it is authentic and can chain to a trusted public root. Windows next uses the public key to decrypt the checksum. The computer then runs the exact same checksum algorithm on the files that are digitally signed and verifies that the resulting checksum matches the now-unencrypted checksum. If it does, the computer knows two facts:

- The software hasn't changed since it was signed by the author. If the software has changed, the computer would have generated a different checksum than the one contained in the software's digital signature.
- The software was, in fact, provided by that specific author. If it was signed by someone else, the author's public key would have been unable to decrypt the digital signature in the first place.

The Dangers of Unsigned Code

So how dangerous is unsigned code? Examining the protections that signed code provides, you can imagine the dangers that unsigned code can represent:

- Software could be sent to you by attackers, yet made to seem as if it came from a reputable author. For example, an attacker could send malicious code and make it seem as if that code had come from Microsoft or another trusted software publisher. This is a common tactic used by attackers.

- Internal file shares can be populated with malicious applications such as trojans and backdoors, or existing business application share points can be replaced with such undesired programs. Users may unknowingly install these applications and expose their computers to attack.

- Legitimate software could be modified to include additional, malicious code. Without the verification provided by a digital signature, virus code could be added to software, compromising your network's security.

- Internal software file shares could be compromised, and normally trusted code could be replaced with malicious code. In this type of attack, a single compromised file could affect many users throughout an organization.

- Many applications have their own application language, such as macros that run within Microsoft Office. These macros can be dangerous and have caused considerable damage in the past. They can now be signed just like any other code to ensure their unaltered state and help provide some assurance against attack.

While not all unsigned software is inherently evil, unsigned software always presents a risk. Even if the software's author is trustworthy, unsigned code provides no assurance that the software wasn't modified after it left the author's hands or even that the software really did come from that author. For example, a software vendor could email you a perfectly innocent update to one of your applications. Without a digital signature, though, you have no way of knowing if someone intercepted the email and modified the software update for her own nefarious purposes. This is referred to as a *man in the middle* attack, because someone between you and your trusted software vendor modified the code. You can assume that most malicious code is unsigned, but that's not an absolute, as many spyware and malware applications are signed by well-known root CAs.

As an extension of these principles, any software produced by your company's own software developers, if you have any, should be signed. Signatures will ensure that the code is never modified to include a virus and that the software really did come from your company's internal software developers. As you'll learn in Chapter 9, you can even issue your own digital certificates for internal use, reducing the cost of signing software.

Medical Office Update Attack

An attack occurred in 2002 that could have been prevented by signed software and ensuring the client computers verified the signature before execution. The names in this example have been omitted to prevent embarrassment.

A well-known software manufacturer has a large installed base for its medical office software. This software is expensive and requires frequent updates because of changing insurance regulations, privacy laws, and the like. Until recently, this manufacturer distributed software updates to customers who paid for maintenance by sending a CD in the mail. However, the rising cost of manufacturing and postage inspired a cost-cutting effort. The manufacturer moved to distribution of its software updates via email. It informed its customers via email and letter that they would be receiving their updates monthly in email. They simply needed to read their email on the computer running the medical office software and double-click the attachment to update their system. For protection, they should ensure that the From: field in email was from the software company.

This worked well, until a group of attackers decided to propagate a virus to the medical offices. The attack was almost too simple. They obtained a list of doctors' offices and their email addresses through a series of social engineering attacks against both the software company and the offices themselves. They then constructed an email body similar to the legitimate body. The attachment contained the virus and some simple code that created a dialog box, informing the user that the update was successful.

To distribute the virus, the attacker spoofed the email so that it appeared to be sent from the software manufacturer's technical support center. Because of the large number of insecure email servers available on the Internet, the attack was launched from several servers to help disguise the true source of the attack. This attack was quite successful; many doctors' offices lost all their records since their last backup, and in more than one case, there was no backup at all.

The flaw that allowed this exploit to occur is the assumption by all parties that email attachments from sources you trust are always safe. This assumption has been exploited in the past but usually not to this extent.

To counter this exploit, the software manufacturer could require all computers running its software to enforce software restriction policies. It could then distribute its code and updates, digitally signed, with confidence that the systems would remain secure. Although this might impact other applications running on the medical office computers until those applications were available with digital signatures, it is almost certainly worth the inconvenience to ensure the security and confidentiality of this information.

Reputable authors have no reason not to sign their code to provide you with those assurances. Signing code requires a software utility, which Microsoft and other vendors provide for free. A code signing encryption key pair costs between $300 and $1000 per year, depending on the certificate vendor the key pair is purchased from.

—continued—

Once purchased, the key pair can be used to sign an unlimited number of software packages. Code signing is not an expensive proposition, and reputable authors can easily justify the expense. Companies can even sign their code with a self-produced key and provide you with the public portion of the key. This technique requires a bit more effort on your part, since you have to download the key, but it allows publishers to sign their code for practically no cost whatsoever.

Enforcing the Use of Secure Code

Code signing applies to two types of software: device drivers and regular software applications. *Device drivers* are pieces of software that interface with hardware, such as a mouse or removable storage device. Signed device drivers are especially important, because device drivers execute with special and powerful permissions under Windows in kernel mode. A maliciously written (or modified) device driver can cause an incredible amount of damage to a computer or network.

Regular software applications are the ones you and your users run on a day-to-day basis. These can do a great deal of damage, too, especially if executed by an administrator, since administrators have such wide-ranging capabilities on the network. In fact, the potential for a malicious application to use your administrator credentials to wreak havoc is a primary reason behind POLA, the principle of least access, as discussed in Chapter 2. If you use your administrator user account only when you actually need to perform administrative tasks, you'll reduce the likelihood that a malicious piece of software can use your credentials.

Driver Signing

Device drivers represent a significant security vulnerability, because drivers run in a very privileged, powerful level of the Windows operating system. Poorly written drivers are behind most operating system crashes. Drivers can be infected with viruses as easily as other software and can do much more damage than regular software because of the driver's privileged relationship with the operating system.

Microsoft provides a special software signing program for device drivers. Device driver authors can submit their drivers to Microsoft, which tests the drivers for operating system compatibility and overall software integrity. Microsoft then applies its own digital signature to the driver, assuring recipients that the driver is compatible and has not been altered since it was tested.

You can configure your computers to reject any device drivers that do not contain a Microsoft digital signature. This is a powerful feature that may help reject a significant number of malicious or poorly written device drivers before they're installed.

Configuring Driver Signing

We'll now take a look at how to put security measures in place that restrict the use of unsigned drivers. This can help both stabilize your environment and increase security. We'll look at these configuration changes exclusively from a security perspective, but you should remember that there may be other benefits to these configuration changes.

Example: Warning When Installing Unsigned Drivers

David Loudon has a laptop computer, which he carries with him on business trips. David often needs to attach his laptop to high-speed Internet connectivity devices in hotels, which sometimes requires that he install networking device drivers. David's laptop is configured with your company's default secure code configuration via local policy, which prevents him from installing unsigned drivers. After discussing the risks of unsigned drivers with David, you decide to modify his computer to simply warn him before installing unsigned drivers, but to allow him to install the drivers anyway if he needs to. Here's what you do:

1. Log on to David's computer as an Administrator.
2. Right-click My Computer and select Properties.
3. On the Hardware tab, click Driver Signing.
4. Select the option to Warn, as shown in Figure 6-1.

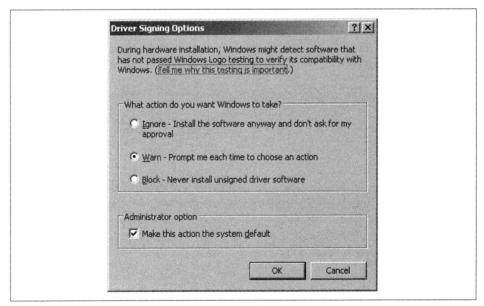

Figure 6-1. Configuring software restriction policy enforcement

5. Select the "Make this action the system default" checkbox.

6. Log off. Test the new configuration by logging on to the computer as David and installing an unsigned device driver.

This scenario allows David to run some unsigned code. While not completely assuring that safe code will run on his computer, it does provide some protection and ensures that David will know the difference between signed and unsigned code. If stability or other issues arise with David's computer after his installation, both you and he have some idea where to begin troubleshooting.

Software Restriction Policies

Software restriction policies (SRP) allow you to classify applications and restrict their use, preventing users from running unauthorized software applications. Software restriction policies use one of four methods to identify applications:

- A hash rule, which is a cryptographic hash (or checksum) that uniquely identifies a particular file
- A certificate rule, which identifies the digital key pair used to sign a particular piece of software
- A path rule, which identifies software by its location on a computer's hard drive
- An Internet zone rule, which identifies software by the Internet domain the software is retrieved from

Software restriction policies can be configured either as part of a local computer's policies or, for more effective centralized management, as part of a group policy applied to all domain computers and users.

Configuring Software Restriction Policy

By default, enforcement of software restriction policies is disabled. To enable enforcement, you need to modify the appropriate policy. To configure the Group Policy settings that apply to software restriction policies, you should follow this procedure. Note that this procedure uses the Default Domain Policy, but you can apply the policy anywhere in your domain.

1. Open the Group Policy Management snap-in.

2. Open the Default Domain Policy Group Policy Object.

3. Navigate to the Software Restriction Policies node as shown in Figure 6-5, later on in this chapter.

4. Right-click the Software Restriction Policies node, and then click New Software Restriction Policies.

Notice that, by default, there are no software restriction policies in force. You cannot configure this policy in detail until you actually create a basic policy by choosing New Software Restriction Policies.

You can now specify what types of files policy enforcement applies to, as well as whether these restrictions apply to members of each computer's local Administrators group. This is done through the Enforcement option of the policy as shown in Figure 6-1, which is displayed when you double-click the Enforcement Group Policy setting.

 Avoid enforcing policies on DLL and other library files. If you do, you'll have to configure rules to allow those files to execute, and it can often be difficult to determine which library files an application needs to use. If you forget to authorize a DLL, applications that need it won't run properly.

By default, all software is allowed to run unless you create a policy that specifically disallows it. Software restriction policies do contain a Disallowed policy under the Security Levels folder, shown in Figure 6-2, which you can configure to be the default action for any software not specifically mentioned in its own policy.

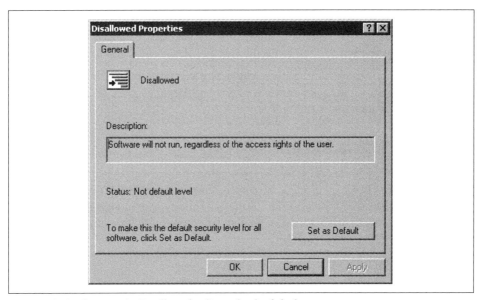

Figure 6-2. Configuring the Disallowed policy to be the default

Once policy enforcement is enabled, the default policy (Unrestricted or Disallowed) will affect all software that does not have a specific software restriction policy defined. For software that does have a defined policy, the policy itself will determine whether the software is allowed to run.

Creating a new hash rule

When you create a new software restriction policy, or rule, you define the software that the rules will apply to and whether Windows should allow the software to run. The following procedure shows how to create a new hash rule that disallows execution of the Windows Calculator.

1. Within the Software Restriction Policy node, right-click Additional Rules, and then click New Hash Rule.
2. Click Browse to find the desired file. In this case, browse to *C:\Windows\ System32* and double-click *calc.exe*.
3. In Security level, select Disallowed as shown in Figure 6-3, and then click OK.

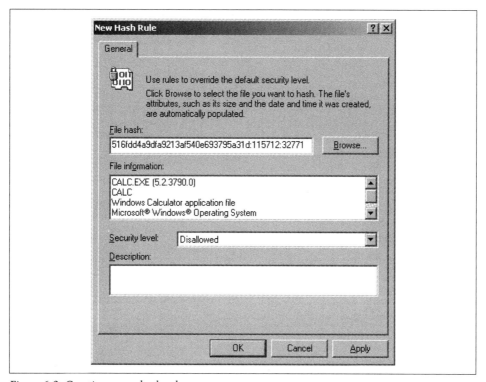

Figure 6-3. Creating a new hash rule

As shown in Figure 6-3, you configure three key items in a hash rule:

The hash

You can use the Browse button to select a file (in this case, *calc.exe*), and Windows will calculate the file's hash for you. Theoretically, you can type in a hash if the file is not available on the local computer, but this is not often done.

The security level for the application
> Which is either Unrestricted or Disallowed.

A description for the rule
> Which helps to identify the rule and its purpose later.

 Once you apply a rule to a computer and enable software restriction policy enforcement, Windows immediately starts restricting software use. If you specified Disallowed as the default policy, only applications you have specified as Unrestricted in a rule will be allowed to run. Be sure you test your software rules thoroughly to ensure users' applications will still run properly.

Creating a certificate rule

Another powerful rule you can create with software restriction policies is a certificate rule. This type of rule applies to all code that chains to a specific root certificate. You can choose to allow or disallow the code based on the root certificate that its signature chains to.

For example, let's assume that the private key of a specific root certificate issued by Thawte has been compromised. You want to block all signed code that chains to this root certificate. You do that with a certificate rule as shown here:

1. Ensure that the certificate exists in a CER file on your hard drive. If it's in your certificate store, you must export it to a file using the process described in Chapter 9.
2. Within the Software Restriction Policy node, right-click Additional Rules, and then click New Certificate Rule.
3. Click Browse to find the desired CER file, and then click Open.
4. In Security level, click Disallowed as shown in Figure 6-4, and then click OK.

Now all signed software that chains to this root certificate will be disallowed and will not run. Note that this can affect software you previously trusted. You should verify the impact of this rule on your network before deploying it.

Example: Allowing an Application to Run on Computers

Kim Yoshida, an employee in one of your company's branch offices, informs you of a new software application that the branch uses. The application allows the branch to calculate local bank tariff fees, which are unique to the county that Kim's branch is located in. Although Kim was able to install the application, your company's software restrictions are preventing her from executing it. Your software restriction poli-

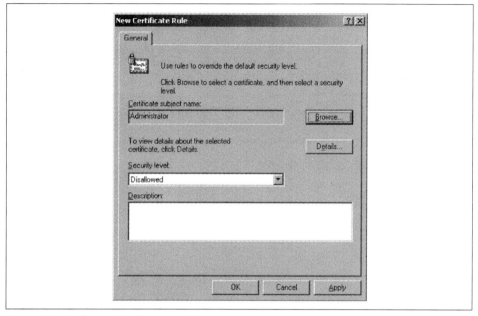

Figure 6-4. Working with software restrictions

cies are enforced through a Group Policy Object. You test the application and determine that it does not adversely affect your company's computers and decide to allow it to run on any company computer. Here's what to do:

1. Open the Group Policy Object that contains your software restrictions.
2. Locate the Software Restriction Policies section, as shown in Figure 6-5.
3. Right-click on the Additional Rules folder, and select New Hash Rule.
4. Click the Browse button, and double-click the new application's executable file.
5. Change the Security level selection to Unrestricted.
6. Type a description for the rule, such as **Rule to allow the new tariff calculator to execute**.
7. Click OK to save the modified Group Policy Object.

If you didn't want to allow the calculator to run on all your company's computers, you could create a new Group Policy Object that contains the hash rule for the calculator's executable and then link that Group Policy Object to an organizational unit that contains only the computers on which the calculator is allowed to run. You could also link the policy to the Active Directory site that represents Kim's branch office, which would allow the calculator to run on the computers in that office.

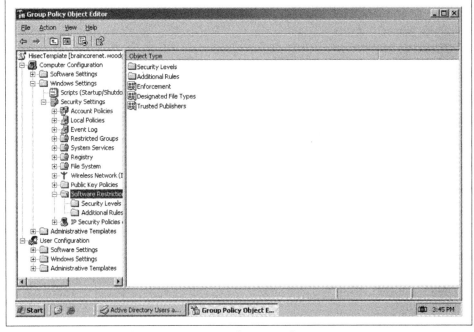

Figure 6-5. Configuring software restrictions to allow an application to run

Example: Allowing Applications with a Specific Extension to Execute

You company's software developers create a new scripting language used in your company's branch offices. The script files are named with a *.wbx* filename extension, and the script processing application is installed on all your company's computers. As the network administrator, you want to ensure that WBX files are treated as executable files by your company's software restriction policies. Your company already has a Group Policy Object named SoftRestrict that defines software restriction policies for each domain in the company. Here's how you can modify the SoftRestrict Group Policy Object to include WBX files:

1. Open the SoftRestrict Group Policy Object and locate the Software Restriction Policies section.

2. Double-click on the Designated File Types policy.

3. Type **WBX** in the File Extension text box, as shown in Figure 6-6, and click Add.

4. Cick OK.

Once the procedure is completed, the appropriate software restriction policies will apply to your WBX files.

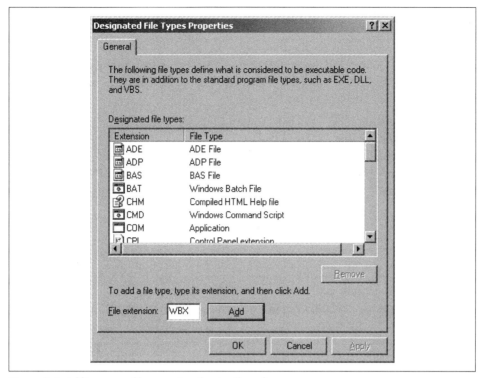

Figure 6-6. Adding a new file extension that is allowed to run

Best Practices for Software Restrictions

Software restrictions can be complex and, if not carefully configured, can cause as much disruption to your users as a virus. Here are some tips for configuring effective software restrictions in your environment:

- If you choose to make the default policy Disallowed, be sure to thoroughly test your software rules on a test computer in a test domain before deploying the rules to your production users. Although this policy can be the most effective at blocking unsafe code, it can also have the largest impact on user productivity and cause a profoundly negative perception of security.

- Use file hash and certificate rules whenever possible, since they are the most accurate and most difficult to circumvent. Path rules can be circumvented by simply copying the software to a different location, and Internet zone rules can be defeated by acquiring the software from a different Internet domain. Hash and certificate rules are nearly impossible to circumvent, because they identify the software itself, not the location the software comes from or resides at.

- Configure policy enforcement so that it doesn't apply to DLL and other libraries. Then, you'll only have to configure rules for actual executable (EXE) files.
- Don't rely on rules to disallow files that are infected with a virus. While a rule can identify an infected executable that you've discovered, the rule will not identify other executables infected with the same virus. Antivirus software is still your best line of defense against viruses.
- Apply SRP at the OU level, and ensure that OUs are created to contain users with similar software needs. This allows you to customize the SRP at every OU to allow exactly the software necessary for the workgroup. The beneficial side effect of this administration is that you get a cheap software metering solution!

Summary

In this chapter, you learned about the security vulnerabilities presented by computer software and how code signing provides assurances that the software your users install is from a particular author. As long as you trust that author, you can trust the code, since the signature guarantees that it hasn't been modified since written. You also learned how to configure Windows Server 2003 to prevent the installation of unsigned software, including unsigned device driver software. As more and more nefarious programmers seek to use software to compromise the security of business information systems, you will need to take stronger steps to protect your systems against unauthorized software. Digitally signed software and effective software restrictions provide the tools you need to protect your network.

CHAPTER 7

Authentication

As you learned in Chapter 2, authentication is the process by which a computer validates the identity of a user or another computer. Authentication is a core functionality of any network operating system, including Windows Server 2003. Windows Server 2003 actually supports several complete authentication protocols: LAN Manager, NT LAN Manager Versions 1 and 2, and Kerberos. In this chapter, I'll introduce you to the two main types of protocols, explain how they're used and configured, and discuss why you might want to use one over the other.

LAN Manager and NTLM

LAN Manager, or LM, is an authentication protocol designed (at its time) to maximize password security in a Windows-based environment. The LM protocol was first used in Microsoft's LAN Manager product a very long time ago and is still the authentication protocol of choice for older operating systems, such as Windows 95 and Windows NT 3.51 and earlier. Later, when Windows NT was introduced, LM was enhanced and renamed the NTLM authentication protocol. Although NTLM has been around for a long time, it's still a basically good authentication protocol, and it is the native network authentication protocol of Windows NT 4.0 and earlier operating systems.

A Brief History of LM and NTLM

LM was introduced, as you might expect, in Microsoft's LAN Manager product of the late 1980s, which evolved over time into Windows NT. It is very similar to NTLM and is supported in most Microsoft products, including Windows for Workgroups 3.11, Windows 95, Windows 98, Windows Me, and all versions of Windows NT through 4.0. LM's long history is reflected in the protocol's priorities. At the time it was invented, most computer networks contained only a single network operating system. The World Wide Web didn't exist, and computer networks from different companies were rarely connected to one another. Computer crime was usually limited to common embezzlement, not the complex intrusion schemes of today. Multitier applications were practically unheard of; most computer networks were used essentially for file and print sharing and the occasional client-server application. Client-server applications usually implemented their own security mechanisms, so the operating system—and LM—wasn't concerned with supporting those applications' security requirements.

LM was designed to combat the security challenges of its day, which primarily involved intruders who stole passwords by eavesdropping on network logon traffic. LM's strength is that it never transmits the user's password across the network, even in an encrypted format.

NTLM is the successor of LM, and it was introduced in 1993 with the release of Windows NT 3.1. In LAN Manager, the hash of each password had to be stored at each LAN Manager server. This presented a security risk as well as a lack of data centralization. NTLM's biggest change to this was its introduction of the concept of a domain controller. These domain controllers kept the password hashes for all users in a domain and were the only servers trusted to keep this information. However, NTLM changed little in the way the authentication mechanism worked.

In Windows NT 4.0 Service Pack 4, Microsoft introduced a new version of this authentication. Called NTLM Version 2 (NTLMv2), it is a great improvement over LM and NTLM. It uses much longer keys for the hash algorithm and takes advantage of passwords longer than 14 characters. These changes, among other cryptographic changes, make NTLMv2 a far more secure authentication protocol than its predecessors.

For the remainder of this book, it is not important to draw the distinction between LM and NTLM authentication, which is mostly in the cryptography used to create the different password hashes. The authentication process itself is similar enough between the two that we can discuss them as one technology. We will call it NTLM.

How NTLM Works

NTLM is based on the concept of a cryptographic hash, which you learned about in Chapter 2. Windows stores user passwords in a special section of the Windows Registry called the Security Accounts Manager, or SAM, or in the Active Directory database in Windows 2000 or later domains. Passwords are never stored in clear text; instead, each password is run though a one-way hash algorithm, and the result is stored in the SAM. This process is illustrated in Figure 7-1.

The main weakness in LM is how it creates its password hash. It really doesn't use a hash algorithm at all; it uses the DES encryption algorithm with some static data. Although this cryptography was considered reasonably secure at the time, it is easily broken today.

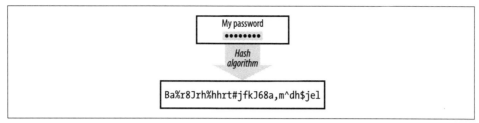

Figure 7-1. Storing hashed passwords in the Windows SAM

Logging on

When a user attempts to log on to a Windows NT domain, NTLM uses the following process (which is illustrated in Figure 7-2):

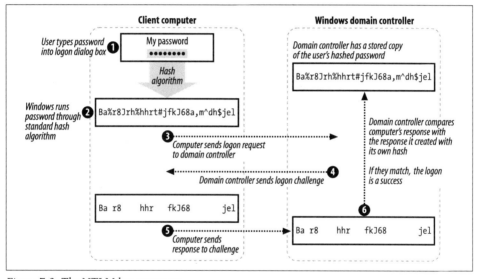

Figure 7-2. The NTLM logon process

1. A user types his password into the logon dialog box on his client computer.

2. The client computer runs the password through the standard NTLM one-way hash, producing a hashed password that should be identical to the one stored on the domain controller.

3. The client computer transmits a logon request to the nearest domain controller, including the username that the user provided.

4. The domain controller sends a logon challenge to the client computer.

5. The client computer responds to the challenge by encrypting the challenge data with the hash of the password.

6. The domain controller creates its own response to the challenge with its copy of the hash.

7. The domain controller compares the responses. If the appropriate pieces match, the logon is successful.

 All communications between the client computer and the domain controller are encrypted using a shared secret key. The shared secret is the client computer's own domain password, which both the client computer and the domain controller store in their SAM.

Security token

When a user successfully authenticates to the domain, the domain controller sends information to the user's logon process. This process builds a *security token* on the user's client computer. The security token contains a list of every security identifier (SID) associated with the user. That list includes the SID for the user's own domain user account, as well as the SIDs for any domain user groups that the user's account is a member of. The user's client computer stores this token for future use. The token is also used to start the user logon session's shell, or interactive session. Whenever a process is started through this session, the original security token is associated with that process. In this way, Windows enforces the requirement that all processes run within the security context of some account. That security context is defined by the security token.

Accessing resources

When an authenticated user attempts to access resources (such as files) on her client computer, the client computer compares the user's security token to the access control list (ACL) on the resource. If the ACL doesn't contain one of the SIDs in the security token, access is denied. If the ACL does contain one of the SIDs in the security token, the user is granted whatever access is associated with that SID on the ACL. If the token contains multiple SIDs (as they often do) because the user is a member of one or more groups, the cumulative permission from more than one SID may be necessary to obtain the desired level of access. This is automatically done by the security subsystem.

When the user attempts to access resources on other computers, such as file servers, the server she contacts must first contact a domain controller to build its own copy of the user's security token. The server can't trust the security token the user's client computer has, because it's possible (although barely) for the user to falsify that token. The server retains a copy of the user's token in its memory for a period of time, so that subsequent requests for access don't require another request to a domain controller.

The token remains in memory until it is expired or replaced. That means that changes to the user's group membership are not automatically picked up—a new user must get a new token. The most certain way to do that is to log out and log back in.

NTLM Pros and Cons

NTLM has several advantages:

- The user's password is never transmitted in its entirety. Only a portion of the hashed password is transmitted, and even that is done over an encrypted communications channel.

- The user's password isn't stored in clear text, so even if the SAM is compromised, the user's password cannot be read. Only the hash can be read.

- The protocol provides a way for the user's security token to be built and exchanged, enabling authorization as well as authentication.

Unfortunately, as computer networks became more common and more interconnected, NTLM started to show a number of significant flaws:

- SAM has several vulnerabilities, which allowed attackers to access the hashed passwords.

- NTLM can use a maximum of 14 characters to create its stored hash. These 14 characters are split into two seven-character strings. Cryptographically, it is reasonably easy to brute force attack two seven-character strings with modern computers.

- NTLM cannot use lowercase letters. It converts all lowercase letters to uppercase before creating the hash. This reduces the character set for the password, making brute force attacks far more likely to succeed.

- The hash algorithm used to store passwords became well known. That allowed attackers to guess users' passwords by running password guesses through the hash until the result matched the result stored in the SAM. Because the algorithm remained constant, large libraries of hashed passwords could be stored and used to quickly attack a SAM.

- NTLM used a mechanism known as pass-through authentication to distribute the authentication task. The way pass-through authentication was designed created a bottleneck at the primary domain controller (PDC) of each domain. Some of the tasks done by the PDC, such as password changes, could not be offloaded to any other server.

- Attackers began accessing passwords by pretending to be trusted servers. Users' client computers would transmit logon information to the attackers, thinking that they were domain controllers or file servers. NTLM provided no way for users to verify that the server they were connecting to was the one they intended to connect to.

- NTLM was largely limited to interoperability with Microsoft products. As computer networks became more heterogeneous, NTLM didn't provide a way to interoperate with non-Microsoft operating systems.

- NTLM provided no way for a middle-tier application to access resources on a user's behalf. When a user's client application accessed a middle-tier application, the middle-tier application usually used a generic administrator credential to access backend resources. This technique works, but presents a security threat, because the middle-tier application is running under powerful security credentials.

When Microsoft began developing Windows 2000, they decided a new authentication protocol was necessary. They chose to implement a well-established, standards-based authentication protocol: Kerberos. Of course, NTLM is also included in Windows 2000 and Windows Server 2003, because older Microsoft clients—Windows NT 4.0 and earlier and all Windows 9x versions—don't support the Kerberos protocol.

 Microsoft has created an Active Directory client for older Microsoft operating systems. This client provides not only enhanced functionality and Active Directory interoperability, but also NTLMv2 functionality. It does not, however, provide Kerberos compatibility. Only Windows 2000 and higher Microsoft operating systems include support for Kerberos.

Configuring LM

Even though NTLM is inferior to Windows Server 2003's native Kerberos protocol (which I'll discuss next), many Windows clients—including Windows 95, Windows 98, Windows NT, and Windows Millennium Edition—can't use anything but LM or NTLM. Even newer client operating systems—Windows 2000 and higher—still support NTLM. In fact, Windows 2000, Windows XP Professional, and Windows Server 2003 will automatically try and use older authentication methods such as LM and NTLM if Kerberos isn't available or doesn't work. This can present a security weakness.

Disabling hash storage

One weakness of LM authentication is that it stores its LM password hashes on domain controllers. While domain controllers are generally pretty secure, storing the hashes at all presents an opportunity for attackers to crack passwords. Because the algorithm used to generate the hashes is well known, attackers with access to the hashes can perform a *dictionary attack* to try and guess passwords. Basically, this type of attack requires an attacker to run common words, and variations on common words, through the hash algorithm. If the attacker can successfully generate a hash that matches one on the domain controller, the attacker knows the clear-text password that goes along with the hash, rendering your domain vulnerable.

Windows 2000 Service Pack 2 introduced the ability to disable the storage of LM hashes. This can be done both on domain controllers and on member computers or even standalone computers, removing the hashes for local user accounts. You can also disable hash storage for local accounts on Windows XP. Just follow these steps:

1. Start the registry editor (*regedit.exe*) on the computer in question.

2. Find the registry key `HKEY_LOCAL_MACHINE\SYSTEM\CurrentControlSet\Control\Lsa`.

3. On Windows 2000, if the key `NoLMHash` does not exist, perform the following steps. From the Edit menu, select New, Key. On Windows XP and Windows Server 2003, select New and then select DWORD Value.

4. Enter **NoLMHash**, set the value to 1, and press Enter.

5. Close the registry editor.

6. Restart the computer for the change to take effect.

The computer will continue to keep any hashes it already has but will not generate or store new LM hashes for new or changed passwords. If you make this change across your domain controllers, consider forcing your users to change their passwords as soon as possible to remove the hashes from the domain. You must also ensure that all client computers and other authenticating hosts are properly upgraded and con-figured to support NTLMv2 or Kerberos authentication. Otherwise, authentication requests from these computers will fail.

 If you store password history, the LM hashes of those previous pass-words are stored in the history. Setting `NoLMHash` does not clear pass-word history, so those hashes are retained. Only cycling through enough passwords will clear that cache.

Disabling NTLM variants

The Windows operating system actually supports several variations of NTLM. I've discussed LAN Manager, or LM, authentication. Next up the ladder is NTLM Version 1, or just NTLM. Since Windows NT 4.0 Service Pack 4, Windows has also sup-ported the newest variant, NTLM Version 2. NTLMv2 is supported natively on Windows 2000 and later operating systems and can be added to Windows 95 and Windows 98 by installing the Microsoft Directory Services Client, first provided on the Windows 2000 CD-ROM.

NTLMv2 is cryptographically much stronger than LM and NTLM. Although still a hash-based process, it uses much stronger cryptography and handles the password differently. It addresses numerous shortcomings of NTLM, including the 14-charac-ter password limit and the uppercase conversion of letters, which allowed for a much larger entropy of password characters. NTLMv2 is strongly preferred over NTLM and should be used whenever down-level clients allow it.

 Although most applications trust Windows to carry out authentication tasks, some require more direct information and may make authentication APIs themselves. You should test all applications in your environment with the restricted authentication configuration before you deploy it.

Once all client computers in your organization support it, you should configure them to use only NTLMv2, and not other variants of NTLM. Doing so will provide the best security for your environment. After installing the Directory Services Client (available from *http://www.microsoft.com/windows2000/server/evaluation/news/ bulletins/adextension.asp*) on Windows 9x computers, you'll still need to explicitly force the use of NTLMv2:

1. Start the registry editor (*regedit.exe*).

2. Locate and click the following key in the registry: HKEY_LOCAL_MACHINE\System\ CurrentControlSet\Control.

3. Create a new registry key named LSA by right-clicking the Control key and selecting New → Key. Type **LSA**, and then press Enter.

4. On the Edit menu, click Add Value, and then add a registry value named LMCompatibility. The value must be a REG_DWORD, and you should set its value to 3.

The LMCompatibility parameter specifies the mode of authentication and session security to be used for network logons. Although I recommend using 3 to require clients to use NTLMv2 authentication and not allow any weaker method (without potentially breaking other LM or NTLM processes in your environment), you can use any of these values:

0   This allows the computer to send the older LM and NTLM response and to never use NTLMv2 session security. Clients will use LM and NTLM authentication and never use NTLMv2 session security. Domain controllers accept LM, NTLM, and NTLMv2 authentication.

1   Allows the computer to use NTLMv2 session security if negotiated. Clients use LM and NTLM authentication and use NTLMv2 session security if the server supports it. Domain controllers accept LM, NTLM, and NTLMv2 authentication.

2   Allows the computer to send NTLM responses only. Clients use only NTLM authentication and use NTLMv2 session security if the server supports it. Domain controllers accept LM, NTLM, and NTLMv2 authentication.

3   This allows the computer to send NTLMv2 responses only. Clients use NTLMv2 authentication and use NTLMv2 session security if the server supports it. Domain controllers accept LM, NTLM, and NTLMv2 authentication.

4   Causes domain controllers to refuse LM responses. Clients use NTLM authentication and use NTLMv2 session security if the server supports it. Domain controllers refuse LM authentication (that is, they accept NTLM and NTLMv2 only).

5   Causes domain controllers to refuse LM and NTLM responses (accepting only NTLMv2). Clients use NTLMv2 authentication and use NTLMv2 session security if the server supports it. Domain controllers refuse NTLM and LM authentication (they accept only NTLMv2).

Notice that the exact function of this registry value depends on whether or not you're working on a client computer or server or on a domain controller. The value should be applied to all computers regardless of role to force them to use the desired authentication protocol first. For more information about deploying this setting through Group Policy, see Chapter 5.

Kerberos

Kerberos is an Internet-standard authentication protocol originally developed at the Massachusetts Institute of Technology (MIT). Kerberos was specifically designed to correct the shortcomings of many older authentication protocols, including Microsoft's LM and a variety of then-popular authentication protocols unique to the Unix platform.

A Brief History of Kerberos

Kerberos is currently in its fifth version and is defined in the Internet Engineering Task Force's (IETF) Request For Comments (RFC) 1510. You can access any of the IETF's RFCs online at *http://www.ietf.org*. Kerberos is the Greek name for the mythological three-headed dog that guards the gates of Hades. The three heads of the mythical Kerberos correspond to the three basic roles in the Kerberos protocol: client, server, and Key Distribution Center (KDC).

How Kerberos Works

RFC 1510 describes in detail how the standard Kerberos protocol works. A number of MIT-standard implementations of Kerberos are available for various flavors of Unix; Microsoft closely adhered to the RFC standard when implementing Kerberos in Windows 2000 and Windows Server 2003.

Kerberos operational theory

To achieve its goals, Kerberos is a fairly complex protocol, involving several layers of encryption. Kerberos relies heavily upon shared secret authentication, which you learned about in Chapter 2. In the next few sections, I'll walk you through the process Kerberos uses to initially authenticate a user, allow a user to access resources, and allow middle-tier applications to access resources on a user's behalf.

All Kerberos transactions involve three parties:

The client
> Who is attempting to access resources.

The server
> Which contains the resources the client is attempting to access.

The Key Distribution Center, or KDC
> Which provides authentication services. In a Windows Server 2003 environment, every domain controller (DC) in a domain is also a KDC.

Logging on. The logon process starts when the user types a username and password into the logon dialog box. From there, Kerberos takes over:

1. As shown in Figure 7-3, the user's client computer runs the password through the standardized one-way hash. The result, in theory, will match what the domain controllers have stored in Active Directory for the user's password. The client computer then builds an authenticator, which includes the current date and time and the user's name. One copy of the authenticator is encrypted, using the user's hashed password as the encryption key. Both copies are then sent to a domain controller.

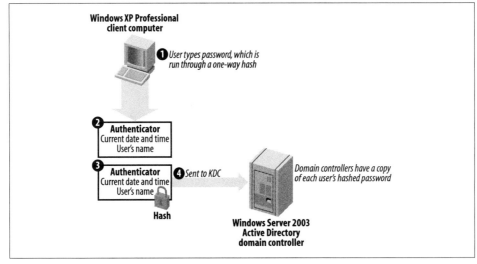

Figure 7-3. Sending the authenticators to the domain controller

2. As shown in Figure 7-4, the domain controller receives the two authenticators. It reads the user's name from the unencrypted authenticator and uses that to look up the user's hashed password in Active Directory. The password is then used to decrypt the encrypted version of the authenticator.

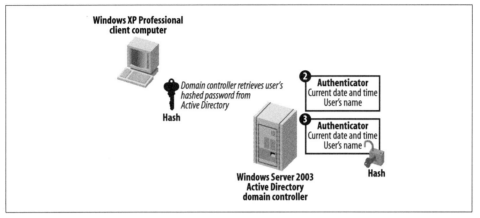

Figure 7-4. Decrypting the authenticator

3. The domain controller analyzes the two authenticators. They must be identical, they must be no more than five minutes old, and they must not have been received before by the domain controller (to ensure an attacker is not trying to replay the authentication sequence). If all those conditions check out, the user is successfully authenticated.

 The five-minute interval described here is known as "skew time" and is discussed later in this chapter.

4. As shown in Figure 7-5, the KDC service builds a special ticket-granting ticket, or TGT, which contains basic information about the user. The TGT also contains a randomly generated session key, which the client and KDC will use to encrypt and decrypt further communications. The KDC uses its own private encryption key to encrypt one copy of the TGT. Both copies are then encrypted by using the user's hashed password as an encryption key, and the combined package is sent to the user's client computer. Note that this is the last time the client or KDC will use the hashed password to encrypt data during this session.

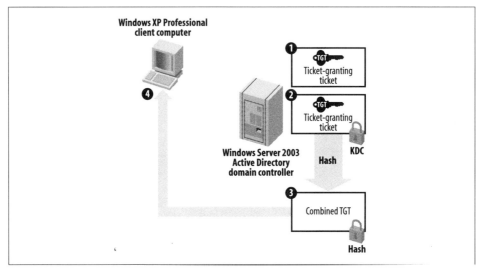

Figure 7-5. Building and sending the ticket-granting tickets

5. As shown in Figure 7-6, the user's client computer uses the user's hashed password to decrypt the combined TGT package. This reveals a clear-text version of the TGT and an encrypted version that the client computer cannot decrypt. Both are stored as a pair in a special volatile area of memory (RAM) as shown in Figure 7-6. All future requests to the KDC will be encrypted using the session key contained within the TGT.

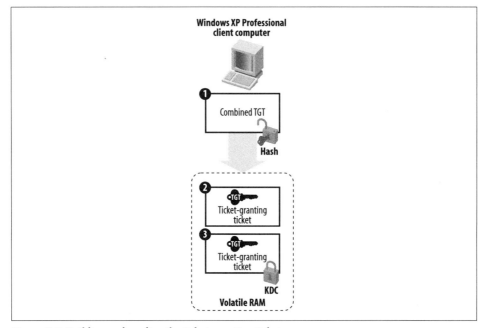

Figure 7-6. Building and sending the ticket-granting tickets

The area of RAM used to store Kerberos tickets is never swapped out to the system page file. Once the system is shut down, or if power is lost, all tickets are destroyed and must be recreated. This is done intentionally to ensure that a nefarious attacker cannot restart a computer and assume a user's credentials.

Once the user's client computer receives the TGT, the authentication process is done.

Accessing resources. When a client needs to access resources on a file server, it uses the TGT it received from the KDC to do so. Here's how it works:

1. As shown in Figure 7-7, the client builds a ticket request, indicating the file server that it needs to access. The request is encrypted using the session key included in the TGT. The encrypted request is bundled along with the encrypted copy of the TGT and sent to the KDC.

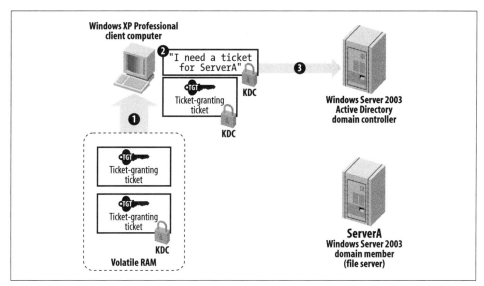

Figure 7-7. Sending a ticket request to the KDC

2. As shown in Figure 7-8, the KDC decrypts the TGT using its private encryption key. That reveals the session key within the TGT, and the fact that the KDC was able to decrypt the TGT ensures that it hasn't been tampered with. The KDC uses the session key to decrypt the main request and uses that information to build a ticket, which includes a list of the user's security group membership. The ticket also includes another randomly generated session key. One copy of the ticket is encrypted using an encryption key shared by the KDC and the target file server. The entire package is encrypted using the session key from the TGT and then sent to the client.

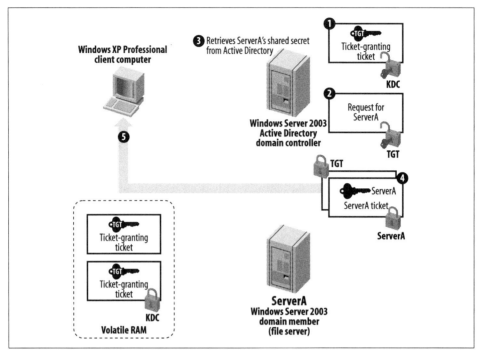

Figure 7-8. Building a ticket for a client

 All computers have their own domain password, which they store after hashing it. They use this hashed password as a shared secret encryption key with the KDC, since the KDC has access to the identical copy of the password in Active Directory.

3. As shown in Figure 7-9, the client receives the ticket from the KDC, decrypts it, and stores it in volatile RAM, along with the TGT and any other tickets. One copy of the ticket is unencrypted, allowing the client to access the ticket's expiration date and the ticket's session key. Until that ticket either expires or is destroyed, the client will continue to use the copy now in RAM to access the file server, rather than asking the KDC for another ticket each time.

4. As shown in Figure 7-10, the client builds an authenticator, encrypts it using the ticket's session key, and sends it to the server. The client also sends the encrypted version of the ticket that the client received from the KDC. The server decrypts the ticket by using its shared secret encryption key, thus revealing the ticket's session key. The server uses the ticket's session key to decrypt the authenticator and verify the timestamp. The server knows that only the KDC could have encrypted the ticket with the server's own private key, and so the server trusts the ticket.

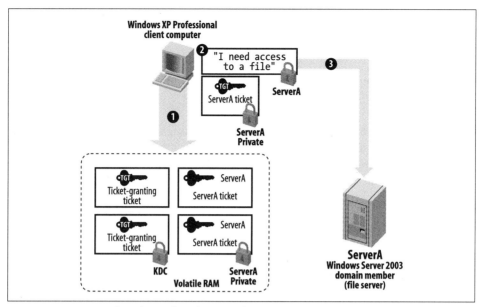

Figure 7-9. Receiving the ticket and sending it to the server

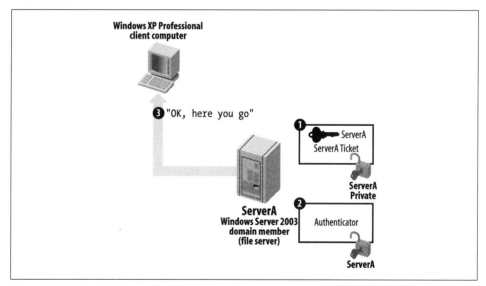

Figure 7-10. Examining the ticket and granting access

The resource request is finished. The file server never had to contact a domain controller to validate the user's identity or security token, and the server doesn't have to keep the user's ticket in memory. The user's computer will resend the ticket every time access is required, preventing the server from having to manage authentication information on its own.

Although the resource request is finished and authentication information is provided, the resource access is not necessarily granted. A second process, authorization, now takes place to determine if the known-authentic entity is allowed to access the requested resource. This authorization is based on the identity of the user and the list of the user's security groups included in the ticket.

Proxy authentication. Multitier applications are becoming more and more common in business environments. In a multitier application, users run a client application, which communicates with one or more middle-tier applications. The middle-tier applications generally perform data validation and other business logic, before passing data on to a backend tier such as a database server. One example is a proxy service that accepts database queries from a web server, sends them to a database on an intranet, and then returns the data to that web server. The proxy service prevents the user from directly accessing the data while providing the desired data access services.

Although the users never physically interact with the backend data, they should be prevented from accessing any data that they are not authorized to view or change. In the past, middle tier applications used powerful administrator credentials to access the backend tier and implemented their own security mechanisms to determine what data the user should have access to. This technique presents a security risk, because if the middle-tier's security mechanism is flawed or circumvented, the middle tier may provide users with data they are not authorized to have. For example, many middle-tier applications are designed to use a powerful administrator account and to determine users' permissions through the use of a simple database table. That table is rarely protected or encrypted, making it easy to modify the information it contains. By modifying the table, an attacker could easily grant himself additional permissions and take advantage of the middle-tier application's full administrator privileges.

Kerberos includes two methods for a middle-tier application to use a user's credentials on their behalf, effectively impersonating the user when accessing upper application tiers. This impersonation assures that the user won't have access to any data she shouldn't, because the backend tier believes that the user, rather than a generic middle-tier application, is actually accessing the data.

Domain policy must be configured to allow either type of impersonation discussed next. Setting domain policy is described in Chapter 5.

Kerberos' first form of impersonation is *proxy tickets*. When a client needs to access backend resources through a middle tier, the client asks the KDC for a proxiable ticket. The KDC generates the ticket and sends it to the client, who then forwards it to the middle-tier application. Because the ticket is marked as proxiable, the middle-tier application is able to use the ticket to access resources on the backend server. The primary disadvantage of proxy tickets is that the client must know the name of the backend server. Most multitier applications don't make that information available to a client, because the backend is often composed of several servers that load-balance work between them.

Kerberos' other form of impersonation is *forwardable tickets*. The process for obtaining and forwarding a ticket is more complex and requires more overall computing power, but it allows clients to access backend resources through a middle-tier application *without* knowing backend server names. Here's how it works:

1. The client contacts the KDC and requests a forwardable TGT. The client provides the name of the middle-tier server it plans to forward the ticket to, and the KDC encrypts the TGT using that server's shared secret. The TGT contains the security group membership list for the requesting user.

2. The KDC sends the forwardable TGT to the client, who is unable to read it but simply forwards it to the middle-tier server.

3. When the middle-tier application needs to access resources, it uses the forwarded TGT to request a ticket from the KDC. The KDC sees the request as coming from the original user and builds a ticket for the backend server that includes the list of the user's security groups.

4. The middle-tier application uses that ticket to access the backend resource. The backend server sees the request as coming from the original user and limits the available resources to those that the user is authorized to access.

Kerberos' ability to allow software applications to impersonate users allows administrators and software developers to create multitier applications that are significantly more manageable and secure than they could using older authentication protocols like NTLM. However, using Kerberos' impersonation features does require extra development effort on the part of software developers, although that extra effort is minimal in most cases.

Microsoft's Kerberos implementation

The Kerberos protocol included in Windows Server 2003 closely adheres to the RFC 1510 standard. In fact, Windows Server 2003 is basically compatible with non-Windows servers and clients that also use a standard MIT implementation of Kerberos, as I'll discuss later in this chapter. While this compatibility is far from turn-key, it can be made to work with a reasonable amount of effort.

Microsoft also wanted a way for Kerberos to work in the broader environment of the Internet. As written, Kerberos relies on shared secrets for its encryption. Shared secrets are fine within an organization, but when you want to authenticate outside users, there's no way for a shared secret to work. Also, as designed in RFC 1510, Kerberos provides no means to interoperate with smart cards, an increasingly popular form of authentication for many companies. Microsoft responded by modifying their implementation of Kerberos to include support for public key infrastructure, or PKI, allowing Kerberos to work with smart cards and, in theory, with any PKI infrastructure. Rather than working in a vacuum, though, Microsoft submitted their modifications as an Internet Draft to the IETF, helping ensure that future versions of the standard MIT Kerberos will include PKI compatibility. As of the time of this writing, this submission is still in Internet Draft form. You can learn more about PKI in Chapter 9 and the Appendix.

Configuring Kerberos

While Kerberos doesn't require any configuration to operate properly, you can customize Kerberos' operation slightly by modifying policies within your domain. The following settings control Kerberos' behavior:

Maximum life for service tickets (default: 600 minutes)
> This is the maximum length of time a service may hold a Kerberos ticket before a new ticket is required. You shouldn't change this policy unless you have a specific reason to do so or have been advised to do so by Microsoft Product Support.

Maximum life for user tickets (default: 10 hours)
> This is the maximum length of time a user may hold a Kerberos ticket before a new ticket is required. Lowering this value will make tickets expire more frequently, placing a heavier load on your DCs to issue replacements. Raising this value allows tickets to remain in effect for much longer, increasing the possibility of their being compromised.

Maximum life for user ticket renewals (default: 7 days)
> When a user's ticket expires, his client computer will automatically try to renew the ticket. Renewing places less load on DCs, because they do not need to look up the user's password or perform other steps associated with issuing a new ticket. By lowering this value, you can increase the load on your DCs, as they will have to issue more new tickets than renewals. You also shorten the time between account lockout or expiration and the time when the ticket is destroyed, which can improve security in environments in which account lockouts and expirations occur frequently.

If your users shut down their computers at the end of the day, their Kerberos tickets are destroyed, and the maximum life or maximum number of renewals for those tickets isn't important. So if your users are in the habit of shutting down their computers at the end of the day, there's no benefit in modifying the maximum life for user ticket renewals.

Maximum tolerance for computer clock synchronization (default: 5 minutes)
This policy determines how much allowance Kerberos makes for other computers' clocks being out of sync. Since Kerberos communications are time-sensitive, this setting may require adjustment on especially busy networks with extremely high network latency and poor time synchronization.

 Keep in mind that, by default, all computers within a domain synchronize their system clocks to a domain controller, and all domain controllers synchronize with the domain controller holding the PDC Emulator role. On a properly functioning network, five minutes of clock tolerance should be sufficient.

You can configure Kerberos' policies in your domain by modifying the domain's Kerberos policy, as shown in Figure 7-11.

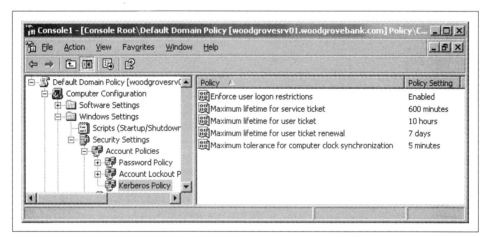

Figure 7-11. Modifying the default domain Kerberos policies

Kerberos Pros and Cons

Kerberos offers a number of advantages over older authentication protocols such as NTLM:

- Mutual authentication of all parties is assured by Kerberos' use of tickets.
- The primary burden of authentication is placed upon the client computer rather than upon servers.
- Kerberos provides a means for middle-tier applications to access resources on behalf of a user, by using that user's credentials in a secure fashion.
- Because all domain controllers function as Kerberos KDCs, there is no central server bottleneck for authentication requests. This is in contrast to earlier versions of Windows NT, with which the primary domain controller (PDC) often became an authentication bottleneck because of its centralized design.
- Kerberos never transmits even a portion of the user's password over the network.
- Kerberos is time-sensitive, preventing attackers from capturing and replaying network packets in an attempt to gain network access. Kerberos also tracks authenticators and will reject an authenticator that is used more than once.
- Kerberos is compatible with many non-Windows operating systems, making it easier to configure centralized authentication on a heterogeneous network.

Kerberos' single disadvantage, if you can call it a disadvantage, is that it isn't compatible with NTLM. For that reason, Windows Server 2003 maintains an NTLM-based security provider for older Windows clients that do not support Kerberos.

Kerberos Interoperability

Since Kerberos is an Internet-standard protocol, Microsoft's implementation is basically compatible with any other MIT-standard version of Kerberos, whether running on the client or on the server. Here are the details about Windows' Kerberos interoperability:

- Unix-based Kerberos clients can authenticate to a Windows KDC by using standard Kerberos utilities such as *kinit* and either DES-CBC-MD5 or DES-CBC-CRC encryption.
- Windows clients can authenticate to Unix-based KDCs in a Kerberos realm.

 Kerberos realms are roughly the equivalent of Active Directory domains.

- Windows provides the ability to map local computer accounts to Kerberos principals, allowing users a single logon that includes non-Windows Kerberos realms.

- Windows can maintain trust relationships with non-Windows Kerberos realms.

- Active Directory includes the means to map user accounts to Kerberos principals in trusted realms.

Most Windows-Unix interoperability problems stem not from Kerberos, but rather from the inherent differences in the way the two operating systems handle authorization. For example, without the proper account mapping in Active Directory, principals in a Kerberos realm cannot provide the information necessary to build an access token and therefore be granted access to domain resources.

Summary

In this chapter, you learned about Windows Server 2003's two authentication protocols, NTLM and Kerberos. You learned how both protocols work and how they interact with Windows' authorization requirements. You also learned how Windows' Kerberos protocol interoperates with non-Windows Kerberos implementations and how to configure Kerberos' behavior on your network.

CHAPTER 8

IP Security

So far, I've examined a number of security mechanisms, including how to store data securely and how to prove your identity to local and network computers. Many nefarious individuals are foiled by strong authentication and secure data storage, but plenty of attackers won't be deterred by them. With IPSec, you can implement an additional security measure on your network that will make it difficult for even the most determined attackers.

An attacker outside your network often attempts to gain access to your network resources by guessing passwords, probing servers for open TCP/IP ports, and so on. Another more subtle method is to capture and analyze data sent to and from the network. Many network services and applications transfer information such as usernames and passwords over the network in clear text, and attackers can use this information to gain access to your network.

For example, if your company uses Windows domains, all your network users are given usernames and generally make up passwords for themselves. They also probably belong to web sites like Yahoo!, where they maintain private accounts. Many users will set their Yahoo! (or other web service) passwords to the same as their company network passwords. After all, one password is easier to remember than a dozen. The problem is that Yahoo!—and many other network services—don't encrypt passwords as a part of their logon process by default. The result is packets of data transmitted from your company network over the Internet to a Yahoo! server, containing user passwords, completely unencrypted. Attackers watch for this type of data and capture it from outside your network. Once they do, they start using the passwords they find as a basis for attacking your network. This potential for data interception is why it's important to use web sites that offer SSL encryption of sensitive data.

The problem of unencrypted network transmissions isn't limited to the Internet, though. Earlier in this book, I discussed the need for physical security of a network. If attackers gain physical access to your network, their work is greatly simplified.

They can simply monitor and record all network communication, and eventually they will get the information they desire. Whether this information is confidential documentation, a database of usernames and passwords, or some other secret information, a physical compromise of the network allows unprotected data to be captured. In this case, attackers don't need to guess passwords or other credentials, as they can simply grab the data they want directly from the network as it's transmitted between computers. IP Security protects against this type of attack by protecting sensitive data on the network. In this chapter, I explain how IPSec works in enough depth to make it clear how it provides security and authenticity. I also show you the right and wrong ways to use IPSec. Because although any fool can deploy an IPSec policy, understanding the technology's strengths and pitfalls will help you make the right decision and provide exactly the right level of security.

What Is IP Security?

Simply put, IP Security (IPSec) is a method to cryptographically process IP packets by encrypting the data, signing the packet, or both. This cryptography is done on the computer before the data is transmitted on the network.

IPSec is standardized in a series of lengthy Internet RFC documents. These include RFCs 2401 through 2412, which define its core functionality, plus another half-dozen or so additions to IPSec functionality or features. These documents describe in painstaking detail exactly how IPSec functions and communicates.

The impact of IPSec is profound. Insecure intermediate networks can easily transport secure data. Because IPSec is an extension of the standard TCP/IP suite, routers and other internetworking devices work well with it. They usually don't know that the traffic is protected, and the protection has no effect on routing (with some minor exceptions I'll discuss later).

Benefits of IPSec

IPSec provides a number of important security benefits.

First, it helps protect data on physical LANs. I've already discussed the need for physical security in an earlier chapter. When the wires that connect your computers are insecure, the data that travels on them is insecure. This happens more often than most people realize. Common walls in a shared office building, network connections in unsecured locations, shallow buried cable in remote locations—any of these will compromise the security of the data on the LAN. An intruder with basic tools and hardware can capture all the data transmitted over these insecure lines. IPSec cannot stop an intruder from capturing this data, but it can protect it in such a way that it is useless to the intruder. Without the cryptographic key, the intruder has a great deal of work to do to decrypt the information.

IPSec and SMB signing sound as if they do the same thing. In a sense, both can provide the authentication of packets on the network. However, SMB signing is very limited in its scope and flexibility. It can only authenticate packets, and only SMB packets at that. It is also limited in its authentication mechanisms. IPSec has the ability to both encrypt and sign packets, and it can be used with any type of data that travels over the TCP/IP protocol suite. You can implement both SMB signing and IPSec simultaneously, but there is no advantage and the overhead may be detrimental to performance.

IPSec also provides protection from eavesdropping when using the Internet. The Internet is an inherently insecure medium for data transfer. However, many corporations use it as a cheap backbone to connect remote office and field personnel. Although a few security technologies—such as SSL—can encrypt data across the Internet, these are most often application-layer technologies. This means the application itself must encrypt and decrypt the data. SSL, for example, is useful only for web browsers and a handful of email applications; you can't use it to protect FTP connections, since FTP applications don't implement SSL or anything like it. IPSec operates at a lower layer, allowing any application to communicate securely. The application simply uses the TCP/IP communications suite as usual, unaware that the data is transparently being protected. The Windows operating system handles the encryption, making it accessible to any and all applications running on the computer.

IPSec provides strong protection from data-insertion attacks. Intruders don't always seek to capture data. Instead, they may want to replace some data on your LAN with their own data. This type of attack may take the form of a virus delivery vehicle or a corporate espionage need, in which intruders profit from your data being replaced with theirs. IPSec provides protection against these attacks through its ability to digitally sign each packet sent on the network, ensuring that each packet is received unchanged from how it was originally sent. Packet signing can be used independently of IPSec's data encryption functionality so that the appropriate amount of cryptography is used.

 Both encrypting and signing the same packet may, on the surface, seem redundant. However, they're not. Encryption protects only the payload of the packet, while signing guarantees the authenticity of the whole packet—including the header. Together they provide very strong data security.

IPSec is based on a set of Internet Requests for Comments (RFCs). The RFC process allows peers from around the world to collaborate and create a widely accepted standard that has been discussed and examined in great detail. This often means many corporations and governments accept the RFC standard and that products from different manufacturers can interoperate if they adhere to the standard.

The main body of IPSec RFCs are RFCs 2401–2412. They constitute the basic set of documentation that virtually all implementations are based on. Many additional RFCs add to or change parts of IPSec, but 2401–2412 are considered the core elements. All these RFCs can be downloaded from *http://www.rfc-editor.org*.

The implementation of IPSec in Windows Server 2003 adheres to the standards, making it interoperable with IPSec implementations running on other operating systems. There have been some concerns in the past about this, which I'll address later in the chapter.

Just because two implementations of IPSec are RFC-compliant doesn't mean that interoperability is a gimme. Often some configuration and testing work must be done before two vendors' IPSec products will work together well. But RFC compatibility is a great indicator that the products will cooperate—eventually.

Drawbacks of IPSec

No matter how it may have sounded up to this point, IPSec isn't the Holy Grail of network security. IPSec has a few drawbacks. None of these should stop you from considering IPSec for your systems, but they are important points to keep in mind.

First, IPSec requires significant system resources of each computer that uses it. If you consider the scale of what IPSec does, you may be surprised that your computer can do it at all. It has to do cryptographic operations on every single packet that is sent. For example, a 1MB file sent on an Ethernet network creates about 750 packets of data. The corresponding decryption or signature verification occurs when each packet is received. In other words, IPSec usage can result in a very large number of cryptographic operations. In addition, IPSec clients have to change encryption keys periodically, which is an even more resource-intensive operation. All this work requires system resources, which can be depleted quickly if IPSec is not implemented correctly. For example, if you decide to use IPSec to encrypt and decrypt every packet of data sent to and from your computer, expect your computer to slow down significantly.

Manufacturers like 3Com and Intel offer IPSec-capable network adapters. With one of these adapters, Windows' own IPSec capabilities aren't used. Instead, dedicated hardware on the adapter is used to perform all IPSec operations. Because the hardware can work hundreds of times faster than Windows' built-in IPSec software, the adapters make it more feasible to use IPSec on a large scale. Check with your network adapter vendor to see what IPSec solutions they offer and how they work with Windows Server 2003.

IPSec makes it nearly impossible to analyze data packets via network capture. When you use IPSec to encrypt the data portion of IP packets, you're protecting them from everyone except the sender and receiver. If problems occur on the network and you want to use a network traffic analyzer, such as Microsoft's Network Monitor, to capture and examine packets, the tool will see the IPSec packets. But because the data portion is encrypted, the network traffic analyzer will be unable to interpret those packets. It will still show the packet's addressing information and that the packet is encrypted with IPSec, but nothing more. To successfully analyze network operations at this level, you may need to temporarily disable IPSec.

Unfortunately, some operating systems do not support IPSec. If you restrict sensitive computers to communicate only using IPSec, you are effectively limiting which clients can connect to those computers. Limiting the computers that can connect to one another may be either desired or undesired, depending on the diversity of your network clients. You should ensure that all clients that must connect to this resource support IPSec.

Finally, IPSec is easy to mess up. It has the power to stop all network communication in your organization. You cannot just sit down and hack together an effective IPSec policy on your production domain. The policies that define how IPSec behaves are complex and must be carefully planned, based on a risk analysis, and then tested prior to any deployment. Shortcuts or omissions during this process have led to many people regretting their decision to explore IPSec.

How Does IPSec Work?

IPSec isn't one single component. The designers of IPSec chose to create it as a number of separate components that work together similarly to TCP/IP, which was created from a number of specifications that are integrated into one large solution, or suite. Also like TCP/IP, IPSec has a large number of components involved and features a very complex set of interactions among those components. IPSec's design provides the benefit of modularity: when a change is made to one component, the others are not necessarily changed. The drawback of this modularity is that IPSec is exceedingly difficult to explain without the use of diagrams, simply because so many different components must work together to make IPSec operate.

The number of components and their interaction is somewhat complex. Administrators, such as yourself, benefit from some discussion of the IPSec architecture, since it's good to know how it works on your network and what burden it will place on your servers and clients. But because there are numerous dedicated references already available, I will not analyze IPSec completely down to the bit level.

IPSec Components

At the core of IPSec are four major components:

IPSec driver or core engine

This is the component of IPSec that does the actual encryption (application of the Encapsulating Security Payload—ESP—protocol), decryption, signing (application of the Authenticated Header—AH—protocol), and signature verification. The driver is also responsible for coordinating the effort of the other IPSec components to ensure that it can complete the necessary tasks. This is the workhorse of IPSec.

IPSec Policy Agent

This is the cognitive function of IPSec. The policy module examines the IPSec settings of a system and determines which traffic should be protected and some generic settings for that protection. It does not do the actual work of protecting the data, it simply alerts the IPSec driver that the traffic must be protected. When the Policy Agent isn't running, no new IPsec policies can be downloaded to the client.

Internet Security Association and Key Management Protocol (ISAKMP, pronounced EYE-suh-kamp)

ISAKMP is the negotiator for Internet security settings. When the computer receives a request to establish a shared secret key with a target computer, it must learn the IPSec configuration on that remote computer to ensure that its settings are acceptable. ISAKMP connects between the computers to negotiate an agreed-upon group of settings to use for encryption and signing. However, ISAKMP does not establish the data encryption keys itself. It uses another component, the Oakley Key Determination Protocol, to establish those data encryption keys.

ISAKMP is a subcomponent of IKE.

ISAKMP connects from a source computer to a destination computer using user datagram protocol (UDP) port 500. If IPSec is not running on the destination computer, it is likely that no service is listening on UDP port 500. The source computer will send several requests to establish an ISAKMP session. If nothing is listening on the destination computer, there will be no response and the source computer will assume that IPSec is unavailable. Whether the connection is made after this failure depends on the IPSec policy, as you will see later in this chapter.

Internet Key Exchange (IKE)

Because IPSec uses shared secret key encryption, there must be some mechanism for the computers to contact each other and agree on a key. IKE manages this by providing generic key agreement services for IPSec. It also stores shared secret keys and configuration information to manage secure connections. IKE can use a myriad of key agreement and encryption protocols, depending on the settings it is provided by ISAKMP.

IPSec Component Interaction

From the information I've presented so far, it's a bit difficult to visualize how IPSec works. Numerous components provide specific functions, but there seems to be no single piece that you can point at and identify as IPSec. The easiest way to explain how all the components of IPSec come together to provide a security solution is to demonstrate how they interact, the order in which they operate, and how an IPSec connection is established. Figure 8-1 illustrates this flow of data between IPSec components.

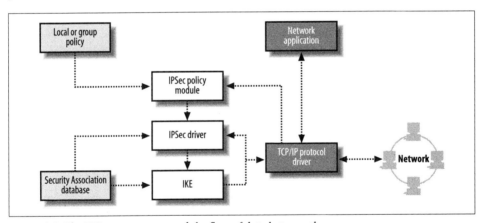

Figure 8-1. The IPSec components and the flow of data between them

The IPSec components work in this fashion:

1. Local or group policy is applied to a computer during startup and periodically while the computer is on. This is not IPSec-specific, but rather the normal operation of Group Policy as described in Chapter 5.

2. Any IPSec policies are retrieved by the IPSec Policy Agent.

3. When one or more IPSec policies exist, the IPSec Policy Agent monitors communication to the TCP/IP protocol from all applications. It's watching for traffic that matches the policy it is configured with—that is, network traffic that it must protect.

4. When network traffic that needs protection is identified, the IPSec Policy Agent communicates with the IPSec driver. It informs the IPSec driver of the type of protection required.

5. The IPSec driver then determines whether a Security Association (SA) exists that can be used to protect the traffic. For the purposes of this discussion, an SA is a set of IPSec settings and key material that is shared between this computer and the destination computer.

6. If no SA exists, the IPSec driver contacts the IKE service. IKE is responsible for negotiating settings between the computers, performing mutual authentication, and establishing shared secret keys that conform to the security policy. IKE uses ISAKMP for this task.

7. IKE provides the SA to the IPSec driver, which then protects the network traffic.

8. The driver returns the protected traffic to the TCP/IP protocol for continued processing.

Whew! This process is complex and can take time to carry out. You might not feel confident explaining this after your first read-through of this explanation. Consider bookmarking this page and referring back to it when you need to review IPSec data flow and components.

Microsoft's Implementation of IPSec in Windows Server 2003

The Microsoft implementation of IPSec in Windows Server 2003 adheres to the appropriate RFCs and is compatible with other hosts running RFC-compliant IPSec software. This includes other computers running Windows 2000 and Windows XP Professional, computers running other operating systems with an IPSec component, and intermediate network devices such as routers. In the next few sections, I'll discuss the specific software components that implement IPSec in Windows Server 2003.

Microsoft IPSec Components

In the Microsoft implementation of IPSec, the IPSec driver acts as a filter driver on top of the TCP/IP protocol stack. The IPSec driver is initialized at the same time that other network services are initialized at system bootup, and the driver receives its policy information from the IPSec Policy Agent. The agent examines local and domain policies (which are set through Group Policy) that apply to IPSec to determine exactly how IPSec should behave. The appropriate configuration information is then delivered to the IPSec driver as a *policy list*. The Policy Agent does little else, but does periodically check for changed IPSec policy settings and delivers those to the IPSec driver as necessary. So the core IPSec work is done by the driver, but the agent is necessary to deliver the driver's configuration information.

The IPSec driver examines all data sent through the TCP/IP protocol stack and destined to be sent over the network. This examination occurs before the protocol stack processes the data, allowing IPSec the opportunity to modify (encrypt or sign) the data prior to transmission. The driver compares all traffic to its policy list to determine if the traffic is supposed to go out encrypted or signed, or possibly not go out at all. When the IPSec driver finds that some data matches one or more of its IPSec policies, the driver does its job and protects that data—signing it, encrypting it, or blocking it as defined in the policies.

Assuming the traffic isn't blocked, if no shared secret keys already exist between the local computer and the destination, ISAKMP and IKE negotiate the keys and provide them to the IPSec driver. These keys are generated only after mutual authentication takes place between the computers. Windows Server 2003 supports three types of authentication for IPSec communication:

Certificate-based
> Each party in the IPSec communication must have a certificate and a corresponding private key. This certificate must chain to a specified trusted root. For more information on certificate chaining, see Chapter 9.

Kerberos
> Each end of the IPSec communication must authenticate using Kerberos, which is explained in Chapter 7.

Shared secret key
> A shared secret key is specified on each host. The hosts must use the same shared secret key to set up communication. When both hosts have the same shared secret key, it indicates that they have prearranged authentication through some other means (such as human interaction). This option is by far the least desirable since the shared secret key is itself a vulnerability.

After authentication, a shared secret key (also known as a session key) is established between the parties and provided to the IPSec driver. Once the IPSec driver has secured the data appropriately using the specified key and rules, the data is passed to the TCP/IP protocol stack and sent over the network.

When the data is received on the destination computer, the packet is examined by the TCP/IP stack, which determines that the data is protected by IPSec. The stack hands the data to the local IPSec driver for decryption, digital signature verification, or both. Because the receiving IPSec driver gets its shared secret key and security settings information from its own ISAKMP and IKE components, it already has all the information it needs to decrypt the data or verify its digital signature. The data is decrypted and/or verified and returned to the TCP/IP stack for distribution to its intended application—such as a web browser, FTP application, or other application.

Network traffic is processed in this fashion until the network communication is terminated. However, continuing to use the same symmetric session key over a long period would present a security risk. If an attacker managed to crack one key, she could decrypt enormous amounts of data. Therefore, IPSec can be configured to periodically generate and use new keys. It does this on the fly without interrupting data transmissions. Normally, the new key is based on the previous authentication and key exchange to save CPU and network utilization and is configured by default to happen infrequently enough to avoid taxing system resources. But you can configure an element of IPSec called *perfect forward secrecy* (PFS) to require IPSec to carry out authentication and rekey from scratch every time. Although PFS tends to consume a lot of computer resources, its cryptographic protection of data is slightly more secure.

You can see how IPSec adds extra work to the tasks of sending and receiving data. Entire additional software modules are loaded into memory, data is encrypted and decrypted, encryption keys are negotiated, and so forth.

Deployment of IPSec to Windows Computers

Computers running Windows 2000, Windows XP Professional, and Windows Server 2003 can all use IPSec to secure network communications. If the client computers are members of an Active Directory domain, they can receive their IPSec settings through Group Policy. As discussed in Chapter 5, Group Policy is a method used to distribute a group of settings to groups of computers. IPSec settings are easily deployed using this mechanism to as many computers as you desire. IPSec settings can also be configured on a per-computer basis using the computers' Local Security Policy snap-in. Because IPSec configuration can be complex, however, local configuration can be arduous and error-prone unless you have a small number of computers to configure. When dealing with a large number of computers, I don't recommend implementing IPSec unless you have an Active Directory domain with which you can centrally configure IPSec settings.

At the beginning of this chapter, I explained that IPSec is a transparent security mechanism, so users cannot easily determine if and when they are using IPSec. Because Group Policy is also transparent and automatic, the combination allows you to deploy and enforce security settings without the cooperation or awareness of your users. This is often a highly desired solution, as users have the propensity to circumvent or simply ignore security requirements when they feel no threat. Users in a physically secured building may feel safe and assume that the path their data takes must also be safe. Conversely, users in a branch office may automatically assume all their data could be intercepted and that they should use extravagant security means to protect it. Using Group Policy and IPSec allows you to make these decisions and removes control over data security from your users' hands.

IPSec Overhead and Offloading

I recently attended a computer conference in Orlando where I delivered a presentation on how to correctly deploy IPSec. This session was attended primarily by network administrators with varying degrees of experience in both security and general network operation.

I got no further than the first technical slide when I saw a hand go up. The question was: "I've heard that IPSec presents a tremendous overhead and will drag my network down to its knees." Well, that's not really a question, but it brought up an excellent point. Most administrators are under the assumption that IPSec is some kind of network Sword of Damocles—always ready to destroy everything. Because this is such a common theme, it's helpful to address it specifically here.

Two aspects of IPSec can have an impact on your systems: network bandwidth and computer performance. Network performance is not significantly impacted by IPSec deployment. The amount of traffic that IPSec adds to the network is minimal. ISAKMP negotiations are very small, and the addition of the AH or ESP headers to the TCP/IP packets is negligible. If network bandwidth consumption is within desired performance guidelines before deploying IPSec, it will almost certainly remain at the same level after IPSec deployment. If, however, the network is already performing improperly due to saturation or other issues, nothing should be added (including IPSec) until that preexisting condition is addressed. IPSec could fail or perform poorly in those conditions or potentially aggravate the existing condition.

Computer performance with IPSec is usually a more realistic concern than network performance. The encryption, decryption, signing, and signature verification functions all take processor and memory resources to complete. In addition, SA and key management on computers with large numbers of simultaneous IPSec sessions can consume even more resources. This resource consumption can range in severity from barely measurable to severe enough to prevent network communication and local console operation.

IPSec-enabled network cards, as mentioned earlier in this chapter, help with the computer performance issues. However, they're not always necessary. A server running with an average of 1% CPU utilization and plenty of available RAM probably doesn't need an IPSec-capable network card and will probably not realize any benefit from such an upgrade. The most appropriate application of such hardware is in marginal performance cases or when IPSec has been demonstrated to deteriorate computer performance.

One other question comes up frequently on this IPSec topic: should I buy an IPSec-capable NIC if I'm planning to purchase a system that will use IPSec? When planning ahead, an IPSec card may be a good idea. IPSec network cards are often a minor change in cost when planned as part of a system purchase. After installation, though, you can forget about the card and use the system as normal. The card may not provide a huge benefit over time, but if it's a small additional cost, it should certainly be considered.

Using IPSec Correctly

IPSec can be used whenever you need to secure data, which you'll pretty much always want to do. The natural inclination of a security-minded administrator is to simply sign and encrypt all traffic on the network, which isn't a bad inclination. With security, erring on the side of caution is desirable. However, IPSec cannot be deployed this way within most organizations.

I've examined the way IPSec works and shown that there is a significant amount of work that the system must do to secure network traffic. If some of that traffic is already secured through another mechanism, such as SSL, what good will IPSec do? Securing data twice sounds fantastic but is simply repetitive and usually offers no more protection than doing it once. Also, some network traffic is inconsequential to security. For example, if an intruder learns that your corporate standard homepage is *www.msn.com*, they gain no advantage. So using IPSec becomes a balance between security, necessity, and the availability of system resources to implement it.

The best strategy is to ensure that any sensitive network traffic is encrypted and any traffic that isn't sensitive, but may be altered en route, is signed. You must also consider the impact on system performance to all computers that will use IPSec. For example, any system that will use more than occasional IPSec, such as a central server that stores sensitive data, should be sized to provide the extra resources necessary—more memory, faster processors, and so forth. If possible, network cards that perform IPSec functions on the card should be used. These cards remove most of the work from the computer's CPU and provide very efficient IPSec processing.

Some examples of good judicious use of IPSec might include:

- Required encryption of all network traffic of a human resources database server. This helps provide confidentiality of the data on the network.

- Requiring data signature between trusted clients in a point-of-sale scenario. Although the data of each transaction may not be considered confidential, you may need to ensure its accuracy and protect against attackers who could modify that data in transit.

- Encrypting all data transported through an Internet-based router-to-router tunnel. Data transfer on either network may not require security, but the data in transit must be secured. This is often the case with branch offices.

- Blocking all communication to a server except over a desired port. IPSec can be used as a very effective policy-based port filter and allow/deny network traffic based on its rules. It doesn't always have to negotiate security; it can simply disallow traffic that doesn't meet specified criteria. For example, a computer designed to allow only Telnet traffic might allow network traffic on port 23 without negotiation and block all other ports. This minimizes the exposure of the computer to attacks that come through other network ports.

Example: Woodgrove Bank Corporate Accounts Payable

Woodgrove Bank is headquartered at Woodgrove Tower in Charlotte, N.C. They own the entire building and use about 75% of the office space for their own business. The other 25% is leased to various companies.

Heide Haupt, a user in corporate accounts payable, has an office on the 30th floor of Woodgrove Tower. She accesses data on the accounting server Wood-Acct-01 that is located in the data center. This data is considered confidential by the bank as it contains corporate financial information as well as personal employee data. Heide is educated in safe data management practices and ensures that the data remains stored on the file server at all times. She does not copy it or print it locally.

An intruder who wants to obtain corporate data learns that there is a network jack in a storage closet on the 30th floor. He gains unnoticed entry and installs a network monitor device to record all data on the network. This includes the data Heide is manipulating.

Don Fink, our IT security manager, wants to ensure that all traffic in and out of Wood-Acct-01 is secured using IPSec. He wants to require data encryption and packet signing and refuse access to any client unable to comply with this requirement. Because Woodgrove Bank uses Active Directory, he wants to allow Kerberos authentication to prove the identity of all parties for IPSec.

Client IPSec configuration through Group Policy

Don must configure the IPSec Group Policy for two objects, the server and the clients. He must require the server to secure the communication and also allow the clients to communicate securely when requested. Don configures the clients first. All client computer accounts reside in the Client Computers OU in the Woodgrove Bank domain. Don implements the following configuration:

1. Start Active Directory Users and Computers snap-in.
2. Expand woodgrovebank.com, right-click the Client Computers OU, and click Properties.
3. Click the Group Policy tab and choose New to create a new GPO. Don names this new GPO **IPSec Policy**.
4. Click Edit to edit the new policy.
5. Navigate to IPSec Policy → Computer Configuration → Windows Settings → Security Settings, then click IP Security Policies on Active Directory. This is shown in Figure 8-2.
6. In the right pane, right-click Client (Respond Only) and click Assign. Verify that the value under Policy Assigned changes to Yes, as shown in Figure 8-3, which indicates that this policy is active. Note that only one policy can be assigned in an IPSec policy, so trying to assign additional policies will unassign the desired one.

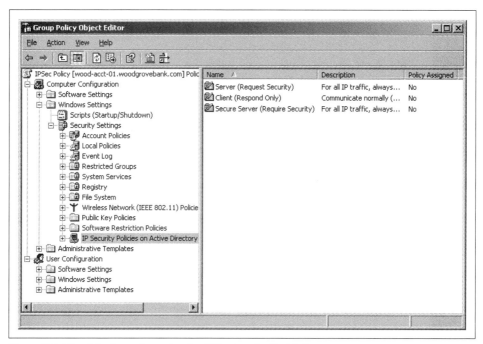

Figure 8-2. The default configuration for IPSec is to be disabled

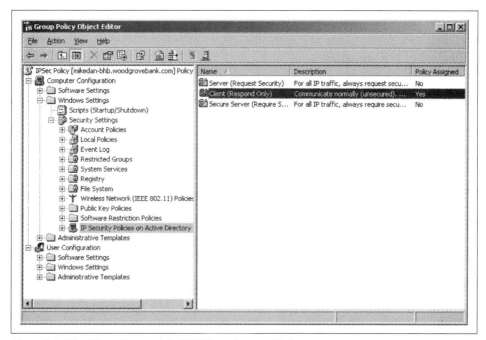

Figure 8-3. The Client (Respond Only) IPSec rule is enabled

Don has now assigned an IPSec policy setting, which will be picked up by the IPSec Policy Agent and sent to the IPSec driver. This enables Don's IPSec settings on the computers.

Server IPSec configuration through Group Policy

Don must now configure the server Wood-Acct-01. I'll assume the server is in an OU called Accounting Servers and that all servers in this OU have the same security requirements as Wood-Acct-01. If that were not the case, Don could easily move the computer accounts to appropriate OUs to apply policy correctly at those OUs.

1. Start Active Directory Users and Computers snap-in.
2. Expand woodgrovebank.com, right-click the Accounting Servers OU, and click Properties.
3. Click the Group Policy tab and choose New to create a new GPO. Don names this new GPO **IPSec Accounting Server Policy**.
4. Click Edit to edit the new policy.
5. Navigate to IPSec Accounting Server Policy → Computer Configuration → Windows Settings → Security Settings, then click IP Security Policies on Active Directory.
6. In the right pane, right-click Secure Server (Require Security) and click Assign. Verify that the value under Policy Assigned changes to Yes.

Note that the Secure Server (Require Security) default configuration allows communication using ESP but not AH as displayed in Figure 8-4. Three settings that may not be self-evident should be explained:

Permit
Configuring a security method for permit essentially removes IPSec from network traffic that matches the pattern we've identified in the previous dialog box. IPSec will permit this traffic to continue on the TCP/IP stack.

Block
Block is the opposite of permit. Whether security negotiation takes place or not, any traffic that matches the identified criteria will be blocked. This traffic is simply erased from memory.

Negotiate
The most complex and useful setting is negotiate. When traffic of the configured pattern is encountered and negotiate is set, IPSec attempts to negotiate a session between computers. This means it will check for an existing SA, and if none exists, IKE will attempt to make a connection and establish settings and a shared secret key.

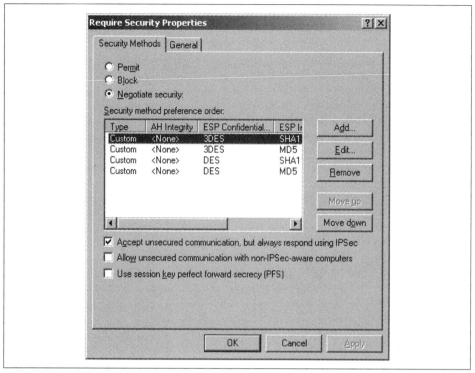

Figure 8-4. The Secure Server IPSec rule does not apply AH because it is redundant with ESP

As discussed earlier, ESP results from negotiated shared secret keys and therefore provides encryption. However, Don wants to customize this policy to use both encryption (ESP) and signing (AH) to ensure that source and destination addresses are never spoofed.

He can customize this policy as follows (assuming he continues following steps from the point he left off earlier):

1. Right-click Secure Server (Require Security) and click Properties.

2. On the IP Security rules list, select All IP Traffic and click Edit. Click the Filter Action tab, select Require Security, and then click Edit. These options should look hauntingly familiar, as they are identical to the settings we saw in Figure 8-4.

3. Click Negotiate Security, and then click Add to create a new security method.

4. Click Custom, then click Settings to display the Custom Security Method Settings page as shown in Figure 8-5.

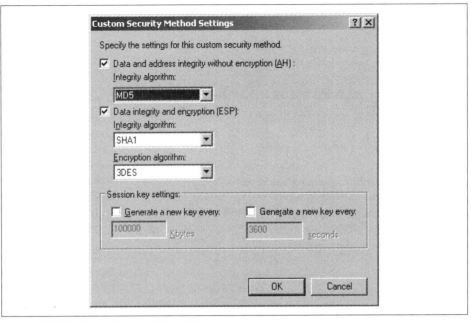

Figure 8-5. The Custom Security Method Settings property page

5. Check the "Data and address integrity without encryption (AH)" option, then choose the desired hash algorithm. You can also choose other advanced encryption options on this page, as well as choose the interval at which to generate a new shared secret key during IPSec communication. Then click OK.

 You can configure an almost infinite number of options for IPSec, including the ones in this dialog box. The settings appropriate for your environment should be carefully analyzed and documented as discussed in Chapter 15 before you deploy them.

6. Click the security method you just created, and then click Move Up until this method appears at the top of the security method preference order.

7. Click OK to all open dialog boxes until the Group Policy Object Editor appears, then close it to save all changes.

At this point, the policy has been edited but not assigned. Unless you specifically right-click this policy and click Assign, this policy will not become active. This is intentional, as it allows you to make changes to many policies without having to implement them every time. Only policies that are explicitly assigned will take effect.

Remember that the policy changes used to deploy IPSec must be replicated and applied to all affected computers before they will take effect. As I discussed in Chapter 5, that can take up several hours.

 Although you can force a client update of Group Policy with the *gpupdate.exe* command, you should do so only in a testing environment in which time is constrained. In a production deployment, allow Group Policy to update normally.

Verifying IPSec Operation

After the clients and server have been configured for IPSec, a prudent administrator must confirm that the desired security is in place and working correctly. This is important because assuming a security implementation worked without verification could leave the network in an insecure state indefinitely, and improper configuration may not always be apparent. For example, IPSec may negotiate to use unprotected communication, which will cause nothing to fail but will not result in the desired security level.

A number of techniques and tools can be used for this purpose. Although IP Security Monitor is the simplest and easiest to understand, I'll provide details on other tools and techniques. You should use whatever method you're most comfortable with.

Verifying IPSec operation with IP Security Monitor

You want to confirm that all communications with an IPSec-configured computer are secure. After all, verification is the last and most important step in applying security. You can use a new Windows Server 2003 tool, the IP Security Monitor MMC snap-in, to get detailed information about the activity and state of IPSec. This tool provides a great deal of useful information in a simple format.

 The IP Security Monitor snap-in replaces the IPSecMon tool that is included in Windows 2000.

To use the IP Security Monitor to verify the state of IPSec on the server, you should perform the following tasks while logged in as an administrator on the desired computer:

1. Click Start, click Run, type **mmc**, and then press Enter.
2. Click File, click Add/Remove Snap-in, and then click Add.
3. Select IP Security Monitor from the list of snap-ins, and then click Add.
4. Click Close and then click OK.

5. Double-click IP Security Monitor, double-click the local computer's name, and then click Active Policy. The active IPSec policy is displayed in the details pane as shown in Figure 8-6.

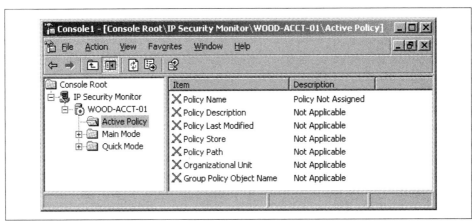

Figure 8-6. IP Security Monitor showing no policy assigned

6. To get more details about what IPSec activities are occurring on this server, you can explore the Main Mode and Quick Mode nodes.

7. To see a list of the computers currently communicating with this one via IPSec, navigate to the Security Associations container as shown in Figure 8-7.

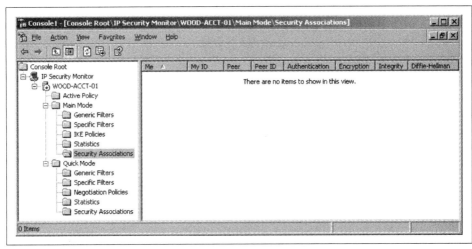

Figure 8-7. No Security Associations means this computer isn't using IPSec at all!

Because no policy is set, no security associations are listed in the details pane. As IPSec policy is implemented and secure connections are established, this list will be populated with the detailed information about each connection.

The IP Security Monitor snap-in displays a great deal of information. Detailed analysis can be accomplished with this tool to verify correct operation, both initially and over time. Within the context of an initial deployment, the tool can be used to quickly determine whether IPSec policy has been deployed correctly and whether computers are using the policy to communicate securely.

Verifying IPSec operation with other tools

Several other methods can be used to determine whether IPSec is working correctly. These methods include both specific tools and general troubleshooting techniques.

IPSecCmd. This command-line tool can be used to either verify current IPSec status or configure local IPSec policy. It is not installed by default, as it's part of the Windows Server 2003 Support Tools installation. For information on installing support tools, see the Help and Support Center in Windows Server 2003.

The following command is the most appropriate and comprehensive for displaying all IPSec configuration information for the local computer:

```
c:\> ipseccmd.exe show all
```

Netsh. This powerful tool is used to configure and diagnose a wide range of networking components. It can gather and display an enormous amount of data about IPSec statistics and configuration. It is similar to IPSecCmd in that it is command-line based and provides much of the same information, so you can use either tool. The following command shows all static IPSec information about the computer, including long-term configuration information and IPSec rules:

```
c:\> netsh IPSec static show all
```

The following command shows all dynamic information about the computer, including current status and statistics:

```
c:\> netsh IPSec dynamic show all
```

Other basic techniques. You can indirectly examine the behavior of IPSec with the following:

- Examine the Application and Security event logs for IPSec-generated events. These are often very self-describing and tell you exactly what failed and why. There are also links from most events to the Microsoft Knowledge Base, which contains detailed descriptions of common IPSec events and methods to troubleshoot those events.

- Connect to the computer using a Windows 98 or Windows Me client. By default, these clients cannot communicate with IPSec and will fail to establish a connection. The error messages will vary depending on the operating system and the application that requests the connection, making it harder to specifically identify communication failures as an IPSec-based problem.

- Connect to the computer from a non-Windows computer that cannot use IPSec. The results should be the same as with Windows 98 or Windows Me.

- Enable detailed IKE logging in the Security Log by setting the registry value

  `HKEY_LOCAL_MACHINE\System\CurrentControlSet\Control\Lsa\Audit\DisableIKEAudits`

  to 1. This may quickly fill your Security Log, so when you've analyzed the data, you should disable this logging by changing the value to 0.

- Use a network capture device or software package to capture network traffic flowing into and out of the desired computer. You should see the ISAKMP and Oakley exchanges and then the traffic should be encrypted (except for the header information).

 You can make other configuration changes to create more detailed and extensive IPSec logs. However, these should be used only for bug identification and troubleshooting.

If you see clear communications traffic, you should verify that the IPSec group policies you configured were created properly and assigned to the correct OUs. If these are verified as correct, you should ensure that Group Policy has replicated to all domain controllers and applied to the desired computers. A common reason IPSec fails is the failure of Group Policy to apply the IPSec policy to a computer. For more information on Group Policy, see Chapter 5.

Example: Restricting a Server to Highly Secure IPSec Communication

You may have a computer on your network that contains only highly sensitive data. For that single computer you may want to configure IPSec in a bit more restrictive way. You decide to implement the following administrative policy and apply it to that sensitive computer:

- IPSec keying material cannot be reused. This limits the success of an attacker who learns one session key by changing the key to one he cannot figure out based on the older key. It is implemented through perfect forward secrecy (PFS), which is the label for the criteria that IPSec uses to determine how to derive keys.

- No communication with this computer can occur unless it is secured with IPSec.

This type of highly restrictive policy can be put in place with a minimum of effort, as I'll describe next.

Creating a policy to use perfect forward secrecy

I'll need to begin by creating a new IPSec policy in Active Directory. This new IPSec policy must enforce both session key and master key perfect forward secrecy (PFS) to ensure key material is not reused. Create this type of policy with the following steps:

1. Ensure the desired computer is in its own organizational unit (OU) or is in one with other computers that will share the same highly restrictive IPSec policy.

2. Create a new Group Policy Object and navigate to the IP Security Policy folder. For detailed instructions, follow the instructions provided in the earlier "Server IPSec configuration through Group Policy" section, up to step 5, to reach the IP Security Policies on Active Directory container for the desired OU.

3. Right-click in the details pane, and then click Create IP Security Policy, which will launch the IP Security Policy Wizard.

4. Follow the wizard to create the new policy using the settings in Table 8-1.

Table 8-1. Highly restrictive IPSec policy settings

IP Security Policy Wizard setting	Value
Name of policy	Highly Restrictive
Activate the default response rule	Selected
Default Response Rule Authentication Method	Active Directory default (Kerberos v5 protocol)
Warning (if prompted)	Yes
Edit properties	Selected

5. The Highly Restrictive policy detail will be shown. Click the General tab, then click Settings. The Key Exchange Settings dialog box will be displayed as shown in Figure 8-8.

Figure 8-8. The IKE Key Exchange Settings page

6. Select "Master key perfect forward secrecy (PFS)," and then click OK.

7. Click the Rules tab and then click Edit to display the Edit Rules Properties dialog box.

8. Remove all security methods listed except for the Encryption and Integrity methods by selecting each and clicking Remove.

9. Click "Use session key perfect forward secrecy (PFS)" to configure the security method as shown in Figure 8-9, and then click OK.

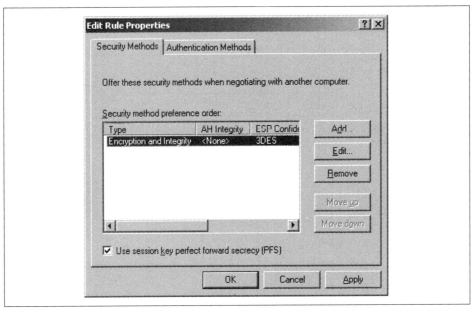

Figure 8-9. The security method shown has session key PFS configured and is the only available method

10. Right-click the Highly Restrictive policy and click Assign to activate it.

11. The new IPSec policy is now configured with restrictive PFS settings and will accept only secure connections with our defined parameters.

Configure IPSec to not allow any traffic to bypass its filter rules

By default, several types of network traffic can bypass IPSec filters and access the network insecurely. This has been done in the past to avoid problems when IPSec tries to secure network traffic that cannot be secured or is being relied on to authenticate for IPSec—a "chicken and the egg" scenario. In Windows Server 2003, the default behavior is not to allow any network traffic to bypass the IPSec filter. However, if you are using servers running Windows 2000 that will be impacted by this new highly secure IPSec policy, you will want to ensure that they also secure all traffic. This can be done by editing the registry on those computers, either through Group

Policy or directly using *Regedit.* You want to ensure that the registry value specified in Table 8-2 is configured under HKLM\SYSTEM\CurrentControlSet\Services\IPSEC.

Table 8-2. Registry value to require all communication to use IPSec

Field	Value
Value Name	NoDefaultExempt
Data type	DWord
Value Data	3

This setting forces IPSec policy to override all communication and apply to all network traffic, no matter its type. However, there is always one exception to the NoDefaultExempt setting. IKE traffic, using UDP port 500, must always be exempt from the IPSec filter. Without IKE negotiating its own security, IPSec would be unable to acquire a security association and would fail to communicate with all hosts.

Example: Using IPSec with a Non-Microsoft Client

Not all clients that want to connect to Windows Server 2003 computers are Microsoft-based clients. Kathie Flood, another user at Woodgrove Tower, uses a Unix-based desktop computer at work. She must access files stored on a secure Woodgrove Bank server in the Red Team Servers OU. Many of the employees in Kathie's department are in the same situation, but this is a small group within the bank. Kathie's computer does not participate in domain-based security, so Don has no way to send appropriate settings to her computer. But he can configure the server in a way that will make it easy for Kathie to connect to the server securely while still providing security for all connections to the server.

Configuring IPSec for certificate-based authentication

Don chooses to obtain a public key certificate for Kathie and her coworkers and for the servers using IPSec. This is the best solution for clients that may not be able to perform implementation-specific authentication such as NTLM or Kerberos but can still use certificate-based authentication. Don configures IPSec on the Red Team Servers OU as follows:

1. Install the trusted root certificate in Active Directory or on the local computer. Details of this process can be found in Chapter 9.

2. Create a new group policy for IPSec settings and edit it in the Group Policy Object Editor. Call the new policy **Red Team IPSec Policy** and create it in the Red Team Servers OU.

3. Navigate to the IP Security Policies container, right-click the container, and choose Create IP Security Policy.

4. Follow the wizard to create the new policy using the settings in Table 8-3.

5. Right-click PKI IPSec Policy and click Assign. Verify that the value under Policy Assigned changes to Yes.

Table 8-3. IPSec settings for certificate-based authentication

IP Security Policy Wizard setting	Value
Name of policy	PKI IPSec Policy.
Activate the default response rule	Selected.
Default Response Rule Authentication Method	Use a certificate from this certification authority (CA).
Warning (if prompted)	Yes.
Select Certificate	Select the Woodgrove Bank root CA certificate or another root CA certificate that all IPSec certificates chain to.
Edit properties	Deselect.

A certificate and private key must be installed on Kathie's computer and Wood-Acct-01 to allow IPSec to authenticate each to each other. Because the installation on Kathie's computer is dependent on the exact type and version of IPSec software used, as well as the specific type of Unix, the exact steps are not provided here.

Once Kathie's computer is configured for IPSec, it can communicate securely with the server. Other clients can still communicate with the server, even without an appropriate certificate, because they authenticate via Kerberos.

Summary

IP Security is a wonderful mechanism to protect data on a possibly insecure physical network. Used correctly, IPSec can protect data in a unique way that is simple and efficient. Its implementation is somewhat complex, as is its configuration through Group Policy. Wizards help with most of the common IPSec configuration tasks, which is a big benefit.

Plan to use IPSec carefully within your organization, remembering the impact IPSec can have on performance. Computers expected to carry a high load of IPSec traffic should be sized accordingly, with faster processors and additional memory. Dedicated IPSec-capable network adapters can also make high-volume IPSec usage more feasible. An Active Directory domain, while not a requirement, is a highly desirable means of centrally configuring your company's computers to use IPSec appropriately.

CHAPTER 9

Certificates and Public Key Infrastructure

Within virtually all modern computer infrastructures is the concept of authentication. I discussed Windows Server 2003's authentication model and mechanisms earlier in Chapter 7. But often this type of authentication does not meet the needs of all technologies. For example, numerous devices, such as routers, do not understand Kerberos or NTLM authentication. These routers may need to trust other entities on the network, such as users or other routers.

I've said that public key certificates from a trusted certification authority provide a mechanism for this trust. Now I'll discuss the specifics of certificates—how they work, what they do, and what benefits they provide. Then I'll show you the certification authority—what it does and why you may need one. I'll also describe how to make a decision on whether to use a public or private certification hierarchy in your enterprise. Each course of action is then explored in great detail. You'll read procedural, process, and conceptual information about each strategy.

If you've already decided to implement a *public key infrastructure* (PKI) and want to get right down to examples, you should skip ahead to the "Implementing a Private Certification Hierarchy" section. That's where I show you exactly what to do to get this all set up and ready to rock.

What Are Certificates?

Imagine that you need to communicate with a secure web site on the internal corporate LAN. This is not an uncommon occurrence, as many web sites provide sensitive data in your environment. In this case, you want to change your health benefits information with your human resources department. You must be sure of two things to be confident that this communication is protected: the data transmission must be encrypted, and the web server must be who it says it is. If the data transmission is insecure, a malicious user could capture the network traffic and obtain or modify the sensitive data. If the web server is replaced or spoofed, your communication is vulnerable to a *man in the middle* attack in which an attacker becomes the middleman between your computer and the intended server.

 A man in the middle attack is also frequently referred to as a *bucket brigade attack*, referring to the historic method of firefighting by passing buckets.

By now you're thinking that authentication by a reasonably secure mechanism such as Kerberos can provide this assurance. However, we must remember we're talking about web traffic as a communications channel. There is no guarantee that the web server understands Kerberos at all, and even less of a chance that there is a safe integration between Kerberos and the web server. (Microsoft's technologies in this area actually do provide this integration, so this is just an example.) Also, remember that Kerberos provides tickets and proves authentication. It is not designed to provide generic keys for any requesting application, and it does not protect any network traffic but its own.

A public key certificate (just *certificate* for short) is simply a document that contains identification information about the holder (or subject) and the public key portion of the key holder's public-private key pair. A certificate is issued by a *certification authority* (CA), which also digitally signs the certificate with its own private key to guarantee the authenticity of the certificate. If the recipient of information protected by a certificate *trusts* the integrity of the certification authority that issued the certificate (in the example, if the recipient trusts the issuer of your certificate), the certificate—and the information it protects—can be trusted. Although private certification authorities within your organization are known to be trustworthy, others may not be and must be evaluated to determine whether you should trust them. Details about establishing trust and the criteria used to decide which public authorities to trust are provided later in this chapter.

Certificates are most often used for identity authentication and secure exchange of information over an untrusted network. Because they contain a public key, a sender can use that key to encrypt information that only the trusted holder of the corresponding private key can decrypt. For example, Alice can obtain Bob's certificate and use the public key it contains to encrypt data. Only Bob has the corresponding private key, so only Bob can decrypt that data.

Similarly, the holder of the certificate's private key can use that key to encrypt information such as a hash of a message, creating a digital signature. All holders of the certificate can use that public key to decrypt and verify the digital signature in the message and verify its authenticity. Bob, for example, may want to reply to Alice with nonconfidential information. However, he wants to prove that the information came from him. He can use his private key to encrypt a hash of the message and send that hash along with the message. When Alice decrypts the hash with Bob's public key (from his certificate) and determines that the hash is authentic, she knows two things: Bob sent the message, and the message hasn't been tampered with.

Certificate Concepts

As I've said earlier in the book, a certificate is a binding of a public key to an identity. Any certificate has three very important components: the public key, the identification information, and the digital signature of the certificate. These components provide enough information to complete our desired tasks such as authentication, encryption, and digital signature creation. Because it contains only essential information, a certificate tends to be rather small—2KB or less is average. As we'll see during our discussion of certificate deployment later in the book, this small size is one element that makes certificate deployment a bit easier than if they were huge. And even when certificates are customized (for example, by use of a custom certificate template) to add additional information, they tend to stay small.

The four separate types of certificates are generally defined by their intended use and subject type (*subject* is just a fancy word for the holder of the certificate):

End-entity or personal certificates
> These certificates are issued to users and are used for commonly recognized certificate tasks such as authentication and digital signature creation. Because certificates may have different purposes and strengths, one user may hold several certificates. Each end-entity certificate is signed with the key of the CA that issued the certificate.

Server and computer certificates
> Servers and many computers on a network must also prove their identity to other entities. In the Windows Server 2003 family, domain controllers must all have certificates to prove their identities. These certificates allow domain controllers to identify themselves to other domain controllers and aid in secure communication.

Software publishing certificates
> These certificates are usually issued to one or more software developers for the purpose of digitally signing software before production or deployment. This digital signature allows the developer to prove that the software comes from a trusted source and that it is unmodified since its creation (e.g., uninfected by a virus). These certificates are usually owned by a *role holder*—that is, someone or something that performs a specific task, such as software signing. It may be one or more people or one or more processes or may be transferred as roles change in a company.

Certification authority certificates

Certification authorities digitally sign all end-entity certificates before issuance. These certificates are signed with a specific private key corresponding to the public key contained in the certification authority's certificate. This private key is usually the most important component in a public key certificate environment, since compromise of this private key jeopardizes the trust of the certification authority. Even the certification authority's certificate is signed—either by its parent in a hierarchy or self-signed in the case of root certification authorities.

Regardless of the type or intended use of the certificate, all certificates contain the same type of information. This information is simply used in a different way, depending on its type and the application using it.

Certificates are formatted in a regimented yet flexible manner. The definition of this format is contained in Request for Comments (RFC) 3280—Internet X.509 Public Key Infrastructure. This RFC defines the *X.509 Version 3 (X.509v3) certificate*, which is the current standard for public key certificates. A large number of associated standards precede and complement RFC 3280, and many technologies interoperate with data formatted to this standard.

This is an example of an X.509v3 certificate in base-64 encoding:

```
-----BEGIN CERTIFICATE-----
MIIB9jCCAWOgAwIBAgIQ+1uhfc1HfJtGmZ3gwO4UTzAJBgUrDgMCHQUAMBIxEDAO
BgNVBAMTB2R1ZmF1bHQwIBcNMDExMjE2MDUzMDI3WhgPMjEwMTExMjIwNTMwMjda
MBIxEDAOBgNVBAMTB2R1ZmF1bHQwgZ8wDQYJKoZIhvcNAQEBBQADgYOAMIGJAoGB
AMjSnqvhhW3k5b3KAcbrZJTfcydV3awYAYzGCDO6mVuiWzLXg9xLODkxGtO6Hu4/
fIiSCL5QI7iH9SR8YvvOJEulZQQ5nMOdny3+cHNnhZdqC+SqmY8G+ukLa/n8Y7Wl
lubaftAuaBA2kyLKyBZh9Oa8AU/dlv/AzKNDXfanakeRAgMBAAGjUzBRMBUGA1Ud
JQQOMAwGCisGAQQBgjcKAwQwLQYDVRORBCYwJKAiBgorBgEEAYI3FAIDoBQMEmR1
ZmF1bHRAQlJJQOtQSUxFADAJBgNVHRMEAjAAMAkGBSsOAwIdBQADgYEAuu6mEZWu
yvZQs3f/BGLWBIQb5gTT3jXGkseOU8+MvTb+FTNg83dbHKuxDGLdRhpjGn8jnlRV
CUVzlarBKLSfUTa8Q4+/ncCsqn5HnNGabS8la55uaB3RVM2dJlJ8eKXnPyHOH7zX
TWIFEdLqOqEw89GvIApT4jsffK3t+SrxUIg=
-----END CERTIFICATE-----
```

Notice two things about this certificate. First, you cannot read it. It is encoded for computer use—not for security as much as for simplified use by the computer. This encoding normally employs the Public Key Cryptography Standard #7 (PKCS #7) format, as defined by RSA Labs. Plenty of programs are available to interpret this information for you. Second, notice how small it is. As I've said, one of the valuable properties of a certificate is its ease of deployment. Because this certificate is so small, it can easily be distributed by almost any means without consuming significant bandwidth.

The same certificate, when viewed through the Windows Certificates snap-in, looks much different. This is because Windows interprets the raw data contained in the certificate and presents it in a simple, readable format. Notice in Figure 9-1 the three tabs to display different information about the certificate:

General

Displays basic information including the state of the certificate, the entity (or *subject*) that it was issued to, and the original issuer. This is a summary-style display of the information.

Details

Displayed in Figure 9-1, this tab contains the information from the certificate including the public key, cryptographic algorithm, and subject name.

Certification Path

Shows the certificate hierarchy that issued the certificate. Each CA in the hierarchy between the issuing CA and the root CA is shown with a status for each of those certificates.

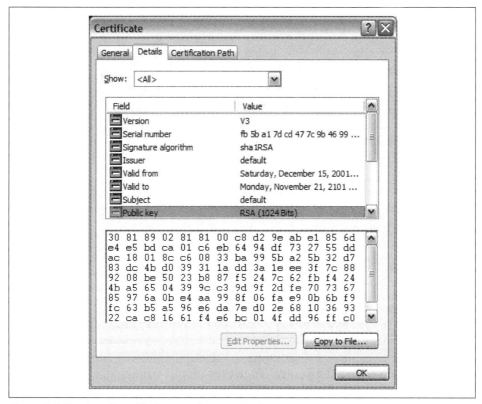

Figure 9-1. Display of a public key certificate in Windows

Benefits of Public Key Certificates

Why would you want to use public key certificates in your corporation? Simply put, they are the best way to establish trust and provide a method for secure communication among users in your corporation.

Numerous applications use certificates for securing their data. In the appendix, I discuss how Microsoft Outlook uses certificates for data encryption and digital signature. But this is only one of a variety of uses. Applications of certificate-based cryptography can also include securing any data communication between users, providing authentication of users, and establishing trust that a user is who he says he is. Applications from Microsoft and other developers that take advantage of these features currently exist. You've already read about IPSec's use of certificates for authentication in Chapter 8. IIS also uses certificates for SSL-based communication and authentication and is covered in Chapter 13.

The one nice advantage that authentication through public key certificates provides is portability. Other online authentication protocols such as NTLM and Kerberos require extensive interaction and a reasonably chatty network protocol to provide their authentication. Public key–based authentication, on the other hand, is more processor intensive but far less interactive. An entity can prove its identity and establish a shared secret key with a minimum of network traffic and without involving many (if any) third-party authentication servers.

Any application has the ability to make use of certificates. As I'll discuss in the next section, a rich set of programming interfaces is made available in Windows Server 2003 to obtain, manage, and use certificates. Similar interfaces are available in many Windows client operating systems. Using these interfaces, custom applications that take advantage of the enormous security that certificates provide can easily be written. The only caveat is that an application must be written specifically to use this type of security. Trying to append public key certificate awareness to an existing application is usually unsuccessful, as the technology is not fully designed and integrated into the application.

Where Do Certificates Come From?

Certificates usually come from dedicated certification authorities. Though there are a few well-known public certification authorities such as Verisign and Thawte, there are as many certification authorities to choose from as there are snowflakes. However, one important question must be answered before selecting a certification authority: do I create my own certification authority within my enterprise, or do I obtain certificates from a third party? To use the correct terminology: do I use a private (internal) or a public (external) certification authority?

Certificates don't always come from certification authorities. Some applications may be unable to function without a certificate that's specifically configured for the application. Most of these applications will check to see if such a certificate exists, and if not, they will generate their own. These certificates are known as self-signed certificates. This is because the local computer—as opposed to a certification authority—provides the digital signature for the certificate. The Encrypting File System (EFS) is one example of an application that behaves in this fashion.

A self-signed certificate is useful for the application that generated it. It will contain the same information as a certificate from a certification authority, but it is its own root certificate. The benefit to this certificate is that it can be created easily and used to provide some application-specific security. However, you do not get the same level of assurance from a self-signed certificate, as it was not issued by a certification authority. There is no real binding of identity to the key.

What Do I Do with Certificates?

Once your enterprise users have obtained certificates, there are a multitude of uses for them. Applications can use them to prove your identity, send encrypted information, and provide nonrepudiation of data. It is important to note that applications must be written specifically to take advantage of certificate-based security. Users cannot take advantage of all the benefits of certificates without supporting software.

Users can, however, manage their certificates and certificate stores. As we'll see in later chapters, very little certificate management is done on the Windows Server 2003 family certification authority. This means that virtually all certificate management happens on or at the request of the user's computer. As we'll see, some of this management is done automatically with no user intervention or knowledge, and some requires user understanding and cooperation.

Distributing Certificates

You have already read that certificates have numerous purposes, depending on the applications deployed. Most of those applications require that you have obtained someone else's certificate—specifically, that of the user or computer you want to securely communicate with. Without that information, you cannot authenticate the recipient and do not have the public key with which to encrypt sensitive data. You must obtain this certificate to proceed with operations that require it.

The most basic way to obtain another user's certificate is to ask her to send it to you. Although this is somewhat risky, if you trust her and the threat of bucket brigade attacks is low, it works just fine. This scenario works for any certificate used on Windows 2000, Windows XP, or Windows Server 2003, no matter what type of certification authority issued the certificate (if any). Although some certificates are sometimes specifically restricted in their uses, these restrictions are based on the application that uses them. You must test applications to ensure they support certificates obtained and used in this way.

Exporting a certificate without the private key

To export a certificate for distribution to other parties or to copy it to multiple computers for distributed use, follow the steps in the later "Archiving a certificate and private key" section to run the Certificate Export Wizard. The only difference is that you must specify that you *do not want to export the private key*. Distribution of your private key defeats the security provided by PKI-based technology, because as mentioned earlier, the fundamental assumption with public key cryptography is that the private key always remains accessible to exactly one entity.

Once the certificate is exported to a file, it can be distributed to anyone you intend to communicate with. This is most often done via email by sending the certificate as an attachment. Other techniques include publishing the certificate on a file share, posting it on a web page, or writing it to a CD-ROM and mailing it. Remember that these certificates are very small so they are easily distributed through virtually any mechanism you can think up.

Importing a received certificate

Once the intended recipient receives the file, it can be easily imported for use by any application that uses the standard Microsoft certificate stores. To import the received file, you can take the following steps:

1. Save the certificate file to the local hard disk or insert a disk that contains the file.
2. Use Windows Explorer to locate the file.
3. Right-click the file and then click Install Certificate. The Certificate Import Wizard will start.
4. Select "Automatically select the certificate store based on the type of certificate" to allow the wizard to determine the correct store based on an analysis of the certificate. This ensures that certificates for CAs and subjects are kept in their proper places and are easily located by applications and the user.
5. Click Next and then click Finish to import the certificate to the appropriate store.

Once the certificate is imported, the file can be discarded. It contains no sensitive information, so no extensive care is required for its container or transportation.

Importing a certificate revocation list

As mentioned earlier in this section, some applications behave differently, depending on the certificate issuance and the validation the application performs. Many newer applications require a check of the certificate's revocation status to ensure it has not been compromised. This is done in Windows by retrieving the certificate revocation list (CRL) for the CA that issued the certificate. I'll discuss certificate revocation and the CRL later in this chapter.

If the computer that imports the certificate cannot retrieve the CRL from its public location, it will fail its revocation check and the certificate may not be usable. This happens most often with computers that are in an offline state, such as laptops or remote office computers. In this case, the CRL can be exported and imported in essentially the same way the certificate was exported and imported in the previous examples. The only difference is that the file is a CRL file instead of a certificate (CER) or PKCS #7 (P7B) file. The CRL is also normally a very small file, similar or slightly larger than the certificate export file.

As a reminder, not all applications require a CRL to use the certificate. You must test the applications that use the certificate to determine whether these steps are necessary; there is no clear-cut way to determine CRL reliance other than extensive testing. Although performing these procedures for both the certificate and CRL will provide a more complete certificate transportation solution, it may not be necessary to transport the CRL. But either way, it won't hurt. If the possibility exists that the CRL will be needed in the future, it's a good idea to go ahead and transport it with the corresponding certificate.

 Both certificates and CRLs have expiration dates. Although certificates may be valid for several years, CRLs are usually valid for only days or weeks. This is because certificates are revoked with some frequency and the CRL must be updated to include those revoked certificates. Therefore, when the CRL must be transported in this manner, you will most likely be required to repeat the procedure periodically. The certificate does not need to be redistributed every time the CRL is; each has its own independent lifetime.

Backing Up the Certificate and Private Key

After the certification hierarchy is set up and configured, the number-one issue that helpdesks encounter is users who have lost the private key associated with a certificate. Often this key has been used to encrypt data using the Encrypting File System (EFS), to send and receive encrypted email, or for some other long-term protected data storage use. The most common reasons for losing a private key are:

- Reinstallation of the operating system
- Deletion of the user's profile
- Hard disk failure and replacement resulting in data loss

When the private key is permanently lost, there is no way to recover the data protected with that key. Many people are surprised to learn that. But if there were a way to recover the data without the private key, the entire public key security concept would be useless. However, as an administrator, you have some options to mitigate this situation.

The only real solution to this problem is to archive the private key before it is lost. This can be done in two distinct ways. Both ways have advantages and drawbacks, so they must be weighed carefully before a decision is made.

One option is to configure the certification authority to store the user's private key when accepting a certificate request. This allows the administrator to maintain the storage of these keys indefinitely and provide a replacement whenever a user loses it. The user does not need to take any additional steps to ensure this level of redundancy. Although archiving the private key on the CA presents some security concerns, there are huge recoverability benefits. This option is frequently referred to as key archival and must be supported on the issuing CA.

The other option is for the user to archive his private key to an external drive, floppy disk, or CD. This is easily accomplished by the user through the Certificates MMC snap-in. A fairly straightforward wizard asks a few questions and then writes the private key to a file specified by the user. This file can be password-protected for an additional level of security. In any case, this file must be physically protected from others to avoid the possibility of this private key copy from falling into the wrong hands. Another drawback to this method is that it is not administrator controlled and cannot be enforced through technology-based policy. Users can simply forget to create the backup.

Archiving a certificate and private key

To archive a private key to a floppy disk or CD, the user must follow these steps:

1. Run the Certificates snap-in (*certmgr.msc*). This snap-in allows certificates and private keys to be displayed for the current user, the computer account of the local computer, or a service account.

2. Identify the correct certificate. There is usually more than one certificate and private key available through the snap-in, as is shown by a typical certificate store in Figure 9-2. Care must be taken to ensure the proper key is archived. But because the certificates and keys are so small, many keys can be archived and stored. Backing up all certificates is recommended, but this cannot be accomplished in a single step.

3. Right-click the certificate and click All Tasks, then click Export to run the Certificate Export Wizard.

4. Specify that you want to export the private key with the certificate. This step is critical, as the private key is the unique data that is truly valuable and cannot be replaced by administrators or other users.

5. Provide a password for the exported private key and certificate. This is used to prevent compromise of the private key if the storage medium is compromised.

6. Export the file directly onto a floppy disk (or writeable CD drive). This ensures that a temporary copy is never stored on the local hard drive.

7. Repeat as necessary for each certificate that has an associated private key.

8. Separate the floppy disk (or CD) from the user to keep them both safe.

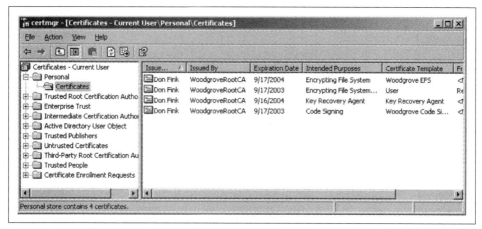

Figure 9-2. Certificates MMC snap-in displaying several certificates

Remember that the private key still exists as a part of the user's profile information on the computer. It has simply been backed up to the floppy disk. If the user's profile is damaged or lost (for example, if the computer's hard drive fails), the floppy disk has a copy of that private key.

Restoring an archived private key

To restore a private key that has been lost, use the following simple procedure:

1. Insert the floppy with the archived private key.
2. Double-click the file on the floppy disk.
3. Provide the password.

The certificate and its private key are now imported into the user's private key store.

The restore procedure does not remove the private key from the floppy disk or make the disk any less valuable. The disk should immediately be returned to its protected storage to ensure its security. If the disk is ever damaged or considered obsolete, it should be destroyed to ensure the unrecoverability of the private key it may still contain.

What Is a Certification Authority?

Public key certificates are the answer to many authentication issues, as you've just seen. The next question is: where does the server get its certificate? From a CA. This is the crux of what I'll be discussing in this section. The web server certificate can come from either a public or private CA, but either way, a CA must provide that certificate by signing the requested certificate with its private key.

Certification authorities primarily provide three functions:

Issue public key certificates
> The heart of any CA is the ability to receive a request from a client for a public key certificate and issue a certificate in response. This process can take many different forms and be governed by both technology-based and administration-based rules. The certificate requests are often governed by certificate templates, which define what information is required for a request and what type of certificate can be issued based on each request.

Publish certificate revocation lists
> When certificates are compromised, there must be a way to notify clients that the certificate is invalid. The CA creates a list of invalid (or revoked) certificates and then distributes (publishes) the list. This list is called a *certificate revocation list* (CRL). It is similar to the old lists of lost or stolen credit cards that were distributed to merchants. A merchant who accepted a credit card would hopefully check the list to ensure the card number was not listed. Similarly, whenever an application makes use of a public key certificate, it would hopefully check the CRL before considering it valid.

Archive private keys
> A relatively recent advancement in public key technology is the ability of the CA to request a copy of the client's private key during the certificate request and issuance process. This key is normally kept in an encrypted fashion on the CA in case the user ever needs her key restored. This feature is available in Windows Server 2003 Enterprise Edition and will be discussed later in this chapter.

How a Certification Authority Works

A certification authority can be thought of as a simple database with an enormous set of complex rules. I'll examine the different conditions that a certification authority will encounter and the rules that apply to each condition. This section applies to Windows Server 2003 Enterprise Edition acting as a certification authority, although most of these terms and concepts apply to any manufacturer's certification authority, including Windows Server 2003 Standard Edition.

Server configuration

Each certification authority must be installed and configured by an administrator, as there is no automatic or default installation. It is absolutely critical to design and plan the deployment of a certification hierarchy well before any certification authorities are deployed. Certification authority planning is discussed later in this chapter.

Subject requesting a certificate

When a subject requests a certificate, some information is always required by the CA. Although some essential information is required for any certificate issued (such as the public key), other information may vary. For example, some certificates might require user principle names from Active Directory, while others may require the IP address of the computer requesting the certificate.

The client must ensure that the right information is provided in the request, in the right format for the CA to interpret. This information will vary based on the issuing CA and the type of certificate requested. For example, a client certificate used for authentication is different from a subordinate CA certificate, because they have very different intended uses and often require different security levels (for example, different cryptographic key lengths). These usage differences often require that their certificate requests contain different data. For example, a request for a passport probably requires different proof of identification than a request for a check cashing card at a grocery store.

Because there are several different ways to request a certificate from a Windows Server 2003 CA, there must be a way for the client to learn the specific type and format of request that the CA can understand as well as the information that must accompany the request. This is accomplished by configuring *certificate templates* on the server.

Certificate templates are containers for the certificate configuration and allow both the server and client to mutually understand the required format for successfully obtaining a certificate. Typically, certificate templates are designed as part of the certificate authority infrastructure and created during the initial configuration. But because these templates are independent of one another and highly configurable, they can be modified, supplemented, or removed whenever a business or security need must be met. But a template is always required so the client and server both know what information is required for enrollment.

Processing the request

A subject requests a certificate from a certification authority by obtaining the certificate template (either directly from the CA or from Active Directory, depending on the type of CA), preparing the proper information in the correct format, and presenting that information to the certification authority. The certification authority is then responsible for either issuing or denying the request. This decision is based on a fairly basic rule: the template either stipulates that requests for a certificate be issued automatically or put into a "pending" state.

 Contrary to popular belief, a certification authority does not generate the public-private key pair used in a certificate. The subject generates the key pair when creating the certificate request (in Windows Server 2003, this is done by the built-in Cryptographic API (CAPI). The public key portion is then included with the certificate request that is sent to the certification authority. The private key never leaves the subject's computer unless exported or for server-based key archival.

Publishing a certificate

The specific processes to be followed before issuing a pending certificate vary greatly. In some cases, an email confirmation that the request is authentic may be all that is required. In other cases, such as with high-value certificates, physical confirmation of the subject or extensive background investigations may be necessary. From the perspective of the administrator, the more valuable the certificate, the more rigorous and comprehensive the verification of the subject must be. From the certification authority's perspective, all pending certificate requests are the same. A certificate manager for that certification authority must manually issue the certificate to complete the request.

Once a certificate is issued by the certification authority (with approval from the certificate manager), the certificate request is signed with the private key of the certification authority. This creates the certificate. The certification authority then stores a copy of the certificate for itself and distributes a copy to the requester, by any method desired. This distribution does not need to be protected, as the certificate does not contain any secret information and its security does not rely on restricted distribution.

In many configurations, the certificate is also sent to a directory service to provide the certificate to any requester who wants to securely communicate with the subject. This provides centralized distribution of certificates and provides an additional layer of assurance that the certificate is unadulterated. However, the client could just provide the certificate to any requester through any desired means. Although this distribution mechanism is less trustworthy and more inconvenient, the digital signature on the certificate is considered sufficient to prove its own authenticity.

 Most certification authorities have the ability to perform one or more additional tasks when a certificate is issued or denied. The Microsoft Windows Server 2003 CA, for example, has the built-in ability to send email or publish the certificate to Active Directory. The Windows Server 2003 CA is built in a modular fashion that allows an administrator to install code that can do anything when a certificate is issued, providing for great customizability of the CA. For more information on customizing the Windows Server 2003 CA, see the MSDN article "Writing Custom Exit Modules" at *http://msdn.microsoft.com/library/en-us/security/Security/writing_custom_exit_modules.asp*.

Server publishing a certificate revocation list

Over time, certificates may become invalid. RFC 3280 defines another common data structure used with certificates, the certificate revocation list (CRL). A CRL is a much simpler structure than the certificate. It is simply a list of serial numbers of certificates that are no longer valid, such as certificates that have had the private key compromised or been replaced. This list is signed and published by the certification authority that issued the invalid certificates. The CRL can be distributed to any URI reachable by the certification authority and the certificate users. The CRL distribution point (CDP) must be established in advance to ensure that all clients that will use certificates from the certification authority can reach the CDP and download the CRL. The CDP is simply the location that stores the CRL. The CDP is often implemented as a location on a web server, but it can be any other URI you want, such as an FTP location, a UNC location, and so forth.

Deciding Between Public and Private Certification Authorities

There are two "flavors" of certification hierarchies that you can use. I'll refer to them as private and public PKI hierarchies. Just as in most decisions, there are benefits and drawbacks to each. I'll briefly discuss these flavors here and show how they will help or hinder you in reaching your goals for your PKI. Later in the chapter, I'll provide more in-depth examinations of each that specifically address the deployment and integration methods for those flavors.

Before we begin, it is helpful to know that the two flavors of PKI—private and public—are not completely isolated. It is possible to integrate a private PKI with other users or organizations, even organizations outside your own company. There are ways to build explicit trusts between organizations, no matter what flavor of PKI is used. These methods are simply more complex than one flavor or the other.

Public Certification Authorities

The criteria for selecting a public certificate authority will vary depending on numerous factors. Some of these factors will help you decide whether to use a public or private CA. Others may help you decide between the many public CAs available if you choose that type of solution.

Cost
> Often the driving factor in these decisions is the cost per certificate desired. This depends on many factors, but in general public certification authorities charge per issued certificate and per validity period. They may also charge for customized certificate revocation lists (CRLs). On the surface, this can seem like an expensive option. Private certification authorities have associated headcount and equipment costs that you don't have with a public CA. Many companies would rather outsource such functions and not incur the liability of permanent costs. In such situations, a public certification authority might be a great solution.

Ease of deployment

Does the public certification authority have an integrated solution for delivering certificates to your users? Is there a delay between request and issuance, and if so will that impact your users' ability to perform their jobs? Can the public certification authority deliver their solution into your infrastructure without any security gaps? Can they issue and deploy computer- and role-based certificates without jumping through hoops? If the answers to these questions are yes (or if the questions aren't important to your business need), consider using a public certification authority. However, this is usually the weakest link in this solution's chain and you can expect some holes in this type of deployment.

Alignment of functionality to need

Many certificate configurations are available for different needs, such as different intended uses and different scopes of trust. Most public certification authorities can provide configurations that specifically meet your needs. However, it comes back to the first item in this list—cost.

Security integrity of issuing corporation

Most public certification authorities today will take as much care as your own internal processes require for an equivalent level of security assurance—or more. This has greatly improved over the last few years, when these companies have risen from one-room offices to large infrastructure providers. Depending on your level of interaction and trust with the company you've selected, you should ask for copies of their security plans and tour their facility. Often, these facilities are more secure than data centers at financial institutions and government installations—and almost certainly more secure than yours.

Financial stability of issuing corporation

If the certification authority is not financially self-sufficient, the solution may not be self-sustaining. In other words, if the public CA you use goes out of business, your entire PKI may suddenly stop working. There are numerous large public certification authority companies today that can provide some level of assurance. This should at least help ensure a guaranteed length of time that the CA's certificate revocation list (CRL) will be available, which will prove critical to the ongoing functionality of your infrastructure.

As you can see, several important questions must be answered when determining whether to use a public certification authority with your deployment. Many of the factors in this decision are out of your control, such as the financial condition of the company. However, most of the questions can be answered without compromising anyone's security. Obtain this information and scrutinize it carefully before any decisions are made. Remember that this company will have the private key used to sign every one of your public key certificates and therefore will have a significant level of control over your public key-based security.

Private Certification Authorities

You can use a Windows Server 2003 system to serve as a certification authority. This allows you to create your own certification hierarchy within your company. This provides several benefits, including:

Lower cost
> Once a certification authority hierarchy is established within your corporation, the cost per certificate is extremely low. It amounts to the cost of purchasing, configuring, and maintaining the certification hierarchy hardware and software, divided by the number of certificates issued. For example, if your server costs $10,000 to purchase and maintain over three years and it issues 20,000 certificates during that time, your cost per certificate is 50¢.

Flexibility
> You can choose to issue certificates for any purpose desired. There is no necessary distinction between certificate issuance methods, types, and purposes. You can, for example, deploy a CA that issues code-signing certificates with no authentication. While not always a great idea, this may be appropriate for your business need.

Ease of deployment
> Because the certification authority is internal to your company, the integration to your infrastructure is already done. You have your choice of deployment method rather than relying on the public certification authority's supported method. This can also contribute to the cost, as some deployment mechanisms are less expensive than others. For example, the certificate autoenrollment feature provided by Windows Server 2003 Enterprise Edition can lower the cost of end user certificate distribution to nearly nothing.

Architectural discrimination
> When you deploy a private certification authority, you can remove or add authorities or complete layers of authorities as appropriate for your business need. This allows you to remain flexible and change your PKI to match the changes in organization or business direction.

I have already discussed the benefits of a public certification authority and the considerations to weigh when making this decision. You must ask several questions before deciding to use a private certification authority. These include:

Do I trust my internal certificate officers?
> Some set of administrators must have the ability to set up and remove certification authorities, issue certificates, manage private key archival, and perform other security-sensitive operations. These administrators are generally referred to as certificate officers. When deciding to use a private certification authority, these officers must be identified within the company. This is important, as all

certificate-based security could be compromised by a malicious officer. Normally, a public certification authority will have a set of procedures that provides checks and balances to prevent malicious employees from causing harm in this way.

Are my internal servers physically secure?

As you've read numerous times in this book already, all security starts with physical security. The private key of your root certification authority is only as secure as the physical computer (or media) where it is stored. Internal security usually consists of data center perimeter and intrusion prevention and detection systems and sometimes uses an HSM for protection of private keys. If you cannot provide absolute physical security for this critical data internally, a public certification authority may be worth considering.

How much control over the certification authority do I require?

When using a public CA for certificates, you must realize that it holds the issuing and root CA's private keys. This means the public CA has complete control over all issued certificates, including renewal and revocation. When a private CA is used, you (or some trusted entity in your organization) retain that private key. Of even larger consequence is that the configuration of the CA is determined by the manager of that CA. Any contract for certification services should include stipulations and operating practices to ensure both parties are aware of the operation and parameters of the CA.

How much money do I want to spend?

Obviously comparative shopping is important. This is usually one of the last questions to be asked, as many other questions may be deciding factors themselves. Weighing the full-term cost of using a public versus a private CA can be a lengthy process, but it is critical to ensure the success of the project. Running out of funding in the middle of a deployment may provoke poor decisions midway through the process, which could be disastrous to the integrity of the project.

Ultimately, you will need to make a decision about what kind of certification authority you're going to use. From this book's perspective, I can only go into great detail about implementing a private PKI with Windows Server 2003, as that's the CA that you can install, configure, and manage yourself that's built into the operating system. If you decide to go with a public PKI (covered in the next section), I recommend you still read the private PKI sections after that so you understand what's going on behind the scenes with the CA you've chosen.

Implementing a Public PKI

Now that you've decided to use a public certification authority and outsource your PKI, you must determine how to incorporate it into your current environment. The vendor you've selected will undoubtedly provide a great deal of consultation and advice on how best to configure your environment to interact with its hierarchy. Because the public certification authority could be running any CA server and client software to create and maintain its certification hierarchy, at some points I cannot provide detailed steps. I will not assume that you've chosen any particular public authority or software, as there is no single best vendor among the numerous options. Therefore, our procedures will focus on Windows Server 2003 family servers and Windows XP client computers. I can summarize the elements of this type of deployment as follows:

1. Set up a secure communication channel between your network and the vendor's. This is normally handled by the vendor.

2. Configure the certificate revocation list (CRL) to be published to a location accessible to your network's subjects and verify its publication. This is normally established with agreement between you and the vendor, as you may want the CRL published to a specific point within your network to reduce bandwidth usage.

3. Verify exactly who needs a certificate and what its intended use will be. This should have already been completed in your planning process based on a risk and needs analysis and incorporated into your vendor contract.

4. Securely enroll your organization's users by verifying their identities and issuing them their certificates. This is normally done by you with guidance from the vendor and the collaboration of appropriate internal management. This step is crucial to the security of your new PKI deployment, as the receipt of a certificate by an unauthorized individual could compromise the entire deployment.

5. Securely enroll any network services or intermediate devices (e.g., routers) and configure them to use their new certificates. This is similar to issuing users their certificates but will require more policy-based guidance and auditing, as multiple individuals may have access to these valuable credentials during the process.

6. Maintain the CRL by promptly informing your PKI vendor whenever a certificate is no longer valid. This is an ongoing collaborative maintenance task.

7. Regularly audit the interaction between your company and the vendor to verify that only authorized transactions are taking place. Again, this is an ongoing task to ensure that no security compromises have quietly occurred. Auditing is frequently the only way to avoid misappropriated but as yet unexploited credentials from compromising security.

As you can see, a number of these tasks are accomplished by the vendor as they are very vendor-specific. Other tasks can be handled by the operating system of both internal servers and clients. The Windows Server 2003 family and Windows XP make many of these tasks simple.

Numerous software-based solutions are available to accomplish the implementation tasks discussed here. These software solutions are often provided by the vendor as part of a negotiated solution package. It is possible that the described tasks will be entirely completed by the vendor and no effort will be required on your part. However, many of the available solutions do not provide this service and will require you to complete these tasks manually. You should scrutinize the vendor agreement to determine which, if any, tasks you must complete yourself.

Deploy Root CA Certificate to All Clients as Trusted Root

The vendor will provide you with a root certificate that all deployed certificates will chain to. This certificate must be trusted by all clients and servers within your enterprise. With Windows Server 2003 family Active Directory, this is accomplished very simply. Group Policy can be used to distribute the desired certificate.

Let's set up a fictitious example. For our example, let's assume that your organization, Woodgrove Bank, has contracted with the Internet security firm Contoso, Inc., to provide certificates for data encryption and digital signatures. As part of the process, Contoso provides you with a root certificate on a floppy disk. You can easily deploy this certificate to all clients by following these steps:

1. Open Active Directory Users and Computers.
2. Right-click on woodgrovebank.com and click Properties.
3. Click the Group Policy tab and choose New to create a new GPO. Name this new GPO **Root Certificates**.
4. Click Edit to edit the new policy.
5. Navigate to Root Certificates → Computer Configuration → Windows Settings → Security Settings → Public Key Policies, then right-click on Trusted Root Certification Authorities and select Import.
6. Import the root certificate from the floppy disk into the policy.
7. Verify that the correct certificate is listed in the Trust Root Certification Authorities Group Policy setting. See Figure 9-3.
8. Close all open windows.
9. Wait for Active Directory replication to complete policy replication, then wait for all clients to retrieve the new policy. This can be accelerated by using the GPUpdate utility, but in normal deployments there is no need to rush the process.

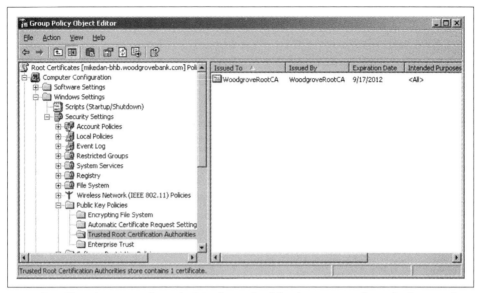

Figure 9-3. The new root certificate for Woodgrove Bank has been imported into the Group Policy settings

Note that you deployed the root certificate to the root of your domain. This is because all clients within the domain should trust this certificate. If the environment were more restrictive and required only a subset of users to trust the certificate, that could be accomplished by restricting the policy to those desired users, groups, or organizational units.

Obtain and Deploy Client Certificates

You have now successfully configured all network clients to trust the new root certificate. But you still need to deploy the client certificates in a trusted manner. This is the most variable aspect of this type of deployment. The method by which you securely authenticate the intended recipients and distribute the certificates is the step most likely to provide unauthorized access to intruders.

Considerations for client certificate deployment

There are as many methods for client certificate deployment as there are environments that will deploy certification hierarchies. Before considering specific mechanisms used to perform the client deployment, you should be aware of some common rules. Which of these rules you will follow, and how strictly, will help you determine which deployment mechanism is best for your environment.

- You must require that users prove their identity to a disinterested third-party (such as a professional auditor or external security company) before being presented with their new certificate. You should not, however, assign this task to nonsecurity personnel such as a manager or group assistant, because such a method is doomed to be compromised. Nor should you use an automated mechanism that would allow an existing intruder to extend the intrusion. Also, these proofs of identity should be audited in some nonintrusive way, such as a video recording device.

- Involve the human resources and legal portions of your company during the planning of your deployment. This will help ensure that you do not violate any privacy laws or policies during your deployment. This step may seem unnecessary and difficult, but it is far better to incorporate these groups during planning than face a lawsuit for an ill-conceived deployment plan. While this is often a time-consuming and expensive task and many companies bypass it, you should consider it a required element in your process.

 I do not offer any specific legal advice in this book for two very important reasons. First, every state and country are different and any legal opinions offered here would not be appropriate for all areas. Second, I'm not a lawyer and do not claim to be an expert on privacy or discrimination law. In my experience, the best course of action is to offer a well-written deployment plan to both HR and legal advisers and have them tell us that there are no problems. I'm not entirely sure what they're looking for, but having their seal of approval means that I don't need to know.

- Deploying certificates to intermediate network devices (e.g., routers) and service accounts should be a task assigned to a group of administrators, not just one. These tasks must be audited by a third party to ensure no collusion occurs during the deployment. This auditing party could be senior management or a vendor contracted specifically to audit security-related tasks.

- Do not attempt to deploy the entire certificate base at once. Phase in your approach so as to not overwhelm the security authentication and auditing people. One popular approach is to deploy certificates to intermediate devices first to catch any errors in policy or technology before users are involved. Next, a small cross-section of the user base is selected and certificates are deployed to them. Once these phases have been completed and any problems that have arisen are addressed, the main deployment has a more reasonable chance of success.

Common ways to deploy certificates

Once you've reviewed the considerations for client certificate deployment, you can examine the various ways certificates can be deployed to clients. There are numerous ways to accomplish this task. This section will discuss the most common and their benefits. This is not a complete list, as each certificate vendor has at least one preferred method and many employ several. Also, keep in mind that most of these solutions do not work for entities other than users. Routers, web servers, and the like will still most likely obtain their certificates through manual enrollment.

 It's important to realize that any automated method for certificate deployment to end entities negates the manual human-to-human authentication that was discussed as a very important consideration. These automated solutions provide a great benefit in that they can make certificate deployment simple. However, they remove one of the best security processes available: face-to-face authentication. You should use these automated deployment solutions only after considering this risk.

Installation of an enrollment application

Many vendors have software-based solutions that run on client computers. This software can often make certificate enrollment transparent to the user and reduce costs resulting from user errors such as enrolling for multiple costly certificates. The deployment of these applications to client computers can often be automated through software publishing.

Logon scripts

Windows Server 2003 and most Windows operating systems support logon scripts. A logon script can easily be created to execute code that enrolls for and installs a certificate on the client computer or on behalf of the user. The level of functionality for these scripts varies depending on the operating system being used. This option is somewhat more costly, as custom scripts must be developed and tested. This solution may be inappropriate for environments in which users remain logged on for extended periods, as logon scripts execute only when the user logs on.

For more information on creating scripts that enroll for certificates, including sample scripts, see "Using Certificate Enrollment Control" at *http://msdn. microsoft.com/library/en-us/security/security/using_certificate_enrollment_control. asp*.

Email web hyperlinks

A simple email can be sent to groups of users asking them to click a link. This link can point to a web page that contains script code similar to the logon script, enrolling the client for a certificate and installing it. There are several limitations to this type of deployment. The largest isn't technical; it's behavioral. Any solution that requires users to interact or perform specific actions will be less effective than a solution that runs without interaction. Expecting users to click a link may be overly optimistic, and if the certificates are required for job functions, you do not want to rely on this behavior.

Use autoenrollment

Autoenrollment is available to clients running Windows XP or Windows Server 2003 computers and automatically enrolls for and retrieves certificates from Windows Server 2003 enterprise certification authorities. If the certificate vendor is using this type of technology and integrates with autoenrollment, the certificate distribution is greatly simplified. Detailed information on autoenrollment is provided later in this chapter.

This sampling of automated enrollment methods is intended to give you some idea of the wide variety of certificate distribution solutions available. If you're integrating a public PKI vendor with your organization, you should determine which solution works best for both your clients and the vendor.

Planning Your Private Certification Hierarchy

In deciding to deploy a private certification hierarchy, you have taken on the task of correctly planning your own architecture and deployment. This is an opportunity for you to revisit your need for a PKI and structure it to meet those needs. Once deployed, it is extremely difficult and expensive to make large changes, so getting it correct from the beginning is quite important.

Numerous considerations will impact the planning of the hierarchy. These should be primarily based on the established business need. The PKI deployment will be supporting and enabling other technologies. The hierarchy should be based on those other technologies and their use of certificates. For example, if your email program does not support certificate chains of a specific length, you may want to plan your deployment to ensure this level of depth is not reached.

The hierarchy is also sometimes based on organizational or political divisions within a company. Many departments have their own IT group that makes decisions for that department and does not coordinate with other groups. Often, managers refuse to allow staff from another department to make security-based decisions that may affect their assets, such as the decision to issue a key recovery agent certificate. These types of situations should be avoided if possible as they unnecessarily complicate the hierarchy and often break technologies that would otherwise work correctly.

Hierarchy Depth

The primary decision in designing a PKI is the number of levels, or depth, of the certification authority hierarchy. The number of tiers in the certification hierarchy is normally two or three. This figure is a direct result of the most commonly planned configurations and their similarities and is a fairly consistent "sweet spot" for well-planned certification hierarchies. There are several reasons to avoid having only one CA in your hierarchy, including:

Lack of redundancy

If your only CA is brought down for maintenance or upgrade, the entire PKI is offline. This is obviously a bad situation in an environment that requires certificates for critical business functions.

Exposure to attack

If you have only one CA, then the issuing CA is also the root CA. Attackers can easily identify the CA and begin to attack it. Once an attacker is able to successfully attack the root CA's private key, he has complete control over the entire PKI. Complete removal and redeployment are required to recover from this type of security breach. Removing the root CA from scrutiny by attackers is an important and highly effective way to provide additional security.

Inability to revoke portions of the issued certificate space

If the single CA is compromised, the entire PKI must be revoked. In a multitier multi-issuer PKI, the problem is more partitioned. If the private key of an issuing CA is compromised, that CA's certificate can be revoked and all certificates issued are rendered invalid. This allows the rest of the hierarchy to function normally. This type of partitioning is critical to disaster planning, as it provides both additional security and redundancy.

Performance

Having a single CA immediately creates a performance bottleneck to administrators. All requests must be submitted to and issued by this CA. When certificates are initially deployed, this CA must generate certificates for all requesting subjects. Even with a very high performance CA issuing 10 certificates per second, it can take a very long time to accept a request, issue the certificate, and present it to the subject for installation. Having more than one CA allows this work to be distributed to all issuing CAs and provides better response times to clients.

One policy and practice statement for the entire hierarchy

A CA can have only one certificate policy and certificate practice statement. If a single CA is employed, these documents must cover all possible scenarios, certificates, and issuance processes for this CA. These documents would almost certainly be too large to be useful for their intended purpose and would become a maintenance headache, as their constant update to reflect the changing hierarchy would be expensive. Smaller, distributed policies and practice statements help ensure that they remain useful and easily managed.

There are also several reasons to avoid certification hierarchies deeper than three levels. These reasons are basic and somewhat obvious. They include being unnecessarily complex, creating more infrastructure than necessary, and requiring more maintenance than a shallower hierarchy. In addition, clients will take longer to validate certificate chains as they get deeper, directly impacting client performance across the organization. Finally, there are very few benefits to having a hierarchy this deep that would justify the expense of an additional middle tier in the hierarchy.

Security Showdown: Two-Tier Versus Three-Tier PKI

A PKI can be designed in any way you see fit, including any number of tiers from the root to the issuing CA. As I've already stated, both two-tier and three-tier architectures are extensively used. In this segment of Security Showdown, Don and Mike will debate the benefits of each.

Don: I like three-tier. You keep your top-level CA offline, literally disconnected from your network and hidden in a locked room full of rabid tigers. That way, absolutely nobody can get to it to compromise it. That root CA is the source of all trust in your entire hierarchy, and you've got to protect it better than the crown jewels. The second tier contains a smaller number of servers, which are authorized by the root—authorized by sneakernet, mind you, since you never connect the root to your network. Just write the certificates to floppy disks and walk them (hence sneakernet) to the second-tier servers.

That second tier gives you a small number of servers to deal with for things like managing revocation and whatnot, which is nice. However, you can't always keep that tier small and manageable *and* use it to issue a zillion certificates to your users, client computers, customers, and what have you. That's where the third tier comes in. Authorized by the second tier, they carry the brunt of your certificate load. Since all they do is issue certificates to actual security principals, you don't have to manage them as much or put them on especially heavy-duty hardware.

The three-tier design works well for the same reasons that three-tier applications, like web sites, work well. You get manageability, scalability, and security all in one neat architecture.

Mike: Good points. I can certainly see the benefits provided by the three-tier design. However, I think it's overkill. Two tiers in a PKI hierarchy is all most administrators will ever need.

A well-managed root CA will do little other than issue the occasional subordinate CA and publish its CRL. The CRL is incredibly short—in most implementations, the root CA's CRL is empty. And the amount of work the root performs to sign CA certificates is trivial. So why would you want to add an additional middle tier that does about the same trivial amount of work? You can maintain a great two-tier hierarchy and the only change is that you may want the root's CRL published a bit more often.

That middle tier in a three-tier hierarchy also requires several intermediate CAs to be set up and maintained. In a smaller organization, that's simply a waste. Most organizations will not need to revoke an entire CA, as its key will be protected and its compromise will be an exceedingly rare event.

As we know, one immutable security law is that complexity is the enemy of security. The flatter we can keep a PKI hierarchy, the happier we will be. There are fewer things to go wrong and less exposure to attack. I simply don't see the benefit of having that third tier unless you honestly expect a CA to be compromised on a regular basis.

—continued—

Don: Excellent points, especially for smaller organizations. However, in a larger company, I'd definitely stick with three-tier. You get your totally protected offline root, a second tier of authorizing servers that can be relatively small and therefore easier to control. Finally, you get as many servers as necessary in the third tier to issue certificates to the masses, like your users. Sure, three-tier takes a bit more hardware and management, but this is enterprise technology we're talking about, and a certificate hierarchy is no place to wimp out.

Once you've determined the depth and basic structure of the hierarchy, you should identify the role of each CA in the hierarchy. This is usually straightforward. Each CA is usually categorized into one of three roles: root, intermediate, or issuing CA. These should be defined before we continue.

Root CA
> Issues certificates to other CAs. It also issues its own CRL, which is usually short or empty. Functionally, that's all it does. It is the "root" of all trust in the organization. Its certificate is deployed to all subjects as a trusted certificate. The root can either be an *online root CA*, meaning it is on the company network and accessible from other computers, or it may be an *offline root CA* that is both physically and logically isolated when it is not being used. It may help to think of the root CA as the king of the PKI. All subjects trust the king, and anyone working in the king's name should also be trusted. The king's workers are the intermediate and issuing CAs.

Intermediate CA
> Does not issue certificates to end entities such as users and computers. Instead, it issues certificates to issuing CAs. It acts as a buffer layer between an issuing CA and the root CA. This allows partition of the PKI to be revoked or modified without affecting the rest. The intermediate CA also publishes its own CRL.

Issuing CA
> Issues certificates to end entities such as users and computers. It is also responsible for revoking end-entity certificates and regularly publishing a CRL. It receives its certificate from either an intermediate or root CA.

These terms are generic industry terms and are applicable to any CA running any available software. Two types of CA are specific to the Microsoft Windows Server 2003 implementation:

Enterprise certification authority
> An authority that is configured to integrate with Active Directory. It requires a connection to an Active Directory domain controller during installation, though the CA itself does not need to be a domain controller. The benefits of using an enterprise CA include the ability to publish certificates and CRLs to Active

Directory and the use of certificate templates (which are detailed later in this section). Enterprise CAs can be installed only on servers running Windows Server 2003 Enterprise Edition.

Standalone certification authority

The opposite of an enterprise CA. It is not connected to Active Directory. There are fewer options available on a standalone CA. However, the standalone CA can be run on any computer running Windows Server 2003. The root CA, especially if it is offline and would not normally be available to integrate with Active Directory, is often configured as a standalone CA.

Having a hierarchy with all CA roles identified is the essential component of any good PKI planning. This document should be reviewed to ensure it meets all business and organizational objectives before continuing.

A typical mixed-tier hierarchy with all roles identified is shown in Figure 9-4. This diagram shows all desired certification authorities with their names and roles. Some portions of the hierarchy are two-tiered and some are three-tiered, depending on the business justification for intermediate CAs in each case. The diagram shows a dotted line from the root CA to the authorities it has issued, which indicates that it will function as an offline root CA. The diagram also shows the CA name for each entity. In Microsoft Windows Server 2003, this is frequently the same as the computer name, although they can be different if desired. For simplicity and because there is no other business rule preventing it, I use the CA name as the computer name.

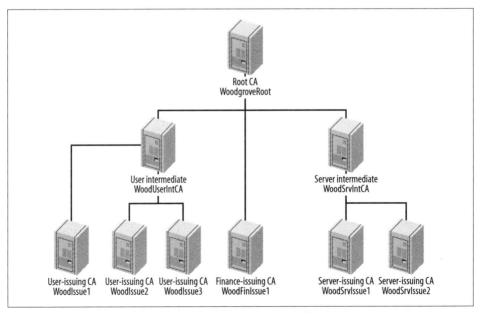

Figure 9-4. A typical certification hierarchy for Woodgrove Bank

Note that finance is isolated from the other portions of the PKI because of the high value and risk of compromise for this department. It also does not require an intermediate due to its low number of issued certificates and high level of assurance.

Desired Certificate Configuration

The purpose of creating a certification authority hierarchy is to create and distribute certificates to clients, which allow them to trust other clients. Early in the planning phase, you should make a careful analysis of the intended uses of certificates. This will allow you to determine the number and configuration of certificates that each type of user will require.

There are two schools of thought on this topic. These two schools are similar to the ways administrators design many technologies with similar flexibility in design. Do you want to issue one multipurpose certificate to each user, or do you want each user to have several certificates, each with its own specific intended use and configuration? Either way can be easily accomplished with the Microsoft Windows Server 2003 CA, so the limitation is not in the technology. The biggest consideration in this area is usually one of application usage and compatibility. Some applications, for example, may use only the first certificate available to them that has a local private key. In those cases, it would be ill-advised to deploy numerous certificates that would confuse and break the application. On the other hand, one multipurpose certificate is beneficial in its ease of administration, and the return on investment (ROI) per certificate is far larger than the multicertificate method.

No matter which decision you make, you will almost certainly want to modify the settings that clients use to obtain a certificate. This can be accomplished by the use of certificate templates. Certificate templates are similar to templates for other data structures in that they define what data is contained and in what format. In this case, certificate templates tell the requester what information to provide to the CA. The CA then uses the template to validate the request's completeness and format, and also to determine what information should be included in the issued certificate. The CA also uses the template to determine various other settings, such as whether the issued certificates should be stored in Active Directory.

Virtually any configuration can be supported with an appropriately customized certificate template. However, there is one caveat for using these templates. There are two versions of certificate templates, Version 1 (v1) and Version 2 (v2). Several v1 templates were included with Windows 2000 Server. They cannot be modified, even in Windows Server 2003, because the v1 templates were created to be static. v2 templates can be created and modified to suit any needs. However, v2 templates can be used only on an enterprise certification authority, because v2 templates are stored in Active Directory. These templates are available to all enterprise CAs in the forest, providing for simplified and centralized certificate template administration.

A typical certificate template used to issue certificates to end users for digitally signing contractual documents might be configured with the values shown in Table 9-1.

Table 9-1. Values for a typical certificate template

Configuration setting	Value
Original Template	User Signature Only
Security Permissions	Authenticated Users: Read, Enroll, Autoenroll
	Certificate Administrators: Full Control
Purpose	Signature
Key Usage Extension	Digital Signature, Signature Is Proof of Origin (Nonrepudiation), Selection Marked Critical
This Number of Authorized Signatures	1
Policy Type Required in Signature	Issuance Policy
Issuance Policy	High Assurance
Validity Period	6 Months
Renewal Period	6 Weeks

This is just one example of the power and flexibility provided by customized v2 certificate templates. Many other settings could be applied to this template based on specific needs. And any number of templates can be created.

Issuing Certificates Automatically

When the certification authority's configuration is set to issue certificates automatically, you need to do some advance planning. The decision to automatically issue certificates based on a template has a profound impact on the overall trustworthiness of a PKI. It should be made through your policy-making decision process and include the support of all stakeholders in the solution. The decision is usually based on one or more factors, including:

Access control on the template or request mechanism

Most certification authorities, including Microsoft's, allow other security mechanisms to be used in conjunction with a certificate request. These are usually placed on the certificate template itself or in the certificate request mechanism. They could also take the form of protecting incoming communications to the certification authority (e.g., an IPSec policy). These access controls ensure that only authentic and appropriate requests can be made for a certificate. Thus, no further safeguards may be necessary. This is the most common case in which certificates are automatically issued.

Low value of certificates

When the value of the issued certificates is not significant, it may be more cost-effective to automatically issue the certificate.

Regular issuance reviews

Instead of limiting the issuance of certificates, you may want to review the certificate issuance logs later to determine if any inappropriate issuances have been made. This is somewhat akin to closing the barn door after the cows have gotten out, but may be appropriate for low-value certificates or low-volume certification authorities.

 Regardless of the type, security, or volume of issuance, you should make regular audits of issued certificates. This is the only way to ensure that the certification authority is being used properly. Virtually all certification authorities have extensive auditing capabilities for this reason. Auditing of a Microsoft certification authority is covered in the "Configuring CA Auditing" section later in this chapter.

In many cases, certificate requests should not be automatically issued, and some type of manual process should be employed before certificate issuance occurs. This is commonly referred to as *pending* certificate requests. The certificate request is retained in the certification authority's database, and the client is notified during the enrollment process that the certificate cannot be issued at that time. The reasons a certificate template may be set to place requests in a queue pending approval include:

High value of issued certificates

Some certificates may have a high value, such as those used for digitally signing contracts or authorizing monetary payments. In these cases, great care must be taken to ensure an unauthorized subject does not receive such a certificate.

Absence of other safeguards

If the certificate template and the certification authority have no access controls placed on certificate requests, any user could potentially submit a certificate request. Often users do not know what they're requesting and may request wholly inappropriate certificates. Placing the request in a pending state allows the certificate manager to determine whether the request is valid and appropriate.

Certificate Revocation Architecture

When a client uses a certificate, she has the ability to extract the CDP information and request the CRL. Because this can happen at any time, it is critical to ensure the CRL is reasonably current at all times. The certification authority can be configured to publish the CRL at any interval required. Several major factors contribute to the decision of how often to publish a CRL:

Size of CRL

The more certificates revoked, the longer the list. Although each entry in the list is quite short (the size of each entry may vary but will almost always be less than 1KB), if a great number of certificates are revoked before they expire, the CRL can increase greatly in size. A CRL can have up to 1000 certificates listed before it reaches its maximum default size and another CRL is automatically created.

Network bandwidth

Each time the CRL is published, it must be distributed to all specified CDPs. If the CRL is published to a distributed location, such as Active Directory, additional replication may take place. In addition, all clients must download their own copy of the CRL when used. This can quickly consume network bandwidth, and if the network is already taxed, this may be an unacceptable drain on resources.

Application CRL support

Remember that applications must support CRL checking for any of this to matter—it is good behavior, but not required. If the applications in your enterprise do not check the CRL or check it only infrequently, frequent distribution could be a waste of time.

 Most certificate-aware applications do not document whether they require, support, or ignore CRLs. In general, the only way to determine CRL support is to test the application by deploying a test PKI, issuing and revoking the certificate, and then using that certificate with the application. It might take a bit of time, but it's the only way to be sure.

Security exposure of issued certificates

As I discussed earlier, when considering whether to automatically issue certificate requests or place them in a queue pending approval, each certificate type has a different value. Certificates from a certification authority that issues high-value certificates obviously require a higher level of protection. This means that, in addition to the appropriate applications checking the CRL, the CRL should be published more frequently by those high-value certification authorities. This helps ensure that a revoked certificate has a shorter window for misuse.

Now I'll examine the considerations to make when deploying your private certification hierarchy. There are two major considerations, including whether to use delta CRLs and defining the CDP.

Delta certificate revocation lists

To help mitigate some of the negative aspects of frequent CRL publication, you can publish *delta CRLs*. A delta CRL is, as its name implies, a CRL with only those certificates that have been revoked since the last CRL (or base CRL) was published. This makes a delta CRL much smaller and more easily replicated. Applications that support delta CRL usage check the base and delta CRL to ensure that no compromised certificates are trusted. If the delta CRL is out of date, a new one can be quickly retrieved without having to replace the full CRL. Eventually the entries in a delta CRL will be listed in the full CRL. These intervals are configurable on most certification authorities, including Microsoft's. Specific configuration of a Microsoft CA's CRL is discussed later in this chapter.

Many newer applications and operating systems support the use of delta CRLs when checking certificate revocation status. However, as always, you should verify that the PKI-aware applications you are using will recognize and correctly process a delta CRL. These applications may be incorrectly written to look for only a single base CRL at the CDP. This is not correct behavior when a delta CRL exists, as the base CRL will include a reference to the delta CRL's CDP. However, you must know whether your PKI-leveraging applications handle delta CRL configuration before beginning your deployment. A quick test in a lab would suffice. The test could easily be accomplished with the following tasks. The detailed steps for each task are covered later in this chapter.

1. Install a root CA.
2. Configure the CA to issue your desired certificate template.
3. Configure the CA to publish both base and delta CRLs. Publish your base CRL.
4. Enroll for and issue a certificate from the test client.
5. Revoke the issued certificate.
6. Publish a delta CRL. You now have a revoked certificate that appears on the delta CRL but not the base CRL.
7. Test the application's use of the certificate. If the application correctly detects that the certificate is invalid, it supports the delta CRL configuration. If the application does not recognize the certificate as revoked, the application does not support the use of a delta CRL.

If your application does not support delta CRLs, you should make one of two decisions. Either modify your deployment plans or obtain an updated version of the application that supports this configuration. If the former option is chosen, you should decide how you will make the CRL shorter. This can be done in several ways, such as shortening the lifetime of issued certificates, separating the users of the misbehaving application to their own CA, or distributing the users to more CAs.

CRL distribution points

Choosing a CRL distribution point (CDP) is a fairly simple matter. The main consideration is whether the CDP must be reachable by clients outside the LAN. If the clients are all within the corporate network, choose a highly available centralized server or Active Directory (or both) to act as the CDP. If you will issue certificates to clients both inside and outside the LAN, another CDP should be added that includes an Internet location (or some other location that the intended clients can reach). This is usually a web server, and the CDP is included in the certificates as an HTTP URL, which provides fairly ubiquitous access.

Hardware Plans

Although a CA can be configured on any computer running Windows Server 2003 family, there is some benefit to having it reside on a computer without other software services. The primary benefit is a reduction of attack surface. If other applications or services are running on the CA, they could potentially expose the CA to an attack. It also allows the CA to be kept current with security updates and patches as the need arises with a minimum of effort.

Most server hardware configurations are more than acceptable for a CA running on the Windows Server 2003 family. The CA is a relatively small consumer of CPU horsepower and memory space. Unless the CA is generating and issuing certificates at a constant pace, as in an initial deployment, the server will usually carry a light load relative to other servers in the enterprise. However, as stated earlier, this does not indicate that you should provide other services with the computer. A somewhat idle CA that doesn't fully use the hardware's capabilities is far more secure than a fully loaded server that carries numerous security exposures that an attacker might probe.

One important consideration when planning hardware investment for the PKI is the physical size and design of the CA hardware. As I've discussed, each CA should be physically secured within a data center specifically designed to provide physical security. The hardware purchase should be a natural extension of that security design. If, for example, the secure data center is configured to support computers in 19-inch racks, the CA hardware should be purchased to fit those racks. This helps ensure there are no surprises during deployment when the computers may be placed in an inappropriate location due to size incompatibility.

Cryptographic hardware for certification authorities

Another major consideration when making hardware decisions for your certification authorities is whether to use hardware security modules (HSMs) or cryptographic accelerators. These dedicated and highly specialized devices mitigate numerous threats, assure multifactor authentication, and provide tamper-proof auditing.

Should I Waste Hardware on a Dedicated Root CA?

Many administrators wonder whether a large amount of dedicated equipment is really necessary to maintain an offline root CA. Once the root CA is established and it issues the intermediate or issuing CA certificates, its only ongoing role is to periodically issue a CRL and renew child CA certificates. Its CRL will include only revoked certificates it has directly issued—intermediate or issuing CA certificates. The CA certificates issued by the root are normally long-lived certificates. So there may be days, weeks, or even months in which there is absolutely no activity on the root CA.

However, the root CA must be readily available if a second-tier's certificate is compromised. It is far more efficient to revoke the CA's certificate than the certificate of all issued certificates from the compromised CA, and the compromised key could always be used to issue new nonrevoked certificates. But this requirement for quick access does not mean that the CA cannot have a small lag interval.

The decision on whether to use dedicated computer hardware for the root CA is entirely yours. In some enterprises the root CA is a hard drive that is periodically installed into a standard hardware configuration to issue a fresh CRL. This is a perfectly valid configuration, as long as the root CA can be brought up quickly in case of urgent need. This configuration also allows the continued use of expensive hardware that would otherwise sit mostly idle.

At the root of the HSM is the importance of the private key of the CA. You already know that the private key of the CA is used to sign all issued certificates. Compromise of this key allows an attacker to sign any certificate requests he desires, as well as decrypt any information encrypted with the CA's public key. Because of the sensitivity of the CA's private key, it must be protected to whatever extent is deemed necessary. There are several methods to protect the CA's private key. One is to split up the private key using a combination of management techniques and software; that will be discussed later. Another method is to use dedicated hardware.

An HSM is simply a device that holds the private key and allows the key's use only when directed. The HSM is frequently implemented as a small device that connects to a computer's bus via SCSI or PCI and may be configured as an internal or external device. HSMs employ specific software that allows them to notify the CA that the key is available only through the device. When the CA requires the private key for an operation, the appropriate party or parties authenticate themselves with the HSM, and the HSM performs the validation of those parties. When the appropriate number and identity of parties are reached, the HSM does the cryptographic work with the key. The actual private key never leaves the device.

Many organizations are required to use an HSM that meets the Federal Information Processing Standard (FIPS) 140-1—Security for Cryptographic Modules. This is a device-independent standard that defines how an HSM protects private keys and how they can be accessed. FIPS 140-1 has different levels of security, with Level 1 being the least secure and Level 4 being the most secure (and most expensive). You should investigate whether your industry has regulations that define a minimum level of FIPS 140-1 protection before you make any HSM purchases. For most environments, Level 3 protection provides more than adequate private key protection, including protecting against physical attack of the HSM itself.

The incorporation of an HSM in your CA hierarchy provides numerous benefits, including:

A hardware security partition between the computer and the HSM
> The cryptographic work with the private key is contained entirely within the HSM. The key is generated on the HSM and remains there forever. Even if the computer is compromised, the key was never known to the computer and cannot be derived from its memory, secondary storage, and so on.

A focal point for security scrutiny
> It can be difficult to perform a detailed security analysis of an entire operating system, but an HSM can be subjected to intense scrutiny with minimal effort. They are frequently certified to very high government and military security specifications because of their limited scope and function. They usually employ better random number generation techniques than a computer-based operating system uses.

Auditing of private key usage
> Most HSM devices provide the ability to audit each use of the private key. This auditing is done entirely on the HSM and, therefore, cannot be erased or tampered with. Regular reviews of an HSM audit log would reveal any inappropriate use of the private key.

Multifactor authentication
> An HSM can easily be configured to perform private key operations only when multiple operators are present. This ensures that no single operator has the opportunity to misuse her privilege and use the private key inappropriately. This goes beyond auditing to be a preventive rather than investigative safeguard.

Acceleration of private key operations
> Because a small amount of specially designed hardware is performing dedicated tasks in an HSM, the hardware is more efficient at cryptographic tasks than a computer's multipurpose CPU is. As a result, cryptographically difficult tasks such as long key generation take far less time when performed by an HSM.

Increased randomness
> Cryptography relies on random number generation for part of its security. The ability of a computer system to generate values as random as possible contributes directly to the cryptographic security of that system. If the computer's random number generation is predictable, an attacker has an advantage when trying to break its security. Many manufacturers build an improved random number

generator into their HSM to help improve randomness. When the CA requires a random number, the HSM uses its own process to generate and return a (hopefully) unpredictable random number. (Note that many security professionals do not believe there is ever a truly random number, and I do not say that an HSM will provide one. However, a number needs to be only sufficiently random as to avoid prediction by an attacker.)

Implementing a Private Certification Hierarchy

The implementation of a private PKI is far more complex than that of a public PKI. The hierarchy must be planned in detail before any deployment can be considered. You may even want to consult legal experts to help create a certificate practice statement. Each CA deployed must be configured for proper security before exposing it to any users or attackers. The description provided on implementing the PKI is sequential and should be followed in the correct order to ensure proper deployment.

This isn't to say that deploying a PKI is hard. The individual tasks associated with the deployment are actually very straightforward and take little time to complete. The planning itself isn't difficult either. But ensuring you've completely thought through all aspects of the PKI and created a solid plan will help avoid missing steps or key elements of the deployment. And recovering from these missed elements or steps is something that's not always possible in the PKI environment.

Create a PKI Deployment Plan

Before you begin to implement your certification hierarchy, you must have your planning completed. You already know how the PKI will work—what templates will be used, who will get certificates, how many tiers will be in the tree, and so forth. That plan tells you what to deploy but not how to deploy it. To get to the next stage, you must determine the exact method and order you will use to properly deploy the technology. This information makes up your deployment plan, which is similar to your plans to deploy any broad-reaching technology across the enterprise.

At its minimum, your PKI deployment plan should include the following information:

A logical map of the desired certification hierarchy
> This will include the computer names and CA names to be used, their specific configurations and equipment locations. This makes the map useful as both a checklist and to show hierarchical relationships at a glance.

A timeline for the deployment
> A timeline is important information for any deployment plan, but especially so for the PKI hierarchy. Because child CAs cannot be installed before their parents

are available to sign CA certificate requests, the hierarchy must be deployed in a top-down fashion beginning with the root CA. Remember that equipment and people rarely show up on time, so allow flexibility in your plan for late equipment arrival and human interruptions such as vacation or illness.

A detailed procedure for the installation of each CA
The installation should be followed without deviation to ensure the correct configuration of all components. This book will provide most of the information necessary to create these procedures.

Identification of parties for CA installation
Each CA should be installed by a minimum of two individuals, a technical person and an auditor or member of upper management. This ensures that no single person has the ability to compromise important private keys or configure the CA with intentionally weak security or backdoors.

Identification of parties to make changes to your network (if necessary)
For example, your domain administrators may have restricted the ability to join computers to the domain. You may also be planning to add customized certificate templates to Active Directory, which requires specific permissions that you may not have. It is necessary to have a user with the appropriate privileges perform these configuration changes. The tasks that require specific privileges will be included in your detailed procedures.

Ensure the deployment is done in your test environment first
Testing a PKI deployment is a critical step that must be done before actual deployment. Do not try to save time by deploying your hierarchy within a test environment and then moving it into production—this rarely works because of differences between the test and production environments. Fully deploy the PKI in your test environment before any CA is set up in production.

Detailed administrative processes that will follow a successful deployment
A secure deployment must be maintained to ensure it does not become either insecure or useless. The procedures used to keep the PKI up and running should be documented before the environment is deployed to avoid these unwanted situations.

In our example Woodgrove Bank implementation, we can assume that the PKI infrastructure shown in Figure 9-4 has been approved by senior management. This diagram can be extended to include the details determined from the deployment planning. A more complete figure including some of these details is shown in Figure 9-5. For the sake of brevity, only the details for the root CA and one intermediate CA are provided.

Once you've got a timeline in place, together with your certification hierarchy and plan, you have exactly what you need to begin your deployment. However, there's a little more documentation that should be completed before you start.

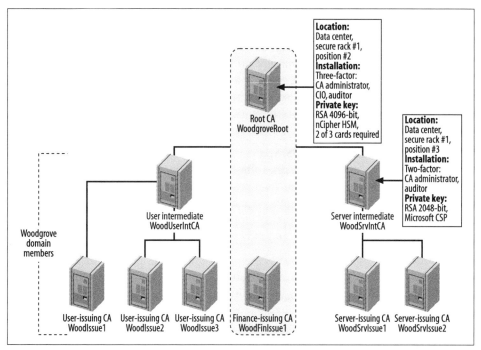

Figure 9-5. Woodgrove Bank's planned certificate hierarchy diagram, including details of deployment for the root and one intermediate CA

Construct Certificate Policy and Certificate Practice Statement

Security isn't just about the technology. It's also about the practices and policies that are used to provide assurance of security. The most secure software in the world doesn't remain secure for long if sloppy computer management allows compromise of the computer or its underlying infrastructure. Within a PKI, there are guidelines for proper management and policy. These guidelines are documented during the planning process as I've already discussed. However, it may be useful to document them in a standardized way that can be integrated with the PKI itself.

The certificate policy and certificate practice statement are two documents that can be created by the PKI administrator. They are used to fully document the intentions and limitations of the PKI as well as the policies and procedures involved in PKI management. Although many administrators consider their procedures and policies internal information and are loath to provide them to end users and external companies, there is often a need for this. I'll describe each type of document briefly and show why it could be beneficial to provide this information.

Certificate policy (CP) is a broad description of the acceptable use of a certificate issued by the relevant PKI. To be more precise, the CP tells users what the intention of each certificate type is and where it can and cannot be used. This is important for all users and certificate consumers to understand, as the intended use of a certificate may not match the actual use. An email encryption certificate, for example, could be used to protect proprietary information on a laptop, which may be an inappropriate use of the certificate. Without a CP, the user has no way to understand how the certificate should be used. The CP also has some legal benefit in that it can provide documentation in case of misuse resulting in loss or liability. When used in this way, a lawyer should be consulted to review and coauthor the CP before deployment.

Certificate practice statement (CPS) is a complementary subset of the CP. It picks up where the CP leaves off and describes the security processes in detail. The CPS can apply to one CA or a portion of the hierarchy. The details normally include, at a minimum, the practices used for issuance such as identity validation and key management. Often a CPS includes details for all CA operation including renewal, revocation, and CA maintenance and may vary in scope from a single CA to all CAs in a certification hierarchy.

The benefit of publishing a CPS is twofold. First, it establishes a well-known and reviewed set of policies. Changes in certificate administration, management, and so on do not affect the CPS unless they specifically undertake to do so. This helps avoid the ball-dropping that often occurs during responsibility handoffs and helps ensure that no gaps in security form. The CPS also provides critical information for partners or vendors when PKI integration is desired. If you already have a detailed document establishing your policies and procedures, it's a simple matter for the other company to review the documents and determine whether your policies match well enough with theirs to establish the trust.

For either the CP or CPS, you are the sole judge of what it should contain. There are several guides and suggested topic lists, and several are included in the RFC mentioned in the following note. However, any information you deem necessary should be included in one or both of these documents. For example, you can add helpful information for holders of certificates such as security contacts within the organization and suggested practices (e.g., safely backing up the private key of valuable certificates).

 For more information on certificate policy and certificate practice statement background and creation, see RFC 2527—Internet X.509 Public Key Infrastructure Certificate Policy and Certification Practices Framework and the new draft of its replacement: *draft-ietf-pkix-ipki-new-rfc2527-01.txt*. For numerous examples of actual CP and CPS documents, use any Internet search engine for the term *CP* or *CPS*. Many companies publish them for public review. Blatant copying is not advisable (and could be illegal), but a review of other documents to ensure your documentation is complete would be a good idea.

The CP and CPS can be very large or very small. A quick search on the Internet at the time of this writing yields readily available statements ranging in size from 1 to 105 pages. Your documents will probably be on the lower end of that range. They are placed in a location that is accessible to holders of certificates and is pointed to by the appropriate fields within each certificate. The CP and CPS are similar to a CRL in that they can reside at any uniform resource locator (URL) that the client can reach. Because the contents are considered open to public scrutiny, the documents can be placed outside your firewall if you have external subjects that must access the statement. Consider mirroring your publication locations when deciding where to place them, and ensure that client computers can reach those locations.

Install the Root Certification Authority

Discussing the order used to deploy a PKI is somewhat irrelevant. A PKI hierarchy can be installed only top-down, with the root CA installed first. While technically some other work could come first, none of it will work properly until the root CA is completely configured and is able to issue certificates to its subordinate CAs. Therefore, I'll discuss deployment in a top-down fashion starting with the root CA.

If there is one thing you need to know about installing a root CA, it is that the private key of the root CA is the most important piece of information in your certification hierarchy. For this reason, it must be safeguarded from the very beginning. Lackluster key management cannot be reversed or mitigated at a later time. This is the reason I've recommended having at least three parties be present when the root CA is installed. You might also consider videotaping the installation for later audit and proof of security.

The hardware assembly and configuration should also be done as part of the root CA installation. A server assembled and configured outside the close scrutiny of a multiparty audit is unacceptable, as many covert security vulnerabilities could be introduced during that window of opportunity. If an HSM will be used on the root CA, it must also be installed and configured during this process prior to the CA software being installed. This ensures that the private key is created as securely and reliably as possible and remains secure throughout the entire process.

I created a diagram for Woodgrove Bank's PKI deployment in Figure 9-5. It's time to examine a portion of the hierarchy and discuss its deployment. Let's assume that you will deploy the hierarchy beginning with the portion inside the box. You're doing this after your testing has succeeded and you're certain that the hierarchy is planned correctly. You want to limit the initial production deployment to as small a group as possible to limit damage should something go wrong.

Your first job, as I discussed, is setting up the root CA. You should follow this plan to accomplish your task:

1. Click Start → Control Panel.

2. Double-click Add or Remove Programs.

3. Click Add/Remove Windows Components.

4. Check the checkbox for Certificate Services. You will be warned that you cannot change the computer name or domain membership once Certificate Services is installed. Click Yes to proceed, then click Next to begin the installation.

5. Click Stand-alone root CA to select the correct type of CA to install, select "Use custom settings to generate the key pair and CA certificate," then click Next. This is an important setting, as it will determine the role of the CA in the hierarchy and allow you to use the desired cryptographic service provider (CSP). The configuration is shown in Figure 9-6.

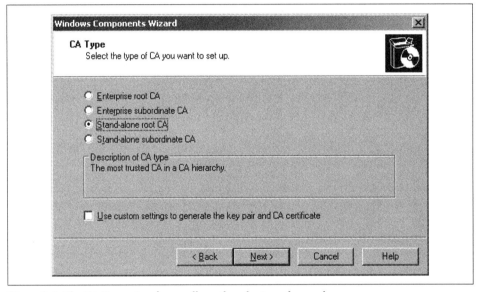

Figure 9-6. The CA Type wizard page allows the selection of any role

6. On the Public and Private Key Pair page, select the desired CSP, algorithm, and key size. You have wisely installed and configured an nCipher HSM, so you choose that CDP and the appropriate key size and algorithm, as shown in Figure 9-7. If you configured the HSM to require authorization to create and use private keys, you'll be prompted to perform that authorization now.

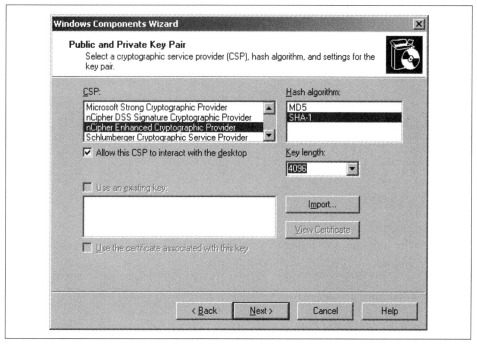

Figure 9-7. The installation wizard allows detailed selection of the cryptographic service provider, hash algorithm, and key size

7. Under Common Name for This CA, type the CA name. In this case, you're installing **WoodgroveRoot**.

8. Provide the validity period for the root CA certificate. This setting is critical, as all certificates within this PKI must have a lifetime shorter than this one. The correct configuration for these options is shown in Figure 9-8. Then click Next.

9. Accept the default certificate database settings and click Next.

10. If the computer is running Internet Information Services (IIS), a prompt will appear asking to stop the service temporarily. If you plan to use web enrollment or this computer is not providing web services (as it shouldn't be), click Yes.

Configuring the root CA's CDP list

The wizard will now copy files from the product CD and announce when it is finished. Now you have a functioning standalone root CA!

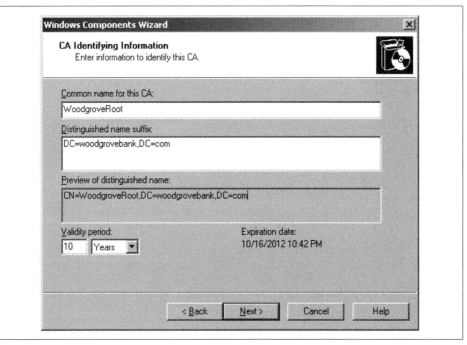

Figure 9-8. The CA Identifying Information wizard page provides entry for two critical pieces of information: the CA common name and the CA certificate's validity period

The first thing you will do is configure the root CA's CDP list to match your plan. To do so, you take the following actions:

1. Click Start → All Programs → Administrative Tools → Certification Authority.

2. Under Certification Authority (Local), right-click WoodgroveRoot and click Properties.

3. Click the Extensions tab to display the default configuration for CRL distribution points.

4. Click Add to add a new path to the list. Provide the path that clients will use to access the root CA's CDP. Note that this setting is CA-specific, so only the root CA's CDP must be provided here. This is shown in Figure 9-9.

5. Select the new path provided and click "Include in the CDP extension of issued certificates." No other options need to be selected as the root CA will neither publish delta CRLs nor use Active Directory to publish its CRL.

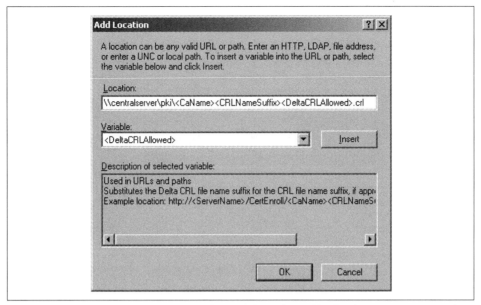

Figure 9-9. Use both static information and a limited set of variables for the CRL name to avoid naming conflicts

6. Remove all paths that do not publish the CRL to the local computer. These paths will be unreachable by client computers and may confuse poorly written client applications. The CDP configuration should now match the configuration shown in Figure 9-10.

7. Click OK. The CA must be restarted to change the CDP configuration. Click Yes to allow this restart.

Protecting the private key without an HSM

If you are not using a HSM, you can use another method to protect the private key of the root CA. Although this method is not the best solution available, it provides far more security than simply leaving the private key on the root CA. This method relies on distributing different pieces of information about the root CA to several different parties. Only when the parties combine their information can they reconstruct the private key.

Note that this method works for the private key of any appropriately configured CA. Portions of the method can also be used to protect any arbitrary private key, not just a CA's private key.

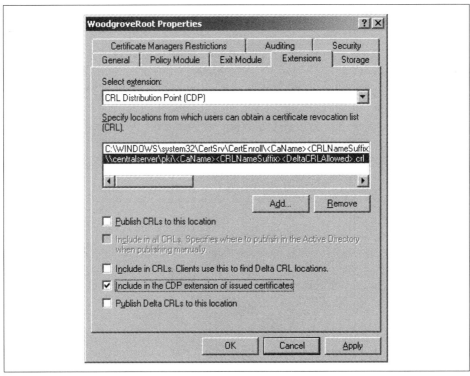

Figure 9-10. The CDP list for WoodgroveRoot is short due to its offline status; the CRL will be manually moved to the UNC path later

You may need one or more floppy disks (or CD-R media if your CA is equipped with a CD writer) depending on the number of parties you want to require when reconstituting the private key. You may also need *splitf.exe* and *joinf.exe* to manually split and rejoin the private key's storage container. These files have been around as freeware for many years and are readily available on the Internet.

 Make sure you don't download a virus or trojan when you obtain these files. Get them from a reputable source!

Essentially, we're making it so that you cannot use the private key alone. To begin, we export the certificate and private key using the Certificate Export Wizard as shown earlier in the chapter in the "Archiving a certificate and private key" section. We select the Remove Private Key checkbox on the wizard to delete the private key from the CA, and we provide a password during the export. The export generates a file that we write to the floppy disk or CD-R. This immediately removes the private key and begins to provide some additional key security. Only the party who has both the password and the floppy disk has access to the private key.

To increase that to two parties, you do the obvious: ensure that the person with the floppy isn't the same person who has the password. Only when these two people act together can the private key be reconstituted and used. For parties of three or more, we use *splitf.exe* to split the private key file into two or more parts. Then we put each of these parts on a separate floppy and distribute them to multiple trusted individuals. In this configuration, only the combination of all floppies plus the password can retrieve the key.

In addition to the root CA's private key, other valuable private keys may be exported and secured in this fashion. Key archival and recovery, a major benefit of a Windows Server 2003 family CA, requires someone to have a private key for recovering other users' private keys. Obviously this key is extremely valuable. As such, it should be exported from the private key store of whatever user obtained it and stored in the method I've described. Because access to the CA's database is required to obtain the encrypted key to recover, an additional factor can be the restriction of the CA officer so that the CA officer must request and provide the encrypted private key for all key recovery operations. This factor requires role separation to be enforced on the CA, which is documented in Windows Server 2003 family Help.

The key protection procedure has two potential security flaws that you must mitigate. First, during the export and key-splitting operation, temporary files will probably be written to the computer's hard disk. Although a long shot, an attacker could potentially scan the hard drive and reconstruct the file. Cipher.exe /W will eliminate that threat by wiping the data from the hard drive. For more information, see Chapter 4. The other flaw is that floppy disks are notorious for going bad over time. Storing unique and critical data on a floppy is idiotic. Multiple copies of each fragment or file should be made and provided to trusted parties for redundancy. Numerous other removable media solutions are far more reliable over time, are affordable, and can store any arbitrary data, including our private key. These can include magneto-optical drives, recordable DVDs, or even technology not commonly used for this purpose such as CompactFlash or Memory Stick media. Any technology that reliably stores data as a file will work.

Publish offline root CA's CRL

Before you finish with the root CA, you must publish its CRL to an accessible location. As I've discussed, you should take the root CA offline and both physically and logically isolate it once its installation is complete. This means that it will not be able to publish its CRL to any CDP not on the computer itself. However, any client that checks the revocation of the root CA's certificate must be able to locate a valid CRL. You configured the root CA's certificate to point to an accessible CDP during installation. Now you need to get that CRL there manually.

To manually publish the offline root CA's CRL, take the following steps:

1. In the same Certification Authority (Local) console that was used earlier to configure the CDP, double-click WoodgroveRoot to expand the CA containers.

2. Right-click Revoked Certificates, click All Tasks, then click Publish.

3. Click OK to publish the new CRL to the configured CDPs. This dialog box is shown in Figure 9-11.

4. Copy the CRL to a floppy disk (yes, they still exist, but you can use any portable data storage you like) and go to a computer that has access to the client-accessible CDP. Manually copy the CRL to the correct CDP.

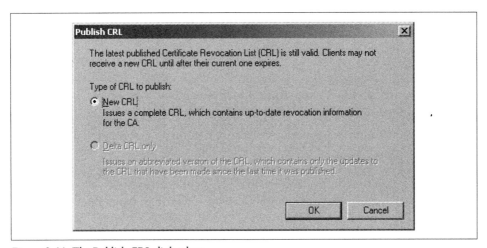

Figure 9-11. The Publish CRL dialog box

This procedure must be done even though the CRL is empty. Clients that validate a chain must be able to retrieve and verify a CRL, even an empty one. Once you're done exporting the CRL, you can secure the root CA. You'll need this CA again once you begin installing the other CAs in the hierarchy, so don't take it completely down yet. You must ensure that only authorized physical access and no network access can occur until the deployment is complete. This is done simply by locking it in an area of the data center that only you or other authorized personnel can access. You could take other steps like locking the hard drive itself in a vault, but that would certainly sacrifice convenience.

 Notice that the Delta CRL Only option is unavailable in the Publish CRL dialog box shown in Figure 9-11. This is because the CA is not configured to publish a delta CRL.

As I mentioned in the earlier sidebar discussion of whether to dedicate hardware to the root CA, once the deployment is complete, the decision can be made to keep it continuously running or not. In any event, any hardware that comprises the root CA must be physically secured to ensure only authorized access occurs in the future. In most enterprises, the only authorized access will be periodic CRL creation and, rarely, the renewal of the root CA certificate or the issuance of a new CA certificate.

Install Intermediate and Issuing CAs

Installing an intermediate or issuing CA is the same as installing a root CA. The process must be documented and secure throughout. There are two major differences between the installation of a root and subordinate (or any CA that is not the root CA and issues certificates based on the trust of a CA higher in the hierarchy). The first is that the CA certificate must be issued by another CA, which slightly complicates our installation process and requires some manual steps. The second is the potential desire to integrate one or more enterprise CAs in the certification hierarchy. This is a simple and important option during installation.

You want to deploy the WoodFinIssue1 CA. This is an enterprise subordinate CA that will issue certificates to the finance department. You can jump right in and start configuring the machine as follows:

1. Ensure the computer is joined to the Woodgrove domain. This is required when the CA is installed as an enterprise subordinate CA.
2. Follow steps 1–4 listed in the steps to install the root CA.
3. Click Enterprise Subordinate CA to select the correct type of CA to install. Also, select "Use custom settings to generate the key pair and CA certificate." Click Next.
4. Select the desired CSP, algorithm, and key length—in this case, the Microsoft Strong Cryptographic Provider using the SHA-1 hash algorithm with a 2048-bit key length is appropriate. Click Next.
5. Under Common Name for This CA, type the CA name. In this case, we're installing WoodFinIssue1.
6. Accept the default settings for certificate database storage and click Next.
7. Select "Save the request to a file" to allow the CA certificate request to be saved to a specific file, as shown in Figure 9-12.
8. The rest of the installation will be the same as the offline root CA installation.

At the end of the installation process, the file specified in step 7 will be created. This is the certificate request for the WoodFinIssue1 CA certificate. This request must be submitted to and issued by the CA's parent, which in this case is WoodgroveRoot.

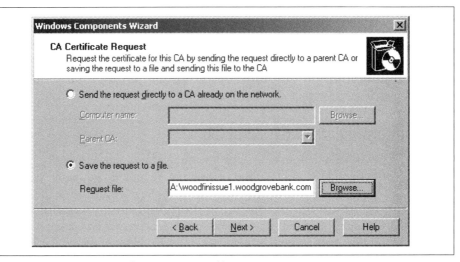

Figure 9-12. Saving a CA certificate request to a file

The file can be transported by any desired means. You will copy the REQ file created on WoodFinIssue1 to the floppy disk and bring it (properly accompanied and audited) to WoodgroveRoot. Once there, you'll follow these steps to request and issue the certificate:

1. Open the Certification Authority MMC snap-in.

2. Right-click WoodgroveRoot, click All Tasks, then click Submit New Request.

3. Specify the REQ on the floppy drive from WoodFinIssue1.

4. Because WoodgroveRoot uses an HSM, the appropriate safeguards must be completed to load the signing key from the HSM onto WoodgroveRoot.

5. Double-click the Pending Requests container to display the submitted request.

6. Right-click the request, click All Tasks, then click Issue.

After the certificate has been issued, it must be exported from the issuing CA and brought back to the requester. Use the same floppy disk to bring the certificate from WoodgroveRoot to WoodFinIssue1, then follow these steps:

1. Double-click the Issued Certificates container to display the newly issued certificate.

2. Double-click the certificate.

3. Click the Details tab, then click Copy to File.

4. Use the Certificate Export Wizard to export the necessary information to a file. The file should be a P7B file that includes all certificates in the chain as shown in Figure 9-13.

All certificates in the chain are exported, as WoodFinIssue1 does not yet have Wood-groveRoot's certificate.

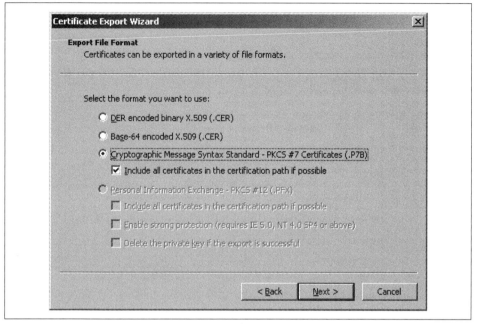

Figure 9-13. Exporting the entire certificate chain into a P7B file from the root CA

You then return the file to WoodFinIssue1 on floppy disk. To load the newly issued certificate and bring WoodFinIssue1 online, follow this final procedure:

1. Open the Certification Authority MMC snap-in.
2. Right-click WoodFinIssue1, click All Tasks, then click Install CA Certificate.
3. Specify the P7B file on the floppy disk.

This allows WoodFinIssue1 to build and validate the certificate chain. At this point it's a short chain, only itself and WoodgroveRoot. Once the chain is validated and an appropriate CRL is retrieved, the CA will come online and provide its services.

Configure Certificate Templates for Desired Certificates

Now that the root and issuing CAs are both installed, you will create the new certificate templates that the WoodFinIssue1 CA will issue. This CA issues two certificates to users: one for digitally signing contracts and one for encrypting data. You want to archive the private key of the data encryption certificates in the event any valuable private keys are lost.

You create two new certificate templates corresponding to the need for two certificate types. For our example, I'll show you how to configure the encryption certificate, because I provided an example of a digital signature certificate template earlier in this chapter. You configure this new certificate template using the following steps at WoodFinIssue1:

1. Click Start → Run, type **mmc**, and press Enter.

2. Click File → Add/Remove Snap-in, click Add, then double-click Certificate Templates. Click Close, then click OK.

3. Double-click the Certificate Templates node to display all certificate templates currently maintained in Active Directory.

4. Right-click the Basic EFS template, then click Duplicate Template. I chose this template to duplicate because its use most closely matches the intended use of our new certificate template. This helps us reduce the number of configuration steps for the new template.

5. For Template display name, enter **Woodgrove Finance Encryption Only**.

6. Click the Purpose tab to verify that the Purpose is listed as encryption. You should also ensure that the Archive Subject's Encryption Private Key box is checked to allow the user to back up his private key in the future.

7. Click the Security tab and verify Certificate Administrators (or whatever group you have configured to contain the PKI administrators) Full Control; Finance Users Read, Enroll, and Autoenroll. Remove all other entries from this ACL, as shown in Figure 9-14.

8. Issuance Requirements: select CA Certificate Manager Approval. Because WoodFinIssue1 is a narrowly focused CA, the administrator is the appropriate entity to authorize and issue certificates.

9. Click OK to create the new certificate template. Note that Active Directory will take a short time to replicate the new certificate template information to all domain controllers. During that time, clients should not attempt to enroll for certificates and administrators should not modify the templates. Strange things can happen if the template is used before it's fully replicated.

Once the certificate template is created and replicated in Active Directory, we can "turn it on" by adding it to the CA. Because Active Directory stores numerous certificate templates, do not assume that every CA will issue certificates based on every template. Each CA must be individually configured with the information about which certificate templates will be issued. To configure WoodFinIssue1 to issue certificates based on the desired templates, configure WoodFinIssue1 as follows:

1. Click Start → All Programs → Administrative Tools → Certification Authority.

2. Right-click the Certificate Templates container, click New, then click Certificate Template to Issue.

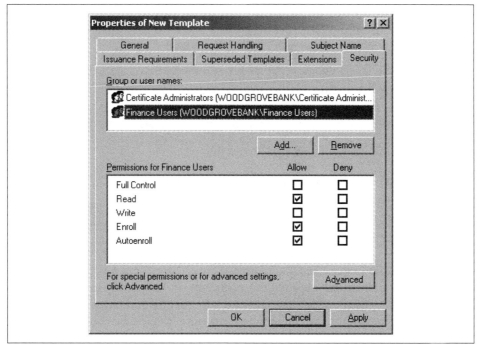

General | Request Handling | Subject Name

Issuance Requirements | Superseded Templates | Extensions | Security

Figure 9-14. The Security tab for the new certificate template shows all granted permissions

3. Click the Woodgrove Finance Encryption Only certificate template, then click OK.

4. Repeat the process to add the Woodgrove Finance Signature Only certificate template.

Configure the Issuing CA

Once the issuing CA is installed, it can be configured with the necessary settings. In the case of WoodFinIssue1, Don must customize the CDP list to place our CRL in the same location as the root CA's CRL. This can be done using the same steps described earlier. You will also be archiving private keys issued from this CA. This is easily done in two parts.

First, obtain a certificate based on the Key Recovery certificate template and secure its private key. Then enable and configure the key archival settings on the desired CA. This is done with the following procedure:

1. Click Start → All Programs → Administrative Tools → Certification Authority.

2. Right-click the name of the CA, then click Properties.

3. Click the Recovery Agents tab. Then click Archive the Key to enable key archival.

4. Click Add to add the existing key recovery agent (KRA) certificates to the CA.

5. Type a number in the "Number of recovery agents to use" box. You can choose a number up to the number of KRA certificates loaded.

6. Click OK. When prompted to restart the CA, click Yes.

Once the CA is restarted, the key archival settings will be enforced. Remember that only clients that support key archival will work with this option. In addition, certificates with a purpose of Signature will not archive the private key to ensure nonrepudiation of digitally signed data.

Configure Autoenrollment for Windows XP

I assume in this example that the clients that will obtain certificates from WoodFinIssue1 are all running Windows XP. This is because Windows XP has the autoenrollment client built into the operating system and allows for simple deployment of appropriately configured certificates. When Windows XP computers are members of a Windows Server 2003 family Active Directory domain, they periodically query the domain for appropriate certificates and obtain them automatically. This is the easiest way to deploy certificates to clients. Several other methods—including web enrollment and Automatic Certificate Request Settings (ACRS)—are available for certificate distribution if the desired clients are running other operating systems.

To deploy these certificates to clients using certificate autoenrollment, you simply ensure the clients are members of the domain that WoodFinIssue1 is in. A limited autoenrollment configuration is turned on automatically in Active Directory. Additionally, if you want to provide additional functionality such as certificate management through autoenrollment, you can do so by configuring Group Policy as follows:

1. Open a Group Policy Object as described in Chapter 5. The group policy should be applied to the OU containing the desired users. In your case, you'll apply the policy to the Finance Users OU.

2. Because Finance has no existing Group Policy Object, you will create one called Default Finance GPO.

3. Edit the GPO.

4. Go to User Configuration → Windows Settings → Public Key Policies. Then double-click Autoenrollment Settings.

5. Verify that the default Enroll Certificates Automatically setting is selected. Then check the "Update certificates that use certificate templates" and "Renew expired certificates, update pending certificates, and remove revoked certificates" options.

6. Click OK to save the settings.

Because the newly configured settings will probably not be needed for some time, Group Policy replication and client application should not be a concern.

Optional: enroll intermediate network devices for certificates using MSCEP

We've assumed that the subjects for all certificate requests so far are computers running Windows XP. Obviously, not all subjects that can use a certificate run this operating system. For Windows 2000 clients, you can configure Automatic Certificate Request Settings (ACRS) to enroll for a limited set of certificate types. ACRS is configured through Group Policy and is fairly straightforward to use.

Numerous other clients will also want certificates. In particular, intermediate devices such as Cisco routers use certificates to provide network-based security through such mechanisms as IP Security (IPSec). These clients obviously don't run Windows, so we need a means for our Windows Server 2003 family CA to receive a request from and provide a certificate to these clients.

The Simple Certification Enrollment Protocol (SCEP) is a generic and device-independent way to request and provide certificates. It's so simple that most networking devices can use SCEP even though they may have little else in the way of client functionality. Many Cisco network products support SCEP and provide IPSec functionality at the router based on the certificates they obtain. Microsoft Windows Server 2003 family's CA supports SCEP enrollment using a tool called *MSCEP.dll*, which is included in the Microsoft Windows Server 2003 Resource Kit. The tool is provided with extensive documentation and is simple to install and configure.

Other enrollment methods

Clients can obtain certificates from a Microsoft CA in a number of ways. To ensure you understand that there are many avenues here, I'll list them with a brief description of each. They include:

Client autoenrollment

> Client autoenrollment is a Group Policy–based method for a client to request and retrieve certificates from a CA. It has been described several times throughout this chapter, including detailed steps on how to complete an autoenrollment-based deployment.

Web enrollment

> Another popular enrollment option is web-based enrollment. In this scenario, clients use their web browser to connect to a CA-aware web site. They can then request, retrieve, and install certificates based on preconfigured settings. This method is generally the most manual and slowest, but is often used because of its simplicity and the universal adoption of web browsers. The web pages are also customizable to allow corporations to control and enhance the user's experience. Plus you can install the web pages on a non-CA to help isolate your PKI from enrollment requests.
>
> For detailed instructions on how to set up and configure web enrollment, see *http://www.microsoft.com/resources/documentation/WindowsServ/2003/standard/proddocs/en-us/sag_CS_CertWebEnroll.asp*.

Certificates MMC snap-in

A little-known option for domain-joined clients to obtain certificates is through the Certificates MMC snap-in. In this snap-in, the user can browse to the \Personal\Certificates node, click Action, click All Tasks, then click Request New Certificate. This is a very limited solution though, because any certificate that cannot be automatically approved and installed must be manually retrieved and installed through another mechanism. For this reason, I don't suggest you enroll for certificates in this manner.

Automatic Certificate Request Settings

ACRS is a holdover from the Windows 2000 PKI architecture. It is a simplistic version of client autoenrollment. You should not use ACRS if you're running Windows Server 2003.

Custom applications

Microsoft provides several API opportunities for you to write your own custom PKI-aware software. This software can request, retrieve, install, and manage certificates for you. Most applications leverage the Microsoft Cryptographic API (CAPI) and the CAPI Component Object Model (CAPICOM). Detailed information on CAPICOM can be found at *http://msdn.microsoft.com/library/en-us/security/security/capicom_reference.asp*.

Test Desired Applications

Once your certification hierarchy is configured to match your deployment and architectural plans, there's one objective left. You must test the deployment. Client applications should be run repeatedly to ensure the newly issued certificates provide the desired functionality. All possible certificate subjects should attempt to enroll (and reenroll) for certificates to make sure this process is functioning. Clients should also attempt to enroll for certificates that they should not have access to, such as CA certificates or Key Recovery Agent certificates. Finally, the root CA's security should be double-checked. An innocent mistake such as plugging a network cable into the root CA by an uneducated system administrator could bring an offline CA online and subject it to compromise.

Maintaining Your Hierarchy

Now that the PKI is operational, maintenance functions must be put in place. Good security starts with a solid and well-analyzed plan and continues with a secure deployment that meets that plan. However, no deployment is secure forever. As the PKI continues to function, the environment will change. These changes may not change the security provided, but you must perform tasks to ensure that appropriate security is maintained. These are the ongoing tasks that ensure that each CA is functioning properly and providing the services it is designed to provide.

Certificate Issuance

The CA's primary job is to issue certificates. In many cases, the CA will issue certificates automatically without any administrative intervention, which is accomplished by configuring the CA and certificate templates with proper security permissions. On many CAs and with many high-value certificate types, however, manual administrative verification may be important. In those cases, the certificate request will be set to Pending when it is received by the CA. Only manual issuance by one or more parties can issue those certificates. For details on configuring certificate templates to require multiple signatures, see the Certificate Templates topic in Windows Server 2003 Enterprise Edition Online Help.

Let's assume you have configured your CA to place all requests in a Pending state. To issue a certificate that's been placed in a Pending state, perform the following simple procedure:

1. In the Certification Authority console, double-click the name of the CA to expand the CA containers.
2. Double-click Pending Requests.
3. Find the certificate request you want to issue in the righthand pane. Right-click that request, click All Tasks, then click Issue. Conversely, if the request is illegitimate or undesired, you can click Deny to remove it from the Pending Requests queue.

Once issued, the client will need to retrieve the certificate. This can be accomplished in many ways, such as autoenrollment, web enrollment, or SCEP enrollment. Most clients will automatically retrieve the request or be instructed on how to later retrieve the certificate during their request submission.

Configuring CA Auditing

As I stress throughout this book, you must audit critical systems to ensure they are not being misused. The CA is no exception to this advice. Auditing CA activity is a new feature in the Windows Server 2003 family CA. It is available on all versions of the Windows Server 2003 family operating system to help ensure the best security possible.

Configuring auditing for the CA is a simple procedure, which can be done during CA postinstallation configuration or at any time after. To configure auditing on a CA, follow these steps:

1. Configure Group Policy for the CA to enable Audit object access. For information about configuring Group Policy, see Chapter 5.
2. In the Certification Authority console, right-click the name of the CA and click Properties.

3. Click the Auditing tab.

4. Check each type of event you want to audit. The descriptions are fairly detailed and should clearly define what is being audited. Only one of these options is likely to generate large numbers of entries: Issue and Manage Certificate Requests.

Whenever an event of the type selected occurs, the CA will create an event in the Event Log. This can be manually retrieved and reviewed at any time. Many great tools are available to combine event logs from disparate computers and automate some of the log reviewing tasks. While I won't specifically recommend any of these tools, they are a good idea to consider when deploying your PKI. Reviewing detailed events from numerous issuing CAs can become time-consuming without automation tools. However, the consequences for not doing these reviews can be devastating.

Renewing CA Certificates

As I discussed earlier, a CA's certificate has a finite lifetime. It is limited by the configuration of its own certificate and the certificate of all its parents up to the root CA. Because of this and other reasons, issuing CAs normally have a shorter lifetime for their certificate than the root CA. This means that the CA's certificate must be periodically renewed.

The first and probably most difficult part of renewing any CA is knowing when its certificate is going to expire. You've documented this well during your earlier process, but years may go by before renewal needs to occur. Personnel turnover, lax process conformity, and so on may cause the security staff to simply forget to do this. Luckily the CA will begin to remind you with Event Log entries when the certificate is about to expire. However, you should manage your own process to ensure nothing is overlooked. Many PKI administrators use calendar or planning software such as Microsoft Outlook. They place an event in the future and set a reminder for days or weeks in advance of the event. In this way, they ensure that they'll be reminded of this task by at least two independent processes.

Renewing a CA's certificate is a simple process. It's similar to initial certificate enrollment in that the root CA can sign its own certificate, but subordinate CAs must submit their requests to the parent for issuance. To start the process of renewal:

1. In the Certification Authority console, right-click the name of the CA, click All Tasks, then click Renew CA certificate.

2. If prompted, click Yes to stop Certificate Services.

3. Choose New or Existing Key Renewal. The decision on whether to use the current key or obtain a new one is based on whether the key has expired (as I've discussed) or whether the key has been compromised. The wizard provides this information, as is shown in Figure 9-15.

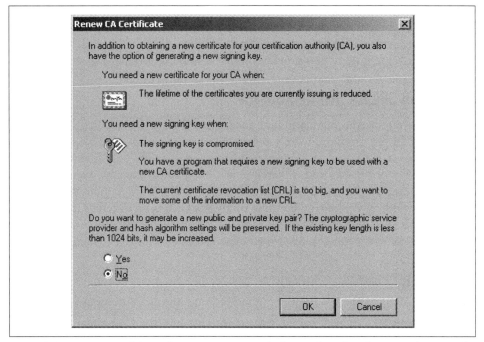

Figure 9-15. Renewing a CA certificate requires a simple decision based on the reason for renewal

The remainder of the tasks will be familiar to you from the CA installation process. If the parent CA is offline, you'll need to manually submit the request and retrieve the issued certificate. If the CA certificate template is set to manual issue, you'll need to issue it as described in the previous section.

Revoking Issued Certificates

I've discussed the CRL and CDP extensively in this chapter and earlier in the book. I've not yet detailed how a certificate gets on the "bad list." This is a fairly anticlimactic event, given the knowledge you now have of the CA process and operation. When you know that a certificate has been compromised or should no longer be honored, you should immediately revoke it. To revoke any issued certificate:

1. In the Certification Authority console for the CA that issued the certificate, double-click the name of the CA to expand the CA containers.

2. Double-click Issued Certificates.

3. Find the certificate you want to revoke in the righthand pane. Right-click that request, then click Revoke Certificate.

4. Provide a Reason code from the drop-down list. Providing a reason code is optional and will default to Unspecified. A certificate that is revoked for a reason of Certificate Hold can be unrevoked later. All other reason codes provide permanent revocation.

Remember that certificates do not appear on the CRL until the CRL is issued or a new delta CRL is published. For high-value certificates or CA certificates that are compromised, you may want to immediately publish a new CRL or delta CRL. To do that, follow the instructions provided earlier in this chapter.

Publishing CRL for Offline Root CA

All CRLs have a specific validity period, configured during CA installation, to ensure that clients do not continue to rely on outdated information. The root CA's CRL usually issues a CRL with a longer validity period than its subordinates, since it issues far fewer certificates and is therefore less likely to revoke any. Even if the CRL is blank, it must be published for clients to locate it when building chains. The procedure to periodically publish the offline root CA's CRL is no different than the procedure we used while setting up the root CA. While a simple process, it must be done periodically to ensure clients do not experience broken trust chains.

Backing Up Your CA

The common principle on backing up data is simple. You back up any data you cannot afford to lose. I've been preaching that for years. So the CA's database is information you cannot afford to lose and you must back it up regularly. Right? Maybe.

The CA's database contains some critical information. The most important thing it contains is the CA's certificate. However, you've already backed that up separately, either manually or using an HSM.

The database also contains configuration information about the CA, such as permissions, issuance templates, and so forth. You've already got that information in your deployment plans and it is easily recreated. Your CA's database also contains the list of certificates you've issued, denied, or set to pending. Do you actually need that data?

There is only one type of unique information in the CA database that cannot be recreated or obtained from another CA: archived private keys issued by this CA. Although the client has its copy of the private key, the client cannot resubmit it to the CA. If the CA's database is lost and a client wants its private key recovered, it's simply not possible.

You can decide for yourself whether to back up each CA's database. If kept in a secure location and access is properly restricted and audited, it doesn't present a security risk. However, there may be little benefit to backing it up. This depends on whether you're archiving private keys on that CA.

Summary

Public key infrastructures come in two flavors: public and private. Incorporating a public PKI within your corporation has numerous benefits and drawbacks. Neither flavor is necessarily more or less secure but rather involves a different strategy of trust. A detailed analysis of your intended uses for the certificates should be made and then both flavors should be considered. Once both flavors are considered for your specific scenario and all benefits and drawbacks are weighed, a decision can be made on which solution to use.

The Windows Server 2003 family provides a great deal of functionality for a private PKI, but vendors generally provide those services when leveraging a public solution. Nevertheless, Windows Server 2003 does provide some essential functionality for using the public PKI model. The real benefit of using Windows Server 2003 with PKI, however, is when using it as a certification authority within your own private PKI.

Designing and deploying a private certification hierarchy can be a daunting task. The plan must be laid out carefully in advance and can be quite complex in many cases. A number of decisions must be made early in the process; without them, the deployment cannot even begin. Once that plan is created and reviewed, it should be tested thoroughly to ensure it meets the design goals while providing the necessary security.

Once the plan is documented and tested, you can begin to deploy and configure the root CA. You now know how to deploy a multitier hierarchy once the root CA is established. After the hierarchy is in place, you can configure it for proper issuance, revocation, and ongoing management. These tasks are no less important than deploying the root CA, as any lapse in security in the chain could result in unintentional trust (or lack of trust).

CHAPTER 10

Smart Card Technology

Smart cards—credit card–sized cards with embedded electronic circuitry—are becoming the preferred way for users to identify themselves. Smart cards are rapidly becoming less expensive and easier to use, and Windows Server 2003's built-in support for smart cards makes them instantly compatible. In this chapter, I'll introduce you to smart cards, explain their advantages and disadvantages, and discuss how Windows Server 2003 interfaces with them.

What Are Smart Cards?

Smart cards most often look like credit cards, with the addition of a small set of electronic contacts embedded in the surface of the card. You've undoubtedly seen such contacts, as they're used in a myriad of places such as credit cards, video arcades, and digital satellite receivers. A typical smart card is shown in Figure 10-1.

Figure 10-1. A typical smart card

Smart cards can take other physical forms, too, such as miniature versions that comfortably fit on key chains. USB key fobs that contain a smart card chip are also becoming popular, as they contain both the interface (reader) and the card. All these varieties operate essentially the same. So although this chapter will refer to them generically as smart cards, they may not take the shape of a card at all.

Smart cards provide one of the best means of electronic identity validation currently available. Consider how a user like David Loudon authenticates himself today, probably by using a username and a password. Both of those pieces of information—called *factors*—are something that the user knows. One of those pieces of information—the username—is a factor almost anyone can discover or deduce, meaning identification must rely primarily on a single factor: the user's password. As you learned in Chapter 2, passwords are subject to compromise by skilled attackers. As a result, the username and password combination is a relatively poor means of identifying users, because it can be easily compromised.

Smart cards, on the other hand, require two different types of factors: something the user *has*—the smart card—and something the user *knows*—a personal identification number, or PIN. Smart cards are practically impossible to duplicate, and PINs are easy for users to remember and difficult to guess. A PIN containing only four digits has more than enough complexity to successfully thwart most attackers, and you can require users to select PINs that contain more digits or contain a mixture of digits and letters, like a regular password. A password's vulnerability to attack is mitigated by the fact that the password by itself is useless—anyone seeking to misuse the password must also obtain the physical smart card associated with the password.

The person who has the smart card doesn't have to have the PIN. If the PIN and card are kept by separate people, then only the combination of the PIN (what someone knows) and the card (what someone else has) provide access to the credentials and key kept on the card. This can be a benefit when you want to ensure that some operations must be carried out by a minimum of two people. You can create a user account that requires a smart card for authentication and then assign only that account the rights necessary to perform the operation. You can then give the card to one trusted administrator and the PIN to another (or you can divide the PIN up between administrators for more than two factors!). Now only the combined efforts of those involved will be sufficient to perform the task.

How Smart Cards Work

Smart cards use public key cryptography and special additions to the Windows software. Special software—usually included with the smart card reader hardware—replaces or interacts with the *graphical identification and authentication* (GINA) component in Windows operating systems. You're already familiar with the GINA, although you may not know it by that name: it's the logon dialog box that appears

Biometrics: Authentication Based Upon You

Biometrics is another means of identifying users, one that's been around since the days of *Star Trek*'s retinal, voice, or palm scans (depending on the season). Biometrics are rapidly moving from the realm of science fiction into the real world. Several vendors currently offer devices that scan fingerprints, voice prints, and even retinas to verify a user's identity. Figure 10-2 shows a typical fingerprint scanner.

Currently, these methods are still fairly expensive and not completely reliable. A user who scratches his finger might not be able to log on until he sees an administrator to change his on-file fingerprint image. A user with a head cold might not be able to make a voiceprint match. A user with a hangover might stumble in Monday morning and be unable to log on with a retinal scanner. Biometric authentication technology is undergoing major improvements, however, and the equipment is becoming smarter and better able to deal with these types of minor variations.

Numerous other biometric factors are being explored, but all have drawbacks. The number of false positives, for example, must be nearly zero while reducing the number of false negatives to a tolerable value. The best biometric authentication in the world is useless if it requires numerous scans to achieve success.

As always, though, companies continue trying to improve biometric technology. In the near future, more accurate, less expensive devices will be available, making them a viable option for identification on your network. However, smart cards provide additional advantages, such as the ability to force a user to log off when the card is removed, easier replacement of lost or broken cards, and so forth. Smart card readers are also much smaller, making smart cards easier to use for mobile users than bulkier biometric scanners. Finally, smart card technology is inexpensive today and is getting less expensive and more feature-rich every day. Because of their wide acceptance and deployment, smart cards will undoubtedly continue to grow in popularity and functionality. Smart cards do have some disadvantages: they are a physical device that can be easily misplaced or even damaged. Users are much less likely to damage (or lose) their eyes or fingers!

when you press Ctrl-Alt-Delete on a Windows 2000, Windows XP, or Windows Server 2003 computer. The default GINA just asks for a username, password, and domain; the GINA provided with most smart card readers asks users to insert their smart card and type a PIN. Depending on the smart card technology, the standard Windows XP and Windows Server 2003 GINA *may* provide this functionality without replacement, prompting the insertion of a smart card when the proper device drivers are loaded and functioning.

Once a user inserts the card and types her PIN, Windows builds an authenticator, which it transmits to the smart card. The smart card verifies that the PIN provided by the user is correct and then encrypts the authenticator using the card's embedded

Figure 10-2. Typical fingerprint scanner

private encryption key. The encrypted authenticator is sent back to Windows, where the authenticator is used to complete the logon process. The smart card–encrypted authenticator replaces the authenticator normally used in Kerberos authentication, and the domain controller authenticating the user retrieves the user's public encryption key from your public key infrastructure (PKI) rather than using a shared secret. The process is illustrated in Figure 10-3. For more information on how Kerberos authentication works, see Chapter 7.

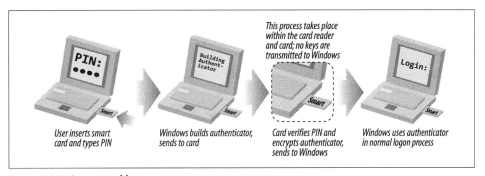

Figure 10-3. Smart card logon process

Notice that no passwords are used. The role of the password during authentication is replaced by the PIN. Although the user account must still have a password, it is not used during the process.

The cryptographic operations that require the smart card's private key are done on the smart card itself. The unencrypted data is sent to the smart card and is returned as ciphertext. The card has enough processing power to encrypt or digitally sign data, albeit far slower than most computers. However, this provides one very important security feature: the private key never leaves the smart card. A compromise of a computer does not compromise any data protected with the smart card's private key. Only a compromise of the card itself would break this security, and as I've discussed, that is extremely unlikely.

Whenever the user needs to validate his identity, the credentials obtained by way of the smart card are used to encrypt an authenticator. The smart card itself is not normally accessed for each operation. Once the user has an access token, the smart card is not needed for each authentication operation. Other applications may access the card though, such as a login over Terminal Services or a signing operation that requires the private key on the smart card.

A core component in this process, of course, is the smart card reader. A typical reader is shown in Figure 10-4. The reader contains the electronics necessary to interface with the smart card and communicate with Windows.

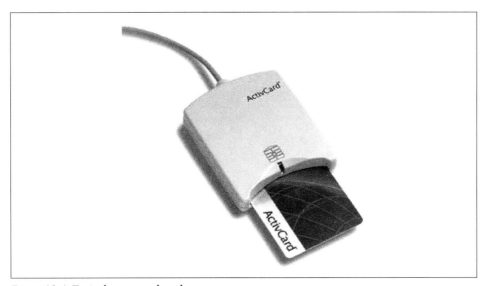

Figure 10-4. Typical smart card reader

A disadvantage of many current readers is that their internal electrical contacts slide over the smart card's when the card is inserted. This wear and tear can eventually damage the card's contacts, rendering it useless. Some types of readers keep their contacts out of the way, lowering them into place when the smart card is fully inserted and reducing wear and tear on the card. Fortunately, most smart cards themselves are inexpensive enough that it's no burden to replace them every couple of years, if necessary. The cost comes from management and operations, not from the cards themselves.

The reader is also responsible for notifying Windows of the state of the smart card. For example, whenever the smart card is removed from the reader, the reader notifies Windows. You can configure a computer's local security policy (either on individual computers or by using a Group Policy Object on a set of computers) to lock the computer or log the user off when her smart card is removed. Figure 10-5 shows this policy setting.

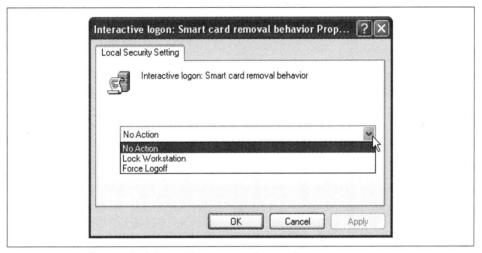

Figure 10-5. Configuring the behavior for smart card removal

Typically, you would always want Windows configured to discontinue access whenever the smart card is removed, helping to ensure the security of the computer. This becomes very effective when combined with administrative policy that requires employees to always have physical possession of their smart cards. This *will* pose a minor inconvenience—say, when a user just gets up to get a drink of water and is forced to reauthenticate on his return. But the reauthentication procedure should take only a few seconds and is simple to accomplish. However, as I've stressed over and over again, you must weigh the usability drawbacks of this security setting against the benefits to determine the best configuration for your environment.

There are times when you might want to continue access when the smart card is removed. For example, you might not require users to use their smart cards to access their client computers, but instead require the card only to access a particular corporate application. In that case, removing the smart card might discontinue access to the application, but not to the computer on which it was running. In addition, many advanced users have more than one computer. Requiring the smart card to remain in the reader of one station makes multiple computer interaction impossible without multiple smart cards, which should never be done.

Smart cards can significantly simplify security for your users. A simple card and an easy-to-remember PIN let them log on and log off, without having to change passwords every 30 days, worry about forgetting a password, and so on. This can also reduce work for your helpdesk support team.

Requirements for Using Smart Cards

Although Windows Server 2003 contains native support for smart cards, you'll need additional hardware and software to actually use them in your environment.

First, you'll need to purchase blank smart cards. A number of vendors offer these at varying prices, currently around $1 to $2 each when purchased in bulk (prices can be somewhat higher for more complex cards). You'll also need to purchase a smart card reader for each computer in your organization. Smart card readers are available in a variety of styles, including some that connect via USB port. Some readers install inside a desktop computer, occupying a 3¹/2-inch drive bay, as shown in Figure 10-6. You can also purchase smart card readers in a PC Card format, designed for use with notebook computers. The smart card readers should come with driver software that is compatible with the operating system the reader will attach to. Most readers provide drivers for Windows 2000, Windows XP, and Windows Server 2003. The reader's bundled software usually includes a replacement GINA, which I discussed in the previous section. Readers often cost less than $10 each when purchased in sufficient quantities.

Figure 10-6. A typical internal smart card reader

Finally, you'll need to implement a public key infrastructure (PKI) in your environment, which you'll use to issue certificates for recording onto the smart cards. Chapter 9 discusses Windows Server 2003's native PKI capabilities. Your smart card vendor may need to provide additional software to request certificates from the PKI and write them to the smart cards. You can also use a commercial certification authority, although doing so can be significantly more expensive than implementing your own PKI. I discuss the benefits and drawbacks of these types of PKI deployments in Chapter 9.

Using Smart Cards

Smart cards can have a variety of uses on your network aside from user logons. They can be used for secure logons, application access, general purpose cryptography, and more. Regardless of how you choose to use smart cards, you'll need to make sure you keep track of them and keep them secure. In the next few sections, I'll give you some tips for effectively using smart cards.

Secure Logon

Smart cards are an effective means of user identification, but as a physical factor, they can be lost or damaged. Deciding to use smart cards in your organization means committing to physical management of those cards. Here are some tips for making smart card management easier:

- Make sure your users have an easy, fast way of reporting lost or damaged smart cards.

- Provide your helpdesk or other organization with the means to quickly disable lost cards by revoking their certificates in your PKI. Exactly how you accomplish this depends on what PKI solution you're using. With a Windows Server 2003 certification authority (CA), you simply open the Certification Authority MMC snap-in from any authorized client, right-click a certificate to revoke it, and then publish an updated certificate revocation list. For detailed instructions on how to complete this task, see the "Revoking Issued Certificates" section in Chapter 9.

- Ensure that your users can quickly obtain replacement cards. Keeping a supply of cards on hand in each of your company's offices, for example, provides faster service than shipping them all from a central location whenever a user needs one.

General Purpose Cryptography

Remember that smart cards never transmit their encryption keys to the host computer. Instead, the computer transmits data to the smart card, which encrypts it and sends it back. This behavior provides increased security for encryption keys, which are tied to the physical card rather than to a specific computer.

However, the increased security of smart cards comes at a price. Because the private key is created on and never leaves the smart card, it cannot be archived. This means that when a smart card is lost, stolen, or damaged, the private key is gone forever. This is compounded by the smart card's portability, which encourages users and administrators to carry them around until they're damaged well before their expected lifetime is up. This can be a drawback if large amounts of data or critical data is protected by this key. Care should be taken to use smart cards in appropriate situations and ensure that backup plans exist in case of smart card key loss. Users should also be cautioned about the proper care of smart cards, which includes the following basic guidelines:

- Do not store the smart card in an eel-skin wallet. Actually, this is a joke: eel-skin wallets damaging magnetic stripe and smart cards is purely a myth.

- Do not use a smart card for any "ancillary" use that you might use a regular credit card for, such as unlocking a door or scraping cheese off the inside of a microwave oven. Smart cards are somewhat flexible, but even a minor scratch or overextension of the chip's circuitry can render it inoperative.

- Carry the card in a protective sleeve. These are available from smart card manufacturers at a nominal cost.

- Remove the smart card when it is not in use or under direct observation. This rule can be used in conjunction with the computer-locking group policy mentioned earlier to lock unused workstations and ensure the smart card is not stolen.

The design of smart cards makes them ideal for all forms of cryptography. In addition to the private key used for logging on, smart cards can contain a general purpose private encryption key. The additional key allows the smart card to be used for all a user's cryptography needs, including conducting e-commerce, digitally signing email, and so forth. Smart cards can actually make cryptography more accessible to your users, since they can use their smart cards on any computer equipped with a reader. Normally, cryptography keys are stored on a computer, making it difficult for users to carry their keys around with them. By storing keys on a smart card, users can carry their keys around with them, making them more likely to use cryptography in appropriate situations.

Distributing Smart Cards

No matter how you choose to use smart cards, remember that they represent your users' identities. You need to ensure that smart cards make it to the correct users and that the users receive the correct PINs for their smart cards. Smart cards should be physically distributed by a person who recognizes each employee. PINs should be communicated via voice or a separate piece of paper, in much the same way that your bank gives you the PIN for a new ATM card. By visually verifying that the correct user has the correct smart card and PIN, you can be assured of the smart card's security.

Many organizations deploying smart cards find it useful to allow the smart card recipient to set her own PIN. Similar to when you activate a new credit card, you provide the card to the individual with reasonable authentication and then require her to further prove her identity before first use. This can be done by creating a custom application that asks the user for some personally identifying piece of information (such as her social security number) and then authenticates that against a database before allowing her to choose an initial PIN. This helps keep management and operation costs down by automating part of the deployment process, which as I mentioned can get quite expensive. For more information on developing this type of custom application, a great reference is The Smart Card Cryptographic Service Provider Cookbook at *http://msdn.microsoft.com/library/en-us/dnscard/html/msdn_ smart_card.asp*.

Implementing Smart Cards in Your Organization

Actually implementing, distributing, and using smart cards for the first time can be a daunting process. With that in mind, here's a complete, step-by-step outline of what you'll need to do to implement smart cards in your own organization.

A great online resource for smart card deployment is Microsoft's Smart Card Deployment Cookbook, available at *www.microsoft.com/ technet/security/topics/smrtcard/smrtcdcb/default.mspx*.

PKI first

Before you can begin using smart cards, you need to have PKI deployed in your environment. I've covered how to do that in Chapter 9. As I've mentioned earlier, your PKI can be an extension of a commercial certification authority, or you can deploy your own root CA. Whichever method you choose, get your PKI up and running, and thoroughly tested, prior to starting your smart card deployment.

Enrolling users

Smart cards show up from the factory without much in the way of "smarts" on board. Specifically, they're lacking the digital certificates that make them useful. During the enrollment process, you'll encode certificates on the cards and issue them to specific users in your organization.

Typically, enrollment is done in person, meaning the smart card recipient actually has to show up and get his card. This can be very inconvenient for users and difficult to schedule, but it's a security requirement. If you simply mailed completed cards out in interoffice memo pouches, you'd have no assurance that the correct users received the correct cards, compromising your entire deployment. The questions surrounding enrollment processes are explored in depth in Chapter 9.

Most organizations like to set up a centralized enrollment station, complete with a dedicated certificate-issuing server and the necessary card readers and burners. If necessary, you can make this station mobile and move it from office to office as you deploy smart cards throughout your organization.

 You'll also need to provide users with smart card readers. Typically, these are USB-connected devices, although laptop users may prefer PC Card–based readers. These readers should be deployed and operational before users show up to claim their new smart cards from your central station.

Preparing to issue cards

You'll need to do some prep work in order to issue a card, and then a simple set of steps will serve to issue all the cards your organization needs. Here's an example of what to do (I'm assuming you're using a Windows Server 2003 certification authority to issue cards; if you're not, you'll need to alter these steps to fit your PKI solution):

1. In the Certification Authority console, ensure that the Enrollment Agent template is present in the Policy Settings folder.

2. Create a new domain user group, named something like Smart Card. Give the group Read and Enroll permissions to the EnrollmentAgent policy template.

3. Open Active Directory Sites and Services, and open the Certificate Templates folder (located under Services → Public Key Services). Locate the Enrollment Agent template's properties, and add the Smart Card group.

4. On the computer you'll be using to issue certificates, open Internet Explorer. From the Tools menu, select Internet Options. In the Trusted Sites category, ensure that the certificate service web page is in the Trusted Sites list.

5. Open the certificate service web page in Internet Explorer, and select Request a Certificate and click Next.

6. Select Advanced Request, and then click Next.

7. Select "Submit a certificate request to this CA using a form," and then click Next.

8. For the Certificate Template, select Enrollment Agent. Then, select Microsoft Enhanced Cryptographic Provider for the CSP. Select a key size—1024 is a common one—and click Next.

9. Click Install This Certificate.

You can also select the Mark Keys as Exportable option to enable the private keys to be exported for backup purposes. Your organization should have policies regarding key backup and recovery, and those policies must dictate how this option is used.

That's it! You're now an *enrollment officer* for your organization and can request certificates on behalf of other users and then install those certificates onto blank smart cards.

Issuing cards to users

When a user shows up for her new smart card, follow these steps:

1. Sign on to your enrollment computer as the enrollment agent, and open the certificate services web page on your certificate-issuing server.

2. Select Request a Certificate and click Next.

3. Select Advanced Request and click Next.

4. Select "Request a certificate on behalf of another user using the Smart Card Enrollment" and click Next. You can perform this step only because you already received an enrollment agent certificate in the previous section.

5. You may be prompted to install a new ActiveX control; allow Internet Explorer to do so. The Enrollment Station Control is required to proceed.

6. Select Standard Logon as the certificate template, select the appropriate certification authority, and select the appropriate cryptographic service provider that corresponds with the smart card hardware you are using. Click Next.

7. In the dialog box that appears, select the issued certificate and click OK. This corresponds to the user's identity.

8. When prompted, insert the user's smart card into the smart card burner, and click OK.

9. When prompted, select the option to change the default PIN (which is usually 1234 but will vary depending on the manufacturer—you should verify this information with the smart card manufacturer in advance). Have the user type her new PIN if possible, or immediately communicate it to her if not. You should record the PIN for backup in accordance with your company's policies (perhaps your company stores a list of PINs in a safe for emergency purposes).

You're done! Your user has a new smart card, and you can move on to the next user.

When the user inserts her card at her own workstation, Windows prompts for her PIN (her identity is already stored in the certificate on the card) and uses this information to send an authentication request to a domain controller. The user experience is very simple and the public key–based Active Directory authentication all happens in the background.

Security Showdown: Passwords Versus Smart Cards and Biometrics

Passwords have been used since the beginning of computer security. It's hard to imagine a system that uses anything else to prove identity. Movies and books show us a future in which computers identify people in a variety of ways. And that future is nearly upon us. In this Security Showdown, we argue about using passwords versus other authentication means in today's technology.

Don: I like complex passwords. Everyone understands how to use them, they work in just about any circumstances, and they're simple. Passwords have no moving parts to break, no circuits to fry, and can't be left on the coffee table at home when you leave for work in the morning. A proper complex password is incredibly hard to guess—so hard, in fact, that it's usually not feasible to even try. And complex passwords don't have to be impossible to remember, either. "L0ves5teak!" is plenty complex, nice and long, and is easy to remember. Heck, coming up with complex passwords can even be fun, like coming up with a cute custom license plate combination.

Mike: Sure, I agree that passwords have their place. But having something other than a password to prove a user's identity is very important. Passwords are far too easy to guess, as even the most complex will have patterns and rules it must conform with. Passwords must be memorized by people, which provides a weak link in that the person must be considered reliable. And passwords that are held by people are susceptible to a specific form of attack we haven't mentioned yet: the "rubber hose" attack, in which the knowledge is simply beaten out of the individual. Plain and simple, there are too many ways to beat a system that relies only on passwords.

Sure, creating complexity by requiring a user to memorize a PIN for a smart card adds difficulty to the security experience. But the more factors that are required to prove a user's identity, the safer the network resources will remain. Even if he uses a simple PIN or reuses one he's already memorized for another purpose, it's far better to require that PIN than a password. The PIN is useless without the smart card and vice versa, providing two-factor authentication. The PIN will almost certainly not be guessed with brute force attacks, and the card cannot be reproduced. A wonderful benefit of this two-factor authentication is that the factors can be split: one administrator can retain the smart card while a second knows the PIN. This allows virtually any company adopting this well-established and inexpensive solution to require multiple parties to agree to perform critical functions.

Advanced biometrics provide even more assurance that a user is who he claims to be. New technologies that measure everything from the classic fingerprint or retina scan to thermal imaging and bone placement recognition are evolving every day. These technologies have their drawbacks at the moment, including false negatives and cost. But they're getting more reliable and cheaper every day.

—continued—

Don: You make a good argument for embracing the next phase of technology. However, I still say that, for backward compatibility and because of human nature, passwords will be with us for a while. Perhaps in the near future all these gadgets will replace passwords and change our perception of computer security, but for now, people will still need to compose and memorize complex passwords or migrate to a simple smart card solution. And passwords will certainly remain with us until technical glitches—such as successfully logging on with a fingerprint reader by using gummy bears (*http://cryptome.org/gummy.htm*)—are worked out.

Ultimately, I think we'll bypass smart cards completely and rely on biometric devices like retinal or fingerprint scanners, which combine the security of a smart card with the ease of use of a password.

Summary

In this chapter, you've learned how smart cards work and how they interact with the native Windows logon process. You understand the hardware and software requirements for smart cards and how smart cards can be used to provide secure general purpose cryptography as well as logon cryptography. While smart cards require a monetary investment and a well-designed PKI, they also provide more secure, more effective user identification and remove much of the burden corporate security usually places on users.

As these smart card solutions become less expensive and security becomes more of a concern for large corporations, smart card solutions will undoubtedly become widespread. In the future, many enterprises may use smart cards to enforce multifactor authentication for all data access. You now have the knowledge to deploy smart cards for your organization and use them to enhance security while keeping the user's login and ongoing security experience pleasant.

CHAPTER 11

DHCP and DNS Security

Lots of elements are involved in a healthy network. Many are provided by hardware, such as the routing and switching of data. Others are provided by software and are frequently based on the network protocols in use. These services are often overlooked by security administrators and implementers. But attackers can use these services to launch, support, or continue an attack. In fact, denial-of-service attacks can be very effectively carried out by just attacking these services alone. This chapter explores two important services that exist on most networks but get very little security attention.

Microsoft has recognized the lack of security in DHCP and DNS. As a result, Windows Server 2003 has several security technologies that are not necessarily standards-based or fully compatible with other operating systems; however, depending on your computing environment and need for security, these technologies can prove beneficial.

In this chapter, I'll explore the core network services of DHCP and DNS. These services are essential to most IP networks today in that they respectively provide automatic addressing and name resolution. However, their security considerations and safe operations are often neglected. I'll show you how these services work, how they're vulnerable to attack, and how to protect them against those attacks when possible.

DHCP

The Dynamic Host Configuration Protocol (DHCP) is a service that most IP-based networks use to greatly simplify the daily management of IP addresses and configuration of client computers. The DHCP Server service is provided as an optional component in Windows Server 2003. Because of its integration with the operating system and the reliance of network clients on DHCP, it is critical to understand how DHCP works and how it impacts the security of the overall system.

What Is DHCP?

DHCP allows network clients using the TCP/IP protocol to automatically obtain an IP address and network configuration information. Two computers are involved in any DHCP transaction, a client and a server. The client computer requests DHCP information from a server, which stores information in a database. The server provides the requested network configuration information to the client, which then configures the TCP/IP protocol with this information and begins communicating on the network.

How DHCP works

Understanding how DHCP works is very useful to the security professional. Such knowledge will help in understanding points made later in this chapter about vulnerabilities and flaws in the protocol that often cannot be addressed. Although a complete academic discussion of DHCP would be overkill, the information provided here will ensure you understand the essential parts of DHCP.

DHCP is based on RFC 2131, "Dynamic Host Configuration Protocol." It defines how DHCP works by defining the interaction between a DHCP client and a DHCP server. This is a great way to look at how it works.

The normal flow of DHCP traffic consists of four separate messages, as shown in Figure 11-1.

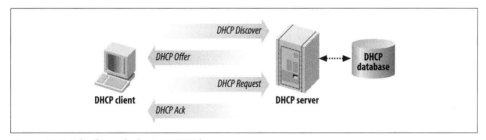

Figure 11-1. The flow of a basic DHCP lease

The messages that make up the basic DHCP interaction are:

DHCP Discover
  This message is broadcast from the client to all hosts on its local subnet.

DHCP Offer
  DHCP servers that have available IP addresses to lease respond to a DHCP Discover with a DHCP Offer. The offer message contains one of the available IP addresses. Essentially, the servers are asking the client if it would like the offered IP address.

DHCP Request

The DHCP client selects one of the received DHCP Offer messages and transmits a DHCP Request to that server. The request contains the information from the DHCP Offer so the server knows who it's talking to. The server identifies the request as a response to its own offer and updates its database to indicate that the offered address has been leased.

DHCP Ack

The DHCP server then responds with the final message to the client, a DHCP Ack. This acknowledgment provides additional configuration settings, called options, for the client, such as DNS name and lease duration. The client uses this information to configure TCP/IP to communicate on the network.

The end result of this interaction is that the DHCP client *leases* an IP address from the DHCP server for a specified time and uses that information to send and receive network traffic. When the client is done communicating on the network (perhaps during shutdown), it sends a DHCP Release to the server. This message informs the server that the address can be made available to other clients on the network. This is normally the final network communication by the client, as it must discard its DHCP settings immediately.

All DHCP addresses are leased from the server by the client. This is because there are a limited number of DHCP addresses available on any given network, and even fewer are available on each DHCP server. To help conserve and reuse unused IP addresses, a specific lease duration is provided whenever a client leases an address. The client can renew its lease at any point during the duration, but per the DHCP standard, must do so after 50% of its lease duration. For example, if a DHCP lease was configured at 48 hours, a client would begin renewing its lease at 24 hours. This is a transparent process to the user.

DHCP security

You may have noticed that there is no security mentioned in the DHCP process. This is because there simply isn't any security built into DHCP. In fact, the author of RFC 2131, Ralph Droms, openly states this drawback in the RFC:

> DHCP is built directly on UDP and IP, which are as yet inherently insecure. Furthermore, DHCP is generally intended to make maintenance of remote and/or diskless hosts easier. While perhaps not impossible, configuring such hosts with passwords or keys may be difficult and inconvenient. Therefore, DHCP in its current form is quite insecure.

An attacker gains numerous advantages when DHCP is used in an environment, such as:

- It is nearly trivial for the attacker to get a valid network address. This provides her the ability to communicate on the network.

- The attacker will get parameters from the DHCP server that identify network service locations, such as DNS and Windows Internet Naming Service (WINS) servers, which may be susceptible to specific attack vectors.

- Because DHCP normally issues IP addresses sequentially, an attacker can identify other hosts on the network by examining her own IP address. Usually any number lower than the attacker's IP address will be leased by a host and active on the network. This is done without probing or even sniffing network traffic.

- An attacker can create her own DHCP server that transmits DHCP Offers and Acks. This could configure the client as the attacker prefers, essentially hijacking the client's network communication. Without any authentication of DHCP, it is nearly impossible for the client to identify this type of attack.

- Simple code can be written to lease DHCP addresses from servers until they run out of available addresses in their database. When this happens, legitimate hosts can no longer lease DHCP addresses, resulting in a denial-of-service attack.

Because security is omitted in the basic design of DHCP, it is hard for us to secure it afterward. I'll explore a few alternative configurations and operations that you can perform to help provide some security when using DHCP. But you should recognize that there is no reasonable way to secure the current version of DHCP.

The principal technology in this area is DHCP server authorization. This is a cooperative server-based scheme in which DHCP servers query Active Directory whenever they start to determine whether they're authorized by the network administrator. If they are authorized, they continue to function normally. If they aren't authorized, the DHCP service shuts down.

This sounds great on the surface. However, the concerns about the security of this technology include:

- Only servers running Windows Server 2003 or Windows 2000 Server with Service Pack 2 or later can be authorized. Any other DHCP server running on any operating system cannot be authorized. This includes third-party DHCP servers running on Windows-based operating systems.

- The DHCP server doesn't have to be authorized. If the DHCP software does not perform this voluntary check, it will begin functioning as normal. This means that an attacker could use another operating system and still launch a DHCP service.

- You must use Active Directory in your network to authorize DHCP servers. If you don't use Active Directory, this feature simply doesn't work.

DHCP server authorization can be useful. It can help prevent misconfigurations on your network, such as when an administrator accidentally brings up a new unauthorized DHCP server. It is also useful for limited prevention against rogue DHCP servers. But it should not be relied upon to stop all attacks of this type.

DHCP and 802.1x

802.1x is a protocol gaining popularity in secure environments. Originally designed to improve on the security flaws of other protocols, 802.1x is used to authenticate clients to network servers before they communicate. This is port-based security, which means that every network port connected to a switch (Ethernet) or access point (wireless) must be authenticated and authorized before any network traffic is passed from that port to another.

802.1x works at a lower layer than DHCP. Therefore, 802.1x can help protect against attackers by requiring authentication before a DHCP lease is obtained.

The problems with 802.1x deployment are simple:

- It requires expensive hardware. 802.1x-compliant switches are not the norm and demand a premium price.
- It requires expensive software. Backend network client software such as RADIUS or Internet Authentication Service (IAS) must be deployed. In addition, because 802.1x uses certificates, most scenarios call for a PKI.
- It requires lots of configuration and management. Clients must be configured with a certificate and the proper settings before they can successfully communicate on the network.

These problems usually outweigh the benefits of deploying 802.1x on a wired network. Therefore, I do not recommend 802.1x as a mitigation for the threats discussed in this chapter.

Using DHCP Securely

There is no such thing as secure DHCP. You'll see it over and over again in this chapter. However, there are ways to make a DHCP-based network a little more resistant to attack. There are several keys to doing this.

First, we must examine the common attack vectors against DHCP. Then we'll examine the countermeasures. And finally, we can look at the system overall and determine whether it's secure enough for our specific needs. If not, there is one simple answer: do not use DHCP. Manually configuring TCP/IP on client computers remains a viable option, and many companies throughout the world do it today. Although it incurs a fairly high TCO and requires a significantly larger IT staff, manual configuration is not without its place.

Overriding all our concerns about DHCP is one basic assumption. To mount a DHCP-based attack of any type, an intruder must have initial access to your network. That is, to hijack clients by sending DHCP Offers, the attacker must put his own computer with a DHCP server on your network. The same is true for all other attack vectors. So one way to help thwart DHCP-based attacks is to tightly control network access. This is discussed throughout the book, but especially in Chapter 14.

All the procedures listed here assume DHCP is already installed on the computer. Installation and normal operation of DHCP are beyond the scope of this book.

Configuring DHCP for proper administration

Windows Server 2003 provides a user group called DHCP Administrators. This group contains all user accounts that are authorized to modify DHCP settings. The membership for this group should be tightly controlled and audited to ensure that no unauthorized users are added to it. This will help prevent both accidental and intentional misconfigurations and help prevent security incidents and denial-of-service occurrences.

Monitoring DHCP for DOS attack

The first and simplest attack against DHCP is to lease all the addresses in its database. As discussed earlier, leasing all the addresses is a fairly simple attack that causes a denial of service by stopping legitimate computers from obtaining DHCP addresses.

A DHCP denial-of-service attack cannot be truly prevented. However, it can be detected early and stopped in its tracks. To do this, you must monitor DHCP. Monitoring DHCP can show you how many leases have been issued over time and can indicate an attack by showing a massive spike or prolonged above-average lease requests. You can also monitor servers to determine when their percentage of available addresses falls below a determined criteria, perhaps 5%. Either of these statistics could indicate a DHCP-focused attack.

To monitor DHCP, you can use the DHCP MMC snap-in, the System Monitor tool, or the Performance Logs and Alerts snap-in. Both the DHCP and System Monitor tools give great snapshots of what's happening with the server at that moment. However, they're not as useful for gathering data over time and identifying trends. To do that, we'll need to use Performance Logs and Alerts.

Knowing what we do about DHCP, we can assume that a denial-of-service attack will take the form of continuous DHCP Discover and DHCP Request messages being received. We can create an administrative alert to tell us when an abnormally high number of DHCP Requests are received on a server.

Before we begin, we must baseline the DHCP traffic. Baselining is, simply put, observing the normal operation of the server to see what it does. In our example, we must baseline the DHCP traffic coming into the server. There are many ways to baseline, but for this book, we'll keep it simple. We'll baseline the DHCP Request traffic over three normal workdays to determine the average traffic that we should expect.

To do this, we follow this procedure:

1. Click Start → Run, type **Perfmon.exe**, and then press Enter. This brings up the Performance snap-in which is a combination of System Monitor and Performance Logs and Alerts.

2. Double-click Performance Logs and Alerts, and then double-click Counter Logs.

3. Right-click Counter Logs, and then click New Log Settings.

4. Type a name for the log, such as **DHCP Offer traffic**. Then click Enter.

5. Click Add Counters.

6. Under Performance Object, select DHCP Server. Then under Select Counters from List, select Requests/sec. Click Add to add this counter. Then click Close.

7. Click the Schedule tab to configure the schedule for monitoring this counter. Because we want to set it for three days, choose beginning and ending times similar to those in Figure 11-2.

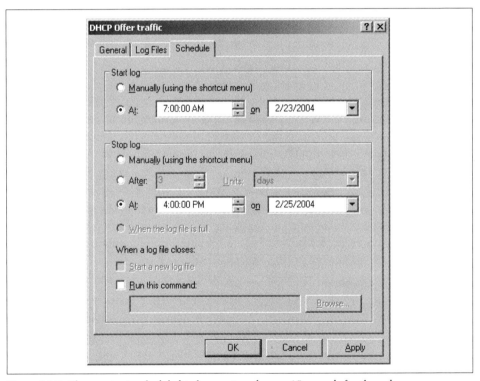

Figure 11-2. The counter is scheduled to be monitored every 15 seconds for three days

8. Click OK. If the folder for the performance log does not exist, you will be prompted to allow its creation. Click Yes.

Once the three days have elapsed, you will be able to view the counter log and determine what the average DHCP Offer traffic is for this computer. Let's assume for brevity that you determine from this log that the maximum DHCP Offers per second the server encountered was 15. This helps us determine when an attack might be taking place.

There is no exact science to determining a number that indicates a problem. You need to decide whether you want more false positives or false negatives. In this case, let's assume a safe number is 20. If your DHCP server encounters more than 20 DHCP Requests per second, you want to know so you can examine the situation and determine whether an attack is taking place.

You can do this by setting up an administrative alert. as shown here:

1. Click Start → Run, type **Perfmon.exe**, and then press Enter. This brings up the Performance snap-in which is a combination of System Monitor and Performance Logs and Alerts.
2. Double-click Performance Logs and Alerts, and then double-click Alerts.
3. Right-click Alerts, and then click New Alert Settings.
4. Provide a name for this alert, such as **DHCP DOS attack**. Then click Enter.
5. Click Add.
6. Under Performance Object, select DHCP Server. Then under Select Counters from List, select Requests/sec. Click Add to add this counter. Then click Close.
7. Configure the alert to alert when the counter exceeds 20 by typing **20** in the Limit box as shown in Figure 11-3.
8. Click the Action tab. This is where you tell the alert what to do when the threshold is met.
9. Click Send a Network Message To, and then type the administrator's login name. Although this works in only limited scenarios, it often helps. You can also configure numerous options to alert you of a problem as shown in Figure 11-4. The application log entry, which is selected, is effective if you have a centralized log management strategy in place.
10. Click OK.

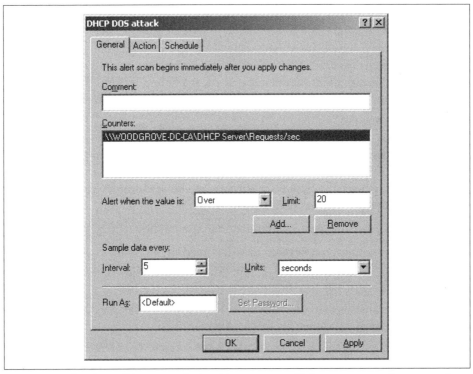

Figure 11-3. This alert will be triggered when 20 or more DHCP Requests are made per second

You now have a tool in place that will help you identify DHCP denial-of-service attacks. There are other tools and processes you could use, to be sure, but this one is included in Windows Server 2003, takes very little time to set up, and is reasonably effective.

Auditing DHCP

Auditing DHCP is, from an attack detection perspective, essentially the same as monitoring the DHCP performance counters. You collect statistical data and determine whether an attack is occurring based on that data. However, auditing DHCP activity can give us more specific information and allow us to examine attacks in greater detail.

Enabling auditing for DHCP is a simple task. Use the following steps:

1. Click Start → All Programs → Administrative Tools → DHCP. This opens the DHCP Management MMC snap-in.

2. Double-click the name of your DHCP server to select it.

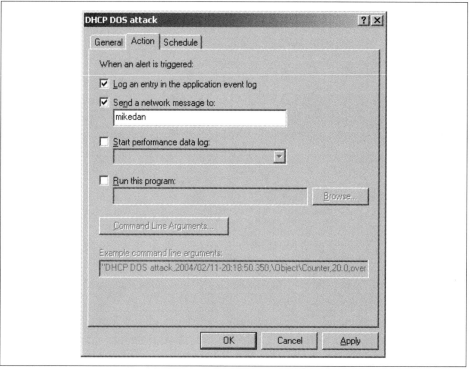

Figure 11-4. This alert logs an event and sends a network message to the author

3. Click Action, and then click Properties.

4. On the General tab, ensure that the Enable DHCP Audit Logging option is selected as shown in Figure 11-5.

Now the DHCP server will log all tasks that it performs. The log is a text file stored in the *%SystemRoot%\System32\dhcp* directory by default. You can change this directory by modifying the path under the Advanced tab in the previous dialog box. The files are stored with the filename of *DhcpSrvLog-day.log* where *day* is a three-letter abbreviation for the day of the week, such as Mon, Tue, and so on.

Analyzing DHCP logs

For our purposes, DHCP logs become interesting only when we see some type of attack occurring. Here's an example portion of a DHCP log showing the beginning few entries in a denial-of-service attack:

```
ID,Date,Time,Description,IP Address,Host Name,MAC Address
24,02/13/04,11:34:07,Database Cleanup Begin,,,
25,02/13/04,11:34:07,0 leases expired and 0 leases deleted,,,,
```

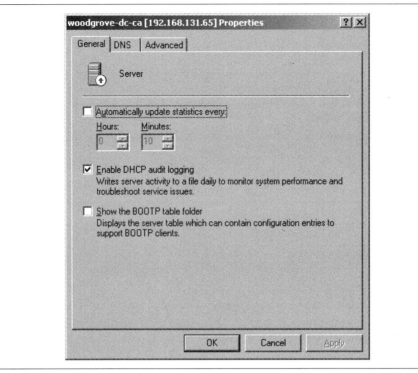

Figure 11-5. The DHCP audit log is enabled

```
25,02/13/04,11:34:07,0 leases expired and 0 leases deleted,,,,
30,02/13/04,11:55:31,DNS Update Request,5.1.168.192,ALICE.contoso.com,,
10,02/13/04,11:55:31,Assign,192.168.1.5,ALICE.wingroup.contoso.com,000BDBD1784E,
32,02/13/04,11:55:31,DNS Update Successful,192.168.1.5,ALICE.contoso.com,,
30,02/13/04,11:55:32,DNS Update Request,6.1.168.192,BOB.contoso.com,,
10,02/13/04,11:55:32,Assign,192.168.1.6,BOB.contoso.com,000BDBF43A0B,
32,02/13/04,11:55:32,DNS Update Successful,192.168.1.6,BOB.contoso.com,,
30,02/13/04,11:55:33,DNS Update Request,7.1.168.192,CAROL.contoso.com,,
10,02/13/04,11:55:33,Assign,192.168.1.7,CAROL.contoso.com,000BDB191D0B,
32,02/13/04,11:55:33,DNS Update Successful,192.168.1.7,CAROL.contoso.com,,
30,02/13/04,11:55:34,DNS Update Request,8.1.168.192,DOUG.contoso.com,,
10,02/13/04,11:55:34,Assign,192.168.1.8,DOUG.contoso.com,000BDBD00B1E,
32,02/13/04,11:55:34,DNS Update Successful,192.168.1.8,DOUG.contoso.com,,
30,02/13/04,11:55:35,DNS Update Request,9.1.168.192,EVAN.contoso.com,,
10,02/13/04,11:55:35,Assign,192.168.1.9,EVAN.contoso.com,000BDBC2929A,
32,02/13/04,11:55:35,DNS Update Successful,192.168.1.9,EVAN.contoso.com,,
30,02/13/04,11:55:36,DNS Update Request,10.1.168.192,FRAN.contoso.com,,
10,02/13/04,11:55:36,Assign,192.168.1.10,FRAN.contoso.com,000BDB42189A,
32,02/13/04,11:55:36,DNS Update Successful,192.168.1.10,FRAN.contoso.com,,
30,02/13/04,11:55:37,DNS Update Request,11.1.168.192,GEORGE.contoso.com,,
10,02/13/04,11:55:37,Assign,192.168.1.11,GEORGE.contoso.com,000BDBBEDEBE,
32,02/13/04,11:55:37,DNS Update Successful,192.168.1.11,GEORGE.contoso.com,,
```

The scenario is that this particular DHCP server serves several client subnets in a moderately sized company. It's one of three DHCP servers. The server is configured to provide 12-hour leases. Its normal baseline (mentioned earlier) usually shows a spike between 8 a.m. and 10 a.m., Monday through Friday, as employees come in and turn their computers on. The load on the DHCP servers is then light throughout the day, mostly consisting of renewals and the occasional new client computer powering up.

At 11:55:31 on Friday the 13th, this server began receiving numerous DHCP requests, of which a small set is shown here. Prior to this time it was relatively idle, occasionally maintaining its leases and leasing new addresses. But all of a sudden, a large number of lease requests began flooding the server. If you notice, the hostnames are all relatively similar and the MAC addresses all share the same prefix. If the names and MAC addresses matched the common host configuration on a network, it might not cause alarm. However, between the massive lease onslaught, the sequential hostnames, and the oddity of the MAC name pattern, it is a distinct possibility that the DHCP server is being attacked.

The other important entry to notice in this log is that the DHCP server is updating the DNS records for its leases. This means that the DHCP denial-of-service attack will cascade into a DNS server denial-of-service attack. On top of that, from the DNS server's perspective, the attack is coming from the DHCP server. So if you noticed the activity on the DNS server first, you might suspect one of your own servers!

This scenario is relatively common, and getting to the root cause is key. When such an attack is detected and is still taking place, you should decide whether your priority is capturing the attacker or ending the attack. Each requires you to perform separate tasks, but in either case you must act quickly. While stopping the attack is usually a simple matter of disconnecting network segments or the DHCP server itself, capturing the attacker is a much more convoluted scenario involving evidence preservation, passive tracing, and data capturing. This falls under the category of incident response and is not covered here. You can refer to many resources for information on incident response, but my favorite is the United States' Computer Emergency Readiness Team (CERT) web site at *http://www.us-cert.gov*.

 Catching an attack in this way while it's still occurring is a very rare occurrence. Don't expect it to ever happen to you. But be prepared if it does.

Monitoring the network for unauthorized DHCP servers

So far we've seen how to protect your authentic DHCP servers from attack—or, more precisely, how to detect an attack as quickly as possible. But there is another common attack that these defenses do not protect against—when an intruder gains physical access to your network and brings up her own rogue DHCP server. That's generally referred to as a DHCP server spoofing attack and can be very harmful on your network.

Once an attacker can lease IP addresses and configuration information to network clients, she essentially owns all network communication with that client. The client uses the DHCP configuration information to determine default gateway and DNS or WINS information, so all communication must go through servers that the rogue DHCP server has identified. This means that the client may be communicating entirely with servers that the attacker owns, and all the network traffic may be either monitored or entirely fabricated.

Windows 2000 and Windows Server 2003 have some basic protection against this type of occurrence. When you install a DHCP server on either operating system, the DHCP server will not start until it is authorized in Active Directory. This is a good basic level of protection against innocent misconfiguration or low-skilled attackers who don't know better.

Most attackers are aware of this authorization requirement. They wouldn't use a Windows-based DHCP server for this type of attack. Numerous DHCP server software packages are available, including several that are free and many that run on non-Windows operating systems. These servers cannot be stopped by Windows Server 2003, as they do not check for authorization before leasing addresses.

To detect when an attacker has introduced a rogue DHCP server to the network, you must use an automated network monitoring package. This package should be configured to search for DHCP Offer packets on the network that originate from a network address that's not on your list of approved DHCP servers. Currently, Microsoft doesn't offer such an automated package. Microsoft's Network Monitor does allow network monitoring capabilities, but it does not have the ability to intelligently monitor for specific events and notify an administrator when those events occur.

Microsoft also provides a little-known tool, *Dhcploc*, to help identify DHCP servers. It is not installed with Windows Server 2003 but can be found on the installation CD in the *\Support\Tools* directory. It is a simple command-line tool that periodically sends out DHCP Discover packets and compares all DHCP Offers it receives against a list of authorized DHCP servers. If an offer comes from a server not on the authorized list, *Dhcploc* sends a network pop-up message to a specified user or computer. Although limited in its use and scalability, this tool can be useful for spot-checking your network.

The best prevention against attacks based on unauthorized DHCP servers is to ensure the physical security of your network. I discussed physical security earlier in the book in Chapter 3 as an essential foundation to any secure network. In this case, physical security is really the only significant prevention against the rogue DHCP server.

Shortening the DHCP lease times on your authentic DHCP servers does not help prevent or recover from this type of attack. The attacker configures the lease time for her rogue DHCP server leases, which may cause the clients to hold those bogus leases for a long time. The best way to recover clients with rogue leases is to use IPConfig /release and IPConfig /renew to obtain a new DHCP lease (or have them reboot).

Eliminating DHCP

I would be remiss if I didn't present the notion of eliminating DHCP from your network. There are three ways client computers can obtain IP addresses:

- DHCP
- Static TCP/IP configuration
- APIPA

The only option I haven't discussed so far is Automatic Private IP Addressing (APIPA, often called Autonet). When a Windows client computer fails to obtain a DHCP lease and has no static or alternate TCP/IP configuration, APIPA takes over. It assigns an IP address in the 169.254.*x.y* range, where *x* and *y* are random numbers. Windows then ARPs for the address to ensure it's not in use before allowing TCP/IP to begin communication with this address. No configuration information is obtained from the network, so external communication is usually unavailable.

APIPA is obviously not a great option for any but the smallest of organizations, and even then it's usually not functional enough to be a viable option because it cannot configure client options such as default gateways and nameservers. Static configuration is, as discussed earlier, an option but has significant drawbacks in cost and scalability. So in *most* cases DHCP must be used to administer network addresses.

DNS

Domain Name System (DNS) is in use on virtually all TCP/IP networks as the predominant name resolution service. Although simple in design, its original specification severely lacked any security considerations. However, many innovations have been made since its original release and now DNS is far more securable than before. In addition, employing a few important best practices can keep this system reasonably safe against attackers.

What Is DNS?

DNS takes the friendly textual name of a computer, such as *www.contoso.com*, and resolves it to an IP address such as 131.107.2.200. That IP address can then be used by TCP/IP to locate and communicate with the desired computer.

DNS is important because humans do not memorize numbers well. We can remember that *www.contoso.com* is a great web site, but we cannot easily remember that to communicate with it we need to type *http://131.107.2.200* into our web browser. DNS solves that problem for us.

Essentially, DNS is just a big distributed database. The data is formatted into individual *records* that store information. DNS allows users and administrators to add records to, manage, and retrieve records from the database it maintains. There are numerous *record types* available in DNS, each representing the type and use of the data it stores. In this chapter, we're mostly concerned with A records (Address records) that map a hostname to an IP address and PTR records (Pointer records) that map an IP address back to a name. However, there are many more record types. They're listed in detail in RFCs 1035 and 1183.

Because the Internet is such a large place, no DNS server has a record for every single computer available. Instead, DNS supports a referral system. If your computer asks DNS to find a record for a computer name it doesn't know about, it has the ability to ask other DNS servers to help you. It can also give you a "next step" referral and allow your computer to contact another DNS server that may be able to resolve that name. These queries are known as *recursive* and *iterative*, respectively. I'll discuss the security concerns about recursive queries and how to mitigate them later in this chapter.

 Because DNS is in such widespread use at this time, a lengthy explanation is avoided here. For more details, the authoritative reference on the topic is *DNS on Windows Server 2003* from O'Reilly.

Requirements for DNS

Windows Server 2003 includes a DNS server component. Installing it requires nothing above the basic system requirements for Windows Server 2003. However, there are some security advantages to installing your DNS server in a domain environment or even on a domain controller.

DNS zone storage

Standard DNS terminology defines zone storage in a single fashion—there's only one kind. Windows Server 2003 offers two types of zones: standard (also called file-baked) and Active Directory-integrated. There is an enormous difference in security functionality between the two. You should be familiar with the benefits and drawbacks of each.

Standard DNS zones. Standard DNS zones are stored in a very simple manner. They're kept in a text file on the hard drive of the DNS server. This file isn't encrypted or protected in any special way. This allows administrators to directly modify the zone file if they so choose. It also provides some simplicity in that the DNS server always has a local copy of the zone file. Windows Server 2003's DNS server allows you to create a standalone DNS server in virtually any configuration, as there are no prerequisites or required underlying technologies needed.

However, standard DNS zones present many security concerns. Primarily, the text file on the hard drive is subject to tampering. The tampering can be done quite easily with an application such as Notepad and may be very difficult to monitor and trace. In addition, no security (beyond the standard NTFS ACL) can be applied to this type of zone for the same reason.

Active Directory–integrated DNS zones. Another place to store the DNS zone data is a database. Conveniently, Windows Server 2003 domains already have a database: Active Directory. Active Directory–integrated zones are simply zones in which the data is stored in Active Directory instead of a text file on the hard disk. While this change of data storage sounds (and is) simple, it provides numerous security advantages. It also has some requirements that standard zones do not.

Active Directory–integrated zones provide several features, including:

Security tab

> The properties of each zone allow you to configure that zone. When you create an Active Directory–integrated zone, the properties of that zone display a security tab. That tab allows you to set permissions on the zone, similar to setting permissions on other objects in Active Directory. For example, you can explicitly deny users of some lesser-trusted groups access to the zone data entirely, while making other groups read-only for the zone data.

Require secure dynamic updates

> In traditional DNS configurations, an administrator maintains the zone database manually. But newer versions of Windows help lessen that maintenance burden. Servers can be configured to allow clients to update their own DNS records automatically through a process called dynamic update. This is especially useful when using DHCP, because addresses may change more frequently than an administrator can handle. If the clients and servers are performing these updates automatically, having stale DNS record information can be avoided.

> Dynamic update has a flaw: anyone can make the update. So someone could replace existing legitimate DNS data with data of their preference. We answer this problem with secure dynamic update. This is a feature of Active Directory–

integrated zones in which the client must prove its identity and perform the DNS update through a secure channel. Unknown clients are unable to change or add DNS data.

Zone replication control
> Because zone information is stored in Active Directory, it can be easily replicated to other servers. DNS allows you to control the zone data replication to ensure that it is not replicated to inappropriate servers where the data might be compromised. This is a desirable security feature, and it helps regulate network bandwidth consumption by zone data.

Of the two types of zones, Active Directory–integrated zones obviously have more security features that we can use to protect against attackers. If you're using Active Directory in your environment already, you should consider using Active Directory–integrated zones. They truly provide huge benefits against denial-of-service attacks and allow you to optimize more of your networking environment. To be fair, standard zones can maintain reasonable security. But if you're already paying the price for the Active Directory–integrated zones, you should use them.

For much more information on zone configuration and requirements, see *DNS on Windows Server 2003* (O'Reilly).

DNS security concerns

The benefits of using DNS in your environment are clear and should already be apparent to you. However, the benefits should be weighed against the drawbacks. None of these threats exists entirely because of DNS. But DNS often makes attacks in this area easier to implement.

When the RFCs that define DNS were created (RFCs 1034 and 1035), the Internet was a small and reasonably secure place. Access was largely restricted to computer übergeeks and military personnel. Because access was restricted and because little or no malicious intent existed on the Internet at that time, DNS was designed without any security considerations. In fact, a search of RFC 1034 and 1035 on the word *security* results in no hits.

Because the world has changed and the Internet is now peopled with malcontents and miscreants, DNS comes under frequent attack. Its fundamental lack of security design makes it vulnerable to a number of attacks. And although new methods are being developed to help provide security, its inherent lack of security design often allows attackers enough leeway to cause harm.

The types of threats that are common to DNS servers are:

Spoofing
> Attackers often try to compromise security by fooling you into thinking that their computer is actually the computer you were looking for. You assume your communication is secure, and it may be, but it's secure to their computer instead

of the one you believe you're communicating with. Such an attack is called *spoofing*. Spoofing is frequently accomplished by attacking DNS and adding false data to its database and cache.

For example, if you attempt to browse to *http://www.woodgrovebank.com*, your computer queries a DNS server. When the DNS server looks up the IP address, it may find a false address added by the attacker. That false IP address is provided to your computer, and your web browser displays the data from that web site. The attacker has, from your perspective, taken the place of *www. woodgrovebank.com*. That's spoofing.

Network footprinting

Footprinting is the practice of learning as much information about a target network as possible. This is usually carried out before an attack to help map out resources and possibly security devices. Because DNS must, by its nature, know about all TCP/IP hosts on a network, it holds much of the information that's necessary to build an accurate footprint of a network. For that reason, attackers often attempt to retrieve all information stored in a DNS server. This gives them details on what resources are available and, often, where they are.

Denial-of-service attacks

You've already read about denial-of-service attacks and that they work by flooding a legitimate server with false requests until it can no longer service the authentic network clients. DNS servers are often the target of such attacks. When a DNS server is taken down with this type of attack, no clients can resolve hostnames to IP addresses, which essentially downs the entire network. Equally damaging is when the target DNS server hosts the records for an Internet presence, such as a web server. Clients can no longer contact the web server in that case, which may result in lost revenue.

Countermeasures, both procedural and technology-based, can help protect DNS against these types of attacks. These countermeasures are discussed in the following section.

Using DNS Securely

The previous sections described the numerous attack vectors provided by DNS. They also described the benefits of having DNS and that, in many networks, it's an indispensable benefit. All these benefits have frequently outweighed the lack of security in DNS for many years. However, some progress has been made in the realm of DNS security. Several new techniques and technologies can help protect both DNS servers and clients and help provide some level of resistance against attackers.

Windows Server 2003 incorporates many of the newer DNS security features. These security features, as well as ways to use them and threats that they help mitigate, are the focus for the rest of this section.

Setting permissions for DNS administration

The first step to securing your DNS server is controlling who has the ability to modify it. Although the default settings are reasonably restrictive, you may want to limit even further the number of users or groups able to configure the server. This is one example of role separation on a DNS server running on a Windows Server 2003 domain controller, where administrators of one component or network service may not require administrative access to another.

You restrict the users and groups that can manage the DNS server by following this procedure:

1. Click Start → All Programs → Administrative Tools → DNS. This displays the DNS Management MMC snap-in.

2. Right-click the DNS server name, and then click Properties.

3. Click the Security tab. You'll see a dialog box similar to Figure 11-6.

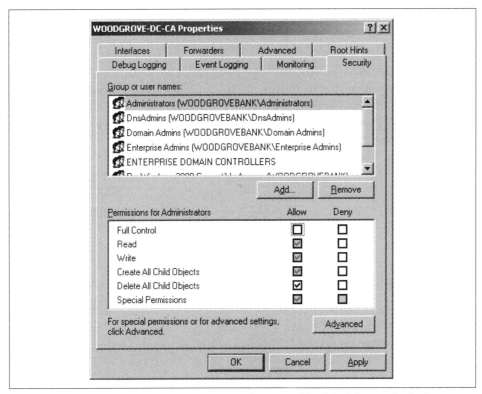

Figure 11-6. DNS server administration is fairly well restricted by default but can be further restricted as needed

4. Click Add to add new security groups to this list, and then select the appropriate permissions for those groups.

5. Click a group in the list and then click Remove to remove the permissions for members of that group.

 The DnsAdmins group has full permissions to the DNS server. That's the built-in group that is designed to contain your DNS administrators. By default, this group is empty. You should add authorized DNS administrators to that group and make as few other changes to the ACL as possible. Ensure you tightly control membership of this group to prevent unauthorized changes to your DHCP configuration.

Setting permissions on DNS objects

Windows Server 2003's DNS server doesn't stop at the basic restriction of a DNS server. You can get very detailed when securing a DNS server. You can set permissions on Active Directory–integrated zones and even records in the same manner as described previously.

For example, perhaps you have an internal DNS domain called research.woodgrove-bank.com. You want to limit access to that domain's data only to members of the Research security group. That's easily accomplished in Windows Server 2003's DNS by doing the following once the Active Directory–integrated zone has been created:

1. Click Start → All Programs → Administrative Tools → DNS.

2. Right-click the domain name (in this case, research.woodgrovebank.com), and then click Properties.

3. Click the Security tab.

4. Click Add to add the Research group to this list. Allow this group Read, Write, Create All Child Objects, and Delete All Child Objects permissions.

5. Also add the DnsAdmins group to allow for administration of this domain later. Allow this group Full Control.

6. Click the Everyone group in the list and then click Remove to remove the permissions for members of that group. Repeat the process to remove the Authenticated Users group and the Administrators group.

7. You should end up with a list similar to Figure 11-7.

This configuration results in a very limited DNS domain. Members of that domain, who are also members of the Research group, can manage their own records and query for other hosts in the same domain. However, outsiders cannot use DNS to identify or footprint the Research group's computers. They don't have permission to get the information from DNS.

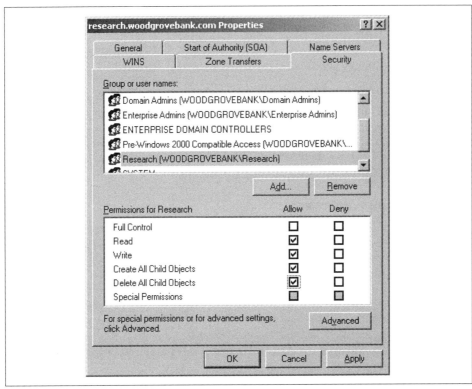

Figure 11-7. The Research group now has permission to use the data in the research. woodgrovebank.com domain

The same procedure can be carried out to set permissions on individual records as well. Although this isn't a very common practice, it can be useful in some scenarios. For example, you may want to secure high-value records for line-of-business servers so that an attacker or errant administrator cannot modify the record and cause a denial of service.

Enabling secure dynamic updates

By default, new Windows Server 2003 DNS servers with Active Directory–integrated zones are configured to allow clients to dynamically update their DNS records. This is allowed because it can be done in a reasonably secure manner.

The fact that the zone is Active Directory–integrated means that Windows Server 2003 can require the client to authenticate with Active Directory. These authenticated credentials can then be passed to the DNS server with the client record update request. The DNS server would then validate the client's credentials before processing the record update.

When DHCP is configured to update DNS, it can potentially add records that it believes are accurate but that are not. This could lead you to believe that the DNS server is attacking the DHCP server. In fact, the attacker is attacking the DNS server through DHCP.

Dynamic updates can also be allowed without the security, principally for standard zones. In this case, all clients are trusted to provide authentic records to the DNS server. This can be dangerous, as it allows clients to pollute the zone data and potentially hijack legitimate resource records, redirecting the client to a host of the attacker's choosing. As described earlier in the chapter, this is bad.

To configure an Active Directory–integrated zone to allow only secure dynamic updates, you should follow these steps:

1. Click Start → All Programs → Administrative Tools → DNS.

2. Right-click a zone, and then click Properties.

3. Under Dynamic Updates, select Secure Only as shown in Figure 11-8.

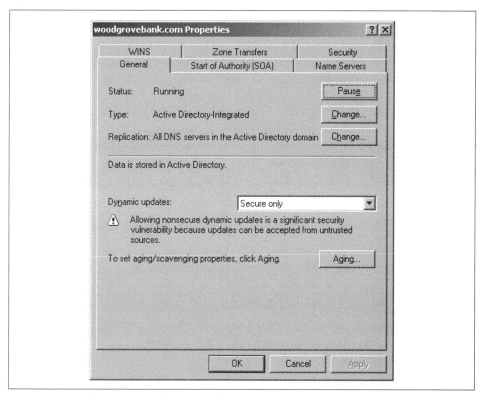

Figure 11-8. Configuring secure dynamic updates

Now the server will accept dynamic updates only from authenticated clients. Note that you can still manually add, delete, and manage records through the DNS Management console. This setting applies only to dynamic client updates.

Restricting zone transfers

Zone transfers are a very common method of network footprinting. If an attacker can obtain a complete zone transfer from either your internal or DMZ-based DNS server, he can use that information to identify hosts. An attacker can often extrapolate computer roles from hostnames, and many record types indicate what type of server is associated with an address. For example, in a Windows Server 2003 domain environment, finding an _ldap._tcp.* record often indicates that the associated host is a domain controller.

To help prevent this from happening, you should restrict zone transfers so that only authorized DNS servers can perform zone transfers with each other. Before you do this, you must identify all DNS servers that need to perform zone transfers with each other. This should be part of your network infrastructure plan and should be accomplished well before DNS is implemented. However, because many networks are not implemented with complete or far-reaching plans, such plans often do not exist.

I mentioned earlier that there are two zone storage types for Windows Server 2003 DNS servers: standard and Active Directory–integrated. Our preferred zone storage type is Active Directory–integrated, as we have far more security options on this type of storage. This is especially true for zone transfers, which by default are secured when you use only Active Directory–integrated zones. In addition, a DNS zone stored in Active Directory takes full advantage of Active Directory's built-in replication. Zone transfers for standard zones must be configured in a different way because of the way they're stored and secured.

Restricting zone transfer for a standard DNS zone can be done with the following steps:

1. Identify and list the IP addresses of all servers that require a zone transfer of this zone.
2. Click Start → All Programs → Administrative Tools → DNS.
3. Expand the DNS server name, and expand the Forward Lookup Zones folder.
4. Right-click the desired standard DNS zone, and click Properties.
5. Click the Zone Transfers tab to show the zone transfer settings. The default setting for a new standard zone is not to allow zone transfers.
6. Click the Only to the Following Servers option.
7. Type in each identified DNS server's IP address, and then click Add. For the example shown in Figure 11-9, we have one DNS server that requires zone transfer.

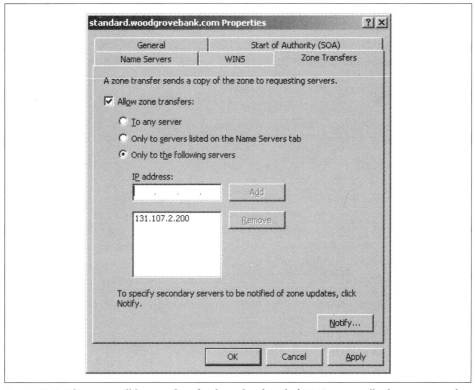

Figure 11-9. This zone will be transferred only to the identified DNS server; all other zone transfer requests will be rejected

Configuring DNS zone replication for Active Directory–integrated zones is far simpler. First, you must decide if you want the zone replicated to any servers other than DNS servers in the same domain. Usually you don't, unless you specifically want to replicate the data for redundancy, reduction in referrals, or some other business need. Also, if you have Windows 2000 DNS servers in the same domain and want them to receive the DNS zone, you can choose that option using this procedure.

Restrict the DNS zone transfer for an Active Directory–integrated zone with these steps:

1. Click Start → All Programs → Administrative Tools → DNS.

2. Expand the DNS server name, and expand the Forward Lookup Zones folder.

3. Right-click the desired DNS zone, and click Properties.

4. On the General tab, next to the Replication option, click Change. This displays the options shown in Figure 11-10.

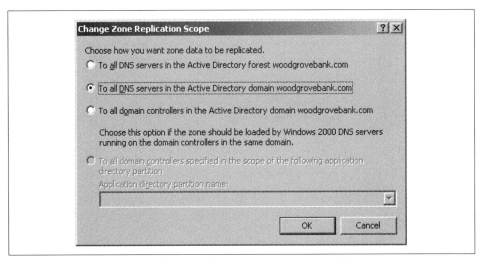

Figure 11-10. Configuring the replication of Active Directory–integrated DNS zones

5. Select the desired option. The default option, "To all DNS servers in the Active Directory domain," is reasonably secure.

Restricting recursive queries

Another restriction you can place on your DNS servers to strengthen security is on recursion. If your infrastructure allows it (if you don't use forwarders), you should disable recursive queries on your Internet-accessible DNS servers. This helps thwart a specific type of spoofing attack in which an attacker sends a recursive query to your DNS server that points back to a DNS server under her control. When that happens, your DNS server essentially trusts all IP information coming from the attacker's DNS server. This can result in a polluted cache and redirected network communications.

Disabling recursion puts your DNS server into a "passive" mode from which it never sends queries on behalf of other servers or clients. Once you've verified that you can disable recursive queries without affecting required network functionality, you can disable DNS recursion by following this procedure:

1. Click Start → All Programs → Administrative Tools → DNS.

2. Right-click the DNS server name, and then click Properties.

3. Click the Advanced tab.

4. Select the "Disable recursion (also disables forwarders)" option as shown in Figure 11-11, and then click OK.

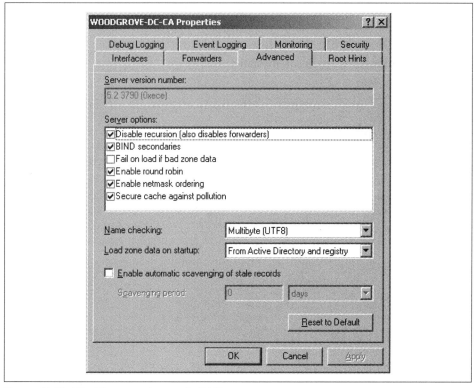

Figure 11-11. Disabling recursion on the DNS server

That's all there is to disabling recursion and preventing an entire class of attack. It's worth mentioning a second time that you should be absolutely certain that this change will not have an impact on your name resolution infrastructure. Disabling recursion without first understanding the implications could adversely affect your network.

Auditing DNS

Unfortunately, DNS provides very little security-oriented event logging. The built-in events and triggers are not sufficient to identify a threat. Therefore, auditing DNS activities through an event log for security analysis is not practical. DNS in Windows Server 2003 provides a configurable debug log feature. However, because this debug logging is intended as a troubleshooting tool, the logging must be manually configured and the resulting log file must be manually retrieved and analyzed. There are no automated tools or processes for doing this work.

However, this does not mean that you should just leave your DNS server alone. The DNS server should be manually audited periodically. These audits should look for common problems such as:

- Misconfiguration, whether intentional or not
- Record pollution
- Access control list conformance to established access control policy

Auditing these problems is simply a matter of using the aforementioned procedures to verify configuration instead of actually establishing that configuration. If any problems arise, you should investigate further to determine how the problem occurred and ensure that it doesn't happen again. For example, if you notice that user David Loudon is a DNS administrator whereas he was not before and is not authorized for that role, you should determine how he became an administrator. That will help you determine a corrective course of action. The action may be as simple as correcting an administrative procedure that allowed David to become an administrator or as difficult as firing David for obtaining administrative permissions through an attack. But without finding the root cause of the problem, you cannot effectively mitigate it.

DNS and DHCP Together

If you're using both DNS and DHCP on the same network, as many of us are, you should consider a couple of specific things that involve the interaction between these two components.

DHCP Service Account

As mentioned often throughout this book, all applications and services run within a user context. This user context provides the access control list (ACL) that's used by the various access control mechanisms in Windows to determine whether access is granted or denied to an object. With the DHCP service, there is a specific concern about what account this service uses.

The DHCP server runs in the Local System security context. When the DHCP server is running on an Active Directory domain controller and contacts a DNS server for record registration, it contacts that DNS server in the domain controller's computer account context. This means that the connection has significantly elevated privileges. Such a connection could be used by an attacker who has compromised one server to "bounce" to another server in a highly privileged context.

To mitigate this threat, you should create a service account specifically for the DHCP service. You must configure your DHCP servers to start the DHCP service in that user context. This will avoid the privileged context problem and help ensure that an attacker has as little leverage as possible against your servers.

Automatic Record Updating

DHCP has a wonderful feature in Windows Server 2003. It can register A and PTR records on behalf of clients that lease addresses from it. The client doesn't have to do any work to make this happen. Client-side settings for this feature are configured through Group Policy, while the DHCP server settings are made in the configuration of the DHCP server itself.

This feature should be used whenever possible and is in fact the default when installing DNS and DHCP on domain controllers. Having the DHCP server update the DNS server allows the DHCP server to control and manage the DNS database for its hosts. This helps prevent attackers from manually modifying zone data. There is some configuration flexibility with this though.

To help provide some flexibility for down DHCP servers and possible record corruption, Windows Server 2003 provides a group called DnsUpdateProxy. If your DHCP servers are joined to the DnsUpdateProxy group, any authenticated user can take ownership of the records registered by DHCP server. This allows for situations in which one DHCP server has gone down and a record needs to be updated by a different server. It also provides some security because users must be authenticated before they can take ownership of a record, and this leaves an audit trail in case of attack or misconfiguration. On the other hand, members of DnsUpdateProxy by definition have elevated privileges on records they don't own. This can be considered a security vulnerability. In this case, you're trading compatibility for security, and you should consider this option carefully before implementing it.

Summary

This chapter is an overview of the security features found in DHCP and DNS on Windows Server 2003. It is not a reference for the operations and technologies behind either DHCP or DNS. You should now be familiar with the basic lack of security in DHCP. Although there are ways to help buttress the security of a DHCP network, the protocol itself simply isn't secure. If this presents an issue that must be addressed, you must address it by finding another IP addressing solution.

DNS, as we've seen, is a name resolution scheme that was designed without security. Unlike with DHCP, there have been significant inroads in appending security to this scheme. There are many ways to help provide additional security on the DNS database. Although some of them are configured by default, all require planning before implementation. And DNS does require periodic manual auditing to ensure that the configuration is correct and that no cache pollution is occurring.

CHAPTER 12

Internet Information Services Security

Internet Information Services (IIS) 6.0 is included with Windows Server 2003. IIS provides a feature-rich set of services for publishing information on the Internet, through a variety of standard Internet protocols. IIS is one of the most popular mechanisms for businesses and organizations to publish information to the public, their business partners, and their employees. Properly configured, IIS is a secure, robust platform; however, as with any complex product, proper configuration of IIS requires careful attention to details.

Surprisingly, proper configuration and management of IIS is less common than you might expect. Many companies take little or no care when installing IIS and leave it vulnerable to many forms of compromise. And because IIS often directly communicates with untrusted people and computers, it's a frequent point of attack. This combination of vulnerability and accessibility to attackers makes it a very common point of security failure.

But this doesn't need to be the case. Simple techniques and procedures can be used to drastically increase the security of IIS. In this chapter, I'll introduce you to IIS and provide some best practices for configuring IIS within your organization.

What Is IIS?

IIS is an integrated collection of services for publishing information on the Internet. IIS is capable of publishing information using any of four Internet-standard protocols:

HyperText Transport Protocol (HTTP)
   The protocol used to publish web pages on the World Wide Web.

File Transfer Protocol (FTP)
   An older but still important protocol used to transfer files between computers.

Simple Mail Transport Protocol (SMTP)
A protocol used for sending email messages across the Internet. IIS' email support is primarily intended to allow web developers to send email messages from web sites. Although IIS does have limited capabilities to receive incoming email, it does not contain the functionality that would make it suitable for use as an email server like Microsoft Exchange Server. The most significant concern around SMTP today is spam, or undesired email, which is beyond the scope of this book.

Network News Transport Protocol (NNTP)
The protocol used to exchange Internet newsgroup (also called Usenet) messages between clients and servers. As of this writing, few exploits and security concerns exist for NNTP.

IIS is administered through the Internet Services Manager, a snap-in to the Microsoft Management Console (MMC), as shown in Figure 12-1.

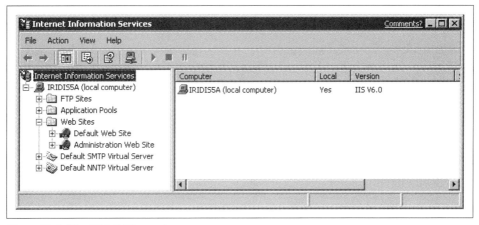

Figure 12-1. The IIS MMC snap-in

IIS is capable of supporting multiple virtual servers. For example, IIS can run three virtual web servers, functioning as three independent (though not physically separate) web servers. This capability makes IIS suitable for large-scale Internet publishing, as well as for smaller-scale needs like a corporate intranet. Figure 12-1 shows the IIS MMC snap-in with multiple virtual web sites.

IIS also contains advanced functionality designed to help web developers quickly create dynamic, interactive web applications. Other web servers require developers to use complicated programming techniques and a special web server interface called the Common Gateway Interface, or CGI. CGI program execution can be time-consuming, because it's not usually as processor efficient as ASP code. While IIS supports CGI applications, it also supports Active Server Pages (ASP), a proprietary Microsoft technology that allows IIS to run server-side scripts written in languages like VBScript or JScript. ASP applications are interpreted on the fly, eliminating a separate compilation step for developers.

The ASP object model also provides developers with enhanced features, such as session management, that make many complex web programming tasks much easier. ASP is a major security concern, primarily because it's so powerful. Improperly secured, IIS can allow attackers to insert their own ASP scripts into a web server and execute them, opening the possibility for an infinite number of attacks.

IIS also supports ASP.NET, Microsoft's completely rewritten version of ASP for the .NET framework. Like ASP, ASP.NET offers an incredible amount of power and flexibility for developers; likewise, it offers a wide array of security vulnerabilities. Fortunately, the .NET framework itself has built-in security features designed to prevent ASP.NET from being used against you. I'll cover those features later in this chapter.

Is IIS Really Secure Enough?

IIS has taken a lot of heat in recent years for its perceived lack of security. Other web server products, including Apache and Sun Java System Web Server (formerly SunOne or iPlanet Web Server), have been touted as significantly more secure than IIS. In some ways, that's true. After initial installation, Apache (for example) is significantly more secure than IIS 5.0 (included in Windows 2000). However, Apache also has significantly less functionality than IIS 5.0 "out of the box," so the comparison between the two isn't quite equal. Were administrators to lock down IIS 5.0 to the degree of functionality supported by a default Apache installation, the two products would measure up pretty much the same as far as security goes.

IIS 5.0's most significant design flaw was that it enabled all its features, such as ASP, in a default installation. This behavior required administrators to proactively disable the pieces of IIS they didn't plan to use, a step most administrators never bothered to take. Because administrators weren't fully aware of the security risk presented by IIS' advanced features, they never took steps to secure the system. Apache looks secure by comparison because it uses the exact opposite approach: its default installation is a minimally functional web server with relatively few security holes. Apache supports advanced functionality similar to ASP, but administrators have to take special steps to install and enable that functionality. In doing so, administrators acknowledge the risk of those features and take steps to secure them. As a result, more Apache installations than IIS installations are fully secured.

IIS 6.0, however, adopts a security philosophy much like Apache's. IIS 6.0 isn't included in a default Windows Server 2003 installation. When you do install IIS 6.0, it's much more locked down and less functional by default. You have to deliberately enable advanced features, making it inherently more secure and ensuring that you're fully aware of the security impact of your configuration choices.

Bear in mind that all web servers are limited by the inherently insecure nature of the Internet protocols they use. Neither HTTP, FTP, SMTP, nor NNTP were originally designed with security in mind. HTTP, the newest of the protocols, is still more than a decade old and was designed at a time when the Internet was very small (and not even called the Internet), and everyone using it knew everyone else. Security wasn't necessary. As long as web servers—including IIS—continue working with these old protocols, despite recent security add-ons to those protocols, web servers have a long way to go before they are *completely* secure.

How Does IIS Work?

IIS runs as a set of services on Windows Server 2003. Each service uses Windows Server 2003 Application Programming Interfaces (APIs) to interact with the operating system's TCP/IP protocol stack. Figure 12-2 illustrates the interaction between IIS and the TCP/IP stack.

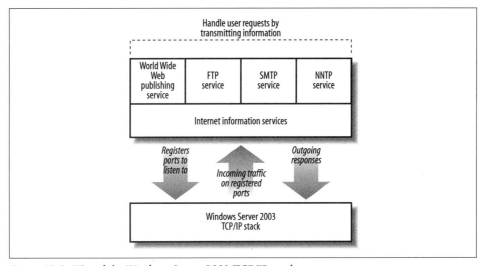

Figure 12-2. IIS and the Windows Server 2003 TCP/IP stack

As shown in Figure 12-2, each IIS service instructs the operating system to listen for incoming network traffic on specific TCP and UDP ports. These ports allow client applications to contact specific applications on a server. For example, web sites typically listen to TCP port 80, while FTP sites usually listen to TCP port 21.

When the TCP/IP stack receives incoming traffic on a port registered to an IIS service, the stack forwards that traffic to the appropriate service. The service can then analyze the traffic, take the appropriate actions, and if necessary, send a response back to the client that sent the request.

IIS Processing

Each IIS service processes incoming and outgoing traffic slightly differently. The FTP, SMTP, and NNTP services are all fairly straightforward, processing and responding to requests as defined in the appropriate Internet Engineering Task Force (IETF) Request for Comment (RFC) documents.

For ASP applications to work, IIS' World Wide Web (WWW) Publishing Service has to do a bit more work. When a user requests a specific web page, IIS loads the page from its location on the server's hard disk. Any pages with an *.asp* or *.aspx* file extension are preprocessed by the ASP DLL files. Other pages are often transmitted as-is to the requesting client.

 .asp files use the older ASP DLL files; *.aspx* files use the newer ASP.NET libraries to process the pages. A single server can process pages of both types, because it can use the filename extension to identify the correct processing libraries.

For an ASP page, IIS uses the ASP processing libraries to execute the script code within the page. The code is removed by the library and replaced with the results of the code, which can include HTML tags, text, graphics, and other elements. The resulting page is passed back to IIS and transmitted to the requesting client.

IIS Security

IIS is integrated with Windows Server 2003's native security. By default, IIS is configured to accept anonymous connections, delivering web pages to anyone who requests them. However, you can configure IIS to require authentication. If authentication is required, IIS will demand logon credentials when a user requests a web page that has restrictive file permissions. IIS will deliver only files that users have permission to access.

IIS supports four primary forms of authentication, as shown in Figure 12-3.

The four types of authentication include .NET Passport authentication, Windows-integrated authentication, Basic authentication, and Digest authentication. All of these authentication types will be discussed later in this chapter.

As shown in Figure 12-4, IIS security also allows you to restrict the computers that IIS will respond to. You can specify that IIS respond to only specific IP addresses or that it respond to all IP addresses *except* a specific list. This capability allows you to, for example, configure IIS to respond to known IP addresses of business partners but not to the general public.

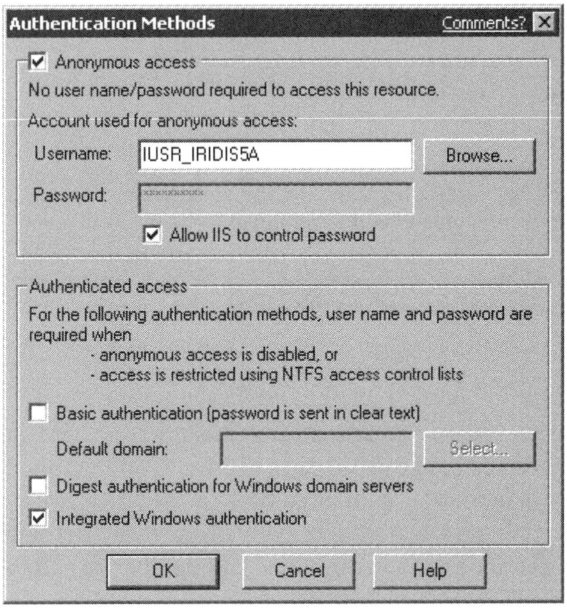

Figure 12-3. IIS authentication methods

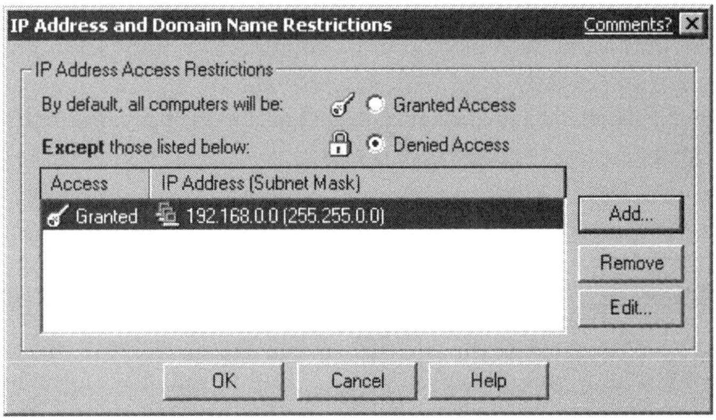

Figure 12-4. IIS IP address restrictions

Using IIS Securely

Network services, by their very nature, accept incoming network traffic and act upon it. Therefore, any network service presents a potential security risk, and a network service as complex and feature-rich as IIS presents a bigger risk, simply because administrators may not understand the security implications of IIS' capabilities. In the next several sections, I'll give you some tips for keeping IIS—and your servers in general—as secure as possible. These tips apply primarily to servers that are accessible to attackers or the general public; the majority of the servers on your network should be shielded by a firewall, preventing the public and potential attackers from accessing the servers in any way.

 You may not feel the need to secure intranet web servers as thoroughly as publicly exposed Internet web servers. After all, you trust your users, right? Don't! Disgruntled or even incompetent employees can cause plenty of damage, and never discount the possibility of your internal network being compromised. Secure *all* your web servers as thoroughly as possible, no matter how safe they may seem.

Installing IIS

IIS is not installed as part of a default Windows Server 2003 installation. That's because only a small percentage of Windows Server 2003 computers need to run IIS; leaving IIS out by default, you're assured that the security risk presented by IIS is present only on computers where you've explicitly installed the software. When IIS is installed, it is not installed with any optional components or services by default, and can serve only static HTML content to clients.

This is a drastic change from Windows 2000, which by default installed its version of IIS and made it active. Unfortunately, this default installation caused all Windows 2000 computers to be vulnerable to a wide variety of IIS-based attacks. Often only administrators who were aware of security vulnerability mitigation and companies that had policies on exactly what software should be running on each computer would remove IIS where it was not required. This is the principal reason that IIS is not installed by default in Windows Server 2003.

 If you upgraded to Windows Server 2003 from an older version of Windows, you most likely already have IIS installed with a hodgepodge of IIS services enabled. In that case, you need to clean up the existing installation. You should skip to "Configuring the Services You Need" and remove the services that aren't necessary. While Microsoft provides a tool, IISLockdown, to help with this, the tool is not as effective as your doing it yourself. I don't recommend you use IISLockdown on Windows Server 2003 for this reason.

When you're ready to install IIS on a server, just follow these steps:

1. From the Control Panel, open Add or Remove Programs.
2. Click on Add/Remove Windows Components.

3. Locate Application Server in the components list and select it. Note that IIS is installed as part of a group of application services rather than as a standalone component as in previous versions of Windows. Because you already know that you want only IIS, this is the only item you select here.

4. Click Details. You'll see the list of Application Server components, including IIS, as shown in Figure 12-5.

5. Select the IIS component. Note that the Enable Network COM+ Access component is automatically selected for you; this component is required to run IIS.

6. Click OK, and then Next. Windows Server 2003 will install the components you selected.

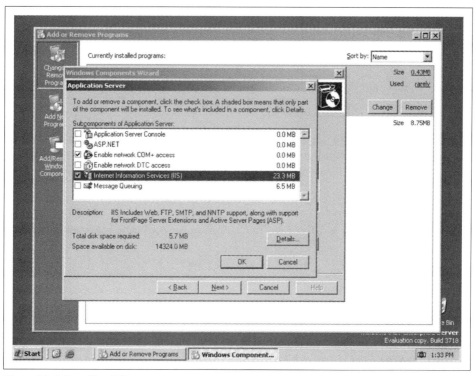

Figure 12-5. Installing IIS

 Don't leave IIS in its default configuration unless you know that's what your organization needs. In fact, you shouldn't even install IIS if you don't know this. In the next few sections, I'll cover the steps to configure IIS. Remember, even though IIS 6.0's default configuration is much more secure, you should always review that configuration to make sure it meets both your business and security requirements.

Configuring the Services You Need

As I've already described, IIS includes a number of different services, including HTTP, NNTP, SMTP, and more. By default, IIS is installed with a single web site, using the HTTP protocol. This is a change from the previous version of IIS, in which FTP and other services were also enabled by default. Figure 12-6 shows the IIS Manager console with the Default Web Site enabled.

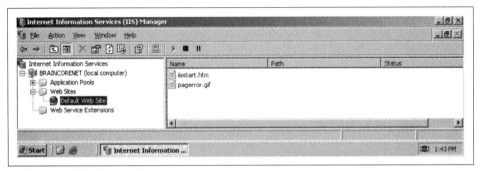

Figure 12-6. The IIS Manager console

Notice, too, that IIS does not configure an administrative web site by default, as previous versions did. IIS' default configuration is designed to provide the minimum functionality necessary for a web server, while preserving as secure a system configuration as possible.

If you want to set up an FTP site or some other IIS service, you'll need to go back into the Control Panel and the Add/Remove Windows Components section. Then follow these steps:

1. Select Application Server and click Details.

2. Select IIS and click Details.

3. As shown in Figure 12-7, select the IIS services that you want to enable. When you installed IIS, only the default services—a set of common files, the IIS Manager console, and the World Wide Web Service—were installed. You can also add other services, such as FTP, BITS, or NNTP, if you wish. Make sure you add only services that you know you need and are part of your written IIS installation procedure (written procedures are described in).

> Don't install any services unless you are going to use them and you have planned defenses around adding them. Planning systemwide defenses is discussed later in this chapter.

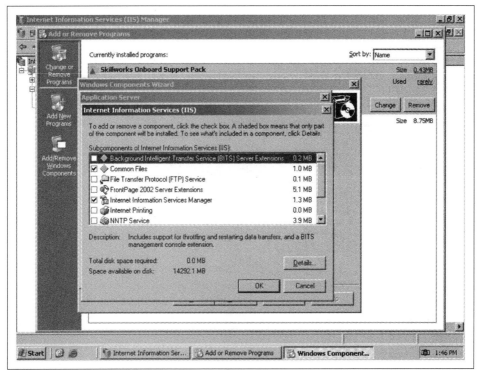

Figure 12-7. Optional IIS components

Even the World Wide Web Service itself has additional components, which you can access by selecting the service and clicking Details. These additional components include ASP, a remote administration web site, WebDAV capabilities, and more. Figure 12-8 shows the components list.

Again, install these components only if you've determined that they're needed in your environment and only if you've researched and understand the security risks. For example:

- ASP is an often-attacked component. While it provides great capabilities to a web developer, developers must also take steps to make sure their code can't be compromised by attackers. Those precautions aren't ones that you as an administrator can easily evaluate; simply ensure that your developers are aware of the risks ASP presents and have taken steps to protect their code from attack.

- Server Side Includes allows IIS to nest web files within one another. This could also allow an attacker to place files on your web server and include them in legitimate files that you've placed there, effectively hijacking your web pages. Carefully thought-out NTFS file permissions can prevent this from happening.

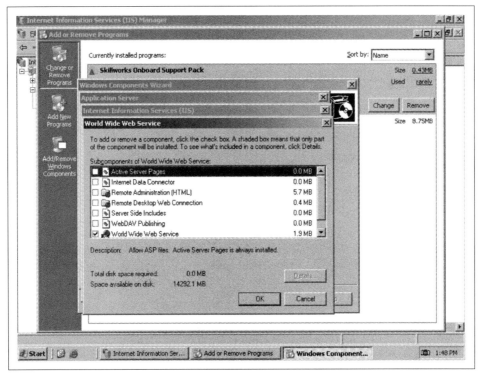

Figure 12-8. Optional World Wide Web Service components

- WebDAV is a publishing service that allows remote users to add and modify files on a web site. Take great care that the WebDAV service permits connections only from authorized users and that attackers will not be able to use the service to upload unauthorized web pages.

Each component shown in Figure 12-8 has its own benefits and security risks. Many of these risks and benefits can be better understood by an experienced web developer, and you should always consult with a developer to help deploy these components in a safe, secure fashion.

Using Secure Sockets Layer

You are probably already familiar with Secure Sockets Layer (SSL). It shows up as that little lock icon (or in the case of Netscape, the unbroken key) and indicates that the server is authentic. It also normally indicates that a secure channel exists between the client and the server and that the data exchanged between them is protected from eavesdroppers. Because this is such a powerful mitigation against different attacks, I'll show you how to set it up with IIS.

Setting up SSL is very simple. You must first obtain a web server certificate and associated private key that chains to a root trusted by the client computers. Chapter 9 went into great depth on this particular topic, so I won't repeat those instructions here. You must load the certificate and private key on the web server by using a wizard. It's this simple:

1. You should already have an appropriate web server certificate and private key, either from a trusted third party or from your own internal PKI.

2. Click Start → All Programs → Administrative Tools → Internet Information Services (IIS) Manager.

3. Right-click the desired web site and select Properties.

4. Click the Directory Security tab, and then click the Server Certificate button.

5. Follow the prompts in the wizard.

Once that's done, IIS automatically finds the certificate and begins using it for SSL traffic on this web site.

Is that it? Well, almost. Most administrators say that they want to require only SSL for sites or entire IIS farms. This isn't normally a good user experience. Allowing only SSL traffic causes normal connections to the server to fail with an ugly IIS error. The better experience is to have a web page that checks the connection state and, if a non-SSL connection is detected, redirects to the HTTPS:// equivalent of the page. This small amount of code should be implemented on all web pages to ensure consistency across the site.

Unencrypted HTTP traffic normally uses port 80. SSL must use a different port. This is normally port 443 but can be any port (they both can). This is important to note when you configure the firewall between your IIS server and the clients and also when configuring port blocking, which is covered later in this chapter. You must allow the SSL port to pass through the firewall. To configure the ports, see "Using Port Numbers" and Figure 12-10, later in this chapter.

Using IP Address Restrictions

One great way to secure internal web servers is to use IP address restrictions. These restrictions tell IIS to accept connections from only specific domain names, computers, or groups of computers, based upon IP address. For an internal server, for example, you might configure IIS to accept connections from only internal IP addresses, ensuring that outsiders—even ones that somehow compromise your firewall—won't be able to easily access IIS.

These restrictions are configured on a per-site basis, as follows:

1. Right-click the site in the IIS Manager console, and select Properties.

2. On the Directory Security tab, click the button to edit IP address restrictions.

3. As shown in Figure 12-9, you can have IIS allow or deny access to all IP addresses by default, and then include a list of exceptions to the default rule. In the example shown, IIS will reject all connections not coming from the internal IP address range shown. Since this address range is a designated private IP range, you can be assured that no Internet-based computers are using it.

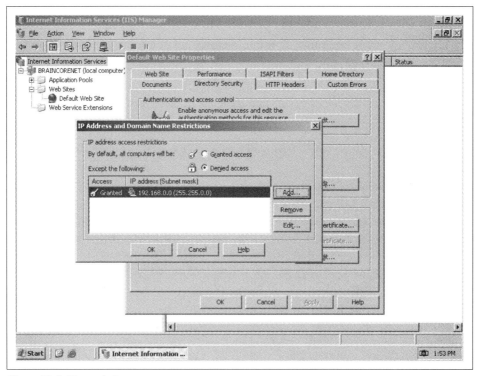

Figure 12-9. IP restrictions

 If an intruder compromises your firewall, he may seem to be using the firewall's internal IP addresses. If IIS should be accessible to only internal users, then you might exclude the firewall's internal IP addresses from the list of allowed addresses. Doing so will help keep all external users out of IIS, no matter how they get into your network.

Using Port Numbers

Web sites typically use TCP port 80 for connections, since that's the default port used by the HTTP protocol. If you have web sites that shouldn't be accessible to the general public, you can "hide" the sites by using a nonstandard port number. Simply provide the correct port number to authorized users, and instruct them to use a different URL to access the web site. For example, suppose you configure a web site on a server named *www.woodgrovebank.com* and assign the web site to use port 85.

Users could access the site only by using the URL *http://www.woodgrovebank.com: 85*.

To configure a web site to use an alternate port number, follow these steps:

1. Right-click the site in the IIS Manager console, and select Properties.
2. On the Web Site tab, provide the desired port number, as shown in Figure 12-10.

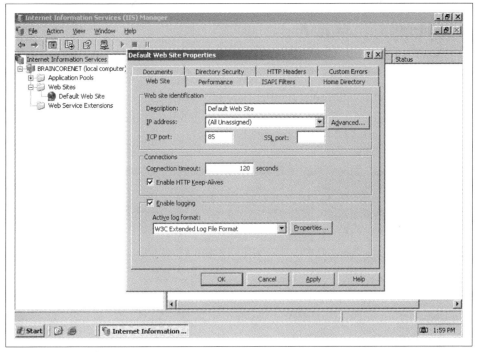

Figure 12-10. Changing a web site's network port

 Be careful not to use port numbers that another service is using. For example, the FTP Service uses port 21 by default, so you can't configure a web site to use the same port number. Doing so will result in both the web and FTP sites working erratically. For a list of standard protocols and associated ports see the following file: *%SystemRoot%\ system32\drivers\etc\services*.

Don't rely on nonstandard port numbers to protect a web site, though. While useful as a means of deterring casual snoopers, sophisticated attackers can use *port scanners* to find your "hidden" sites. A port scanner attempts to connect to all possible ports, or a range of ports, looking for ports on which the attacked computer responds. When the scanner finds such a port, it logs it, allowing the attacker to focus on that port for more specific attacks.

Using File Permissions

You should always use NTFS file permissions to secure web pages that you care about. This is especially true for web pages that shouldn't be generally accessible, as it provides another layer of protection against attackers. When a user requests a web page, IIS checks the NTFS permissions on the page and will deliver the page to the user only if the user is on the file's access control list. If necessary, IIS will ask the user to provide credentials proving she should have access to the file.

Configuring Authentication

IIS supports four different means of authenticating users, which you can adjust as follows:

1. In the IIS Manager console, right-click a web site and select Properties.

2. Click the Directory Security tab and edit the authentication and access control methods. Figure 12-11 shows the dialog box.

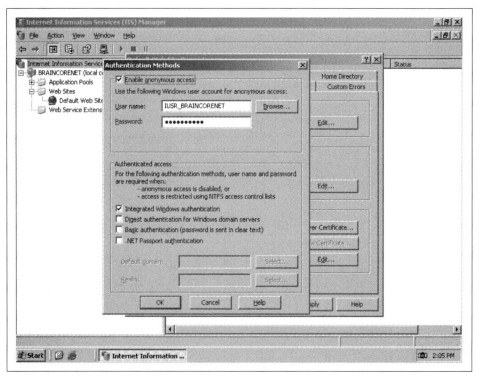

Figure 12-11. IIS authentication

IIS' authentication methods are:

Integrated Windows authentication
Allows users to log on with a server or domain username and password. Users logged onto a domain will have their domain credentials automatically presented to IIS, if necessary. Note that this method works only when users are using Internet Explorer as their web browser.

Digest authentication
Similar to Basic authentication but is compatible with a wider range of web browsers and somewhat more secure. Credentials are protected during transmission, which helps prevent against eavesdroppers learning a user's password.

Basic authentication
Simply sends the user's credentials in clear text. Never select this option unless the web site is already secured by an SSL connection. Clear-text credentials can be easily captured while in transit and used for unauthorized access at a later time.

.NET Passport authentication
Uses Microsoft's .NET Passport system to authenticate users. This method requires a bit of extra setup and may require fees to use the Passport service; see the IIS documentation for details.

 By default, IIS enables anonymous access to web pages. Users will be authenticated only if an authentication method is selected and either anonymous access is disabled or users attempt to access a file that is secured with NTFS file permissions.

Of special note for setting file permissions are two user accounts. They are:

IUSR_computername
When an anonymous connection is made to IIS and no authentication is possible or configured, the connection must still have some user context for access control to work properly. IIS assigns all anonymous connections the same access that the IUSR_computername account (the IUSR account) has. That is, all connections to the IIS server have the same access to resources as the IUSR_computername account.

IWAM_computername
This account is used by IIS as another security context. Specifically, when IIS must launch another process, it launches that process in the IWAM_computername account (the IWAM account) context.

When you plan your file and directory access for IIS files, you must consider whether the IUSR and IWAM accounts need access. In many cases involving anonymous-accessible web sites, the IUSR account must have at least Read access to the files that make up the web site.

Allow Only Needed Functionality

By default, IIS disables most of its advanced functionality. These features are typically enabled through Web Service Extensions, and managed through the IIS Manager console, as shown in Figure 12-12.

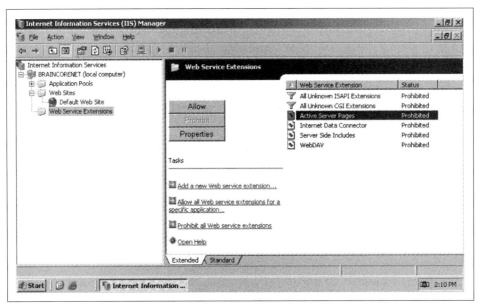

Figure 12-12. Web Service Extensions

As shown, IIS by default disables all unknown ISAPI and CGI extensions, ASP, the Internet Data Connector, Server Side Includes, and WebDAV. You can click the appropriate button to allow or prohibit any service extension, or click the provided links to add new extensions.

 Never allow unknown ISAPI or CGI extensions. Doing so could allow an attacker to place an unauthorized extension on your system and execute it, doing who knows what kind of damage to your network. By allowing only specific extensions, you can control what vulnerabilities your system is open to.

Review Web Server Logs

Your web server log files can provide valuable clues when an attacker is attempting to compromise the server. Unfortunately, these log files can be long and difficult to read, especially on complex, busy web sites. I recommend using a third-party log scanning tool, such as WebTrends (*www.webtrends.com*), which can provide site statistics as well as scan for potential security problems.

Without some type of log analysis tool that can review the logs in a reasonable amount of time, the logs are not effective in identifying and helping mitigate attacks. The amount and complexity of information saved in the logs is simply too much for an administrator to sit down and sort through manually. The logs do still have some value for proving an attack occurred or learning about attack patterns, but for any type of IDS, you need an automated system.

 Many firewall products can serve in this same capacity to analyze patterns in real time and notify you when something bad is happening. Of course, your IIS server should always be behind a firewall.

All IIS web sites create log files by default. These are saved in *%SystemRoot%\System32\LogFiles*, under a subfolder for each specific web site. However, you can change where your log files are saved. To do so:

1. Right-click the web site and select Properties.

2. On the Web Site tab, click Properties.

3. As shown in Figure 12-13, modify the log properties to save to the desired location. You can also control how often IIS will start a new log file: Hourly, Daily, Weekly, and so forth.

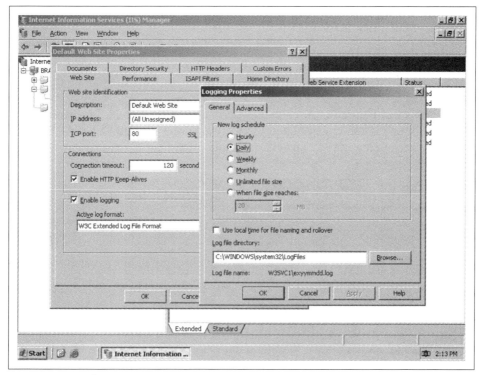

Figure 12-13. IIS log options

Log files can also provide valuable forensic evidence in the event an attack is detected. Forensic analysis is often carried out over weeks or months, so the real-time analysis tool isn't critical to that process. You should archive and save your log files for however long your organization's written security policies require. For more information on implementing log preservation, see the Event Log topic in the Windows Server 2003 Technical Reference (formerly the Resource Kit) at *http://www. microsoft.com/resources/documentation/WindowsServ/2003/all/techref/enus/W2K3TR_ sepol_event_set.asp*.

Using Port Filtering

Windows Server 2003 includes TCP/IP port filtering capabilities. You can use port filtering on a web server to ensure that only web server traffic is received by the server. This helps close the holes opened by any other services or applications that might be running on the server by preventing any traffic from reaching them.

 As you saw in Chapter 8, IPSec can also be used as a port restriction mechanism. Although it may seem redundant and increase management overhead, using both methods helps ensure the most consistent and effective port restrictions possible. Multiple layers of security like this provide for defense in depth, which was discussed in Chapter 2.

To configure port filtering:

1. Modify the TCP/IP properties of any installed network adapter.

2. Click Advanced.

3. On the Options tab, click Properties.

4. As shown in Figure 12-14, configure port filtering as desired. In this example, port filtering is configured to accept TCP traffic only on ports 80 and 443, most commonly used for HTTP and HTTPS traffic.

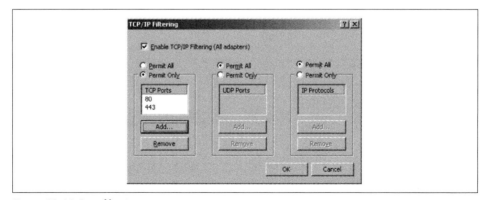

Figure 12-14. Port filtering

Port filtering does have some significant caveats:

- Filtering is effective for all installed adapters, not just the adapter on which you configure it.
- Filtering can prevent key operating system services from functioning. For example, if the configuration shown in Figure 12-14 were applied to a domain controller, the domain controller would be nonfunctional except as a basic web server, because the ports necessary for domain controller and Active Directory communications aren't allowed.

Port filtering is best used on standalone servers that don't belong to a domain and don't do anything except provide a limited set of network services, such as a web site or FTP site. This limited set makes it easy to determine the ports necessary for the server to function. In a domain environment, you can use IPSec instead of, or as a redundant complement to, port filtering.

Blocking ports can provide greatly increased security, but at a cost. You may no longer be able to use remote management tools, access file shares, and so forth if you restrict the system's network communication. You should ensure that port filtering is planned properly to allow for all approved network functionality based on the computer's role.

It's important to note that port filtering and IPSec restrictions should not take the place of a firewall solution. Your IIS servers should always be separated from the Internet by a dedicated stateful inspection firewall that ensures the traffic that passes to your IIS server is appropriate. Microsoft Internet Security and Acceleration Server (ISA) is one such firewall, but many are available. The firewall you choose should inspect all contents of each packet to ensure that the data is appropriate. This helps stop attacks such as malformed URLs and content bombs from even reaching the IIS server.

Dedicating IIS Servers

Avoid running a publicly accessible IIS site on a server that performs other functions. Some server products require IIS in order to operate, but that doesn't mean IIS also needs to host a public web site. Let the server product use IIS, but configure port filters to prevent the public from accessing the IIS server at all, if possible. In addition, you should remove all web content and services that are not required for the product to operate. The less exposure the web server presents, the less likely it is to become a victim of a virus or Internet-based attack.

Specialized Administration: Good or Bad?

Specialized administration isn't always a benefit. Everyone has read about or experienced web-based attacks that affect IIS. The severity and impact of these attacks varies greatly from organization to organization. However, the attacks had their greatest impact in poorly managed environments. One such environment is City Power & Light (CP&L). As usual, I've changed the name to protect the innocent.

CP&L is a large corporation with a deep reliance on technology. Like most companies of this nature, it has a large IT group in which most administrators specialize in their own technology. This allows CP&L to employ gurus in various technologies such as IIS, Active Directory, and security. While specialization is a benefit to the deep technical knowledge required by CP&L, it often leads to isolation between technologies and results in environments that are well configured for one task—and poorly configured for others.

When the PKI was created at CP&L, the PKI guru was careful. He planned out the hierarchy well in advance and took every precaution he could think of. He applied Group Policy to restrict access, required biometric authentication, and used an HSM for key storage on his root CA. However, this guru was unfamiliar with the other services on the CA. He installed IIS because he was informed that web-based enrollment worked only if IIS were installed. He never configured IIS further than necessary to ensure that clients could enroll for certificates on the CA. Because the PKI guru was unfamiliar with IIS, he was simply unaware that the IIS guru should be involved so that they could work together to secure the computer.

The results of this story are predictable. The CA was attacked by a worm that affects poorly configured IIS installations. This worm destroyed the CA database and ran rampant throughout the PKI, destroying every CA except the offline root. The computers had to be completely restored from an outdated backup and manually secured before they could be brought back online. The cost to CP&L was enormous and resulted in significant downtime for the PKI, which was unable to issue CRLs, issue new certificates, or renew existing certificates for several days.

All because one guru didn't confer with another.

Summary

In this chapter, I introduced you to IIS, Windows Server 2003's integrated Internet publishing system. You learned how IIS, like any network-centric service, presents a potential security risk on your network and how to minimize those risks while maintaining the benefit of IIS' capabilities and features. You learned how IIS integrates with Windows Server 2003's own security and how Windows Server 2003 provides a minimal default set of IIS features to help minimize security risks.

CHAPTER 13

Active Directory Security

One area that is sometimes overlooked with regard to security is Active Directory. Active Directory is the center of your IT infrastructure, but many administrators forget to lock it down and take advantage of the built-in security features that it offers. Some administrators feel that it is secure after a default installation or after an upgrade, but this is not the case. Active Directory needs special attention to ensure that it has been properly configured to secure access for creating, modifying, or even reading the contents of the directory.

Don't let me scare you into unplugging your domain controllers as you read this. Rather, understand that there are small, but sometimes significant, changes that you need to make to ensure that your Active Directory infrastructure is secure. You will need to consider security starting at the domain controllers themselves, all the way to the entire forest, and including everything in between, such as domains, organizational units, and objects such as user, computer, and group accounts.

Active Directory security can be very deceptive. Take, for example, an upgrade from a Windows NT 4.0 domain controller to a Windows Server 2003 domain controller. The steps are easy, right? Insert the Windows Server 2003 media and follow the wizard as it takes your Windows NT domain controller and transforms it to a Windows Server 2003 domain controller. The process is quite amazing if you think about it. But if you think about the amazing part only, you might miss the security implications that jeopardize the security of your new domain controller.

In this chapter, I explain how to successfully secure your Active Directory deployment. I will explain how the Microsoft security technologies work and how to configure the domain, forest, and domain controllers to protect the directory database. It is true that anyone can install Active Directory, but I have found that only a few know how to secure it properly.

What Is Active Directory?

Active Directory is the directory database used by Windows Server 2003 to control the collection of user, group, and computer accounts used for authentication and authorization. Active Directory centralizes the administrative task of creating, modifying, removing, troubleshooting, and securing all accounts in the IT infrastructure.

Active Directory consists mainly of domain controllers, member servers, client computers, user accounts, and group accounts. Some objects represent physical objects, such as a computer account representing a person's laptop, while other objects represent logical entities, such as groups, which help administrators control access to resources throughout the IT infrastructure.

The chief purpose of Active Directory is to provide centralized administration and access control over accounts and other objects, plus ultimate control over your desktops with the use of Group Policy.

Benefits of Active Directory

With so many companies moving to Active Directory over the past four years, there must be compelling and overwhelming reasons for the mass migration. There are indeed, especially if you are coming from a Windows NT environment. Next, I'll describe some of the most compelling reasons to move to Active Directory in case you haven't already.

Extensible database

A Windows NT domain is not very elaborate and is very static. The Security Accounts Manager (SAM) offers no options to add additional information to user, group, or computer accounts. The only real option is to use Exchange 5.5 to extend the information that we associate with user accounts. Active Directory fixes this by giving the administrator the flexibility to add custom properties (or as they are more properly referred to, *attributes*) to almost any object that is stored in the Active Directory.

Active Directory user accounts have dozens of attributes ranging from employee ID to fax number. These new attributes are added to the schema and then populated by using Active Directory Services Interface (ADSI) or a Lightweight Directory Access Protocol (LDAP) interface. With some of the new attributes that are added, such as social security number, you will need to ensure that these attributes are secured. This can be accomplished by using the built-in security that is associated with Active Directory. Each Active Directory object has its own access control list (ACL), which controls who has permission to modify or read the object.

Multimaster domain

The multimaster domain concept is a radical new approach for a Microsoft directory service. With Windows NT domains, you were limited to having only a single computer in the domain on which administrators could perform updates to objects. This computer is called the primary domain controller (PDC) in the Windows NT domain. The biggest problem with this was that if the PDC was offline, or unavailable due to network problems, you could not update the database.

Active Directory eliminates this problem by allowing an administrator to add, modify, or delete objects on any domain controller in a domain. Therefore, as long as there is at least one domain controller online, updates can be made to the database. On the backend of the multimaster domain model is a new replication technology that can reconcile multiple changes to a single object from different sources by accepting only the latest change. When you boil it down, the last domain controller to make a change to an object wins.

Object support

Windows NT by default could support only a very limited number of objects; somewhere around 20,000 user, computer, and group accounts. For many organizations, this 20,000-object limit was reached quickly, forcing administrators to take the chance of modifying the registry size for the domain or to create additional domains just to accommodate the number of objects.

With Active Directory, the number of objects that is supported is in the millions, which should accommodate almost any company. There have been tests that have taken the number of objects in Active Directory to nearly a billion. Granted, there will be some overall performance degradation with this many objects, but the possibility exists.

Software deployment with GPOs

Most companies have hundreds of applications that they must support throughout the organization, so ideally they need a simple and efficient method to deploy software. Active Directory, in conjunction with Group Policy Objects (GPOs), provides that solution. By using GPOs, you can target software to specific user or computer accounts. What this means is that you can ensure that all users in the marketing department have the special marketing software package, without having to manually install that software on each computer.

From a security or management standpoint, since the software is deployed using GPOs, only the user or computer accounts that are targeted by the GPO will be able to use the software application. This ensures that you not only meet the software licensing agreements but also control which users have access to potentially dangerous software or to software that is used to access private and confidential data for the company. Group Policy was covered in more depth in Chapter 5.

Security Benefits of Active Directory

Beyond the directory service and administration benefits that Active Directory provides are some security benefits that have persuaded many companies to make the move to Active Directory. However, like almost anything else that is security related, you really have to know how to use the security features to take greatest advantage of them after Active Directory is installed. In other situations, a security feature might require specific operating systems, which may prevent other legacy operating systems from running properly.

Kerberos

Kerberos was first introduced for a Microsoft domain with Windows 2000 Active Directory. Having Kerberos as the authentication protocol for your domain provides better security than its predecessor, NTLM. Here are the main benefits that Kerberos provides for Active Directory:

Efficient authentication to member servers
> Because the client computer receives information from the domain controller when it initially logs on and by subsequent touches to the domain controller, the member servers that the client is communicating with do not need to connect to a domain controller to authenticate each client. The member server will rely on the credentials that the client computer initially obtains from the domain controller for accessing the resources located on the server. The client computer needs to obtain credentials for a particular server only one time, and then it can reuse these credentials for the duration of the logon session.

Mutual authentication
> The Kerberos protocol process is responsible for ensuring that the client computer is who it says it is and the server is who it says it is. This provides a much more secure environment than NTLM authentication, which did not provide any mechanism for client computers to verify a server's identity. This promotes a more secure environment and reduces the possibility of someone pretending to be a server in the domain.

Delegated authentication
> Kerberos has a built-in proxy option that will allow a client to pose as a user identity when connecting to certain network services. This allows a frontend service to connect to a backend service with a client impersonation. Both Kerberos and NTLM provide this option when they are impersonating the client locally, but only Kerberos provides this option for services that reside on different computers.

Interoperability

Now that Microsoft supports industry standards for name resolution (DNS), directory structure (LDAP), and authentication (Kerberos), interoperability with other platforms and devices is more easily achieved.

Trusts

Kerberos is the foundation for the trust model in an Active Directory forest. For those of you who are coming from a complex array of Windows NT domains that needed to trust one another, this is wonderful news. The old Windows NT trusts are:

Manual

Any trust created between Windows NT domains is manual. This means that the trust must be established by the administrator. During the creation of the trust, both domain names need to be known, and a trust password is established to verify the trust. The password is not needed after the initial creation of the trust.

One-way

The trust allows traffic to flow in only one direction for resource access. For example, if DomainA trusts DomainB, then the user accounts in DomainB could be given permission to access the resources in DomainA. However, the user accounts in DomainA could not be given permission to access the resources in DomainB, unless another trust was established from DomainB to DomainA.

Nontransitive

A transitive trust allows a common domain to span two nonadjacent domains. Figure 13-1 illustrates nontransitive trusts: DomainA trusts DomainB and DomainB trusts DomainC. If the trusts were transitive, DomainA would also trust DomainC. Windows NT trusts are nontransitive. This means that the only way that DomainA would trust DomainC is to create another explicit trust between DomainA and DomainC.

Figure 13-1. Nontransitive trusts

NTLM authenticated

The trusts used by Windows NT use NTLM authentication, which is proprietary to Microsoft and reduces the interoperability needed to communicate effectively with other operating systems. Any external trust that goes from a Windows Active Directory domain to any domain (Windows NT, Windows 2000, or Windows Server 2003) outside of the forest will use NTLM trusts.

Active Directory domains break almost every rule that the Windows NT domain trust exhibited. The trusts internal to the forest that are inherent to Active Directory domains are:

Automatic

When a domain is introduced into an Active Directory forest, it is placed in the hierarchy of the namespace. This placement also produces a trust relationship. If the domain is a child domain to an existing domain, the child domain has an automatic trust established with the parent domain. If the domain is the first domain in a new tree of domains, then the domain automatically has a trust relationship with the adjacent domain at the top of the next tree in the forest.

Two-way

To reduce the administrative overhead and logical connections required to maintain one-way trusts, Active Directory implements two-way trusts. These trusts allow users in both domains that are involved in the trust to have the ability to be given permission to access resources in the other domain. This in no way compromises any security; it only provides an easy solution for administrators to have an option to give users access to resources if they need to.

Transitive

All trusts within an Active Directory forest are transitive. This produces an environment that allows all users the ability to gain access resources in every domain in the entire forest. This feature reduces the number of trusts needed, as well as reduces the administration requirements to create, maintain, and troubleshoot nontransitive trusts.

Kerberos authenticated

Kerberos is the driving force behind the other benefits of the Active Directory trusts. Because Kerberos provides the mutual authentication, the trusts can be two-way and transitive.

Smart card support

Active Directory, Windows 2000, Windows XP Professional, and Windows Server 2003 all support smart card authentication. When a smart card reader is installed on a computer, a new graphical identification and authentication (GINA) will be presented to the user, allowing for the PIN to be input after the smart card is inserted into the reader. I covered smart card technology in depth in Chapter 10.

Group Policy Objects

It is impossible to talk about providing security for Active Directory without a lengthy discussion on Group Policy Objects (GPOs). There are two default GPOs in every domain. These GPOs always configure the same settings by default. This provides an administrator with a starting point for additional settings in these GPOs, as well as the foundation to create additional GPOs, if necessary. The two default GPOs are:

Default Domain Policy
> This GPO is linked to the domain and is responsible for establishing the Account Policies for domain user accounts. This GPO is unique in that it is the only location in which you can configure account policies for domain users.

Default Domain Controller Policy
> This GPO is linked to the only OU in a freshly installed domain, the Domain Controllers OU. This GPO applies only to domain controllers and is designed to configure the user rights for the domain controllers. This provides the base security of *who* can do *what* on a domain controller.

GPOs are so integral to the security of the Active Directory and computers on the network that Chapter 5 is dedicated to them. It should provide an in-depth understanding of what a GPO is and what GPOs can do in your Active Directory domain.

Delegation

The lack of delegation options has frustrated more than one domain administrator during the Windows NT era. The ability to give users just a few privileges has never been a viable built-in option before Active Directory. With groups that provide widespread capabilities over the entire directory, it was almost impossible to implement delegation in a Windows NT domain. Groups such as Account Operators and Server Operators gave too many privileges for the accounts and servers over which they had reign.

With Active Directory delegation (or delegation of administration as it is sometimes called), the administrators responsible for Active Directory have the capabilities to provide almost any degree of granular delegation they desire. This is accomplished by configuring security permissions on objects within Active Directory in such a way that only a few user accounts have the privilege to control a limited set of options for the objects.

For example, assume that you are the domain administrator for an Active Directory domain. The marketing department is constantly working on new projects, which require different employees from that department to be moved from group to group. These groups are used to assign permissions to access the resources for the new projects. However, when these new projects are developed, you are asked to create and configure the members of these groups. It is always the marketing director who walks you through who should be in what group, as well as the group structure itself. What you would like to do is remove your role from the creation, modification, and deletion of groups for the marketing department projects. Of course, you don't want the "standard marketing groups" to be controlled by the marketing director, but these special project groups are an ideal opportunity for your control to be delegated to the director. The standard marketing groups are used by the administrative staff to control access to network resources both in the marketing group, as well as for the entire company. For the solution to this problem, you can give the marketing director delegated permission to control just the groups for the marketing projects but not the standard marketing groups. This delegated privilege can include creation, modification, and deletion of these groups, and you can always remove some of the delegated privilege if the director can't seem to control creation or deletion of the groups. If that happens, you can restrict the director to modifying the group membership, which still removes much of the administrative burden from your plate.

This is just one example of delegation. Delegation can include control over user accounts, group accounts, computer accounts, GPOs, organizational units, and more. Delegation is a very powerful feature of Active Directory, and planning for its design is essential to a secure implementation. I will go further into delegation later in this chapter.

Structural Components of Active Directory

You must understand how Active Directory is put together to make good security decisions. Five key structural components make up Active Directory. Each component has a distinct function and security considerations that follow. To understand how each component fits into the overall scheme of Active Directory, you must first understand the details about each component. Then we can start to put the different components together with regard to functionality and security. The key components include domain, tree, forest, organizational unit, and site.

As you read through each structural component description, consider that domains, trees, forest, and sites are not only integral with Active Directory but also integral with DNS. Active Directory relies on DNS to ensure that the information stored in the DNS database is reliable and secured. If DNS is compromised or becomes unstable, aspects such as name resolution, domain controller location, Kerberos, and GPOs would fail. This will leave the IT infrastructure vulnerable and in a state of weakened security.

Domains

The domain is foundational for Active Directory. In all versions of Windows, the domain is the key administrative component that most administrators deal with day in and day out. To understand domains, we need to investigate what a domain is and what a domain is not. If we look at the configuration options required during setup of a domain, we can understand much of what is included in the domain. First off, you are required to give a domain a name. With Active Directory, there are two names for every domain:

NetBIOS domain name

This is the downlevel domain name used to communicate with client computers and applications that don't use DNS to find domain services, such as domain controllers, but instead use NetBIOS. Operating systems that rely on the NetBIOS domain name include Windows 95, 98, and NT.

DNS domain name

The DNS domain name is used throughout the administration tools, as well as by client computers during authentication. Only clients that support Kerberos can use the DNS domain name when they authenticate to Active Directory. Operating systems that rely on the DNS domain name include Windows 2000, XP, Server 2003, and earlier Windows operating systems running DSCLIENT.

Next, the domain is a policy and replication boundary for Active Directory. When we get to the forest definition, we will see how the forest provides a security boundary, but the domain does provide a replication boundary for policy-based security settings, including Account Policy, Group Policy Objects, and replication.

Account Policy

The Account Policy for domain users is established at the domain level. The Account Policy for the domain level includes control over passwords, account lockout, and Kerberos authentication. This means that domain user accounts cannot be controlled at the organizational unit level; they must be controlled at the domain level. Also, the Account Policy is not inherited from the parent domain, if we are focusing in on a child domain. There is no possible way to get a parent domain to push down Account Policies to child domains.

Group Policy Objects

GPOs are the main form of pushing out security to computers in the domain. However, GPOs that are configured within a domain do not and cannot span multiple domains by inheritance or hierarchy. The GPOs can be available to other domains, but there is no option to configure GPOs to span domains with a single configuration.

Replication boundary for the domain naming context

Active Directory's database is split into four main contexts: domain naming, configuration, schema, and application directory. The domain naming context is responsible for user accounts, group accounts, and computer accounts. When domain controllers replicate to exchange and synchronize the changes from other domain controllers, the domain naming context is synchronized with only domain controllers in the same domain. This provides security in that user accounts that are configured in one domain don't have access to resources in other domains until an administrator configures that access. The Application Directory Partition is new for Windows Server 2003 domain controllers and can be used to handle dynamic data. Most Active Directory installations that use this partition use it to store DNS information.

Trees

The concept of an Active Directory tree is tied to DNS namespace. When you bring a new domain into an existing Active Directory forest, you are forced to indicate where the new domain name will be located in comparison to the other domain names that are in Active Directory. You can either locate the new domain name under an existing domain name, making it a child domain, or you can place the new domain name adjacent to the first domain name you created (forest root domain). Figure 13-2 illustrates both of these options.

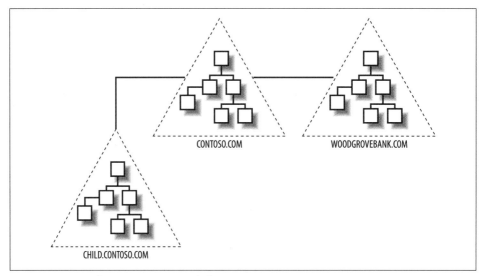

Figure 13-2. Two domain trees in a single forest

The main item to notice in the representation of an Active Directory tree is the contiguous namespace. Figure 13-2 shows two trees. One tree has the namespace contoso.com, and the other tree has the namespace woodgrovebank.com. You can see that the child domain to contoso.com shares the same DNS extension as the parent. From a security standpoint, there is really no difference between having a child domain or a domain that starts a new tree, as woodgrovebank.com does. So, in essence, the definition of an Active Directory tree is contiguous namespace, that is all!

To reiterate the point from our discussion about domains, the domain administrators in the contoso.com domain would not have any administrative capabilities in the child.contoso.com domain nor the woodgrovebank.com domain.

What all the domains do have in common is connected access by the automatic, two-way, transitive trusts that are created by being installed into the same forest. These trust relationships provide a means for administrators to allow users from other domains to access resources in their domain. The key to remember is that the access for users is not available by default; it must be granted by the administrator of the resource first.

Forests

A forest contains at least one Active Directory tree. The forest structure is also determined at the installation of the first domain controller for a new domain. When the domain controller is configured, the wizard will ask if you want to have a new forest of domains, and you will respond with a yes. At this time, you have made a distinct decision to disjoin the new domain from the other domains in almost every way. Without good documentation or a tool that can graphically represent the forest structure, you will have a difficult time determining where a forest ends and where the next forest begins. Figure 13-3 illustrates graphically what multiple forests would look like.

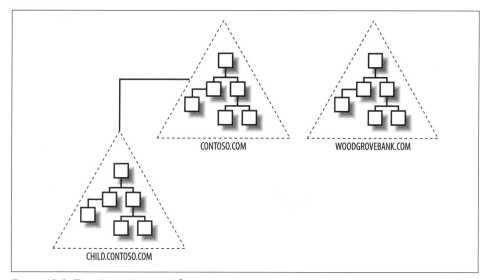

Figure 13-3. Two Active Directory forests

It is very important to note that there is no trust relationship between the two forests in the figure. This is the true separation of domains in different forests. If there is no trust between domains in different forests, it is clear that the users in one forest don't have access to resources in the other forest. For many companies, this is the driving decision to create different forests. For some business or political reasons, some of the users and resources need to be completely disjoined from one another.

From the ultimate security standpoint of domains, trees, and forests, the forest is the true security boundary among the Active Directory structural components. Nothing is shared between forests, not the schema, GPOs, or administration. Some functions, however, do have forestwide effects, including the following:

Global catalog

   The global catalog is the "phone directory" for the forest. Every object from every domain is represented in the global catalog, just not every attribute of every object. The attributes that users would need to search for are included in the global catalog. Some of these attributes include phone number, address, and email address. When a user does a search for an object in the Active Directory using the built-in search tool, the global catalog is referenced to help find the object.

Schema

   As noted earlier, the schema is the foundation of object structures for the entire forest. Every domain in the forest shares the same set of object structures that are defined in the schema. If an attacker accesses or modifies the schema, every domain in the forest will be affected. The schema is one-third of the directory database, which is stored on all domain controllers in every domain. Only one domain controller in the forest can update the schema—the Schema Master.

Configuration context

   One-third of the directory database is the configuration context. The configuration context is responsible for tracking forestwide information, such as sites and subnets related to the site configuration. The configuration context is stored on all domain controllers in every domain.

Organizational Units

Organizational units (OUs) are objects within a domain that help organize the other objects in the domain. OUs can't span multiple domains, but they can be configured in a hierarchy within the domain.

There are two primary reasons, both security focused, for designing and implementing OUs. The first is delegation, which as we have already seen helps administrators to delegate administrative tasks to other administrators or even employees. The other is the deployment of GPOs. GPOs span security settings, software deployment, desktop configuration, folder redirection, and more.

Delegation

   By far one of the most important features of Active Directory is delegation. However, delegation without a solid OU design is almost impossible to implement. OUs need to be designed to delegate administration. The key to delegation is to have the OU contain the objects that the delegate will control. For example, if you have delegated the ability for the HR manager to reset passwords for only the HR employees, then there needs to be an OU for these user accounts. A good design would have an OU named HR_employees, which contains only the user accounts of the HR employees. The design would have this OU low in the OU hierarchy, so that no other OUs are below it. In that design, the HR manager will not have control over any other user accounts by default.

GPO deployment

Many administrators leave out the consideration of GPO deployment when they design OUs. This is a mistake, mainly for security reasons. The GPO deployment should be interwoven with delegation considerations. If there is a conflict between the two design needs, the delegation needs usually win. In this case, the GPO deployment will be taken care of by filtering the GPO (setting permissions on the GPO). An example of a typical GPO design would be the configuration of the Internet Explorer proxy settings for a branch office. All employees in the branch office need to have the same proxy settings for IE, which can easily be set by using GPOs. In this case, there would be an OU named Branch1_employees, which contains the user accounts for only the branch office. This OU would be low in the OU hierarchy, with no other OUs below it.

An error that many companies make is to duplicate their company's organizational chart for their OU design. The OUs are not well suited for this model, since this model usually breaks how the administration of objects and deployment of GPOs are implemented. This is not to say that a small percentage of companies have not successfully used the org chart for the OU design, but in most cases it will cause more anguish than benefit.

 OUs should not be confused with containers. A *container* is a default folder in Active Directory. Default containers include Users and Computers. These are used by Active Directory to store the default user accounts and computer accounts. The main difference between OUs and containers is that GPOs can be linked only to OUs, not containers.

Sites

Although sites don't directly affect security, the reasons for and implementation of them are important to the overall Active Directory structure. If you are using VLANs for security reasons, the design of your VLANs could impact the design of your sites. So security of other network criteria might play a part in the site design. Sites themselves are designed primarily to control replication between domain controllers. A secondary reason for sites is to control access to resources, by directing users to resources in their site, before going across the WAN. By default, domain controllers in the same site replicate every 15 seconds and have a convergence time of 45 seconds within a default Active Directory environment. This is usually a good design, as long as the domain controllers have enough bandwidth between them and the bandwidth is available for this schedule of replication.

If sufficient bandwidth is not available, a less frequent replication schedule is desired. With the default site configuration of only a single site, there is no method to reduce the replication that occurs between domain controllers. To solve this, additional sites are created and domain controllers are moved to sites, which allows for controlled replication between the domain controllers in the sites.

Here are some characteristics of sites:

- Sites can contain domain controllers from different domains.
- Sites are represented by subnets. The subnets are extremely important for sites, since this is how the client computers track down resources in their own site using DNS.
- Sites are typically associated with regions, but not always. Sites are usually configured for networks that are "highly connected"—usually defined as 10 Mbps or higher.

When designing and implementing sites, key configurations need to be addressed:

1. The schedule of the replication needs to be defined. The default schedule is to have the sites replicate every three hours. For most cases, this may be sufficient, but if sites are in close proximity to one another or on different floors of the same building, this may not be fast enough.
2. The domain controllers need to be located in the sites. If a domain controller fails to be placed in a site, it will most likely not be used by the network clients, because the IP address will not fall into the correct subnet configured for the site.
3. The subnets need to be configured for the sites. A single subnet can't span multiple sites, but a site can, and usually does, contain multiple subnets.
4. The overall convergence time needs to be considered. If numerous sites are configured, how the sites will replicate to one another needs to be considered, which will help determine how long it will take a change to replicate to all the domain controllers in each site.

Domain Controllers

If it were not for domain controllers, you would not have an Active Directory. The domain controllers are responsible for the entire authentication of users, storage of objects, control of GPOs, and control of the Active Directory database. This is a lot of responsibility, which also requires a lot of security. The following is a list of key responsibilities of a domain controller in Active Directory:

Authentication of users

The domain controllers are responsible for authenticating all the users that submit credentials. The desired authentication protocol is Kerberos, but if the computer that is generating the authentication does not support Kerberos, a form of

NTLM will be used. In most cases, NTLM v2 will be used in place of Kerberos. Table 13-1 breaks down which scenarios use Kerberos and which use NTLM.

Storage of the Active Directory database

The domain controllers store the Active Directory database locally in the file system. This is just a single file, with some accompanying files for support. The *NTDS.DIT* file is the real Active Directory database; it lives in the *%systemroot%\NTDS* folder. If this file is compromised or corrupted, it can bring down the entire Active Directory. Ideally, the database for Active Directory should be located on a dedicated physical drive that does not include the system volume.

Storage of GPOs and logon scripts

The domain controllers are also responsible for the GPOs (both default and new) as well as the logon scripts. Both the GPOs and the logon scripts are stored in folders under the *%systemroot%\SYSVOL* folder. The GPOs are under the *%systemroot%\SYSVOL\sysvol\<domainname>\Policies* folder. Each is listed by its Global Unique Identifier (GUID). The scripts are all located under the GPOs if they are configured through GPOs. However, if they are the "traditional" logon scripts that are configured via the user account properties, they will be stored under *%systemroot%\SYSVOL\sysvol\<domainname>\scripts*. Here, scripts are shared as *NETLOGON*, just as in Windows NT. GPOs or scripts that are modified or corrupted may not run, which could leave some or all computers without the proper security configuration. Also, if an attacker modifies a GPO or script from this location, she could give herself additional access to resources if enough information is known about the network.

Table 13-1. Windows Server 2003 authentication protocols

Operating system sending credentials	Windows Server 2003 role receiving credentials	Authentication protocol used
Windows NT	Standalone server	NTLM v2
Windows 9x or NT	Domain controller	NTLM or NTLM v2
Windows 2000, XP, or Server 2003	Standalone or untrusted server	NTLM v2
Windows 2000, XP, or Server 2003	Domain controller	Kerberos

The folder structure of the domain controllers is determined at the time a server is promoted to be a domain controller. You have the opportunity to place the directory database file, the transaction logs for the database file, and the *SYSVOL* folder. Regardless, you need to place all these key files on an NTFS volume. Then, make sure that these folders are kept secure, so that an attacker is not able to access or corrupt the files.

Default Security Through GPOs

The domain controllers are the key to ensuring your Active Directory is safe and secure. However, many aspects of your domain controllers may go unnoticed unless you are 100% aware what is happening behind the scenes. An important consideration is the point at which domain controllers receive many of their default security settings. You will recall that two default GPOs help configure the environment: the Default Domain Policy, targeted to the entire domain, and the Default Domain Controller Policy, targeted to the domain controllers. Finally, if you are upgrading from Windows NT to Windows 2000 or Server 2003, you will need to be aware of how the security is different on upgraded servers from those that are freshly installed.

Default Domain Policy

The GPO that is linked to the domain is primarily targeted to configure the domain user's Account Policies. This includes the Password Policy, Account Lockout Policy, and Kerberos Policy. Figure 13-4 shows you the Default Domain Policy regarding the Account Policies.

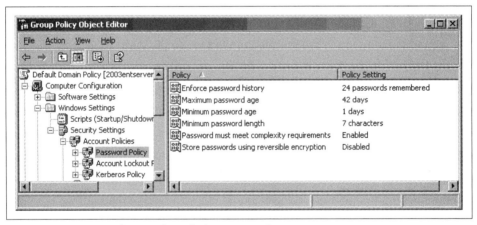

Figure 13-4. Account Policies in the Default Domain Policy

The Default Domain Policy controls more than just the Account Policies. Table 13-2 lists the default settings in the Default Domain Policy.

Table 13-2. Default Domain Policy default configurations and values

Computer configuration	Policy setting	Value
Password Policy	Enforce password history	24 passwords remembered
	Maximum password age	42 days
	Minimum password age	1 day

Table 13-2. Default Domain Policy default configurations and values (continued)

Computer configuration	Policy setting	Value
	Minimum password length	7 characters
	Password must meet complexity requirements	Enabled
	Store passwords using reversible encryption	Disabled
Account Lockout Policy	Account lockout duration	Not defined
	Account lockout threshold	0 invalid logon attempts
	Reset account lockout counter after	Not defined
Kerberos Policy	Enforce user logon restrictions	Enabled
	Maximum lifetime for service ticket	600 minutes
	Maximum lifetime for user ticket	10 hours
	Maximum lifetime for user ticket renewal	7 days
	Maximum tolerance for computer clock synchronization	5 minutes
Local Polices\Security Options	Network security: force logoff when logon hours expire	Disabled
Public Key Policies	Encrypting File System	Administrator is configured as a Data Recovery Agent

The User Configuration portion of the Default Domain Policy is not configured for any setting.

Default Domain Controller Policy

The GPO that is linked to the domain controllers OU is targeted to configure only the domain controllers. This primary focus is on the user rights for the domain controllers, as shown in Figure 13-5.

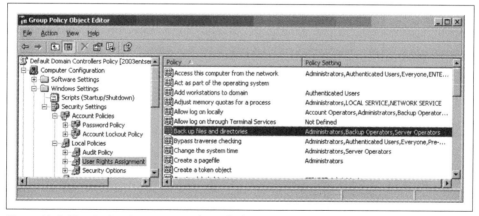

Figure 13-5. User Rights Assignment in the Default Domain Controller Policy

The Default Domain Controller Policy does more than just configure user rights for the domain controllers. Table 13-3 lists the default settings in the Default Domain Controller Policy.

Table 13-3. Default Domain Controller Policy default configurations and values

Computer configuration	Policy setting	Value
Audit Policy	Audit account logon events	Success
	Audit account management	No auditing
	Audit directory service access	No auditing
	Audit logon events	Success
	Audit object access	No auditing
	Audit policy change	No auditing
	Audit privilege use	No auditing
	Audit process tracking	No auditing
	Audit system events	No auditing
User Rights Assignment[a]	Access this computer from the network	Administrators
		Authenticated Users
		ENTERPRISE DOMAIN CONTROLLERS
		Everyone
		Pre-Windows 2000 Compatible Access
	Add workstations to domain	Authenticated Users
	Adjust memory quotas for a process	Administrators
		LOCAL SERVICE
		NETWORK SERVICE
	Allow logon locally	Account Operators
		Administrators
		Backup Operators
		Print Operators
		Server Operators
	Back up files and directories	Administrators
		Backup Operators
		Server Operators
	Bypass traverse checking	Authenticated Users
		Administrators
		Everyone
		Pre-Windows 2000 Compatible Access
	Change the system time	Administrators
		Server Operators

Computer configuration	Policy setting	Value
	Create a pagefile	Administrators
	Debug programs	Administrators
	Deny access to this computer from the network	<domain>\Support_*
	Deny logon locally	<domain>\Support_*
	Enable computer and user accounts to be trusted for delegation	Administrators
	Force shutdown from a remote system	Administrators
		Server Operators
	Generate security audits	LOCAL SERVICE
		NETWORK SERVICE
	Increase scheduling priority	Administrators
	Load and unload device drivers	Administrators
		Print Operators
	Log on as a batch job	<domain>\IIS
		<domain>\IUSR
		<domain>\IWAM
		<domain>\Support_*
		LOCAL SERVICE
	Log on as a service	NETWORK SERVICE
	Manage Auditing and Security Log	Administrators
	Modify firmware environment variables	Administrators
	Profile system performance	Administrators
	Remove computer from docking station	Administrators
	Replace a process level token	<domain>\IWAM
		LOCAL SERVICE
		NETWORK SERVICE
	Restore files and directories	Administrators
		Backup Operators
		Server Operators
	Shut down the system	Administrators
		Backup Operators
		Print Operators
		Server Operators
	Take ownership of files and other objects	Administrators

Table 13-3. Default Domain Controller Policy default configurations and values (continued)

Computer configuration	Policy setting	Value
Local Policies/Security Options	Domain controller: LDAP server signing requirements	None
	Domain controller: digitally encrypt or sign secure channel data (always)	Enabled
	Microsoft network server: digitally sign communications (always)	Enabled
	Microsoft network server: digitally sign communications (if client agrees)	Enabled
	Network security: LAN Manager authentication level	Send NTLM response only

a User rights not included here are either not defined or are defined but are left empty.

The User Configuration portion of the Default Domain Controller Policy is not configured for any setting.

Default Security for Upgrades

If the domain controllers are upgraded from Windows NT 4.0 domain controllers, the security for these settings is much different. In such cases, a special security template is used to configure many of these settings for both the Default Domain Policy and Default Domain Controller Policy. The security template is named *DCUP.INF* and is automatically applied to the domain controller being upgraded.

This watered-down security template is used for an upgrade to ensure compatibility of the existing applications with Windows Server 2003. The proper method to boost the security of upgraded domain controllers is to configure them with a security template that is provided by Microsoft or one of the leading security institutes that provide security templates of their own. Web sites where you can find additional security templates include:

> *www.microsoft.com/windowsserver2003/security/default.mspx*
> *www.cisecurity.com*

 Not all the security templates that you find are supported by Microsoft. However, they are still excellent references and include good combinations of security settings.

These templates will typically reconfigure the weak security areas that the *DCUP. INF* file left open. The following include the main areas that are left insecure by the default template:

- Registry
- File system (including SYSVOL and Windows)
- User rights
- Account Policies (if they were weak in Windows NT)

Providing Security for Domains

Now that we have a good understanding of Active Directory, the infrastructure components, default security, and how to apply security, we are going to investigate each component individually, including how to provide security for it. We start with the domain. The domain has many areas that need to be secured to ensure that an attacker has few areas to focus on. Some of these focus areas could fall under domain controllers, since the objects are stored there, but these are really domainwide considerations, not just domain controller considerations.

Users, Groups, and Computers

As we have seen in earlier chapters, the SID is the mechanism used by the operating system to control and manage the security principals. Remember, the security principals include user, group, and computer accounts. You will want to protect all security principals above all other objects, because it is the security principals that are given access to resources. If an attacker can access a resource as an account that has elevated privileges or administrative privileges, there is almost no way to stop him from doing as he pleases with that resource.

The following simple rules will help you protect user, group, and computer accounts.

Clean up stale accounts

If an account (especially a user or computer account) has not been used in a while, be sure to have a process to remove it from the Active Directory. The new feature to run Saved Queries in the Active Directory will help you quickly find stale accounts. For user accounts, you can query Disabled accounts and accounts that have not logged on for x days. For computer accounts, you can query Disabled accounts and quickly delete those that are no longer needed. The Saved Queries node is the first one listed when you open Active Directory Users and Computers. To create a new query, like the ones mentioned, right-click on the Saved Queries node and then click New → Query. The new window will prompt you for the name for your new query. After you insert a new name for your query, click the Define Query button, which will display the Find Common Queries window shown in Figure 13-6.

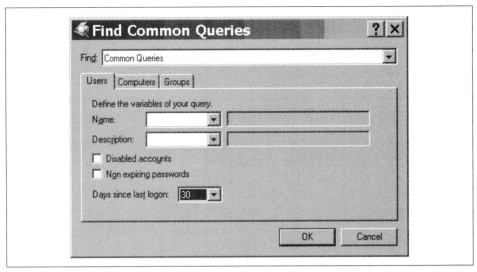

Figure 13-6. Saved Query interface used inside Active Directory Users and Computers

Protect user accounts

It seems obvious, but the passwords for user accounts are rarely protected to the level that they should be. In protecting the user accounts, make sure that the password complexity is configured in the Password Policy. Windows 2000 did not require this, but Windows Server 2003 Active Directory has this as the default, if the domain is installed new. Another step to protecting user accounts is to have a safe and secure process for users to recover from lost passwords. If the process is simply to have a user call with her username to ask for a new password, the door is left wide open for "social engineering." Implement a process that requires some other form of user verification, and then make sure the password is securely sent to the user and that the old password is changed as soon as the user logs in.

Use proper group nesting

The group "mantra" has been around since the early Windows NT days: *Users go into Global Groups, Global Groups go into Local Groups, and Local Groups are given permissions.*

The reason for this structure is really multifold. First, it provides a process that is easy to follow and straightforward to troubleshoot. Second, it allows domain administrators to control the Global Groups on the domain controllers and local administrators of the servers to control the Local Groups. Finally, it repels the worse configuration of all, which is to place a user account into a Local Group directly! The reason this is so insecure is because it is almost impossible to track down memberships in Local Groups.

For example, let's assume that you have a user account named Derek. Derek is an administrator who is given free reign like most domain administrators. So, Derek places his user account in almost every Local Group on every file server in the company. There are 5000 file servers in your company, each with an average of 50 Local Groups. Today, Derek is leaving the IT administration role to become a director. Your company has intelligently restricted directors from having administrative access. However, with Derek shotgunned out to all the Local Groups, he is in essence an administrator with the access that he possesses. If the mantra had been followed, Derek's user account could have been reassigned to different Global Groups, removing the administrative access, giving him the director access that he needs.

Protect service accounts

We all know that a service account is responsible for running a service, which normally spans multiple computers. Services such as backup/restore, Exchange 5.5, SQL, and so on need to have access to multiple computers and are given elevated privilege on these computers. Some key configurations need to occur for these accounts. First, it might be a good idea to provide a dual-user password for the critical service accounts. This will require that at least two administrators be present, to change or log on as a service account. Another good idea for these accounts is to give them a very long and complex password. It is not uncommon to provide a password with more than 20 characters for a service account that controls Exchange or SQL. Finally, it is a good practice to configure the Logon Workstations attribute for these service accounts, as shown in Figure 13-7.

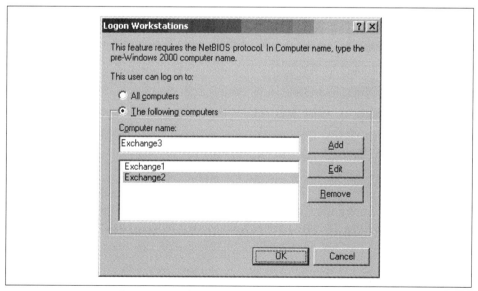

Figure 13-7. Logon Workstations restriction setting for user accounts

To configure the Logon Workstations attribute for a user account, follow these steps:

1. Open Active Directory Users and Computers.
2. Right-click on a user account, then click on the Properties menu option.
3. Select the Account tab.
4. Click on Log on To.
5. Select the The Following Computers radio button in the Logon Workstations window.
6. Type the name of the workstation in the Computer Name text box, then click the Add button.
7. Repeat step 6 until all computer names are added.
8. Click the OK button in the Logon Workstation window.
9. Click the OK button in the user Properties window.

This option is successful only if NetBIOS is enabled on the network connections, which is almost a requirement for most networks. This will allow the service accounts to log on successfully only to the computers they need to, which will prohibit an attacker from trying to log on as one of these accounts. If you have older Windows 9x and Windows NT computers, they too can be listed for this configuration.

Beyond the preceding security concerns and suggestions for locking down service accounts are some additional ideas that can help protect these accounts: First, do not use the same service account across services. This will expose more than just one service at one time if the username and password are compromised. Next, these accounts should not be allowed to have nonexpiring passwords. These user accounts should be as restricted as (if not more restricted than) other user accounts. This will require a documented and regular procedure to change the password on each service account. Finally, use the Network Service account instead of a user account if possible. This account is designed to be used as a network service, functioning on the network as the computer on which it is configured.

Administrative Groups

The domain is full of default, built-in groups. These groups give immediate privilege access to domain controllers, services, accounts, and more. The membership in these groups needs to be monitored and limited to reduce exposure to attacks and vulnerability. Some administrative type groups have more privileges than others. The most essential groups that reside on domain controllers that you need to be concerned with for every domain include:

Domain Admins

The only member of this group to begin with is the Administrator user account. The members of this group can administer all domain controllers for the domain, as well as all computers that are members of the domain. The reason this occurs is that the Domain Admins group is automatically placed in the local Administrators group for every computer that joins the domain.

Administrators

The purpose of this group is to allow the members to control the domain controllers for this domain. By default, the only member is the Administrator. This group has a smaller scope of influence than the Domain Admins group, since the members in this group can administer only the domain controllers, not every computer in the domain.

DNSAdmins

The purpose of this group is to allow the members to control the DNS servers, both standalone and Active Directory–integrated.

Cert Publishers

The members of this group are allowed to publish certificates to Active Directory.

DNSUpdateProxy

The members of this group are able to perform dynamic updates to DNS on behalf of other clients. The only members in this group should be DHCP server computer accounts.

Pre-Windows 2000 Compatible Access

This group is designed to provide backward compatibility. The members of this group are allowed Read access on all users and groups in the domain.

 Two forestwide groups, Enterprise Admins and Schema Admins, will be discussed in the "Providing Security for Forests" section later in this chapter.

Other groups are listed in a default Active Directory domain but don't have the widespread notoriety and vulnerabilities as these groups. Membership in these groups should be kept to a minimum, and all members of the group should be aware of the privilege that is given to them, so they can protect the account while logged in to the domain.

Administrator Accounts

The domain has one built-in Administrator account, but this section will focus on all potential administrators that are given elevated privileges. First, I want to focus on the real Administrator account. This account needs to be protected! There is no other way to say it. This means you should consider the following points for this account:

- Don't allow any user to use the account for logon.
- Don't use this account as a service account.
- Rename the account (most use a common name, to have it fit in with the other accounts).
- Give this account a special, complex password (preferably more than 15 characters, using characters from each possible character range in the password, maybe dual administrator so that it takes two administrators to log on with the account).
- Change the Description for this account.
- Create a bogus Administrator account (make sure the description of this account is the same as the original Administrator account).

Other administrator accounts will have to be created to allow the IT staff to perform their jobs, in addition to their normal user accounts. These additional accounts need to be protected as well. Here are some considerations for these accounts:

- Allow this account to be used only for administrative tasks.
- Don't use any of these accounts as a service account.
- Ensure these accounts have lengthy, complex passwords.
- Consider a company policy requiring that these admin accounts change their passwords more frequently than the normal user password policy demands. Unfortunately, you cannot currently enforce this with Group Policy but can audit the password ages with scripts and management tools.

The key here is to not allow the administrators to use this account for their routine duties as an employee. When they check their email, write memos, surf the Internet, and so forth, they should do so through a typical user account, not an account with elevated privileges.

Finally, some administrative accounts are not placed in Admin groups but are rather given administrative privilege through user rights or delegation. These accounts include service accounts and those for server administrators and helpdesk personnel. In addition to accounts that have administrative privileges, accounts that are given elevated privileges to control applications should be protected. These accounts should be protected in these ways:

- Allow these accounts to be used only for administrative tasks.
- Ensure these accounts have complex passwords.

Object Security and ACLs

We saw in Chapter 7 how users are able to access resources. It can't be stated strongly enough how important this process is to the overall security of your domain. If a user, group, or computer account is compromised by an attacker, your entire network could be in jeopardy. Remember, when a user authenticates, he receives a token that contains the user SID, group SIDs, and user rights.

To see the contents of a token, just run the whoami /all command on any computer. You will get results similar to those shown in Figure 13-8.

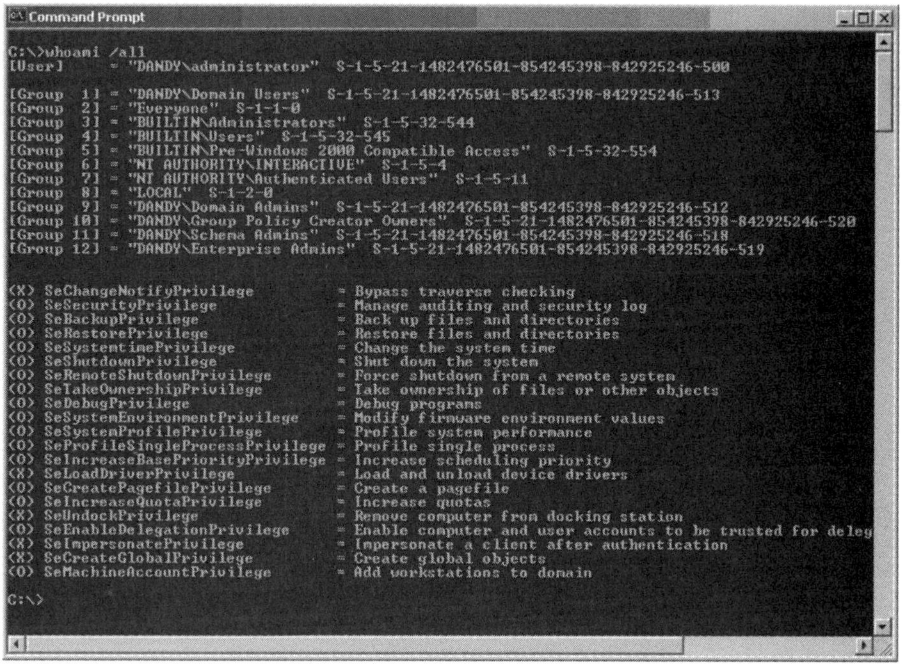

Figure 13-8. Contents of a user token displayed by running whoami /all

Since the output of the whoami command shows the SIDs for the user and group accounts, you can investigate the SIDs, using a tool such as *user2sid* or *sid2user*, to verify that these SIDs should be on this user's token. This falls into the auditing function that should be performed by both the IT staff and security auditing staff on a regular basis.

Example: Configuring Domain User Accounts to Access Resources

Derek is the domain administrator responsible for group management and Active Directory administration. Yvette has been hired to run a new HR file-based database that will run on an existing server named FS1. Derek has not created the new user account for Yvette, but he will be receiving the paperwork from the HR manager soon. Derek needs to configure the user account, groups, and resource permissions to give Yvette Full Control access to the database.

To set the stage completely, it is important to understand the structure of the Active Directory forest. The domain is configured in Windows 2000 mixed functional level, however, there are no Windows NT BDCs. FS1 is a member of the domain and Derek has administrative privileges to FS1.

Derek would follow these steps to properly configure the access for Yvette:

1. Open Active Directory Users and Computers.
2. Right-click on the domain node, then click the New → Organizational Unit menu option.
3. Type **HR** in the Name text box, then click the OK button.
4. Right-click the HR OU, then click the New → User menu option.
5. Type **Yvette** in the First Name text box, **yvette** in the User Logon Name text box, then click the Next button.
6. Type in a password that meets the password complexity for the domain, confirm the password in the Confirm text box, then click the Next button.
7. Click the Finish button.
8. Right-click on the HR OU, then click the New → Group menu option.
9. Type **HR_DBM** in the Group Name text box, select the Global radio button, select the Security radio button, then click the OK button.
10. Right-click the Yvette user account, then click the Add to a Group menu option.
11. Make sure the domain name is listed in the From This Location text box. If it is not, click the Locations button, select the domain name from the Locations window, then click the OK button.
12. Type **HR_DBM** in the "Enter the object name to select" text box, then click the OK button.
13. On FS1, click Start → Control Panel.
14. In the Control Panel, double-click the Administrative Tools icon.
15. In the Administrative Tools window, double-click the Computer Management icon.

16. Expand the Local Users and Groups node in the Computer Management window.

17. Right-click on the Groups folder in the right pane, then click the New Group menu option.

18. Type **DB1_FullControl** into the Group Name text box.

19. Click the Add button.

20. Make sure the domain name is listed in the From This Location text box. If it is not, click the Locations button, select the domain name from the Locations window, then click the OK button.

21. Type **DB_DBM** into the Enter the object name to select textbox, and then click the OK button

22. Click the Create button.

23. Click Start → My Computer.

24. Double-click the C:\ option.

25. Right-click on the HRDatabase folder, then click Properties menu option (this is the folder containing the new database file).

26. Select the Security tab.

27. Select the Authenticated Users in the Group or User Names window, then click the Remove button.

28. Click the Add button.

29. Make sure the computer name is listed in the From This Location text box. If it is not, click the Locations button, select the computer name from the Locations window, then click the OK button.

30. Type **DB1_FullControl** into the Enter the object name to select textbox, then click the OK button.

31. Click on the Full Control checkbox under the Allow column, then click the OK button.

This is the typical method to configure groups within a Windows domain. Note that the user account and global group are located on the domain controllers, whereas the local group and ACL for the resource are located on the member server. With this configuration, Yvette will have Full Control access to the new database, as long as she logs on to the domain.

Configuring correct user group nesting structures

If Derek were to convert the domain to Windows 2000 native functional level or higher, he could and should use a different group strategy. Remember that when a domain is in mixed mode, the Domain Local Groups are not visible to the domain members; they are visible only to the domain controllers (they act like Local Groups did on Windows NT 4.0 domain controllers). The new group strategy would bypass the Local Group on FS1 and would take advantage of the centralized administration capabilities of Domain Local Groups in Active Directory. Derek would follow these steps for the domain with this configuration (the first 11 steps from the preceding process are the same, so we will start where the Domain Local Group is created):

1. Right-click on the HR OU, then click the New → Group menu option.

2. Type **HR_DB1_FullControl** in the Group Name text box, select the Domain Local radio button, select the Security radio button, then click the OK button.

3. Right-click the **HR_DB1_FullControl** group account, then click the Properties menu option.

4. Select the Member Of tab.

5. Click the Add button.

6. Make sure the domain name is listed in the From This Location text box. If it is not, click the Locations button, select the domain name from the Locations window, then click the OK button.

7. Type **HR_DBM** in the "Enter the object name to select" text box, then click the OK button.

8. On FS1, click Start → My Computer.

9. Double-click the C:\ option.

10. Right-click on the HRDatabase folder, then click Properties menu option (this is the folder containing the new database file).

11. Select the Security tab.

12. Select the Authenticated Users in the Group or User Names window, then click the Remove button.

13. Click the Add button.

14. Make sure the domain name is listed in the From This Location text box. If it is not, click the Locations button, select the domain name from the Locations window, then click the OK button.

15. Type **HR_DB1_FullControl** into the Enter the object name to select textbox, and then click the OK button

16. Click on the Full Control checkbox under the Allow column, then click the OK button.

The benefit of using this group structure is that now all groups are located in Active Directory. Also, if DB1 is ever duplicated for load balancing or testing purposes, there is no need to configure a new Local Group on the new server; rather, the ACL of the resource just needs to be configured with the Domain Local Group. This can reduce the overall number of groups that are spread throughout the IT infrastructure, if enough design is mixed in with the implementation. Also, all groups are centralized, which makes administration a bit easier.

Account Policies

One of the most important aspects of any domain is the Account Policies that restrict the passwords for the domain users. To fully protect the domain, you must implement an Account Policy that prohibits an attacker from easily gaining access to the network. This "ease" is from either guessing easy passwords, social engineering, or even reading sticky notes attached to the monitors of users who feel this is the only way to remember their password.

From this, you can see there is a middle ground where passwords should not be too easy, or too hard. For each company, this does differ. Earlier we discussed what the default settings for the Password Policies are in Windows Server 2003 Active Directory, as shown in Table 13-2. These settings are a great place to start, but you should configure any additional settings to strengthen your security that won't force your users to start writing passwords on sticky notes. This might include longer passwords, shorter password ages, or even a custom password filter that makes the password pass a dictionary list omission before allowing it to be configured.

 Account Policies for upgraded domains will retain their original settings. If you have upgraded from Windows NT or Windows 2000 Active Directory, be sure to reconfigure the Account Policies to meet at least the minimum settings established in a default Windows Server 2003 Active Directory domain, for the best security.

You can find more information on creating your own custom password filter at the following Microsoft link: *http://msdn.microsoft.com/library/default.asp?url=/library/ en-us/security/security/sample_password_filter.asp*.

Account Policies at the OU level

Many administrators feel that they should be able to configure the Account Policies in a GPO and link it to the OU. The goal is to have the user accounts in the OU have only the more stringent Password Policy settings configured in the GPO. However, this will fail! The reasons it will fail are logical, as well as a feature of the operating system.

As for the logic, the Account Policies are not user configurations. This means that the Account Policies configure the Computer object, not the User objects. (See Chapter 5 for details.) The Account Policies will configure either Active Directory on domain controllers or the Local SAM on computers in the domain. This last statement drives home the feature of the operating system. The only location where you can modify the Account Policies for domain users is at the domain-linked GPO. There is no other way, custom or built-in, to accomplish this. It is a feature of the operating system!

What do the Account Policies configured in a GPO linked to an OU configure, you might ask. These Account Policy settings will modify the Local SAM on the computer accounts that exist in the OU, forcing the users who log on locally to these computers to adhere to the GPO linked to the OU, not the GPO linked to the domain.

Trusts

To secure your trust relationships, you really need to focus on the external trusts and not be as concerned with the internal trusts. The reason for this is that the internal trusts are automatic and you can't delete them (well, if you did, you would cause severe damage).

The trusts that are a concern are any trust relationships that go outside the forest. This could be to any of the following domain types:

- Windows NT 4 domain
- Windows 2000 domain
- Windows Server 2003 domain
- Kerberos realm

When you evaluate making a trust, make sure you consider the reason the domains are not in the same forest to begin with. You will want to keep cross-domain administration to a minimum; otherwise, it can become a security issue and vulnerability. You also want to match the Account Policies in domains that trust one another. If the Account Policy in one domain is weaker than the other domain, the user accounts in the weak-password domain are vulnerable, which makes your domain vulnerable, since they have access to your domain.

Providing Security for Forests

There is not a lot to secure with the forest, but what there is to secure is extremely important. Remember from our earlier discussion, a forest is a logical structural component of Active Directory. So, there won't be any setting that you make to the forest, although with Windows Server 2003 you can make a forest trust, which does deal with the forest itself.

Forestwide Components

Three areas of Active Directory are forestwide: the global catalog, configuration context, and schema context. Every domain controller contains a copy of the configuration and schema contexts. By default, there is only one global catalog server, the first domain controller in the forest. It is typical to configure multiple global catalog servers, which can be any domain controller.

A global catalog server can become a security issue if the administrator configures security-related information to be stored in the global catalog. If this secure information is located in the global catalog server, anyone who has Read access to this portion of the Active Directory database could obtain the secure information using a tool such as LDP or ADSIEdit. This is not the case by default, but caution needs to be upheld as novice administrators and applications are installed. If a green administrator starts to configure the attributes that are stored in the global catalog, it is very easy to make an attribute a part of the global catalog. Also, applications that modify the schema can also modify which attributes are included in the global catalog.

If an attacker were to get into the configuration or schema context, she could glean only a few bits of information. For example, she could obtain information about the site topology and replication structure and get a listing of all domains in the forest. Although this information is not enough to gain access to Active Directory, it does provide some information that an intruder would need. In addition to the problems that could ensue from information obtained from these contexts, any changes made to them would be widespread and damage could be catastrophic since these contexts are stored on every domain controller in the entire forest. Incorrect configurations in the configuration context could render sites unrecognizable and replication could stop completely. A change to the schema can modify which attributes are associated with certain objects. The loss of these attributes can break applications, cause email to malfunction, and stop production for days.

Forestwide Groups

The best way to ensure that forestwide functions are secure is to manage the groups that are forestwide. These groups include the Schema Admins and Enterprise Admins. There is no reason to have members in these groups as a standard practice. Instead, just place the domain administrators in the Domain Admins group, where they can manage the domain but not the IT infrastructure. Then, when a task needs to be performed by the privileges that are granted to members of the Schema and Enterprise Admins groups, an administrator can be manually placed into these groups to complete the task.

The reasons for having membership in these groups are very simple. If a change needs to occur to the schema, which is rare, a user account needs to be in the Schema Admins group to perform this activity. This could include maintenance on the schema or the installation of an application that needs to modify the schema.

Some applications modify the schema but don't explicitly instruct you that they do. If you attempt to install an application that requires schema access, but you are installing the application with a user account that is not in the Schema Admins group, you will receive an error message. This is a good way to tell if applications update or access the schema in any way during installation.

For the Enterprise Admins group, management of sites and creation of new domains are examples of tasks that require membership in this group. Like the Schema Admins group membership, not having a user account in the group will quickly indicate a problem if the privilege that the group provides is required for the activity.

Forest Trusts

With Windows Server 2003 Active Directory, the limitation of not having two forests joined by a trust has been eliminated. Although many prefer the separation of two different forests for security purposes, many companies had a need to connect different companies that were in different forests. These companies usually had merged or had acquired another company. It is unreasonable in most instances to have these companies combine the domains in each forest to a single forest, so the forest trust was created.

To take advantage of the forest trust, some upgrades and configurations must first be made to the domain controllers, domains, and forest. The domain controllers must all be running Windows Server 2003. Any Windows NT or Windows 2000 Server domain controllers need to be decommissioned or upgraded, since they cannot function in a forest that is trusted by another forest. Every domain in both forests that will be trusted need to be upgraded to the Windows Server 2003 domain functional level. Finally, both forests need to be upgraded to the Windows Server 2003 forest functional level. After these steps have been accomplished, the two forests can establish a trust, so that users in one forest can have the ability to access resources in the other forest.

The forest trust is established between the root domains of each forest. The trust that you create can either be a one-way or two-way trust, allowing for more granular control of which users can access resources. The trusts are Kerberos-based and transitive, but are transitive only for the domains that are in the trusted forest, not additional domains or forests that are outside of the trusted forest.

Providing forestwide access to your resources might make you feel a bit nervous. During the creation of the forest trust, you can control whether the trust allows the entire trusted forest to access resources or only certain accounts from the trusted forest. You will have two:

Forestwide authentication
> Windows will allow all users from the trusted forest to be authenticated for all resources in the trusting forest.

Selective authentication
> This restricts which users from the trusted forest will be authenticated for access to resources in the trusting forest. This will require that individual access be

specified to each resource that you want to make available to users in the trusted forest. By default, no user from the trusted domain has access to any resource in the trusting forest. The Allowed to Authenticate permission on the user account properties will provide the means for the account to be authenticated by the trusting forest.

SID Filtering

A key feature that is now turned on by default with domain controllers running Windows Server 2003 and Windows 2000 Server with Service Pack 4 (or higher) is SID filtering. This is a very important feature that protects the trusts that are created to other forests, as well as to external domains. The concept of SID filtering protects against someone modifying the SIDHistory attribute for a user account in the trusted domain to include SIDs for the trusting domain.

SID filtering works by checking the SIDs for all authenticating requests from trusted domains. The incoming security principal SIDs are checked to ensure that they are all related to the trusted domain, not the trusting domain. The trust removes any SIDs associated with the trusting domain.

SID filtering can be disabled, although it is not a good security practice to do so. Also, old SIDs from a migrated Windows NT domain that are in the SIDHistory attribute are to be removed by the trust. This will not allow the user to access resources that are still associated to the old Windows NT SID. Another problem that might occur from SID filtering relates to universal groups. If a user is a member of a universal group that was not created in the trusted domain, this group SID will be removed by the trust too.

Providing Security for Active Directory Objects

The concept of providing security for Active Directory objects can be viewed in two different ways. First, you can consider the idea that you need to secure the object itself, so that no one can access it. By default, this is taken care of in the operating system and was discussed in the earlier "Providing Security for the Domain" section. However, we need to discuss another approach: delegation of administrative control.

Delegation of administration control, or just *delegation* as it is usually referred to, is not as complex as the name implies. Delegation is nothing more than setting permissions on objects in Active Directory. The permissions are set on objects in Active

Directory the exact same way that you set permissions on files and folders on an NTFS volume. There is a Delegation Wizard, which is useful for some tasks, but more complex permissions require manual attention. Examples of delegation include:

- Giving the HR managers the ability to change group membership for the HR groups
- Giving the branch office staff the ability to create their own global groups
- Giving the helpdesk the ability to reset passwords for all user accounts, except for the IT staff

One thing to keep in mind as you secure objects in Active Directory is the OU design. The OU design must be considered before the delegation is performed. Otherwise, you might be giving too much control or affecting the wrong objects with the delegation.

Delegation is typically provided to give administration over user accounts, group accounts, and GPO linking. Very little can be delegated to control for a computer account, printer, or shared folder.

One of the more complex aspects of delegation is whether to use user accounts or group accounts to delegate control to. If you consider OUs to be like folders and user accounts (and the other objects) like files, it becomes easy.

 Microsoft has developed extensive documentation on delegation of administration. To obtain this documentation, go to: *http://www. microsoft.com/downloads/details.aspx?familyid=631747a3-79e1-48fa-9730-dae7c0a1d6d3&displaylang=en.*

Example: Delegating Control for Helpdesk Admins

Mary is the domain administrator for Contoso. The Contoso Corporation has a main office and a branch office. The branch office has an IT staff that completely controls all aspects of the user, computer, and group objects for that office. The main office has more than 10,000 employees, so the administration of Active Directory is more time-consuming than for the branch office. To help the domain administrators off-load tasks, the IT director is going to allow the helpdesk staff to reset passwords for main office employees who forget them. This will reduce the calls to the domain administrators who have taken care of this issue since migrating from Windows NT. The IT director does not want the helpdesk staff to be able to reset passwords for the IT staff or any employee at the branch office.

To accommodate the delegation and GPO deployment, the top-level OU structure has been determined and implemented, as shown in Figure 13-9.

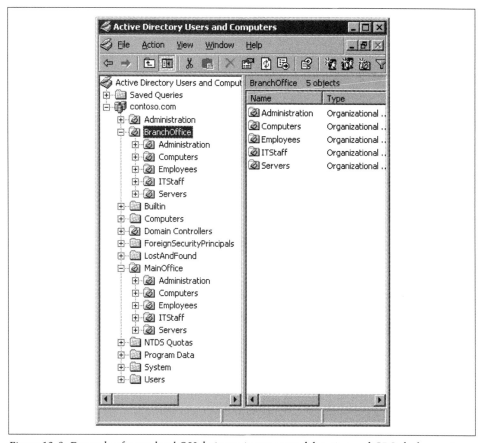

Figure 13-9. Example of a top-level OU design to incorporate delegation and GPO deployment

There are some important design decisions to note regarding the OU design. First, notice how the IT staff and the employees for the main office are separated into different OUs. Also, the branch office is in a separate OU structure than the main office. This allows for the separation that is needed for the delegation of administration. However, note that all the user accounts are under a top-level OU, which allows for "global" delegation to be made at the top-level OU, without making a user a domain administrator or giving him too many privileges. Finally, notice that there is an Administrative OU at each level of OUs. This OU provides a holding area for all "administrative groups" that have delegated privileges over the OUs directly below it. This is to keep track of groups that are used to provide access to resources on the network versus the groups that are used to delegate administration to objects in the Active Directory.

The creation of the Administrative OUs is not necessary for a fully functional and successful delegation model. However, it has provided an excellent method for administrators to keep track of each type of group in a complex Active Directory implementation.

Delegating control

John, Paul, George, and Ringo are all on the helpdesk staff. Mary needs to give them delegated privileges that meet the requirements of the IT director. She would take the following steps to complete the delegation:

1. Open Active Directory Users and Computers.
2. Expand the domain structure down to the Administrative OU under the Main-Office OU.
3. Right-click on the Administrative OU, then click the New → Group menu option.
4. Type **Reset_PW_Main_Emp** in the Group Name text box, select the Global radio button, select the Security radio button, then click the OK button.
5. Right-click the Reset_PW_Main_Emp group account, then click the Properties menu option.
6. Select the Member Of tab.
7. Click the Add button.
8. Make sure the domain name is listed in the From This Location text box. If it is not, click the Locations button, select the domain name from the Locations window, then click the OK button.
9. Type **John** in the "Enter the object name to select" text box, then click the OK button.
10. Repeat step 9 for Paul, George, and Ringo.
11. Right-click on the Employees OU under the MainOffice OU, then click the Delegate Control menu option.
12. Click Next.
13. Click the Add button.
14. Find the Reset_PW_Main_Emp group and add it to the list.
15. Click the OK button.
16. Click the Next button.
17. Select the "Reset user passwords and force password change at next logon" checkbox, then click the Next button.
18. Click the Finish button.

The power of delegation is tremendous, if executed properly and maintained well. Here, you can see that the members of the Reset_PW_Main_Emp group can now take care of all the password reset needs for the employees located in a single OU. This provides ultimate control for the domain administrators, while allowing junior-level administrators and other employees to help with routine tasks. The other benefit of the delegation as you can see from the example is that the scope of influence is limited by a good OU design and delegation model. A final note is that delegation was required here rather than just adding these user accounts to the Account Operators group, due to this action providing these users too broad administrative privileges.

Example: Auditing Management of AD

Derek is the enterprise administrator for Contoso. His company is responsible for more than 250 training facilities throughout the United States. The company has three Active Directory domains, one the empty root. Derek has two domain administrators, Ashelley and Alexandrea, who are responsible for the other two domains. The domain administrators have been reporting that changes have been made to Active Directory objects without their knowledge or written documentation. When a problem occurs from a change, no one is confessing to the change.

You know that auditing the Active Directory management can solve much of the confusion, as long as one of the domain administrators reviews the logs generated from the audit. You instruct each domain administrator to configure auditing for Active Directory to track when any object is managed within her respective domain.

Configuring auditing for DCs

Ashelley and Alexandrea need to configure auditing for their respective domains but wonder whether they can make a single setting in the root domain. After much research and failure, they realize that they can't configure a single setting in the root domain that configures auditing on their domains. They realize that there is no GPO setting that they can configure in the root domain that flows down to the child domains.

They then realize that they can just configure the same settings within their respective domain to configure auditing for Active Directory management. To configure their domain, they perform the following steps:

1. Edit the Default Domain Controller Policy using the Group Policy Editor. (This can be done in many ways: use the Group Policy tab from the Domain Controllers OU property sheet and select Edit, use the GPMC, or configure the Domain Controller Security Policy from any domain controller.)

2. Under Computer Configuration, expand the nodes down to the *Windows Settings\Security Settings\Local Policies\Audit Policy*.

3. Double-click Audit Account Management from the righthand pane.

4. Select the Define These Policy Settings checkbox.

5. Select the Success and Failure checkboxes.

6. Select the OK button.

7. Close the Group Policy Editor window.

Enabling success and failure is not required but will indicate when someone makes a change to an Active Directory account, as well as when someone attempts and fails to make a change. The GPO changes made here will be effective upon the next refresh of the GPOs to the domain controllers in the domain. If any sites need to be spanned with the replication, the convergence time to all domain controllers might be hours or days, depending on the replication schedule.

Viewing Security Log in Event Viewer

After all the domain controllers have received the new audit setting, they will immediately begin to log when accounts are managed within Active Directory. Each domain will log only the activity performed on the domain controllers and Active Directory from its domain. The logs will be logged on the domain controller where the management occurred. To simplify the management of the audit logs, Ashelley and Alexandrea could configure which domain controller the other administrators use when they update objects in Active Directory. If this is not done, the domain administrators would need to gather the logs from each domain controller manually. For more information on auditing and collecting audit logs, see Chapter 15.

 A tool such as EventComb could also be used. EventComb allows an administrator to gather logged entries from the domain controllers and then place them into files that are centrally located. The EventComb tool is a free download available at *http://www.microsoft.com/downloads/details.aspx?displaylang=en&FamilyID=9989D151-5C55-4BD3-A9D2-B95A15C73E92.*

To review the audited events from auditing of Active Directory management, you need to go into the Event Viewer and find the Security Logs. These are the steps:

1. Click Start → All Programs → Administrative Tools → Event Viewer.

2. Select the Security Log from the left pane.

3. Scroll down the right pane until you find an event that you want to review.

4. To view events related to account management, look for those that say Account Management in the Category column.

5. Double-click the event to open the Event properties sheet.

6. The Event describes the Date, Time, Source, User, Computer, and description of the event. The Description will include the object that was modified, as well as any particular information regarding the domain controller and supporting information related to management of the object.

If you have not reviewed many Event log files, you may be shocked with how much information is logged in such a short period of time. Be prepared to spend plenty of time going through the logs, to look for security problems or attacks. Be sure to use tools like EventComb to organize and gather all the events from computers around the network.

If you are having trouble trying to decrypt the description for a logged entry, be sure to use TechNet (either on the CD/DVD format or the online version at *www.technet. com*) and *www.eventid.net* to help you find better descriptions for the logged entries. The best search uses the ID number and a portion of the description that seems to be unique wording or phrasing.

Providing Security for Domain Controllers

Since the domain controllers hold the keys to the kingdom, they need to receive special attention. Domain controllers offer two primary types of access: physical access and network access. With physical access, someone can physically access the computer, such as putting a CD in the CD-ROM drive and typing at the keyboard. Physical access could also result in someone stealing the computer. Network access requires a bit more sophistication from the attacker, but there are plenty of avenues into the domain controller. The network access that needs to be considered includes acquiring user account names, share names, data, and communications with the domain controller.

Physical Access

One of the most important security measures you can take for your domain controllers is to secure them physically. The actual box, tower, or blade needs to be secured. This means behind a door with a lock that only administrators have the key to. In addition to placing the domain controller in a locked room, you need to consider providing these additional security measures to lock down your domain controllers:

- Use physical access controls to secure the lock to the server room as described in Chapter 2.

- Use smart cards on the servers as described in Chapter 10, so users must use two-factor authentication to access the domain controllers.

- Do not leave users logged on to the domain controllers. It is a misconception that a user must log on to the domain controller for it to function. The services that run on the domain controller start without any user logging on.

Another important factor for physical access to a domain controller is providing security access control when the domain controller is restarted. The Syskey utility is described in full detail in Chapter 4.

Network Access

Domain controllers also need to be protected from access across the network. Primarily, you need to protect the administrator account that resides on the domain controllers most of all. The administrator account is the golden user account that an attacker seeks to find and log on as. To protect the domain controller from network access:

Allow only administrators the ability to log on locally to the domain controllers
> This behavior is controlled by using user rights. For domain controllers, this is the default behavior and should not be changed. Standard users who can log on locally to a domain controller can access all the resources that are stored on the computer, not just those that are available over the network.

Remove the ability for the Administrator account to access the domain controllers from across the network
> It should be agreed upon that the Administrator account should not be used for typical administration. This account needs to be protected and not used for routine tasks. This account will be used if there is a problem with a domain controller or recovery needs to be performed on a domain controller. These special uses of this account do not require network access to the domain controllers. Therefore, it is ideal to deny network access to the domain controllers for this account.

Don't use the Administrator account as a service account on the domain controllers
> If the Administrator account is used as a service account, it breaks the rule that this account should not be used for routine tasks. Service accounts log on to servers and domain controllers as if they are physical users. If a virus attacks this computer, it can use the context of the service account to attack other computers on the network. With this highest privileged access, there is almost nothing that the virus could not do.

> The solution to not using the Administrator account as a service account is to create special accounts to be used for services. After the new user accounts are created, you can narrow the computers that the account can log on to, by using the Logon to Workstations option that was discussed earlier in this chapter.

Don't allow SID/name translation
> Many attackers want to know the name of the built-in Administrator account so they can attempt to log on with this account. After you take the precautions to hide this account by renaming it, the only way to identify this account is by its security identifier (SID). This is possible because all Administrator accounts end in 500 on a Windows computer. If the attacker is able to enumerate or translate names and SIDs, the attacker will be able to find the built-in Administrator's new name.

> To combat against this, disable the GPO setting labeled Allow Anonymous SID/Name Translation, shown in Figure 13-10.

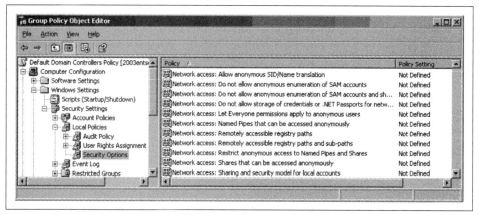

Figure 13-10. Default Domain Controller Policy showing location to lock down SID/name translation, anonymous access, and enumeration of SAM and shares

Don't allow anonymous share enumeration

An attacker that acquires a list of shares on a target computer in a different network can attack that target computer through many avenues. This list of shares is not easily obtained by browsing for the shares when the target computers are on different networks. However, if an attacker is able to access the target computer with anonymous credentials, the list of shares can be obtained and used as an entry point to the target computer.

To combat against this, enable the GPO setting labeled "Do not allow anonymous enumeration of SAM accounts and shares." There is no GPO setting that directly controls access to shares only, so this GPO setting must be used. We will talk about controlling the SAM next.

Don't allow anonymous SAM enumeration

If an attacker can obtain a list of users from the SAM or Active Directory, she will have many opportunities to try to falsify the user credentials to access the network. This list is well protected by default from an attacker without administrative privileges. However, if an attacker is able to access the target computer with anonymous credentials, the list of user accounts can be obtained and used to try and falsify credentials to get access to other computers on the network.

To combat against this, enable the GPO setting labeled "Do not allow anonymous enumeration of SAM accounts and shares" and "Do not allow anonymous enumeration of SAM accounts." Of course, if you want to target only the SAM accounts and not the shares, you will use the second option. Microsoft has separated these out to give you more control over what you want to restrict.

Don't allow the Everyone group to include anonymous

Anonymous users are allowed to perform certain activities in a Windows computer, such as list the user accounts and shares. This allows system services and functions to access the operating system without special requirements. In Windows Server 2003, the Everyone group by default is not included on the access token for the anonymous logon, so permissions that are applied to the Everyone group will not pertain to the anonymous logon. This will restrict the access that anonymous users have for the computer and should be maintained. This is desired behavior, to not have the anonymous logon access resources that the Everyone group can access.

To ensure this behavior, disable the GPO setting labeled "Let Everyone permissions apply to anonymous users."

The final suggestions listed are completed using the Default Domain Controller Policy. Figure 13-10 illustrates the location and settings within the GPO to control anonymous access to domain controllers.

Domain Controller Communications

Domain controllers communicate constantly to exchange Active Directory and GPO information. This replication that domain controllers rely on can be compromised if the network traffic is captured. There are methods to protect this vulnerability, depending on where the network traffic is being transmitted and how secure the network is. If the network is trusted but contains two different segments that don't trust each other, a firewall can be used to separate the two network segments. If this method is used, the domain controller replication traffic may be filtered out by the firewall. So, the firewall needs to be opened up to allow this domain controller replication traffic.

Another scenario might be that the domain controller replication and communication traffic needs to be protected, over either a trusted or untrusted network. This protection can be handled by opening up firewalls for domain controller replication traffic, which we just saw in the previous example, or by using two different IPSec methods. These three solutions are discussed in the following three subsections.

Open firewall ports on trusted network

Your company may have installed and configured firewalls between different networks within your IT infrastructure. This is designed to control the traffic that passes from one network to another, even though all networks are trusted. Although this configuration allows for a secure environment, which is controlled, it does cause grief for domain controllers attempting to communicate across these networks.

If your situation fits into this scenario, you can open the ports on the firewalls that are required for domain controllers to communicate with one another. To do this, you will need to open up a few ports on each firewall to allow domain controller communication. Table 13-4 lists each service and port that you will need to open.

Table 13-4. Services and ports needed for domain controller replication

Service	Port/protocol
DNS	53/tcp and 53/udp
Global catalog LDAP	3268/tcp
Global catalog LDAP over SSL	3269/tcp
Kerberos	88/tcp and 88/udp
LDAP	389/tcp
LDAP over SSL	636/tcp
NetBIOS name service	137/tcp and 137/udp
NetBIOS datagram service	138/udp
NetBIOS session service	139/tcp
Network time protocol (NTP)	123/udp
RPC dynamic assignment	*<fixed-port>*/tcp
RPC endpoint mapper	135/tcp and 135/udp
SMB over IP (Microsoft-DS)	445/tcp and 445/udp
WINS replication (if required)	42/tcp and 42/udp
WINS resolution (if required)	1512/tcp and 1512/udp

This solution does not increase the security of domain controller communication; rather, it allows domain controllers to work in the secure infrastructure that has been created with the firewalls. One variable on the list, RPC dynamic assignment, will require additional attention to configure the communication. This is the value that is used when connecting to an RPC endpoint. This endpoint either can be a random number between 1024 and 65535 or can be statically assigned. Here, you are statically assigning the value, instead of having the firewall open the entire range. The static value that you provide for this port needs to fall between the range of 49152 and 65535. This must be configured in the registry of every domain controller in the domain. To complete the registry update:

1. Open the registry editing tool by typing **regedit** at the Start → Run prompt.

2. Expand the HKLM window to the following path: *HKEY_LOCAL_MACHINE\ SYSTEM\CurrentControlSet\Services\NTDS\Parameters*.

3. Click on the Edit → New → DWORD Value menu option.

4. Type **TCP/IP Port** into the text field, then press the Enter key.

5. Double-click on the TPC/IP Port value.

6. Type a number between 49152 and 65535 into the Value Data text box, then click on the OK button.

7. Exit the registry editing tool.

8. Restart the computer.

This will not increase security for the communication between domain controllers. However, it will allow domain controllers to communicate between different networks where there is a firewall restricting ports.

IPSec for DC communication and replication

A lot of information is replicated between domain controllers that you don't want an attacker to get hold of. Replication between domain controllers includes user account names, group account names, replication schedules, and more. About the only method that you have to secure this communication is to configure IPSec for communicating between the domain controllers.

IPSec will encrypt the data as it is sent across the network. IPSec is a good solution because it encapsulates RPC traffic, which is normally prone to attacks. Another benefit from IPSec for this communication is that it provides mutual authentication, allowing the domain controllers to identify each other before any vital information is sent across the network.

To configure IPSec for all communication between domain controllers, you will need to configure each domain controller's IPSec settings. The following is a general overview of the steps that need to be performed on each domain controller, with some tips to help you configure each step correctly:

1. Create an IPSec IP filter list and filter action using the Local Security Policy.
   a. Make these configurations on each domain controller.
   b. Make sure you set the filter list to control only domain controller–to–domain controller communication.
   c. Include all protocols, to secure all communication. (Refer to the earlier section on RPC communication to specify certain communication protocols to be included in the IPSec filter.)
2. Create an IPSec policy for replication using the Local Security Policy.
   a. Note this is not a tunnel.
   b. This will be for LAN, not RAS access.
   c. You will need to choose authentication methods.
   d. Match up filter list and filter action to this IPSec policy.
3. Assign the policy!

 You could also use the `netsh ipsec` command to manage the IPSec policies.

After this is configured, the domain controllers will use IPSec for all communication. They will not use IPSec for communication with other domain members, which is not a horrible decision. You should not attempt to configure IPSec for all computers on the network, due to the complexity of the IPSec policies and lack of support for IPSec with so many client computers that still exist on corporate networks.

If you need to send IPSec traffic across a firewall, you don't need to open up the myriad of ports that we did in the previous section. You need to open up only the ports related to IPSec. These would include those listed in Table 13-5.

Table 13-5. Services and protocol needed for IPSec to pass through a firewall

Service	Port/protocol
DNS	53/tcp and 53/udp
Kerberos	88/tcp and 88/udp
Internet Key Exchange (IKE)	500/udp
IPSec encapsulated security payload (ESP)	IP protocol 50
IPSec authenticated header (AH)	IP protocol 51

Domain controller communication across untrusted network with IPSec tunnel

If your domain controllers are crossing an untrusted network with replication and basic communication, you need to look into another solution for securing the network traffic. The ideal solution is to use an IPSec tunnel. (If you are using a remote connection for the communication, you can use L2TP/IPSec for the remote access VPN.)

IPSec tunnels are used to increase the security of the server-to-server communication. The IPSec encapsulated packets will have the same benefits that you read about in Chapter 8 on IP Security. The IPSec tunnel is an advanced IPSec policy setting that will have more configurations than our previous example in which we used IPSec transport mode to secure the network traffic.

A minor difference that you will need to keep in mind when establishing your IPSec tunnel is that you can't mirror the filters for tunneled traffic. You will need to have two rules: one for the outbound traffic and one for the inbound traffic. When you establish the two rules, you will need to configure the tunnel endpoints. For the outbound tunnel endpoint, it will be the IP address for the computer on the other end of the tunnel. For the inbound tunnel endpoint, it will be the IP address configured on the local computer. See Chapter 8 for more information about configuring IPSec policies, filters, and rules.

Locating Domain Controllers in Active Directory

Although this may seem silly, many people want to move the domain controller computer accounts to different OUs. This is a mistake, considering the importance of the Default Domain Controller Policy preconfigured at the Domain Controllers OU.

Therefore, additional OUs can be created below the Domain Controllers OU to contain different domain controller accounts, but domain controllers should not be moved outside of the Domain Controllers OU.

Roles and Responsibilities

Domain controllers have a crucial role in housing and protecting the Active Directory. They are also very busy keeping up with changes among other domain controllers and authenticating user logons. With all this activity and security responsibility, domain controllers should be limited to performing the domain controller duties.

Additional duties that domain controllers may properly be responsible for include:

- Flexible single master operator role
- Global catalog

Domain controllers should not be running other services that can be handled by member servers, which don't have the responsibility of Active Directory or authenticating user logons. Services that should be handed off to member servers include:

- Antivirus monitoring
- Backup
- Management
- Monitoring
- Asset control

Summary

Active Directory is a large, complex component of your network. Many aspects of this book—such as IP Security, certificates, DNS, and authentication—relate to providing security for Active Directory. Combining those technologies with the security suggestions that are laid out in this chapter will provide a reasonably secure environment for Active Directory.

If you take only one thing from this chapter, remember that the primary mechanisms to secure Active Directory include GPOs, delegation, and administrative privileges. If you apply security in these areas, the majority of the work for locking down Active Directory will be complete.

CHAPTER 14

Remote Access Security

Remote access presents one of the biggest potential security risks in any network. In fact, remote access is a risk by its very nature: remote access is intended to allow remote computers to access your private network. The key to mitigating the risk is to ensure that the individuals who are accessing your network are legitimate and that the data they transmit to and from your network is protected. In this chapter, I'll discuss the ways Windows Server 2003 lets you deploy secure remote access solutions.

 This chapter isn't intended to be an exhaustive how-to guide for remote access. Entire books on that subject—many of them larger than your phone book—are available. Instead, this chapter is designed to help you understand the security implications of remote access and show you how Windows Server 2003 can help mitigate any security risks that remote access creates. For the ultimate remote access reference, see the *Deploying Virtual Private Networks with Microsoft Windows Server 2003 Technical Reference* (MS Press).

Because remote access is such a significant security risk, some organizations prefer to cut it off entirely, refusing to offer remote access services to their users. That's usually a mistake, because the benefits of remote access are usually just as significant as the security risks. Many administrators, for example, require remote access in order to respond to evening emergencies and to perform other administrative tasks. Refusing to offer remote access services simply isn't an option, because the administrators can't operate any other way. And many employees work very effectively from remote locations, including homebound or traveling employees. Cutting these employees off from any resources could mean cutting productivity and ROI. Some companies see remote access pay for itself in increased employee effectiveness.

What Is Remote Access?

Back in the early days of computing, some things were simple. If you wanted to use a computer, you had to go to it and stay with it while you worked with it. This working method was acceptable for a while, but convenience and accessibility needs were eventually considered. How does a remote salesperson access data if in the office only once a month? How does a homebound employee continue to use computing resources? How can an administrator check errors or logs during off hours without having to get to the computer? For these and other reasons, remote access needed to be addressed.

Remote access in Windows Server 2003 is a set of features that allows remote users to access resources on a remote network. Generally, users can connect to a corporate network and use the resources as if directly connected to that network. Connections to the corporate network can be via direct dial-up networking or through virtual private networking (VPN), in which the computer uses an intermediate network (such as the Internet) to connect to the corporate network. VPN connections can use either of two tunneling protocol varieties in Windows Server 2003: Point-to-Point Tunneling Protocol (PPTP) and its newer version, Layer 2 Tunneling Protocol (L2TP). As you'll see later, L2TP has some significant security advantages over PPTP.

 Because of the proliferation of high-speed Internet connections around the world, most corporations no longer provide dial-up access. For that reason, this chapter focuses on VPN access.

Windows Server 2003 offers several new features for remote access. The most important is its extensive integration with IPSec. Using IPSec to protect VPN connections was introduced in Windows 2000, but several specific needs were not met until Windows Server 2003. These included using preshared keys for VPNs and the ability to create tunnels when connected to network address translation (NAT) networks.

Remote access functionality adds enormous flexibility for users to connect to corporate resources. It also adds opportunities for attackers to connect to those same resources. An attacker that makes a VPN connection to your corporate network is essentially sitting at a desk at your company. Therefore, you must provide protection against such attackers. This chapter describes how to put such protection into place.

Controlling Access

The best way to make remote access more secure is to strictly control who is allowed to access your network remotely, either via virtual private networks (VPNs) or dial-up connections. Instead of allowing all company users to dial in, restrict the service to employees who actually need it. If an employee is going on a business trip, enable dial-up access for his account; when he returns from the trip, remove his dial-up authorization. While the cost of managing this user may be relatively high, the practice of carefully limiting remote access usually provides greatly enhanced security.

Windows Server 2003 uses remote access policies to determine who is and who is not allowed to access a remote access server. Windows Server 2003 can use Remote Authentication for Dial-in User Services (RADIUS) to provide centralized remote access policies for a group of remote access servers and to allow Windows Server 2003's remote access policies to manage non-Windows dial-up gateways.

Remote Access Policies

Windows Server 2003 uses remote access policies to determine whether it will accept incoming remote access connections. Remote access policies can apply to a number of different connection types, including VPN, dial-up, and wireless. Windows Server 2003 provides the Routing and Remote Access Microsoft Management Console (MMC) snap-in, shown in Figure 14-1, which allows you to manage remote access policies and all configuration for Routing and Remote Access (also known as remote access services, or RAS).

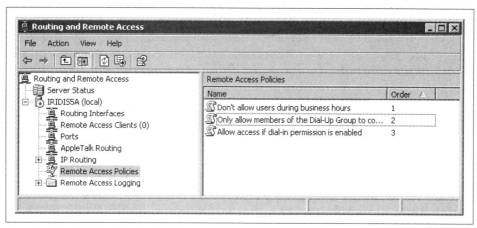

Figure 14-1. Managing remote access policies with the Routing and Remote Access snap-in

When a user attempts to connect to Routing and Remote Access, the service evaluates the remote access policies in the order that they're listed in the snap-in. Each policy specifies conditions, such as user groups, connection types, time of day, and so forth, which the server attempts to match to the requested connection. If the server finds a policy with conditions that match the requested connection, it uses the policy's Allow or Disallow state to permit or deny the connection. If the server is unable to match a policy to the conditions of the connection, the connection is denied.

For example, suppose you create a policy that applies to dial-up connections made between the hours of 6 p.m. and 6 a.m. and mark that policy to allow connections. Any authenticated user attempting to dial in to the server during those hours will be permitted. You can also have policies check for group membership or examine the user's Active Directory account to see if dial-up permissions have been granted to the account.

Written remote access security policies

The technology-based solution to remote access policy is described in detail throughout this chapter. However, these policies must be examined and documented before they can be implemented with the steps I provide. This documentation is in the form of a written remote access policy.

Chapter 15 provides guidelines and processes for creating written security policy for your organization. A number of considerations for these policies are specific to remote access, including:

Login hours
> Do you want to allow your users to connect via remote access at all hours? If policy requires users to work from the office during normal working hours, RAS can be disabled during those hours. This blocks attackers during a significant portion of the day as well as conserves resources on the remote access servers. Bandwidth consumption is also minimized during the important working hours if VPN support is disabled at that time.

Restricted use of remote access
> Do all employees need the ability to dial in? Most corporations require written authorization from management to enable a user to connect via remote access. Restricting use of remote access improves security by minimizing the number of authorized RAS credentials. This restriction also makes the best use of limited resources by stopping unauthorized users from consuming corporate bandwidth.

Temporary remote access
> If a user needs temporary remote access (for example, a normally office bound employee makes an extended business trip), ensure the authorization is revoked after an approved time period. This should be considered part of the authorization process.

Minimum security for connection
> If your users frequently access sensitive data across RAS, you should ensure the connection is as secure as possible. This includes encrypting network traffic between the client and RAS server.

Security for remote computer
> Internet viruses and worms often make successful attacks against unprotected home computers. If those computers are then allowed to connect to your corporate network, the viruses and worms can quickly spread to internal computers.

This effectively bypasses normal firewalls and other protection devices, as the RAS connection is trusted. Many corporations now require that all computers connecting via RAS run current antivirus and firewall software. This is not a foolproof solution, but it does reduce the likelihood that a home or mobile user will infect the corporate network.

An emerging RAS technology group called *Network Quarantine* generically allows administrators to isolate computers connecting via RAS (and often via LAN) and perform some security checks before exposing those computers to the rest of the network. At the time of this writing, Microsoft does not yet have a quarantine product and has not officially announced a date for its availability.

Allowing users to connect via RAS increases the need for defense-in-depth protection of your network resources. Because viruses and worms can lay dormant on remote computers for extended periods before attacking resources, a user could easily transport malicious code into the network. If there is insufficient protection within the network (e.g., each server running virus-scanning software, layers of firewalls, etc.), this malicious code could run amok.

RADIUS and IAS

Normally, remote access policies apply only to the Windows Server 2003 system on which they are configured. If you have multiple servers acting as remote access gateways, or if you have non-Windows remote access gateways, remote access policy management can become cumbersome. Fortunately, Windows Server 2003 provides a solution.

Rather than using its own remote access policies, Windows Server 2003 can be configured to use a centralized RADIUS server. RADIUS is an industry-standard protocol that remote access gateways use to communicate with a central authorization server on your network. The central server uses its own configuration to instruct the gateways to accept or decline incoming connections. Figure 14-2 shows the properties of Routing and Remote Access configured to use a RADIUS server rather than the server's own remote access policies. This was accessed by right-clicking on the server name (in this case, IRIDIS5A) in the Routing and Remote Access MMC snap-in and then clicking Properties.

Windows Server 2003 also includes its own RADIUS-compatible server, called Internet Authentication Service (IAS). IAS is designed to run on Windows Server 2003 and use that server's local remote access policies to authenticate users for other RADIUS-compatible remote access gateways. Since most remote access gateways are RADIUS-compatible (including those produced by Shiva, Cisco, Nortel, and others), you can use IAS to enforce Windows Server 2003 remote access policies on those other gateways.

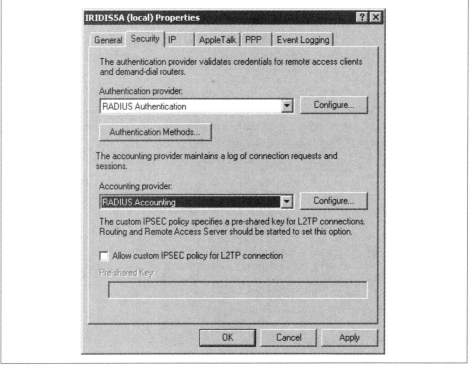

Figure 14-2. Configuring Routing and Remote Access to use a RADIUS server for authentication

You can also use IAS to centralize policy management if you use only Windows Server 2003 and Routing and Remote Access to provide remote access services to your users. Simply install IAS on one remote access server and configure remote access policies on that server. Configure the other remote access servers to use RADIUS for authentication, and configure their RADIUS settings to use the server on which IAS is installed.

Using IAS and RADIUS to centralize remote access authentication management provides more consistent and reliable security than configuring individual policies on a number of remote access gateway servers or devices.

Authentication and Encryption Protocols

Windows Server 2003 supports a number of authentication and encryption protocols, which are designed to support a wide range of remote access clients. Selecting the strongest possible protocols that your clients support provides the best security for your remote access infrastructure.

Authentication and Accounting

Most RADIUS servers, including IAS, can provide *accounting* functionality in addition to their authorization capabilities. Accounting creates detailed log files of remote user access, including logon times and session information. Many organizations use these logs to charge each company department for their remote access usage or to plan for remote access capacity. You can also audit these logs on a periodic basis to check for unauthorized access attempts, overlong sessions from users who normally aren't online for very long, and so forth.

In an especially large remote access environment, the tasks of authorization and accounting might be more than one RADIUS server can handle. Accounting in particular can be very resource intensive, since every remote access connection constantly generates a stream of status messages. For this reason, most RADIUS clients—including Routing and Remote Access—can be configured to use one RADIUS server for authorization and another for accounting, effectively dividing the load and creating a more scalable solution.

Authentication Protocols

Windows Server 2003 supports several remote access authentication protocols. You can use remote access policies to determine which protocols your server will accept, as shown in Figure 14-3.

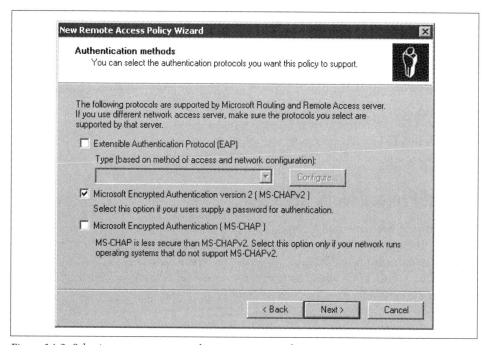

Figure 14-3. Selecting remote access authentication protocols in a remote access policy

The three basic protocols that Windows Server 2003 supports are:

Extensible Authentication Protocol (EAP)
> EAP is primarily used to support advanced authentication mechanisms such as smart cards and requires additional configuration settings depending on how your environment is set up to handle those mechanisms.

Microsoft Challenge-Handshake Authentication Protocol (MS-CHAP)
> MS-CHAP is an older authentication protocol used by client operating systems like Windows 95.

MS-CHAP v2
> Version 2 of the MS-CHAP protocol is native to Windows 2000 and Windows Server 2003 (and is included in Windows NT 4.0 Service Pack 4 and later) and provides more secure authentication than the older MS-CHAP.

Be sure your remote access policies will accept older authentication protocols if your remote access clients need them. However, always allow your policies to accept connections on the strongest protocols as well. Newer clients like Windows XP will attempt to use MS-CHAP v2 first, if your server permits it.

Your remote access clients must be configured to use the same authentication protocols as your server. Figure 14-4 shows the dial-up configuration for a typical Windows client. Selecting the strongest authentication method will cause the client to disconnect if the server does not support that method.

By selecting the Advanced configuration on the client's dial-up properties, you can manually select the protocols that the client will attempt to use. The Advanced configuration dialog box is shown in Figure 14-5.

Encryption Protocols

Windows Server 2003 also allows you to restrict remote access connections to those that use specific levels of data encryption. As with authentication protocols, dial-up clients must be configured to use data encryption. Figure 14-6 shows a Windows client configured to use the strongest possible data encryption and to disconnect if the server does not support that level of encryption.

Virtual Private Networks

Virtual private networks, or VPNs, allow you to use public networks, such as the Internet, as your own private, secure network connection. Many companies use VPNs to connect branch offices to headquarters via the Internet. VPNs rely on data encapsulation and encryption to work and provide reliable, secure connectivity options for remote access.

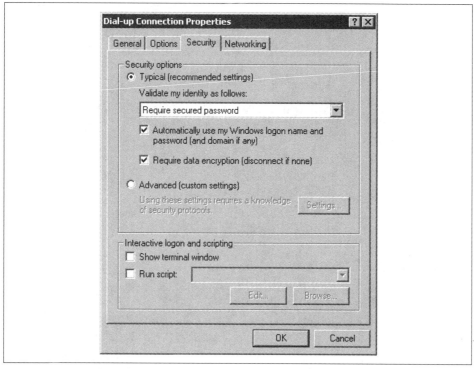

Figure 14-4. Typical Windows client dial-up configuration

Operating Theory

Understanding how a VPN works requires you to first understand the basic nature of modern networking. Networks use layered protocols, called *stacks*, to perform various functions. Users interact most directly with the *application layer*, which is located at the top of the network stack. A web browser, for example, uses the application-level protocol HTTP.

The collection of wires and electrical signals that form a network exists at the bottom layer of the stack. In between the high- and low-level protocols are midlevel protocols that package data for delivery to specific machines and make sure the data arrives safely at its destination.

When your web browser transmits an HTTP request, your computer's IP stack packages, or *encapsulates*, that request in a packet that uses the TCP protocol. The TCP packet is then encapsulated within a lower-level IP packet, then again within an Ethernet packet. The Ethernet packet contains the information necessary for the data to be translated into electrical signals and placed onto the network. The IP and TCP

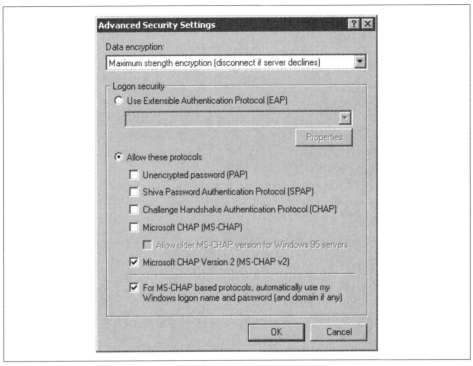

Figure 14-5. Advanced Windows client dial-up configuration

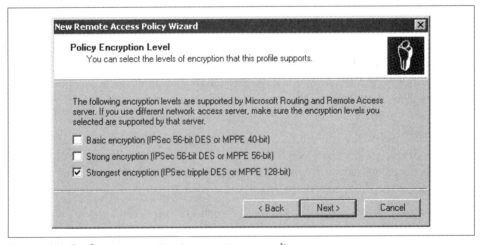

Figure 14-6. Configuring encryption in a remote access policy

protocols contain information necessary for routers to get the data to the correct destination. Once the packet arrives at its destination, its various layers are stripped away by the recipient's network stack, revealing the original HTTP request. Figure 14-7 shows a logical diagram of how encapsulation works.

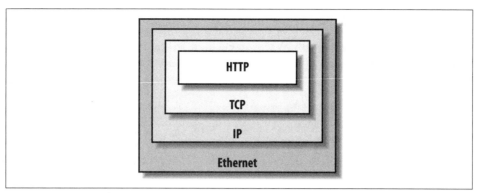

Figure 14-7. Encapsulating an HTTP request

VPN protocols step in before packets are handed off to your computer's network hardware. They encapsulate the data one more time, within a VPN packet. In fact, your computer often sees a VPN as a "virtual network adapter" and passes packets to that "adapter" for final transmission. The VPN adapter encapsulates the data and passes it to your computer's real network interface card (NIC), which places the packet onto the network. Figure 14-8 shows the virtual adapter in action.

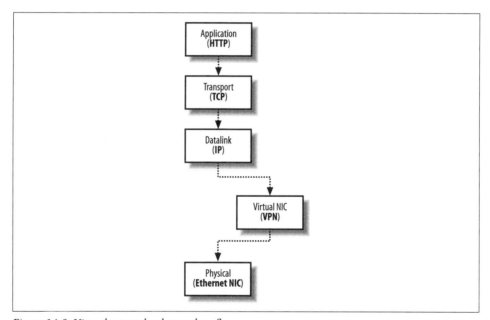

Figure 14-8. Virtual network adapter data flow

Once the data arrives at its destination, the recipient's network adapter passes the data to another virtual network adapter, which strips off the VPN packet information and passes the remaining data to the computer's TCP/IP stack, where the data is processed normally.

Because your computer treats the virtual adapter as a real network adapter, your computer thinks that it has established a private, point-to-point connection with the computer on the other end of the VPN. In effect, a virtual *tunnel* exists between the two computers. All data entering the tunnel is packaged by the VPN protocol and sent directly to the other end of the tunnel, where the data can be unpackaged and read.

VPN Protocols

There are two common VPN protocols, which are supported by Windows Server 2003.

Point-to-Point Tunneling Protocol (PPTP)

PPTP was originally created by Microsoft and introduced in Windows NT 4.0's Routing and Remote Access Services. PPTP encrypts the data it encapsulates, but it does not encrypt the VPN's header data. That means an eavesdropper can detect that a PPTP tunnel is in use and can identify the packets "contained" within the tunnel. However, the eavesdropper would still have to break the decryption on the tunnel's contents to read the data moving through the tunnel. PPTP is widely supported within the Windows product line all the way back to Windows 95.

Layer 2 Tunneling Protocol (L2TP)

L2TP is the newest VPN protocol and provides only the tunneling aspect of a VPN, not encryption. However, L2TP is usually used in conjunction with IPSec, which encrypts the entire L2TP packet. A primary advantage of L2TP over PPTP is that eavesdroppers cannot tell that a VPN is in use, because IPSec encrypts even the L2TP header information. L2TP also enjoys wider industry support outside of Microsoft. Within the Microsoft product line, L2TP is supported natively on Windows 2000, Windows XP, and Windows Server 2003.

Making VPNs More Secure

VPNs are inherently rather secure end-to-end connections, simply because of the way they work. However, the way you build a VPN solution into your network can enhance the security of your overall network as well. Here are some tips:

- Use remote access policies to restrict the users who can use the VPN, just as you would restrict users who can dial in to your network. VPN connections can be authenticated through RADIUS, allowing you to use IAS for centralized policy management, even if you aren't using Windows-based VPN servers. Instructions for restricting the users of VPNs are provided later in this chapter.

- Use L2TP VPNs whenever possible, since they encrypt more of the packets passing through the tunnel. They also provide much stronger encryption than earlier VPN security models.

Where your VPN server is placed on your network is an important security consideration. One technique is to place the VPN server behind your firewall, as shown in Figure 14-9.

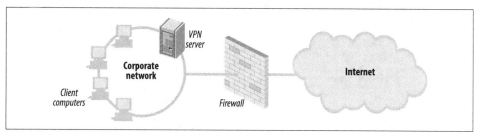

Figure 14-9. Placing your VPN server behind a firewall

That placement works only under a small number of circumstances, though. Depending on the age and patch level of your clients, they may not be able to access the VPN server through the firewall. You may, however, need to configure the firewall to allow the ports and protocols required for RAS. PPTP uses TCP port 1723 and IP Protocol 47. L2TP uses UDP port 1701. If you're using IPSec with L2TP, you must allow IP Protocols 50 and 51 and TCP and UDP port 500.

More commonly, administrators place their VPN server directly on the Internet, as shown in Figure 14-10.

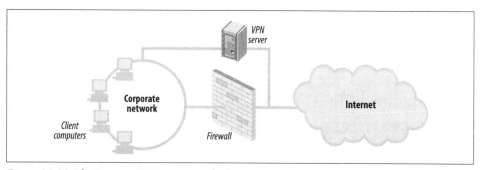

Figure 14-10. Placing your VPN server on the Internet

This placement avoids the problems caused by firewalls, but makes your VPN server a target for attackers, who will try and access your corporate network by exploiting security vulnerabilities in the VPN server itself. If the VPN server runs Windows

Server 2003, you can lock it down by enabling VPN filters. As shown in Figure 14-11, you can configure the network interface connected to the Internet so that it drops all packets unrelated to the VPN protocol in use (in this example, PPTP, which uses a destination TCP port of 1723). These settings are available as properties of the RAS interface.

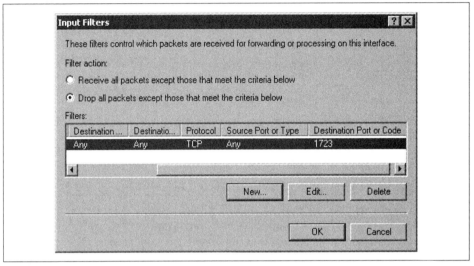

Figure 14-11. Configuring IP filters

 Some firewalls are capable of acting as VPN servers, also. Whenever possible, consider using your firewall as a VPN endpoint, since it is already protecting itself and your network from attackers. Using your firewall as a VPN server eliminates many common VPN configuration problems and avoids the need to connect an additional server to both the Internet and your network.

Example Implementations for Remote Access

RAS is a complex technology that can be implemented in almost as many ways as there are customers to implement it. The scope of remote access configuration is far beyond what can be addressed within the security focus of this book. However, I can address some common configurations and examine the security-specific configurations and concerns.

Setting Up Remote Access Authentication for Dial-in Users

The most common use of RAS is for dial-up users to connect to the corporate network from remote locations with their modems. In this example, I'll assume a third-party modem bank is used and configured to use a separate RADIUS server for authentication and accounting. This customer has allocated a Windows Server 2003 computer specifically to be used for IAS.

The written security requirements for remote users connecting to the corporate network include restriction on the hours allowed for dial-in connections to ensure the resources are used appropriately. In addition, security policy dictates that users must authenticate against an Active Directory domain.

To configure remote access to provide this functionality, follow these steps:

1. Install IAS on the server. You'll find IAS in the Add or Remove Programs application on the Control Panel; just click Add/Remove Windows Components and select Internet Authentication Service from the Networking Services component's Details list.

2. Open the Internet Authentication Service console from the Administrative Tools program group.

3. Examine the default remote access policies for applicability by clicking Remote Access Policies. Generally, you'll want to delete the two default policies and create your own, which is what I'll do in this example.

4. Right-click Remote Access Policies and select New Policy from the pop-up menu.

5. Click Next to begin, then click Set Up A Custom Policy. Then provide a policy name. In this example, the policy will be used to restrict dial-up access to evening hours, so I'll name the policy Evening Hours Only. Click Next to continue.

6. Click Add to add a policy condition.

7. Double-click Day-And-Time-Restriction in the list.

8. In the Time of Day Constraints dialog, highlight the hours during which dial-up access will be allowed. Then click Permitted to change the highlighted hours to blue, indicating that dial-up access will be permitted during those times. This is shown in Figure 14-12.

9. Click OK.

10. Click Add to add a new policy condition.

11. Double-click Windows Groups in the list.

12. Click Add.

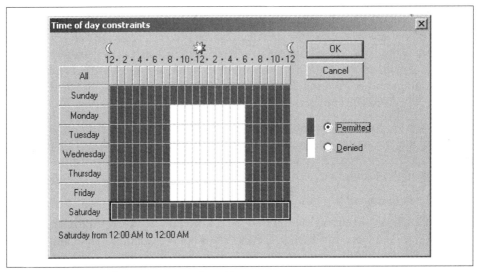

Figure 14-12. Date and time restrictions for RAS users

13. Type **Domain Users** in the list and click OK, then click OK again. Your policy conditions will appear similar to those shown in Figure 14-13.

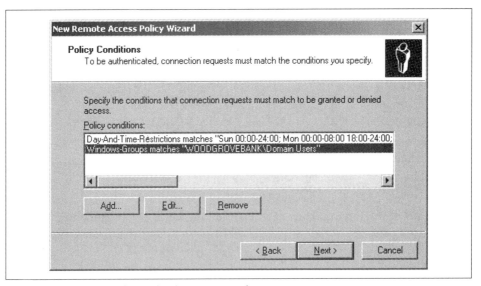

Figure 14-13. Policy conditions for the new RAS policy

14. Click Next.

15. Click Grant Remote Access Permission. This will grant remote access permission if the policy conditions are met. Then click Next.

16. Click Next, and then click Finish to create the policy.

The new policy will allow dial-up access for members of the Domain Users group only during the specified hours. If users attempt to dial in at other times, they will not match the policy conditions and will be denied dial-up access. You'll also need to ensure that users' Active Directory accounts are configured to adhere to the remote policy conditions. This is the default in Windows Server 2003, so unless you've previously modified it (on the Dial-in tab of each account's Properties dialog), you're good to go.

Now, you'll need to configure your dial-up devices to use IAS for authentication. Consult their documentation for details on doing so. You also have to let IAS know that the devices will be using it, by adding them as RADIUS clients:

1. In the Internet Authentication Service console, right-click RADIUS Clients and select New RADIUS Client from the pop-up menu.

2. Type a name and the IP address of the first device that will use IAS for authentication. Click Next.

3. Generally, you'll select RADIUS Standard for the Client-Vendor. However, if your device's documentation specifies a different setting (such as US Robotics or Shiva), use that.

4. Specify a shared secret. This is essentially a password that the device will use to contact IAS. IAS and the device must be configured with the same password.

5. Click Next.

That's it! Once your device is configured, IAS will provide central control over dial-up authentication.

Setting Up a VPN Server

Another very common example in the modern workforce involves work-at-home employees. Many companies allow employees to work from home or a remote location. As high-speed Internet connections proliferate, the dial-up RAS scenario is often being replaced with virtual private networking that provides a high-speed connection through the Internet to the corporate network.

However, this scenario presents a very important security concern. Many attackers prowl the Internet and can be indistinguishable from authorized users. I must ensure that all communication received over the Internet is secure, providing access to authorized clients while blocking unauthorized attackers.

To configure RAS to provide secure VPN connections, follow these steps:

1. Open the Routing and Remote Access console. This example assumes that you haven't previously configured Routing and Remote Access.

2. Right-click the server name and select Configure and Enable Routing and Remote Access from the pop-up menu.

3. Click Next.

4. Select Custom Configuration and click Next.

5. Select VPN Access and click Next.

6. Click Finish to complete the wizard.

7. Select Yes to start Routing and Remote Access. This prompt appears because the Routing and Remote Access service is not yet started on this computer and Windows assumes that, because you are configuring Routing and Remote Access, you want to start it.

Routing and Remote Access automatically creates a number of VPN ports, including 1 PPPOE port, 128 PPTP ports, and 128 L2TP ports. You should disable any that you don't plan to use and ensure that the others meet your configuration needs. To modify these ports:

1. Right-click Ports in the Routing and Remote Access console. Select Properties from the pop-up menu.

2. Select a port from the list and click Configure.

3. Select the appropriate options to enable inbound VPN access or both inbound and outbound. In this example, only inbound PPTP access is required; I'll enable that for PPTP. In this example, the default of 128 PPTP ports is sufficient, and I leave that alone as shown in Figure 14-14.

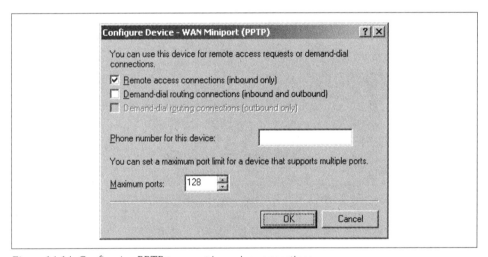

Figure 14-14. Configuring PPTP to accept incoming connections

4. I'll disable the other VPN ports since I don't plan to use them right now. I do this by clicking each of them, clicking Configure, then deselecting all connection types as shown in Figure 14-15. Eventually the only device that has a Used By listing is PPTP.

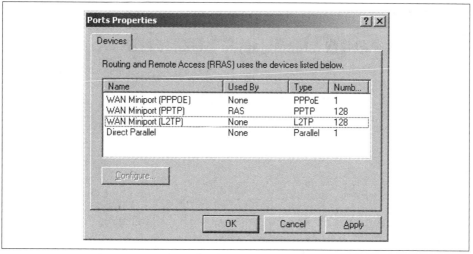

Figure 14-15. Disabling RAS devices is simple

Setting up Routing and Remote Access to accept VPN connections is easy. You'll likely have more trouble dealing with users' ISPs, which may not provide the routing support necessary for PPTP or L2TP connections. If users aren't able to make a VPN connection, contact both your corporate ISP and the user's ISP to ensure that they support the VPN protocol you are attempting to use.

 Routing and Remote Access can be configured to use IAS or another RADIUS server to authenticate VPN users. To do so, modify the properties of the server in the Routing and Remote Access console and select RADIUS Authentication for the authentication provider on the Security tab.

Summary

In this chapter, you learned how remote access to your network presents an inherent security risk and how Windows Server 2003 provides mechanisms to make remote access more secure. Remote access can be controlled through the use of remote access policies and centralized RADIUS servers, and dial-up access can be made more secure by selecting appropriate authentication and encryption protocols. Understanding how VPNs work allows you to design a VPN solution to provide maximum security.

It is important to remember that no security is absolute. This is especially true when talking about allowing remote users to access your network. There is simply no attacker-proof way to allow access. However, many different security options help you lessen the risks. You should carefully weigh the risks of allowing remote access against the benefits before you provide remote access in your environment.

Auditing and Ongoing Security

Computer security is not an absolute. No sane person will tell you, "Your network is secure." There are various levels of assurance and threats that can be mitigated, but ultimately all security is a trade-off. We decide how much time and money we want to spend to provide a given level of security, and then we determine whether the user experience will be acceptable with that security. Time, money, and user experience have nothing to do with security, but they shape the security design.

One of the most common misconceptions is that computer security should be entirely technology-based. Security must be a combination of technology and policy. The technology enables security, but only well-defined policies can ensure the security is employed, maintained, and scrutinized properly. The remainder of this chapter will discuss how these policies can be created and put in place to help ensure the ongoing security of the network. Then I'll discuss the two most important ongoing security tasks: auditing and patching.

Security Policies and Procedures

Network administrators are truly amazing. They have to master numerous technologies. They must know user environments better than the user, even though they may never use them personally. Most must memorize the layout of server rooms and portions of the corporate network infrastructure. With this incredible amount of information in their brains, there's always the chance that minor details could be forgotten or unimportant housekeeping tasks could be put off. That's simply what happens when network administrators get busy or overloaded.

Overloaded administrators who attempt to perform tasks from memory or rely on their brains to remember to do routine jobs are the enemies of security. Invariably, the tasks that are put off are security-related tasks, such as backing up Audit Logs or verifying current patch levels on servers. These tasks are routine, after all, and there's no current attack or vulnerability to be concerned about. Putting off security-related

Rogue Administrator

This scenario is one that makes even the most experienced security professional cringe. There are no perfect solutions to this scenario, but you'll quickly see where improvements could be made. As usual, the names have been changed.

Kathie Flood was a domain administrator at her company. She became aware that a downsizing effort was underway and her job was in jeopardy. For a plethora of personal reasons, Kathie was very upset about this development. She determined that her continued presence would be felt even after she was fired.

Before her dismissal, Kathie created a new user account in the domain. She created a fictitious user named Scott Culp and propagated the various fields in the user account details to make it look as if Scott were a legitimate user in the same department as Kathie. Kathie then added this account to the Domain Admins group and ensured that it had RAS permissions to access the company remotely.

The results of this scenario are predictable. Once Kathie was dismissed, she waited until the company's most vulnerable time—for this company, the fifth of each month is a critical time for customer billing. She then connected to the company's network remotely using Scott Culp's credentials and began attacking the company's critical line-of-business servers. With the Scott account in the Domain Admins group, she was able to choose the method of attack. In this particular case, Kathie wrote a script that remotely destroyed critical parts of the operating system and then forced a reboot.

The company had disabled Kathie's user account and retrieved her building access card at the moment she was dismissed. However, this company had no policy in place to audit sensitive group membership, such as the members of the Domain Admins group. No procedures required sign-off or multiple existing administrators to make the changes Kathie made. Before Kathie attacked the network, she was the only person who knew that the Scott Culp account existed or that it was a member of Domain Admins.

Forensics and postmortem analysis eventually provided enough evidence to point to the culprit. Although Kathie was eventually prosecuted for her crime, it made little difference. Because of another administrator's unintentional but complementary failure, there were no recent backups of the data critical to the company's business. The company lost most of its accounts because of the delay caused by this attack. Eventually the company went under.

Simple auditing would have prevented most of this scenario. The creation of Scott Culp, a user who didn't exist in the human resources database, should have been detected immediately. His addition to the Domain Admins group should have also been detected immediately and reviewed against security policy for administration of that group. And though backup procedures normally fall outside the role of the security administrator, they are often the best way to recover from an attack. Security policies should have been created to periodically audit the backups to ensure they were uncorrupted and useful in case of an attack such as this.

tasks is unfortunately common and often leads to vulnerable networks and success-fully attacked servers. When tasks are delayed and then attempted from memory, this problem could be compounded by tasks being performed incorrectly or incompletely, such as updating a virus scanner but not reenabling it. Although technology is ultimately the vulnerability, human error is directly responsible for many of the computer security problems we experience.

To mitigate the problems of human error when performing security-related tasks, policies and procedures should be developed. They act as documentation to tell administrators exactly what to do and when to do it, as well as what tasks can and cannot be done. These policies and procedures help ensure that complacency does not create vulnerabilities in your network security.

A *policy* is a high-level statement of requirements. Policies do not define exactly how do to something, but rather they broadly state that something must be done. Policies often come from management or cross-organizational groups with the support of upper management.

A *procedure* is a repeatable series of steps that define a task. Procedures should naturally flow from well-written policies as the low-level step-by-step processes that actually implement policies. This is the distinction between policy and procedure: policy defines what to do, and procedure defines how to do it.

> Some policy references define a third component of overall security policy called *standards*, which define normal practices. Many organizations consider standards to be part of both policy and procedure. This helps simplify the policy process. For the purpose of this book, I will discuss policy and procedure, which together include standards.

The relationship between policy and procedure is not 1:1. For example, one of your company's security policies may state, "All web clients must authenticate using Windows integrated authentication." Many procedures must be written to configure clients and servers to enforce this policy. Policies are broader in scope and provide direction, while procedures are very focused on accomplishing a specific task.

There are also security *standards*. Standards are specifications or exact configurations for various elements of your IT infrastructure. They may include software and hardware requirements for computers in different roles or they may work with policies and procedures to define some external control (for example, a standard might dictate how long a procedure takes).

For security considerations, a standard is usually implemented as a *baseline*—a beginning configuration for a computer or user based on established policy. Your company may already have a baseline configuration that requires a virus scanner to be installed on all computers, that the latest service packs and hot fixes are installed, and so on. These often vary by computer role but usually have a great deal of commonality across the company.

Benefits of Establishing Security Policies and Procedures

Well-defined security policies and procedures are critical to the total security of the enterprise. As stated before, security is partially a technology problem and partially an administrative problem. The administrative portion of the problem cannot be solved without specific rules, which in this case are our policies and procedures. In helping to solve the administrative portion of the security problem, security policies and procedures provide the following benefits:

Define acceptable behavior

> People cannot comply with arbitrary policy unless they know what it is in advance. For example, an administrator cannot tell a user to use a more secure password without having defined parameters for that secure password in advance. The administrator also cannot give different employees different rules about their passwords. Having a policy created in advance allows the administrator to simply refer to that document to ensure that the appropriate rule is applied evenhandedly across the organization.

Provide a forum for collaboration of all interested parties

> These parties all have input into the policies, which are formed by consensus. This collaboration often involves upper management, network administration, IT management, and user representatives. This helps to ensure that security policy is well balanced and provides needed security without imposing an undue burden on the users of the secured systems.

Legally assign ownership of actions to appropriate parties

> Without clearly documented policies and procedures, a security breach could be argued to be unintentional or without malice. From a legal perspective, you must clearly establish what behaviors are unacceptable in an organization and what liability is associated with noncompliance.

Reduce the likelihood of security breaches

> Once policies and procedures are defined and applied throughout an organization, the opportunity for security breaches is severely limited. As long as the policies are implemented as designed, the threats they were designed to reduce remain in check. For example, a policy that states that all firewall software must be updated every 30 days helps reduce security breaches by ensuring that the firewall software is current and can deal with the latest known threats.

Reduce the likelihood of misconfigurations

> As I'll show throughout this chapter, administrator-caused misconfiguration is a leading cause of network security holes. Policy is designed to identify those potential holes, and detailed procedures ensure that holes are not created accidentally.

Establish penalties for noncompliance

> Unless upper management decides in advance to apply evenhanded penalties for noncompliance with established policy and procedures, they are ineffective.

Involving these decision-makers in the policy creation process assures all levels of the organization that the policies are appropriate, fair, and well documented. These decision-makers will ultimately be the ones who must discipline or terminate employees who do not follow these procedures, or enforce whatever penalties are established. Therefore, their involvement from the beginning is beneficial.

There are few downsides to creating security policies and procedures. The one of most concern is the time involved. Because careful examination of computer environments and configurations is required, the creation of these documents can take a very long time and become a costly endeavor. Once created, these documents must be approved by upper management before being put in place, which can consume even more resources. Often upper management presents concerns not previously considered, which will require revision of the documents and another full round of approvals.

Creating Security Policies

The policy creation process is not a simple lockstep process like those for installing and configuring software. Administrative decision-making and documentation are often a lengthy and iterative process.

First, you should decide on a process to follow. Guidelines are available to help you design, document, and implement administrative policies. These include the Microsoft Solutions Framework (MSF) and the Microsoft Operations Framework (MOF), both of which are extensively documented on Microsoft TechNet at *www.microsoft.com/msf*. The guidelines will help ensure you do not miss any components of planning or implementation while driving toward a solution.

Once you've decided on a strategy for designing the policies, you must assemble a working group. This group should represent all aspects of the policy process and should include representatives of the following functional groups:

Senior management
>   To provide authorization and support of policies as well as strategic guidance. Management must also agree to enforce any policy created by the body, so their involvement is critical.

Human resources representation
>   To ensure policies do not interfere with employees' liberties as a whole and to ensure that policy enforcement is possible.

Legal representation
>   To provide guidance on policies that are designed to provide forensic evidence as well as ensure that proper wording is used.

Network and security administration
> To verify that policies can actually be implemented and are specific enough to derive procedures from.

Representative(s) of users affected by the policy
> To determine whether policies will interfere with their work.

These teams normally have five to eight members. Too many representatives might bog the group down in debate, and too few might not represent all interests. This number may vary depending on the size of the organization.

 Speaking of groups bogging down, there should be provisions in place for "emergency response" working groups that can quickly assemble and make authoritative decisions in times of crisis. For example, if a simple patch can resolve a spreading worm on your network but it takes six weeks for the full process to authorize this patch, there should be a method to immediately decide to take action.

Now that the group is assembled, a decision must be made on the goals and scope of the policy. The goals will define what the policy will do, such as a data privacy policy with a goal of protecting client data from unauthorized access. Most policies also contain a scope statement that clearly defines who the policy applies to and under what specific conditions, if any.

Once the goals and scope of the policy are documented, the policy can be written. Policies should:

Be separate atomic objects
> Most companies employ one or two broad policies that encompass all users, and then they write several policies specific to different activities or technologies. For example, you might create one broad policy for handling of sensitive customer data that applies to all employees. Because the loss or compromise of this sensitive data would impact your entire business, the policy should apply to everyone. However, a policy regarding data encryption on portable company laptops is far narrower in scope. Both should be created, but you should avoid trying to group all administrative policy into one large blanket policy.

Be enforceable
> It is easy to create a policy that simply cannot be achieved. An example might be, "All data will be secured at all times against all attacks, both known and unknown." While this is a great goal, we cannot create procedures to achieve this goal. Therefore, this is not a policy that can actually be implemented. The administrative resources on the policy team should provide input to ensure the written policy can be implemented with available technology within the current infrastructure.

Balance usability and productivity with security

As I've discussed several times throughout this book, all security is an informed trade-off between usability and security. Realistic analysis should be done to ensure that a policy is not written that stops users from completing their jobs, or that impedes them so that their productivity is significantly impacted.

Be specific

Vague references lead to misinterpretation at all levels and can cause a policy to become unenforceable and potentially backfire. An example might be "No knives or guns can be brought to the workplace" versus "No dangerous objects can be brought to the workplace." The former is specific and easily enforceable, while the latter is completely open to debate and presents an enormous gray area that includes letter openers, screwdrivers, and toothpicks.

Describe the penalties for noncompliance

This is often handled by a lawyer with words similar to "Noncompliance may result in disciplinary action or termination." Management should not approve any policies without specific penalty descriptions, as they have agreed to enforce these policies.

Should not specifically state steps for implementation

Policies are not technology-specific implementation guides; they are high-level administrative documents. The implementation details are documented in procedures, which are discussed in the next section.

Once the policy is created and approved by all members of the policy creation team, it should be made available for review for a brief period. This allows the team to review and possibly incorporate feedback from affected users, management, and other concerned parties. It also gives notice that this policy is being created and will be implemented in the near future. This often has a positive effect, encouraging currently noncompliant users and administrators to become compliant before the written policy provides formal penalties.

The final phase of policy creation is the publication of the policy and handoff to the procedure team. This is the team that will create detailed procedures for the implementation and management of the policy.

Remember that once a policy is created, it should periodically be reviewed to ensure it still reflects the state of the business and the security needs of the organization. A stale policy is sometimes worse than no policy at all. Users and administrators alike will dismiss an inappropriate or stale policy and may apply that dismissal to all policies. Ensuring the continual refreshing of policy actually helps enforce that policy. For that reason, you should consider adding a "seal of freshness" to your policy that requires defined reviews over time and provides for expiration of the policy without such reviews. This provides both business justification for periodic reviews and allows you to plan accordingly.

For more information on creating security policies, consult the SANS Security Policy Project at *http://www.sans.org/resources/policies*. This web site contains a wealth of information on creating security policies and provides numerous examples of both focused and broad security policies. Reviewing the material available from SANS on security policies should be required for all members of your policy team as the first step in your policy creation process.

Creating Procedures

You already know how to create and follow a procedure. You've read numerous procedures in this book. A documented security procedure is not very different. You simply document the steps necessary to complete the tasks that must be done and verify that these steps satisfy the security policies that you've established.

Creating security procedures is a simple process that can be accomplished by following these steps:

1. Complete the security policy creation and acceptance process. Appropriate security procedures cannot be created until policies are finalized.

2. Examine the security policy to determine what tasks must be accomplished to comply with the policy.

3. Create a top-level procedure that will enforce the policy. This procedure will almost always be broken out into smaller tasks. The application of all tasks defined in the procedure must enforce the associated policy.

4. Document the steps required to accomplish each task. These tasks should be focused and narrowly scoped to ensure their portability. For example, applying ACLs on a file should be defined as its own task to allow this task to be reused for all policies that require ACL application. Often a single task will be broken out into subtasks to provide this portability. Each task should define, at a minimum, the following variables:

    a. User rights and privileges required to accomplish the task. For example, a user who is a member of the Domain Admins group may be required to complete the task.

    b. Number and role of individuals required to complete the task. Many sensitive tasks may require that more than one administrator be present to ensure accountability.

    c. Any other tasks that must be completed before this task, as well as any tasks that must follow the completion of this one. Some tasks, for example, might leave a computer in a semiunprotected state and must be immediately followed by a task that corrects that condition.

d. The exact steps required to accomplish the task. For example, "Launch ADUC" is a vague step, while "Click Start, click Programs, click Administrative Tools, then click Active Directory Users and Computers" is far more precise. It may seem that these procedures are unnecessarily wordy, but in these cases, it takes far less effort to be precise than to have a task fail due to imprecision. At the very least, links and references for proper tasks should be provided.

5. Verify that the documented tasks, when applied in the defined order, complete the procedure and enforce the written policy. This verification must be done with a variety of computer configurations to ensure it will always work.

6. Obtain senior-level corporate approval (not just IT management approval) to use the defined procedures and require their use as part of standard operating procedures.

 Just as with policy, senior-level management approval is critical to procedure creation. Without commitment that the procedure is correct and will be supported by all levels, it could be circumvented or completely ignored by employees. Senior management can also scrutinize the procedures to determine if they cannot apply through contractual relationships such as vendor-based computer management. This type of information may not be known to the procedure creation team, and procedures may not be enforceable universally unless modified by senior management.

7. Publish the procedures. Procedures cannot be a secret, especially from the administrators who must use them. However, distribution of the procedures may be limited on a need-to-know basis in some cases, such as forensic or auditing practices that might give an attacker useful information. Review of these procedures should be required whenever the tasks are performed.

8. Educate all parties affected by the procedures. This allows confusion to be resolved prior to the procedures being applied and helps ensure smooth application and continued security.

9. Audit the tasks regularly as they're accomplished to ensure the procedures are being followed. Just auditing the result isn't enough—you must ensure that the actual procedure is being used correctly. Many companies use either video surveillance or direct on-the-job observation to ensure compliance with procedures.

Once you've got your procedures in place, you're ready to securely configure and maintain your environment. You can be reasonably certain that the policies create a secure environment and that the procedures fully implement the policies. However, a good administrator must be ever vigilant. The policies and procedures, when properly implemented and enforced, are great tools. But how can you be certain that they are being implemented correctly? You must monitor your systems and analyze all pertinent activity to ensure it conforms to the policy. Monitoring identifies deviations from policy and procedure as well as alerts you to potentially dangerous conditions. One way to implement this monitoring is through auditing.

Auditing

You've configured your environment to meet the documented security requirements by following the security procedures and plans. These plans were created by technology-specific experts with a thorough review by security administrators and upper management. This should ensure that the initial configuration is secure.

However, you must keep continually vigilant against attacks. The plans you followed almost certainly call for ongoing monitoring of the components that you've installed and configured. This monitoring can be done in a variety of ways. Some applications create log files on the local hard disk. Others send SNMP messages on the network. Many of the newer applications and services, including those included with Windows Server 2003, create entries in the Event Log that can be viewed with Event Viewer.

This centralized location for storing and reviewing audit events provides a great benefit to the security administrator. Event Viewer is a simple tool that can be used to examine these audit events, as well as other system messages, in a single interface. Because other programs know about the Event Log database, these messages can be gathered from disparate systems and combined into one large log file. This log file can then be parsed, either by a security administrator or an automated program, such as Microsoft Operations Manager or Sunbelt Software's Event Archiver Enterprise, to identify security-related events and analyze these events to determine if any unauthorized behavior is taking place.

How Auditing Works

Auditing is specifically designed into most features in Windows Server 2003. When events that might be of interest to administrators or computer owners take place, an audit entry is created in the Event Log.

Audit events can be broken down into two general types of events: success and failure. Each event's audit code is specifically written to detect either success or failure. The resulting condition, along with the event that occurred, the system date and time when it occurred, and potentially helpful supplemental information, are entered into the Event Log as an audit event.

Each application or service may have its own configuration for auditing. Frequently, applications allow several levels of audit event logging. These levels might range from auditing only the most important events to auditing virtually every operation that occurs and creating entries for both the success and failure of each. As you might guess, this can quickly spiral out of control and fill up the logs with useless information. Therefore, discretion should be exercised to ensure you audit the events that will help you detect security issues without auditing so much that the entries become a nuisance.

Overriding the auditing settings is the global auditing configuration. This is similar to an on/off switch for auditing of broad audit categories on the computer. In most configurations, you will turn auditing on for all computers in a domain or OU and then configure specific auditing for services and applications on a per-computer or per-OU basis. This strategy allows you to audit only the necessary events on the computers you're most concerned about and helps you identify and address security issues more effectively.

Configuring Auditing

To correctly configure auditing, you must know what to audit first. Just as with the deployment of all other technologies in this book, you should create a plan for auditing within your organization. This plan should be included in the overall plan for deployment of the technology in question. The considerations when creating an audit plan include:

Are both the success and failure of this event useful in determining what happened?
For example, you may not be interested in auditing successful login events from client computers. This is a normal event that happens thousands of times a day and could quickly clog your event database with useless information. However, logon failure might be far more interesting, especially when it occurs at a domain controller or when a single account shows repeated logon failures.

What is the expected frequency of the event?
You should consider the frequency of the event to ensure you plan for Event Log analysis correctly. If important events happen often, they will require more time to analyze than will occasional events. If you use automated Event Log analysis tools, you will need to know how many of these events to expect in order to set triggers that will fire when that number of events is exceeded. You must also configure Event Log size behavior based on the number of expected events—the more audit entries, the larger the log must be.

What should happen when the Event Log is full?
Microsoft Windows Server 2003 allows you to tailor the behavior of the Event Logs to meet your specific needs. If audit events are critical to capture and your policy states that all defined events must be audited, you can configure the server to require those events to be saved and for the server to crash when audits can no longer be saved. Other configurations may not require such rigid Audit Log requirements.

Once the audit policy is written and reviewed, it can be implemented easily. Auditing is one of the simplest technologies to implement in Windows Server 2003. I provide several example scenarios to show the most common audit requirements implemented. I'll provide the details on how to get to the specific Group Policy section that applies to auditing in the first example. Thereafter, I'll simply show the different options you'd select in that same area of the Group Policy Object Editor.

 The simplicity of enabling auditing is both a benefit and a detriment. If you have a clear plan and know what you're doing, the task is simple to implement and verify. However, this also makes it easy to misconfigure. Many administrators simply switch on auditing for every event they can with no clear plan or goal. Their Audit Logs quickly fill up and become a useless nuisance. This is the reason planning is stressed repeatedly. Without a plan, auditing can cause far more harm than good.

Configuring auditing for domain controllers

Domain controllers are often the first computers to be attacked when an attacker reaches your internal network. They are also the point at which you can catch casual and unsophisticated internal attackers. Because a domain controller must authenticate domain user account logon activity, it's a great place to monitor for unsuccessful logon attempts. As an added bonus, configuring account logon activity for domain controllers will show us all local logon attempts at those domain controllers. We almost certainly have an administrative policy that restricts the local logon events at these computers, and capturing an Audit Log will allow us to verify compliance with the policy.

Follow these steps to configure logon auditing on domain controllers in the default Domain Controllers OU:

1. Click Start → All Programs → Administrative Tools → Active Directory Users and Computers. This can be done on a domain controller or a computer with the Windows Server 2003 Administration Pack installed.

2. Expand your domain, right-click on the Domain Controllers OU, then click Properties.

3. Click the Group Policy tab, then click Edit to edit the Default Domain Controllers Policy. This starts the Group Policy Object Editor.

 If you have a different policy or more than one policy, you can use any of those. Alternately, you can create a new policy by clicking New. Deciding whether to create one large policy or several small policies is discussed in detail in Chapter 5.

4. Double-click Default Domain Controller Policy (or whatever policy name you are editing), double-click Computer Configuration → Windows Settings → Security Settings → Local Policies → Audit Policy. The default domain controller audit policy settings will be listed as shown in Figure 15-1.

5. Double-click Audit Account Logon Events to display the details of the policy. Select both Success and Failure as shown in Figure 15-2.

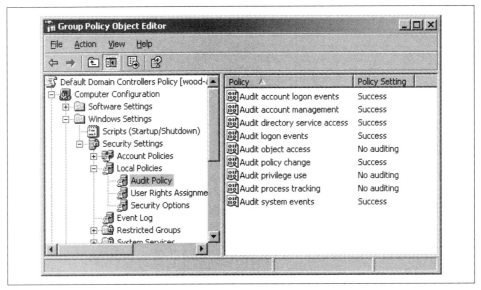

Figure 15-1. Default Domain Controller Audit Policy

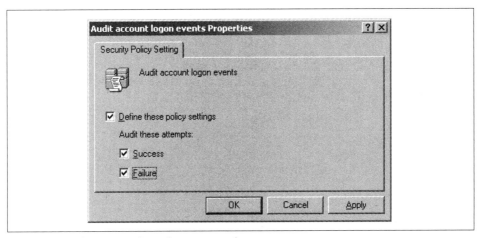

Figure 15-2. Policy settings for auditing account logon events

The domain controllers will now create an audit event for each logon attempt, both successful and unsuccessful. This can prove useful by showing what accounts logged in and where they logged in. For example, if a trusted administrator is on sick leave and you detect a large number of logon failure audits, you can be fairly certain that an attack is being conducted against that account. You can then either take preventive action to stop the account or gather evidence and contact the authorities to prosecute the attacker.

> In a domain environment, this configuration will show all logon attempts using domain credentials. However, if you're using the same policy settings to monitor an important computer that is not a domain controller, an attacker could attempt to log in using local credentials. In that case, you must audit both the *account logon events* (generated when a domain user account is authenticated on a domain controller) and *logon events* (generated when a user logs onto a computer) to ensure you capture both types of logon attempts.

Configuring the Event Log and audit failure behavior

Auditing should be part of your written security policy by now. The different behaviors that must be audited are documented. In addition, the amount of audit data that must be retained should also be documented. Most corporations don't require audit histories to be retained indefinitely; this creates both legal and administrative difficulties. Most corporate data retention policies extend to cover audit and security event data, so this policy should be consulted when configuring auditing.

Auditing may also be required, to the extent that if audit data cannot be captured, data access should not be allowed. This should also be an extension of written security policy. The policy should take into account possible denial-of-service attacks that can leverage such a policy (for example, generating numerous Event Log entries until a computer will no longer allow access).

These settings can easily be applied by Group Policy. To configure the computer to shut down when it can no longer generate security log events:

1. Follow steps 1–4 of the preceding procedure.
2. Under Local Policies at the same level as Audit Policy is the Security Options container. Click this container to show its settings.
3. Double-click the policy object "Audit: shut down system immediately if unable to log security audits."
4. Click Define This Policy Setting, then click Enabled as shown in Figure 15-3.

When a computer with this policy applied is unable to generate any kind of security event, including an audit event, it will crash. Your other monitoring software should detect this crash and alert you to the issue so you can correct the situation. To avoid the situation in advance or correct the existing situation, you should modify the settings of the Event Log. These settings should reflect your specific environment and

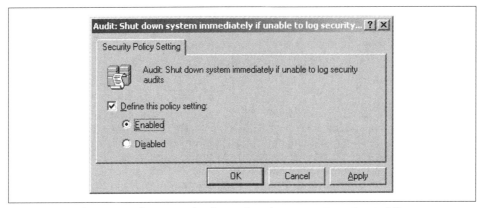

Figure 15-3. Policy settings for system shutdown when the security Event Log is full

policy to ensure that the events are rolled up into the proper database and then cleared.

To configure the Event Log settings to retain 32MB of security logs (a nice big size that shouldn't burden your system) and never delete security log entries automatically:

1. Follow steps 1–4 of the first procedure in this section to open Group Policy Object Editor to the Local Policies node.

2. Under Security Settings at the same level as Local Policies is the Event Log container. Click this container to display the Event Log settings as shown in Figure 15-4.

3. Double-click Retention Method for Security Log.

4. Click Define This Policy Setting, then select "Do not overwrite events (clear log manually)" as shown in Figure 15-5.

5. Double-click Maximum Security Log Size.

6. Click Define This Policy Setting, then set the size as 32768KB.

You have now configured Windows Server 2003 to retain a maximum of 32MB of security log entries and to never overwrite events. The Event Log must be manually cleared (after being saved or transferred per your policy) before the security Event Log reaches this maximum size. If the security Event Log does reach this size and "Audit: shut down system immediately if unable to log security audits" is enabled, the computer will crash, and an administrator will have to manually restart it.

Auditing account management

Now that I've shown how to configure auditing settings, the configuration of additional audit settings is almost entirely the same. You may, for example, want to audit account management functions such as user account creation or group membership

---

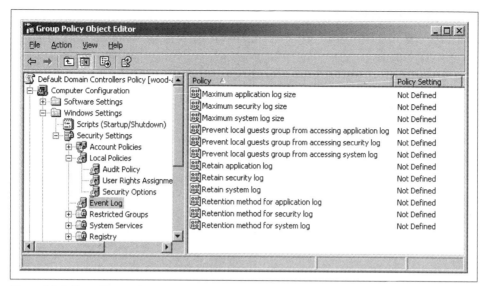

Figure 15-4. Event Log settings

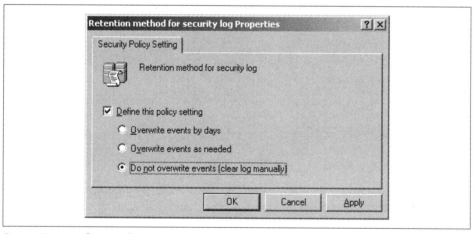

Figure 15-5. Configuring the security policy log to never overwrite events; this setting can be potentially disastrous if you don't plan it properly

modification. Again, this will tie in with your established security policies and provide the ability to review activity to ensure no improper actions have been taken.

To configure account management auditing, simply follow the steps listed in the earlier "Configuring auditing for domain controllers" section. However, you should configure the Audit Account Management policy setting for success and failure actions. This will provide details on all account management activities with a single Audit Policy modification.

Setting up a honey pot

Attackers will find their way onto your network eventually. Whether it's a disgruntled employee searching for blackmail material on her boss or an industrial espionage attack that penetrates your firewall, nothing is impervious. A common administrative tactic is to entice the attacker to find what you want her to find and attack that particular resource. It's akin to setting mousetraps around the perimeter of your house and then putting a particularly yummy piece of gouda in the middle of your living room. But that gouda isn't for the mouse's benefit; it's rigged with video cameras and mouse-seeking missiles.

In computer security, we call this piece of tasty cheese a *honey pot*. Honey pots are computers placed at locations where an attacker is likely to find her way, such as just inside a DMZ. We give these computers tempting names such as DataCentral or HRServer and install unpatched operating systems with services known to contain well-documented exploits such as IIS. When an attacker sees this kind of server, she is drawn to it like a bee to honey. Hence the name.

What attackers don't realize is that administrators have placed triggers and surveillance devices all over the honey pot. From the moment an attacker attempts to access the honey pot, Audit Logs are being generated and monitoring software is alerting administrators that some activity is taking place. Steps can then be taken to trace the network traffic back to its origin and begin compiling evidence of the break-in. This evidence can be used both to enhance future security by determining the point of entry and to prosecute the attacker.

To set up a honey pot, you first configure a computer as mentioned earlier. I would recommend you install Windows 2000 Server and do not apply any service packs or hot fixes. This lures the attacker into believing that this is simply a neglected server on your network. Common configuration errors, such as an administrator account with a weak or blank password, should be used.

Next, configure auditing as shown earlier in this section. The auditing should capture all logon success and failure activity, as well as account management activity (in case the attacker plants or elevates credentials).

Shares should be created on the computer. These shares should have tempting names such as HRDocs or Unfiled Patents and contain concocted datafiles that may have very little data but will serve as bait. Although these names sound a bit too tempting within this context, try to consider it from an attacker's viewpoint. If an attacker saw a share with this name, would she immediately double-click it? The shares should be set for Everyone: Read permission. The files on the share should have filenames consistent with the share name and should be in application-specific format such as Microsoft Word or Microsoft Excel files.

Finally, file auditing should be set on the directory that contains the files acting as bait. To configure file auditing for the HRDocs directory and its contents:

---

1. Configure Audit Object Access to audit Success and Failure audits as shown earlier in this chapter.
2. In Windows Explorer, right-click the HRDocs directory, then click Properties.
3. Click the Security tab, then click Advanced.
4. Click the Auditing tab to show the auditing entries for this directory.
5. Click Add to add an auditing entry to this directory.
6. Type **Everyone**, then press Enter to audit all users' access to this folder. This is done because we don't know what user context the attacker will use to access the folder.
7. In the Full Control row, click both the Successful and Failed checkboxes as shown in Figure 15-6. This will ensure we capture all types of access attempts to the contents of this folder. Then click OK.
8. Click "Replace auditing entries on all child objects with entries shown here that apply to child objects." This will show the completed file auditing settings shown in Figure 15-7. Click OK to apply these settings.

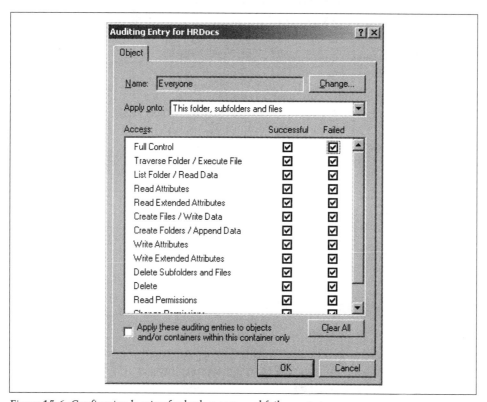

Figure 15-6. Configuring logging for both success and failure events

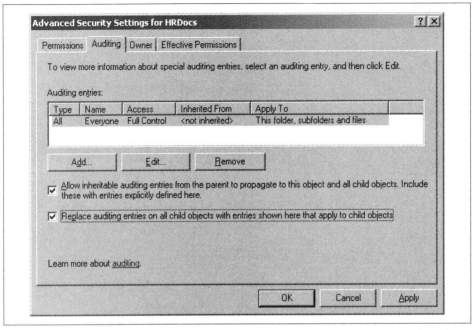

Figure 15-7. Replacing audit entries on child objects helps to ensure application of your desired settings to all necessary objects

Now the honey pot is fully configured from the Windows side. You should ensure that your Audit Log monitoring software is obtaining frequent log updates from the honey pot computer and is configured to page the on-duty security administrator as soon as the log entries begin to appear. This will allow your group to quickly respond and identify the attacker as well as capture and retain all pertinent evidence.

 Before taking any type of legal action based on this book, you'll obviously consult with a lawyer experienced in this field. The information you gather by using the steps in this book may or may not be considered evidence in court. Also, honey pots do walk a fine line between enticement and entrapment that only lawyers and judges can help clarify.

Operating System Updates

When Microsoft ships an operating system, it does its best to find and remove all security vulnerabilities. In a perfect world, that would mean that the operating system was perfect from a security standpoint. In our imperfect world, however, operating systems are large and complex. As we know, complexity is the enemy of security. This means that the complexity of these large operating systems provides plenty of opportunities for security vulnerabilities to crop up.

Security vulnerabilities are discovered every day both by vendors and by customers who purchased the products. Microsoft, like virtually all other hardware and software vendors, continuously refines its products based on the discovery of these vulnerabilities. When a particularly critical vulnerability is discovered, Microsoft quickly writes and releases a software patch to address the issue.

Microsoft almost never writes patches to address configuration issues. This may seem obvious, but many administrators believe that any improper configuration is a bug. The extensive documentation available for Microsoft products, including this book, help you determine the proper configuration to implement. If you implement it incorrectly or without a proper plan in place, you may create your own security vulnerability. Because this isn't improper behavior of the software, Microsoft doesn't patch it.

The quicker you apply a patch to your systems, the quicker you become resistant to attacks that exploit that particular vulnerability. This doesn't mean that you should watch the TechNet web site all day and immediately apply every security patch to every computer in your enterprise. Nor does it mean that you should apply patches only when Microsoft sends email specifically indicating that you have a product with a known vulnerability. The proper patch management strategy for your environment lies somewhere in between.

Patch management is essential to ensure the ongoing security of all components in your network. This book focuses specifically on Windows Server 2003, but the same consideration should be given to other software and hardware that can be updated. Some software, such as virus scanners and software firewalls, should be regularly updated to ensure they provide defense against the latest attack vectors. Routers, hardware firewalls, and other intermediate network devices also have software or firmware that should be regularly updated to ensure they remain resistant to known attacks and patch known vulnerabilities.

Optimally you will plan a software update strategy before you deploy the computers in your enterprise. Realistically, however, this isn't usually the case. Computer systems are deployed with little or no regard for regular software maintenance. We often have to take systems that have various levels of software updates and bring them all to a single version of software. This section addresses the various strategies you can use to determine the software patches installed and the ways you can ensure patches are installed on necessary computers.

The remainder of this chapter will cover updating only operating systems, focusing on Windows Server 2003 and Windows XP Professional in a corporate environment. Most of these strategies can be extended to other software packages and Windows operating systems. As you develop your policy and procedures, you can simply extend the information provided here to encompass your specific environment.

All computer systems are not equal. Some may be critical to your business, while others could be removed with little notice. Because you cannot apply patches to all computers simultaneously, you must determine an order and priority for your patch application activities. Some basic rules apply to your decisions regarding patch application, including the following:

Some systems are more exposed to attacks than others
Web-based attacks that exploit a flaw in IIS, for example, would be most dangerous to computers that have direct exposure to the Internet. When a patch is available for a computer that publicly exposes the functionality that the patch addresses, it should be given a high priority. The patch should be applied to all computers as appropriate, but the more immediate need is to patch those computers most likely to be attacked.

Critical business systems should be patched quickly
While your product support web site may not be essential to your continued business operation, your central database server may be critical, and its loss would mean the demise of the company. When an update strategy and procedure is created, you should keep this in mind and assign priorities according to business need.

Defense-in-depth helps reduce the need to apply patches immediately
If you have internal firewalls and desktop-based virus scanners, your computers may be reasonably resistant to new attacks. This could give you enough time to test the patch and ensure its compatibility with your environment before deploying it. If your computers are completely undefended inside the corporate network, any exposure to an attack could be catastrophic until a patch is deployed to the entire company. Unfortunately, it is common for worms and viruses to "jump" firewalls through a variety of means, such as portable laptops and computers with modems.

 A recent Internet worm called Code Red that attacked IIS was highly successful. A little-known fact about this worm is that there was a patch available for months before the worm became widespread. Vigilant network administrators who had patched their IIS-based web servers quickly thwarted the worm. Those who did not have an update strategy, on the other hand, were susceptible to this attack. They had to repair the damage done in addition to patching all servers to ensure the worm did not continue to spread.

Windows Update

Since the Windows 9x days, Microsoft has provided Windows Update (*http://windowsupdate.microsoft.com*), a web-based service that integrates with Windows to provide operating system updates and new features. You've probably used Windows Update yourself to download and install updates. Windows XP Professional and later versions of Windows even include Automatic Updates, a feature that can periodically check Windows Update for new updates, download them in the background, and apply them for you.

Windows Update is primarily intended for individual users and doesn't always make sense in an enterprise. Imagine, for example, that you configure thousands of client computers to automatically download and apply updates. Each time an update is available, each client computer will independently download a copy, which is an inefficient use of your company's Internet connection. Additionally, you won't have any opportunity to test and approve the updates before they are deployed to your client computers.

Microsoft Software Update Services provides a kind of "corporate edition" of Windows Update and is a more efficient and controllable means of managing security updates within your organization.

Microsoft Software Update Services

Software Update Services (SUS, pronounced suss) is a free download from the Windows web site (*www.microsoft.com/windows*). SUS consists of two components: a server and a client. The server component can run on Windows 2000 Server or Windows Server 2003; the client component is included in Windows 2000 Service Pack 3 and Windows XP Service Pack 1.

> By the time you read this, SUS may be called Windows Update Services (WUS, pronounced wuss, no pun intended).

The SUS client is also available as a standalone download. However, the easiest way to deploy and configure it is to simply deploy the appropriate service pack to your client computers. You'll also receive the other benefits of the service pack, including bug fixes and security updates.

Once installed and configured, your SUS server will automatically download new updates from Windows Update. You'll be able to test and approve these updates, which will then be made available to computers running the SUS client. SUS handles only updates marked by Microsoft as critical, which includes all security updates. New features and other noncritical updates aren't handled by SUS, although client computers can still use Windows Update to obtain these updates.

> The SUS client software is also referred to as Automatic Update. Windows XP Professional ships with Automatic Update but isn't compatible with SUS. Windows XP Service Pack 1 and Windows 2000 Service Pack 3 include a new version of Automatic Update that is SUS compatible.

Installing and configuring SUS server

To install SUS server, simply launch the Microsoft installer (MSI) file containing the software. As part of the installation, you'll specify a location where SUS will store its updates, as shown in Figure 15-8. This location should contain sufficient space for a large number of updates. Keep in mind that SUS server can download all available critical updates for all Microsoft operating systems, Internet Explorer, and other products.

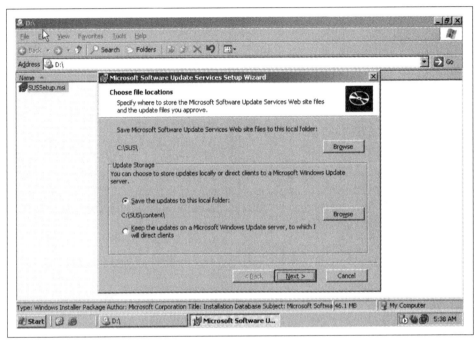

Figure 15-8. Installing SUS and configuring the location for storage of updates

After installing SUS, you can connect to the SUS administrative interface by using a web browser. Simply point the browser to *http://server/SUSAdmin*, replacing *server* with the name of the computer running SUS server.

> You can require the use of SSL on the */SUSAdmin* directory in IIS. In that case, the URL is *https://server/SUSAdmin*.

You may need to configure one or more of SUS server's options, as shown in Figure 15-9. These options control SUS' use of proxy servers, allowing SUS to operate within your network.

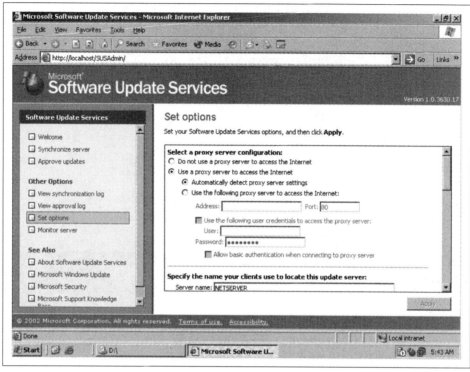

Figure 15-9. SUS configuration options

Your first administrative step should be to configure a synchronization schedule as shown in Figure 15-10. This schedule allows SUS to automatically download new critical updates from Microsoft's servers (or from another SUS server in your organization). A weekly schedule is usually sufficient.

You can also manually trigger synchronization whenever you like, although a scheduled synchronization ensures that your SUS server always has the latest updates. Remember that SUS won't actually deploy these updates to clients until you've approved them, so there's no danger in having the latest updates on the SUS server.

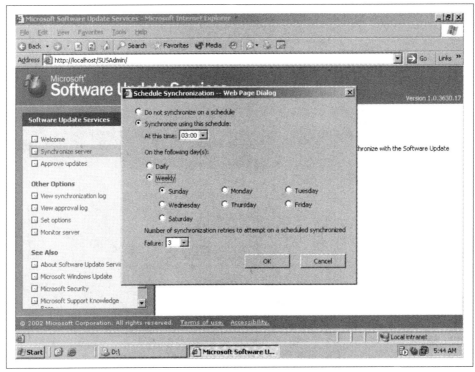

Figure 15-10. SUS update schedule configuration

After synchronization completes, you can use the Monitor Server tab of the SUS admin page to view the number of available updates, as shown in Figure 15-11. SUS categorizes updates by product, including versions of IE and Windows.

However, just because updates are available doesn't mean your client computers will receive them. First, you must approve the updates, giving you the opportunity to test them for compatibility in your environment. As shown in Figure 15-12, you can review the available updates and indicate which ones you approve for deployment to your clients. When client computers contact the SUS server, they will receive all approved, applicable updates for their operating system and other installed products (such as IE).

Notice that the update approval list indicates which updates will require a client computer restart after installation. You can centrally configure the SUS client software's restart behavior to avoid disrupting your users; I'll cover that in the next section.

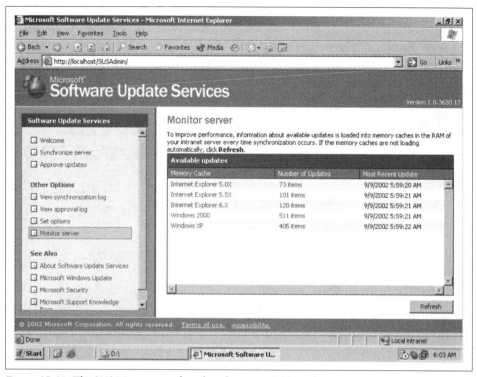

Figure 15-11. The SUS Monitor window that shows available updates

Configuring SUS clients

Once you have installed one or more SUS servers on your network, you'll need to configure the SUS client software on your client computers. Although you can manually configure the software on a per-client basis, it's far more efficient to use Group Policy to centrally configure all your client computers at once. First, determine the right place to apply a Group Policy Object (GPO).

For example, if you want all domain computers to use a centralized SUS server, you might apply an appropriately configured GPO to the domain. However, it's more likely that you'll deploy a SUS server for each major site within your organization. Doing so will allow clients to retrieve their updates locally, rather than using WAN bandwidth. In that case, it would make the most sense to configure a GPO and link it to Active Directory sites, creating a consistent, location-aware configuration for SUS.

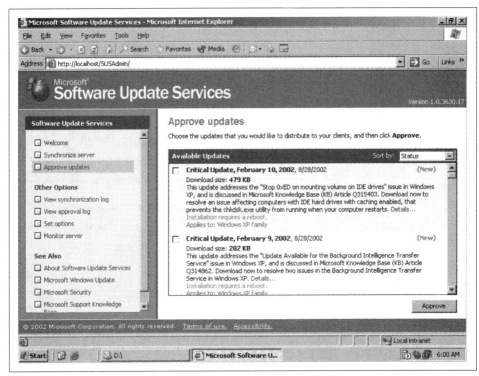

Figure 15-12. Approving updates in SUS

Configuring SUS couldn't be easier: Simply open the Group Policy Editor. Under Computer Configuration, open Administrative Templates, then Windows Update. As shown in Figure 15-13, four policy settings control the SUS client software.

Configure Automatic Updates

This policy setting activates the SUS client software and configures its primary behavior. You can configure client computers to automatically download and apply updates, to notify their users prior to downloading or installation, or to automatically download and notify prior to installation. The best choice is usually full automation, ensuring that users don't prevent the installation of important updates. You can also select the day of the week and time that available updates should be installed. For example, if users typically leave their computers on in the evenings, you might schedule installation for every night at 10 p.m., when users won't be impacted should a restart be required.

Specify intranet Microsoft update service location

This is where you provide the URL of the SUS server that clients should use, which should be the URL of the SUS server that you've set up on your corporate network.

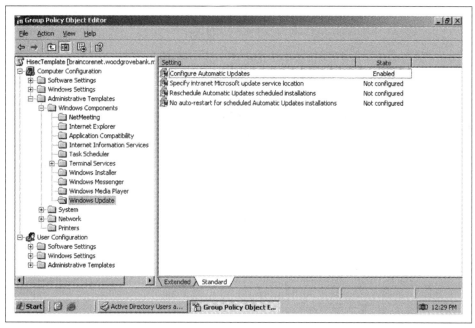

Figure 15-13. SUS client policy configuration

Reschedule Automatic Updates scheduled installations

You can specify how long the client software should wait after system startup to begin installing updates that were missed. For example, if a user turns off his system in the middle of an update installation, the SUS client will not attempt to install the update again until the next scheduled time. By configuring this option, you can have SUS retry five minutes after the system restarts.

No auto-restart for scheduled Automatic Updates installations

This policy allows you to prevent SUS from automatically restarting a client computer after installing updates that require a restart. When this policy is enabled, SUS will complete the update installation the next time the computer is restarted, rather than restarting it automatically.

Remember that these policies apply only to computers running Windows XP SP 1, Windows 2000 SP 3, or Windows Server 2003.

Using MBSA to Determine Current Security Status

The Microsoft Baseline Security Analyzer (MBSA) is a tool used to verify the current state of security patches and settings on a computer. It is a direct result of customer feedback that there was no centralized tool to determine the security state of a computer.

MBSA has two goals for most Microsoft Windows operating systems and applications, including Windows Server 2003 and Windows XP:

- Identify common security misconfigurations such as a blank administrator password or excessive users in the Administrators group
- Identify missing security patches

MBSA has both a graphical interface and a command-line interface. This allows you to tailor your use of MBSA to the needs of your environment. For example, the command-line version of MBSA can be scripted or run as a regularly scheduled batch process. However, for ad hoc usage of MBSA, you may prefer the graphical interface. It provides a simple way to configure and launch the tool as well as view the report and take corrective action.

Among its numerous customer-driven features that make it a powerful and useful tool, MBSA can:

Scan multiple computers
> This can be done by selecting a domain name to scan or a range of IP addresses. Figure 15-14 shows the configuration range options.

Target specific security areas of concern
> This is also shown in Figure 15-14. This feature allows you to target specific MBSA checks. This saves time by scanning only the areas you feel are vulnerable or must verify.

Integrate with SUS
> MBSA can check the patch level of a targeted computer based on its own data or based on the patches loaded on your internal SUS computer. This is also shown in Figure 15-14 as the administrator has selected Woodgrove-sus.

Provide detailed reporting
> When MBSA is done with its scan, it displays the results of the scan as shown in Figure 15-15. All scans and their results are shown, and the areas of security concern are highlighted. You can get more information on the exact criteria used for the scan, as well as the recommended corrective action, from this report. Furthermore, the reports are stored in XML so you can parse them with any XML-savvy program to create charts, analyze trends, or predict future statistics.

Using MBSA should not be part of your daily routine. An appropriately planned and implemented update strategy, as described earlier in this chapter, should eliminate your daily need for tools such as MBSA. It should be used in limited situations such as:

- When a new widespread virus or worm appears that takes advantage of a known security flaw. At that time, you should use MBSA to ensure that your most vulnerable computers are protected with the appropriate patches. This allows you to spot-check those vulnerable servers. Although your update strategy should have already protected those servers, there's no harm in double-checking.

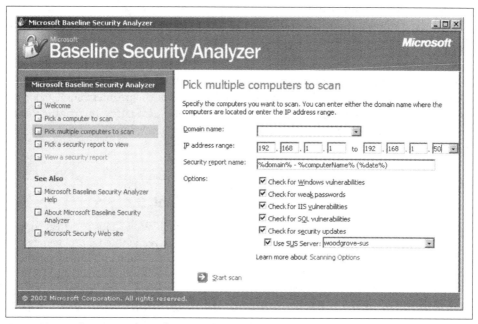

Figure 15-14. The Microsoft Baseline Security Analyzer targeting computers in a specific IP address range

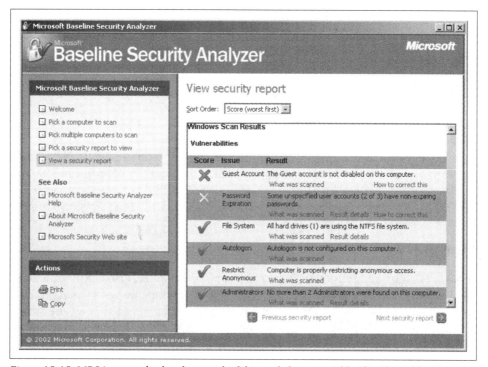

Figure 15-15. MBSA report display: large, colorful icons help you quickly identify problem areas

- As a periodic audit tool to ensure your patch update strategy is working. You will be reviewing Audit Logs of these updates anyway, but MBSA allows you to periodically choose a critical server and examine it for security vulnerabilities.

Any problems that MBSA exposes should not be fixed manually unless there is a time-critical need, such as protecting against a spreading attack. Rather, you should address discovered vulnerabilities by locating the cause of the problem such as a misconfigured update server or violation of a security policy. Locating the root cause of the problem ensures that the problem will not reappear later due to some fundamental flaw or loophole in your security strategy.

MBSA as an Attacker's Tool

You may say to yourself, when first reading about MBSA, "Wow! This is a great tool that can help me identify vulnerabilities." As you begin to read more reports and discover more vulnerabilities and misconfigurations in your environment, however, you may develop a different attitude. You may, as many people do, think that this tool is a little too aware of your misconfigurations. It seems to find so many problems.

You may also realize that you're not the only person who's downloaded MBSA. And that Microsoft doesn't require any type of "good deed oath" to download it. An attacker could use it to footprint your network and get the same information. She could then launch an attack based on a vulnerability from an MBSA report.

While this is true, it's a little shortsighted. Literally hundreds of existing attacker tools are available on the Internet right now. Many of them are redundant with MBSA and many are legitimate tools used by security professionals for penetration testing. An attacker could easily get the same information using a different, non-Microsoft tool.

So don't blame Microsoft for telling anyone who cares to listen about your vulnerabilities. Just fix them!

MBSA can be downloaded from *http://www.microsoft.com/technet/security/tools/tools/MBSAHome.mspx*. Details on exactly what vulnerabilities MBSA scans for and how it determines patch levels are included in the Baseline Security Analyzer white paper located at *http://www.microsoft.com/technet/security/tools/tools/mbsawp.mspx*.

Summary

Security is an ongoing process. Once you complete an initial installation or a complete deployment, you must remain vigilant. Evildoers are constantly trying to gain access to your resources. You must remain watchful and continuously ensure strong security is applied and verified throughout your organization to have a good chance of defending your assets.

Sending Secure Email

As we rely more and more on email to provide essential business communications, protecting the privacy and authenticity of email becomes more and more crucial. Most modern email software applications provide the means to secure your email and provide recipients with proof of the email's validity; Windows Server 2003 provides the public key infrastructure (PKI) necessary to issue the cryptographic keys that make secure email possible.

What Is Secure Email?

Secure email takes one of two forms, each designed for a specific purpose:

Digitally signed
> Designed to provide email recipients with proof that a message was, in fact, written by you and that the message was unaltered since you sent it

Encrypted
> Helps protect the contents of a message, ensuring that only the recipient can successfully read it

Digital signatures recognize that not all email is private and that the means to transmit email are highly susceptible to tampering. Skilled attackers can intercept email in transit, modify it, and send it to the original recipient. In this way, attackers can falsify information, give conflicting instructions, and generally disrupt business. Digital signatures place a relatively small additional load on an email, because they encrypt only a small portion of the email: the signature itself.

 How often would digitally signed email be beneficial? Consider that almost everyone has received spam email claiming to be from a bank or a celebrity. If these messages were digitally signed, you could be sure of the source. Without digital signatures, you must take the email at face value and recognize that it could be a forgery.

Encryption is designed to protect a message by rendering it useless to anyone but the recipient. Encrypted messages require more processing power than unencrypted messages, but provide the assurance that the message will arrive unaltered (it becomes indecipherable if altered) and uncompromised. Encryption can be combined with digital signatures to provide both privacy and proof of the sender's identity.

Encrypting and digitally signing email are two separate security processes. However, they can be used together on the same email message to provide both authentication and confidentiality of the information. Although encryption often implies authenticity, the additional signature is not a large added burden. In fact, these operations can be done with separate keys to provide two-factor proof of the message's security.

How Does Secure Email Work?

Like the Kerberos authentication protocol, which you learned about in Chapter 7, secure email uses cryptography to validate the sender's identify (in the case of digitally signed messages) or to protect the message's content (in the case of encrypted messages).

Digitally Signed Messages

Figure A-1 illustrates how a user can send a digitally signed message using email software such as Microsoft Outlook.

Here's how it works:

1. The user types a regular email and tells Outlook to digitally sign the message.
2. Outlook calculates a checksum on the message. The checksum is the result of a mathematical hash algorithm and is different for every message. Changing a single character in the email would change the resulting checksum. (Remember that we discussed hash algorithms in Chapter 2.)
3. Outlook retrieves the user's private encryption key from local storage and uses it to encrypt the checksum. The checksum is now a digital signature.
4. Both the unencrypted message and the signature are sent to the recipient.

 Digital signatures do not prevent others from reading the text of the message. The message is sent in clear text; only the signature uses encryption. This encrypted signature is easily decrypted by anyone, as we will see.

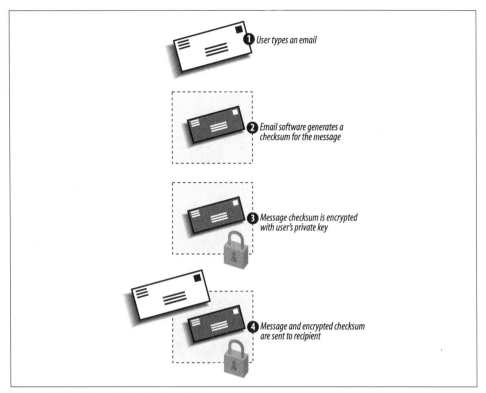

Figure A-1. Sending a digitally signed message

The recipient must perform a somewhat more complex process to validate the digital signature, as illustrated in Figure A-2.

When the message reaches its destination:

1. The recipient receives both the clear-text message and the digital signature. The recipient's email software handles each piece individually.

2. The email text is immediately readable, because it was not encrypted.

3. The email software retrieves the sender's public key. This can be obtained from a certification authority, or the public key may be included along with the message in the form of a certificate. If the certificate accompanies the message, it is verified to ensure it is authentic and chains to a trusted root certification authority.

4. The email software uses the public key to decrypt the signature, revealing the original checksum sent by the message's sender.

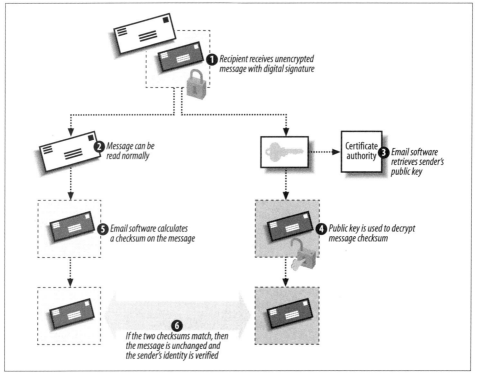

Figure A-2. Receiving a digitally signed message

5. The email software uses the same algorithm that the sender used to calculate a checksum on the clear-text message.

6. The email software compares the checksum it calculated with the now-unencrypted checksum from the signature. If they match, the sender's identity is verified—because only the sender could have encrypted the checksum with his private key—and the contents of the message are verified—because the two checksums match.

Encrypted Messages

Encrypted messages go a step further than digital signatures by encrypting the entire message. The message's contents are protected from eavesdroppers, and the message cannot be altered without making it undecryptable. Because of the nature of public key cryptography, encrypted messages do *not* provide validation of the sender's identity unless a digital signature is used in conjunction with the message encryption.

How Do They Find My Public Key?

Anything encrypted with a digital certificate contains unencrypted information about the certificate that was used. This information allows the recipient to contact the appropriate certification authority and obtain your public key. In Chapter 9, I discussed how certificates can be published to a variety of locations and retrieved when necessary to encrypt, decrypt, or verify data.

More commonly, however, email software simply bundles a copy of your public key along with the message, making it immediately available to your recipient. Your recipient must still trust the certificate, which is a concept I'll discuss later in this chapter. The recipient will also verify its authenticity to ensure that you didn't send along a forged certificate.

Figure A-3 illustrates how encrypted email can easily be sent. Note that this is a generic example and not specific to any implementation. Many implementations do things differently, such as S/MIME creating a symmetric key for message encryption. Figure A-3 shows the easiest way to implement email encryption.

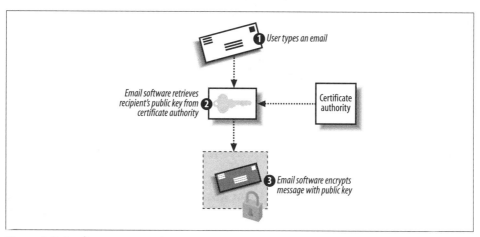

Figure A-3. Sending an encrypted message

In the simplest encrypted email:

1. The sender types an email message and tells her email software to encrypt it.
2. The email software retrieves the recipient's public key. This can be obtained from a certification authority, although many enterprise mail servers, including Microsoft Exchange Server, allow recipients' public keys to be stored along with their email addresses in the server's address book.
3. The email software uses the public key to encrypt the entire message, which is then sent to the recipient.

Messages encrypted with your own private key can also be sent. However, anyone with access to your public key—pretty much anybody—will be able to decrypt the message. Using your private key to encrypt messages provides a similar form of security as digital signatures, although more information is encrypted, thus making the message larger and more difficult to process.

When the recipient receives the email, the corresponding email software simply decrypts the message using the recipient's private key, as illustrated in Figure A-4.

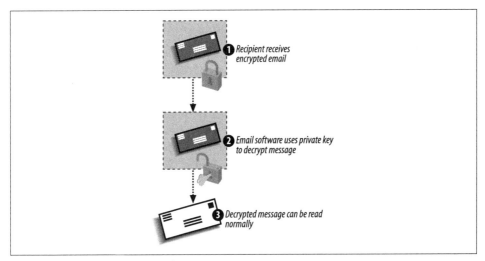

Figure A-4. Receiving an encrypted message

Considerations for Secure Email

Secure email provides a number of advantages to both senders and recipients. These advantages were shown in the beginning of this appendix. However, there are some downsides to using secure email. You must consider a number of factors when deciding whether to use secure email in your company or between trusted parties across an untrusted network. Some of these considerations may not have an impact on your decision, but in all likelihood you'll need to address them all to make secure email work.

The considerations for using secure email include:

- Digitally signed messages require that the recipient trust the digital certificate used by the sender. That may require the recipient to accept a new certificate publisher to trust. Some recipients' computers may be configured so that only an administrator can add a new trusted publisher; unless the administrator trusts the sender's certificate (and the publisher of that certificate), digital signatures are useless.

- Encryption makes email messages (and their attachments) larger, depending on the algorithm, requiring more network bandwidth to transmit them, storage space to retain them, and processing power to decrypt them. Recipients with older computers may not be able to read encrypted messages because their computers may lack power or the more modern cryptographic algorithms.

- Encryption requires that you obtain a public encryption key for your recipient. If your recipient doesn't have a public key, or if their public key is issued by a private certification authority that you don't have access to, then encryption is impossible.

- Both signatures and encryption require both the sender and the recipient to have email software that supports secure email. While most new email applications provide such support, users with older software will be unable to participate. Also, many text-based email programs do not support cryptographic operations and will be unable to correctly process the receipt of a signed or encrypted message.

Once you've reviewed these considerations and addressed them in your overall secure email strategy, you're ready to move on to implementation of your system.

Secure Email Implementation

Implementing secure email requires some form of PKI, either your own or a commercial certificate vendor. There are pros and cons to using either, as I'll discuss in the next two sections.

Using a Commercial Certification Authority

Commercial certification authorities like VeriSign and Equifax sell digital certificates (which contain asymmetric keys) to anyone who wants them. Certification authorities require that certificate purchasers prove their identity before certificates can be issued; each uses a different method to verify an individual's identity. Thawte, one of the leading public PKI vendor brands, maintains a national network of "digital notaries" who use traditional forms of identification, such as a passport, to verify a purchaser's identity in person before issuing a digital certificate.

As you learned in Chapter 9, certificates are useless unless you trust the person or company who issued them. The advantage of purchasing certificates from a commercial certification authority is that your computer is preconfigured to trust most of them. If you look in Internet Explorer's list of trusted certificate publishers, shown in Figure A-5 and accessed through the Internet Options icon in Control Panel, you'll see a list of publishers whose certificates are automatically trusted by your computer.

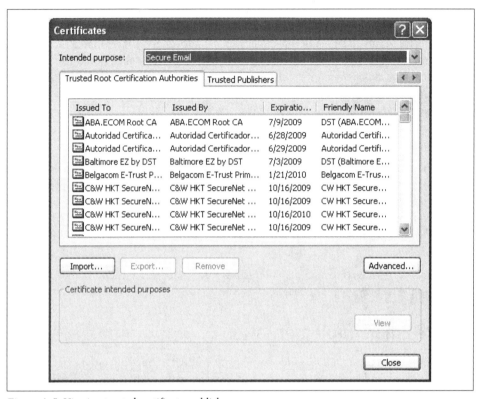

Figure A-5. Viewing trusted certificate publishers

The disadvantage of using a commercial certification authority is that they charge money for the certificates—from a few dollars to hundreds, depending on the vendor. The certificates usually expire after a year, so the cost of the certificate recurs.

As shown in Figure A-6, commercial vendors usually provide a web-based enrollment mechanism, although they often require offline verification of your identity before they will issue a certificate.

Using Your Own Certification Authority

If you need to issue certificates to everyone in your organization, a commercial certification authority can become expensive. You can set up your own certification authority, as described in Chapter 9, to issue certificates to users. The disadvantage of using your own certification authority is that computers, by default, won't necessarily trust the certificates you issue. There are two ways to make them trust you:

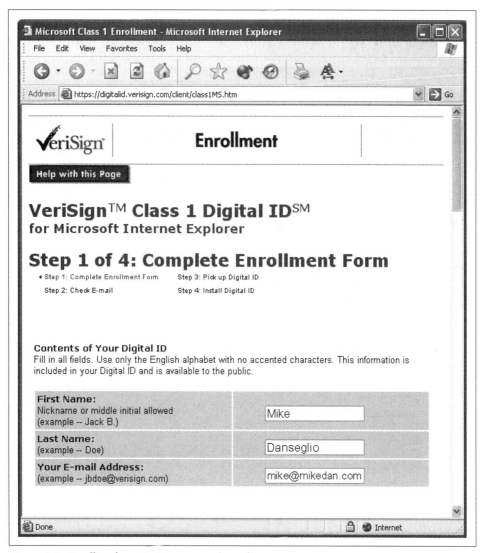

Figure A-6. Enrolling for a VeriSign personal certificate

Obtain a certification authority certificate from a commercial certification authority

These are expensive, but they make your certification authority a part of the commercial authority's chain of trust, meaning any computer that trusts the commercial authority will also trust your certificates.

Configure your computers to trust your certification authority

This is especially easy if the only computers that need to trust your authority are on your network, because you can use group policies to add your certification authority to your computers' trust lists. For information on how to configure clients to trust certificates, see Chapter 9.

Issuing certificates

Windows Server 2003's Certificate Services is capable of issuing email certificates right out of the box. Certificate Services sets up a virtual directory under the server's default web site, which users can connect to in order to request certificates. Figure A-7 shows the web site where users can request a new certificate.

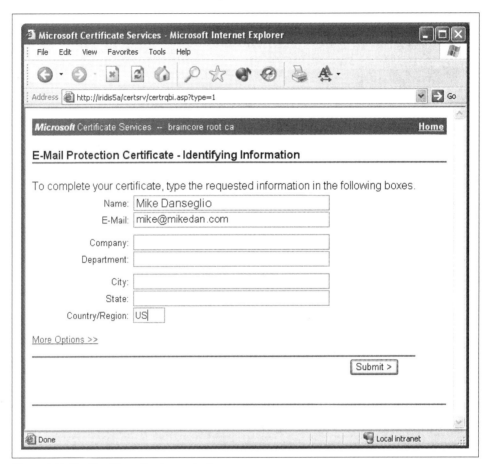

Figure A-7. The Certificate Services web site

When users request a new certificate, Certificate Services' default behavior is to hold the request until an administrator approves it. You should approve certificate requests only after satisfactorily proving that the user requesting the certificate has provided the correct credentials for the certificate. In other words, if you see a request from Maria, make sure Maria actually requested it before you issue it. Failure to properly verify user identity could result in certificates being issued to the wrong users, allowing them to impersonate one another.

Once you issue a certificate, users can retrieve the certificate from the Certificate Services web site, as shown in Figure A-8.

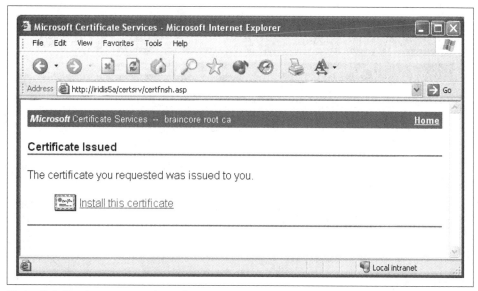

Figure A-8. Retrieving an issued certificate

Configuring clients to trust you

One way to configure clients to trust the certificates issued by your certification authority is to install a certification authority certificate on their computers. The Certificate Services web site allows users to retrieve such a certificate on their own, as shown in Figure A-9.

When users download the certificate, they should store it in their computers' Trusted Root Certification Authorities store, as shown in Figure A-10.

Once they do, your certification authority will be added to the list of certificate publishers their computer trusts, as shown in Figure A-11.

You can also create a Group Policy Object (GPO) that modifies the list of trusted publishers on all your company's computers. You'll find this policy in *Computer Configuration\Windows Settings\Security Settings\ Public Key Policies\Trusted Root Certification Authorities*. This is a great way to configure all the computers on your network to trust your certification authority, although it won't allow you to configure outside computers.

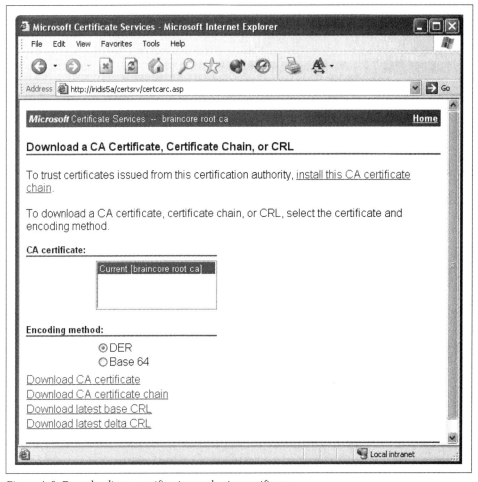

Figure A-9. Downloading a certification authority certificate

Configuring Your Email Client

Users' email software usually requires some configuration in order to use their newly issued digital certificates. A wide variety of email clients—including Microsoft Outlook Express, Microsoft Outlook, Netscape Communicator, and Lotus Notes—support secure email.

 In this section, I'll focus on configuring Microsoft Outlook Secure email for other email software is very similar, although you should consult your software's documentation for details.

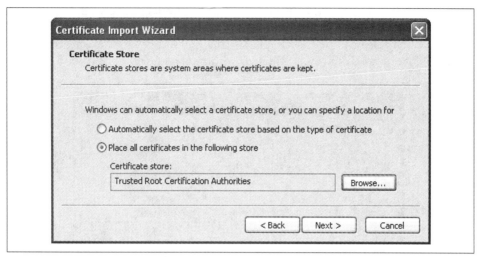

Figure A-10. Selecting a certificate store for the new certificate

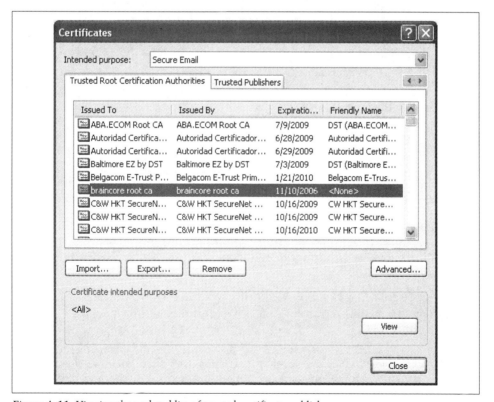

Figure A-11. Viewing the updated list of trusted certificate publishers

Outlook 2002's Options dialog box includes a Security panel, shown in Figure A-12. The Security panel lets you configure Outlook to encrypt or sign *all* outgoing messages. You may also choose to encrypt or sign specific messages by using the appropriate toolbar buttons or menu commands within each message you type.

Figure A-12. Outlook security options

Clicking the Settings button displays Outlook's Change Security Settings dialog box, shown in Figure A-13. As shown, you can specify encryption methods and, most importantly, select the certificates that Outlook will use to digitally sign and encrypt messages.

When you select a certificate, Outlook displays the list of certificates installed on your system that are marked as usable for email security, as shown in Figure A-14.

All certificates are not created equal. When a certification authority issues a certificate, it marks the certificate with certain approved uses. Email software cannot use a certificate unless that certificate is marked for use with secure email.

Figure A-13. Outlook secure email settings

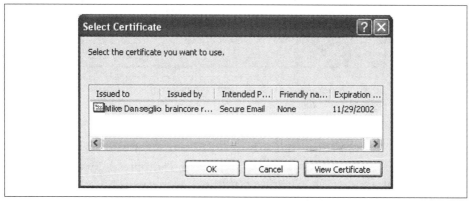

Figure A-14. Selecting a certificate for Outlook to use

In the certificate selection dialog box, you can select any certificate and then click View Certificate to see the details, as shown in Figure A-15. The certificate's details will show the uses the certificate is good for and indicate whether you have the private key associated with the certificate. The certificate's private key is required for Outlook to work properly. Outlook's configuration must also be changed from the default, as described in the "Outlook's Default Encryption Settings" sidebar.

Figure A-15. Viewing certificate details; note the very bottom line of text, which indicates that you have the private key for this certificate

Non-Microsoft Secure Email

What if you're not using Microsoft Outlook, or a similar solution, for email? What if you don't want to invest in expensive certificates or implement a certificate hierarchy? For years, Internet users have been using Pretty Good Privacy (PGP), a powerful and flexible solution for secure email, even across operating systems.

 How good is "pretty good" privacy? Since the newest editions of PGP use top-notch 128-bit encryption, the answer is "pretty great." While it's certainly possible to break PGP's encryption, doing so would take several powerful computers several *years* of dedicated effort. Odds are, by the time they broke the encryption, the information thus revealed would be useless. In practice, because of the time and resources required to break this level of encryption, pretty much nobody tries.

PGP is an open source (*www.opensource.org*) project of the PGP Corporation (*www. pgp.com*). The PGP product is available in a variety of editions, including free editions, enterprise-ready editions, and more. PGP provides 128-bit encryption for email and attachments, tools to manage PGP deployments within an enterprise, and robust cross-platform support, including the latest Windows, Linux, Apple, and Unix operating systems. PGP even integrates directly with Outlook, Notes, Group-Wise, Eudora, and a number of other email clients for easier operation. In addition to providing encrypted email, PGP can also be used to digitally sign email, ensuring that recipients know your email is from you and was not altered in transit.

A number of online services—including HushMail (*www.hushmail.com*)—provide secure email delivery. These online services allow you to establish an SSL-secured session in your web browser, compose or upload an email, and have that email digitally encrypted and sent. These web-based services are great for users who have only an occasional need for secure email and don't want to implement a complete secure email solution.

PGP, by the way (along with the many PGP-compatible products out there), requires PKI, too. Generally, you'll obtain a certificate from a commercial certification authority so that everyone will trust your certificate and have access to your public keys. Solutions like HushMail don't generally require a key purchase, although they do often require their own registration and usage fees that offset any savings you might see in not buying a certificate.

Summary

In this appendix, I've introduced you to the concept of secure email and explained how it works from both the sender's and recipient's point of view. You've also learned the requirements for secure email, as well as the pros and cons of using a commercial certification authority instead of your own certification authority. Finally, you learned the basic steps to configure an email client to use secure email. As businesses rely more and more upon email for mission-critical communications, secure email will become more and more prevalent, ensuring that critical communications are authentic and secure.

Index

We'd like to hear your suggestions for improving our indexes. Send email to *index@oreilly.com*.

baselining DHCP traffic, 249
Basic authentication, 276, 287
best practices
    for physical security, 42–43
    for software restrictions, 121
biometrics, 232
    vs. passwords, 242
blocking ports as security measure, 291
blocking/overriding capabilities of GPOs, 79
boundary security, 26
brute force attacks on passwords, 23
bucket brigade attacks, 170
built-in security templates, 95–97

C

CA (see certification authority)
cable plants
    as risk factors, 34
    securing, 41
cables
    as risk factors, 36
    securing transmissions, 41
cameras, securing data centers with, 39, 43
CAPI (Cryptographic API), 67
    requesting certificates and, 181
    writing custom PKI-aware software, 224
CAPICOM (CAPI Component Object
        Model), 224
card key systems, 33
    controlling security vulnerabilities, 39, 43
CDPs (CRL distribution points), 183
    choosing for private certification
            hierarchies, 202
    configuring for root CA, 211–214
    publishing CRL of offline root CA, 215
centralizing remote access
        authentication, 346
Cert Publishers group, 317
Certificate Export Wizard, 175
certificate hierarchy, 173
certificate policy (CP),
        constructing, 207–209
certificate practice statement (CPS),
        constructing, 207–209
certificate revocation lists (see CRLs)
certificate rules
    best practices suggest using, 121
    creating new rules, 118
    for identifying applications, 115
Certificate Services
    issuing email certificates with, 400
    in Windows Server 2003, 5

certificate templates, 8, 181
    configuring digital signature
            certificates, 197
    configuring encryption certificates, 219
certificate-based authentication, configuring
        IPSec for, 167
certificates, 169–175
    archiving private keys and, 178, 180
    backing up private keys and, 177
    benefits of, 173
    deploying client certificates, 189–192
    distributing, 175
    enrollment applications, 191
    expiration dates of, 177
    exporting
        to floppy disks, 63
        without private keys, 175
    formatting, 172
    importing received certificates, 176
    issued by certification authorities, 180
    origins of, 174
    processing requests for, 181
    publishing, 182
    requesting, 180
    supported by Windows Server 2003 for
            IPSec communication, 152
    types of, 171
    Windows Certificates snap-in, 172
    (see also private certification hierarchies)
Certificates MMC snap-in, 178, 224
certification authority, 170–186
    commercial vendors, 397
    configurable certificate templates and, 8
    configuring clients to trust your
            certificates, 401
    functions of, 180
    how it works, 180–183
    improvements to, 7
    private, 185
    processing requests for certificates, 181
    public, 183
    requesting certificates from, 180
    role separation and, 9
    sending digitally signed email, 393
    using your own, 398–401
certification authority certificates, 172
certification hierarchies
    choosing between public/private
            CAs, 183–186
    private (see private certification
            hierarchies)
CGI (Common Gateway Interface)
        applications, supported by IIS, 273

L

L2TP (Layer 2 Tunneling Protocol), 352
laptops
  chain locks and, 42
  educating users about traveling with, 75
  lost-and-found scenario at Sea-Tac
    airport, 59
  protecting, using multilayered
    approach, 72–74
  as risk factors, 33, 57
  securing, 39
Layer 2 Tunneling Protocol (L2TP), 352
layered security, 43
LDAP (Lightweight Directory Access
    Protocol) interface, 294
LM (LAN Manager)
  configuring, 128–131
  disabling NTLM variants, 129–131
  disabling storage of password hashes, 128
  history of, 123
LMCompatibility parameter, 130
local file security for shared computers, 53
Local Group Policy, 77
Local Security Policy snap-in (MMC), 26
lock icon (public key cryptography), 22
locks
  account lockout policies, 84–87
  controlling security vulnerabilities, 33, 43
  for laptops, 39, 42, 75
  for wiring closets, 41
logon auditing on domain controllers,
    configuring, 371–373
logon events, auditing, 373
logon process using smart cards, 233
logon scripts
  enrolling/installing certificates with, 191
  stored in domain controllers, 307
Logon Workstations attribute, 334
  configuring, 316
logs
  analyzing DHCP logs, 253–255
  clearing when full, 93
  for IPSec-generated events, 163
  providing forensic evidence of
    attacks, 290
  reviewing web server logs, 288
  security/system logs used in
    auditing, 91–93
lost private keys, restoring, 179
lost smart cards, 237
LSDOU (local, site, domain, organizational
    unit), 79

M

MAC addresses, 37
malicious code dangers, 111
man in the middle attacks, 111, 170
manual trusts (Windows NT), 297
Mark Keys as Exportable option, 241
master key perfect forward secrecy (PFS), 164
master keys, protecting with Syskey, 70
maximum life for
  renewals of user tickets, 140
  service tickets, 140
  user tickets, 140
maximum tolerance for computer clock
    synchronization, 141
MBSA (Microsoft Baseline Security Analyzer)
  as an attacker's tool, 390
  determining current security status
    with, 387–390
Microsoft CA (certificate authority), 223
Microsoft Management Console (MMC)
  Local Security Policy snap-in, 26
  Routing and Remote Access snap-in, 343,
    345, 358
  Security Configuration and Analysis
    console snap-in, 98
Microsoft Operations Framework
    (MOF), 364
Microsoft Outlook, configuring for secure
    email, 402–406
Microsoft Software Update Services, 381
  integrating with MBSA, 388
Microsoft Solutions Framework (MSF), 364
middle-tier applications and Kerberos
    impersonation, 138
misconfigurations, reducing likelihood of, 363
Mitnick, Kevin, 31
MMC (Microsoft Management Console)
  Local Security Policy snap-in, 26
  Routing and Remote Access snap-in, 343,
    345, 358
  Security Configuration and Analysis
    console snap-in, 98
modes of protection used by Syskey, 70
  configuring mode 2, 72
MS-CHAP (Microsoft Challenge-Handshake
    Authentication Protocol), 348
MS-CHAP v2 (Microsoft
    Challenge-Handshake
    Authentication Protocol,
    Version 2), 348
multimaster domain concept (Active
    Directory), 295

secure configurations, deploying with
   security templates, 95–108
Secure Domain Controller Security
   template, 96
secure dynamic updates (DNS), 259
   enabling, 264
secure email
   digitally signed messages,
      sending, 392–395
   downsides to using, 396
   encrypted messages, sending, 394–396
   HushMail online service, 407
   implementing, 397–407
   non-Microsoft products, 406
   PGP (Pretty Good Privacy) product, 406
   two forms of, 391
secure file shares, setting up, 50–53
Secure Server (Require Security) default
   configuration, 158
Secure Sockets Layer (SSL)
   public key encryption and, 22
Secure Workstation Security template, 96
securedc.inf template, 96
securews.inf template, 96
security
   Active Directory features, 296–300
   awareness and education programs, 32
   basics of, 10–29
   checklist, example of, 28
   concerns with DNS, 260
   default settings
      for upgrades, 312
      through GPOs, 308–313
   determining status of, using
      MBSA, 387–390
   DHCP server authorization, 247
   enforcement mechanisms, 14–17
      administration-based, 16
      technology-based, 15
   enforcing with Group Policy, 82–94
   for files, provided by NTFS, 47
   importance of, 10–13
   lack of, in DHCP, 246
   layered, 43
   for networks, 26–28
   physical (see physical security)
   problems with web servers, 273–275
   providing for
      Active Directory objects, 327–333
      domain controllers, 333–340
      domains, 313–324
      forests, 324–327

remote access and its risks, 341–359
smart cards and, 230–243
for wireless networks, 42
Security Accounts Manager (see SAM)
Security Association (SA) and IPSec
   drivers, 151
security breaches, reducing likelihood
   of, 363
Security Configuration and Analysis (SCA)
   toolset, 97–103
   analyzing security settings, 101–103
   creating SCA console, 98
   creating security databases, 98
   importing security templates, 99
security databases
   analyzing security settings, 101–103
   creating, 98
   creating templates from, 105
   importing security templates, 99
security design in Windows Server 2003, 3
security enhancements in Windows Server
   2003
   Enterprise Server Edition, 8
   Standard Server Edition, 7–8
   and Windows XP, 5, 57
security features in Windows Server
   2003, 3–5
security identifiers (SIDs), 126
Security Log, 28
   verifying IPSec operation with IKE
      logging, 164
security policies, 11, 360–362
   attributes of, 365
   benefits of, 363
   common characteristics of, 12–13
   components of, 16
   creating, 364–367
   keeping passwords secret, 25
   monitoring, 368
   political aspects of, 11
security procedures, 360–362
   benefits of, 363
   creating, 367–369
   monitoring, 368
security settings
   analyzing, 101–103
   audit policy, controlling, 92
   built-in security templates and, 95
   controlling, 107
   identifying security needs, 82
   password policy, controlling, 86

About the Author

Mike Danseglio is a Program Manager in the Security Solutions group at Microsoft Corporation. He has worked in the fields of security and technology for the last decade. He holds several technical certifications, including MCSE and CISSP. He has developed training seminars and taught extensively on topics such as cryptography, security technology, and attacks and countermeasures. His recent projects include writing security documentation for Windows XP and the Windows Server 2003 family, as well as working on a host of white papers and articles. He also works on security feature development for Microsoft Windows.

Colophon

Our look is the result of reader comments, our own experimentation, and feedback from distribution channels. Distinctive covers complement our distinctive approach to technical topics, breathing personality and life into potentially dry subjects.

The animal on the cover of *Securing Windows Server 2003* is a wandering albatross (*Diomedea exulans*). Named for its unique flying ability, the wandering albatross covers the Southern hemisphere by wing, landing only to mate and scavenge. In nonbreeding years, it has been known to circumnavigate the globe.

The largest of the seabirds, the wandering albatross can achieve a wingspan of almost 3.5 meters and can reach up to 1.35 meters in length. (Females are somewhat smaller than males.) From a distance, the bird appears entirely white, except for its pinkish beak. Viewed up close, however, it has fine black lines on its neck, breast, tail, and wingtips.

The wandering albatross can live up to 60 years. It matures at around 12 years of age. The albatross socializes and courts during its adolescent years, then mates for life. During its lifetime, it will breed every two years. Its preferred food and drink include saltwater, cuttlefish, squid, and food scraps cast off from ships.

An endangered species, the wandering albatross is threatened by surface longline fishing for tuna. The albatross may ingest baited hooks used in such fishing. Tending to follow sailing ships, the wandering albatross has been the inspiration for much marine folklore and poetry.

Claire Cloutier was the production editor for *Securing Windows Server 2003*. Brian MacDonald was the developmental editor; Norma Emory was the copyeditor; and Linley Dolby was the proofreader. Linley Dolby, Philip Dangler, and Darren Kelly provided quality control. Caitrin McCullough, Marlowe Shaeffer, and Mary Agner provided production assistance. Judy Hoer wrote the index.

Emma Colby designed the cover of this book, based on a series design by Edie Freedman. The cover image is a 19th-century engraving from the Dover Pictorial

Archive. Emma Colby produced the cover layout with QuarkXPress 4.1 using Adobe's ITC Garamond font.

Melanie Wang designed the interior layout, based on a series design by David Futato. This book was converted by Joe Wizda to FrameMaker 5.5.6 with a format conversion tool created by Erik Ray, Jason McIntosh, Neil Walls, and Mike Sierra that uses Perl and XML technologies. The text font is Linotype Birka; the heading font is Adobe Myriad Condensed; and the code font is LucasFont's TheSans Mono Condensed. The illustrations that appear in the book were produced by Robert Romano and Jessamyn Read using Macromedia FreeHand MX and Adobe Photoshop CS. The tip and warning icons were drawn by Christopher Bing. This colophon was written by Meghan Lydon.

Better than e-books

Search
inside electronic versions of thousands of books

Browse
books by category. With Safari researching any topic is a snap

Find
answers in an instant

Read books from cover to cover. Or, simply click to the page you need.

Search Safari! The premier electronic reference library for programmers and IT professionals

Related Titles Available from O'Reilly

Security

802.11 Security

Building Internet Firewalls, *2nd Edition*

Building Secure Servers with Linux

Cisco IOS Access Lists

Database Nation

Hardening Cisco Routers

Java Security

Kerberos: The Definitive Guide

Linux iptables Pocket Reference

Linux Security Cookbook

Malicious Mobile Code

Managing RAID on Linux

Network Security Assessment

Network Security Hacks

Network Security with OpenSSL

Practical Unix and Internet Security, *3rd Edition*

Programming .NET Security

RADIUS

Secure Coding: Principles and Practices

Secure Programming Cookbook with C and C++

Securing Windows NT/2000 Servers for the Internet

Security Warrior

SSH, The Secure Shell: The Definitive Guide

Web Security, Privacy and Commerce, *2nd Edition*

O'REILLY®

Our books are available at most retail and online bookstores.
To order direct: 1-800-998-9938 • *order@oreilly.com* • *www.oreilly.com*
Online editions of most O'Reilly titles are available by subscription at *safari.oreilly.com*

Keep in touch with O'Reilly

1. Download examples from our books

To find example files for a book, go to:

www.oreilly.com/catalog

select the book, and follow the "Examples" link.

2. Register your O'Reilly books

Register your book at *register.oreilly.com*

Why register your books?
Once you've registered your O'Reilly books you can:

- Win O'Reilly books, T-shirts or discount coupons in our monthly drawing.
- Get special offers available only to registered O'Reilly customers.
- Get catalogs announcing new books (US and UK only).
- Get email notification of new editions of the O'Reilly books you own.

3. Join our email lists

Sign up to get topic-specific email announcements of new books and conferences, special offers, and O'Reilly Network technology newsletters at:

elists.oreilly.com

It's easy to customize your free elists subscription so you'll get exactly the O'Reilly news you want.

4. Get the latest news, tips, and tools

www.oreilly.com

- "Top 100 Sites on the Web"—PC Magazine
- CIO Magazine's Web Business 50 Awards

Our web site contains a library of comprehensive product information (including book excerpts and tables of contents), downloadable software, background articles, interviews with technology leaders, links to relevant sites, book cover art, and more.

5. Work for O'Reilly

Check out our web site for current employment opportunities:

jobs.oreilly.com

6. Contact us

O'Reilly & Associates
1005 Gravenstein Hwy North
Sebastopol, CA 95472 USA

TEL: 707-827-7000 or 800-998-9938
(6am to 5pm PST)

FAX: 707-829-0104

order@oreilly.com
For answers to problems regarding your order or our products. To place a book order online, visit:

www.oreilly.com/order_new

catalog@oreilly.com
To request a copy of our latest catalog.

booktech@oreilly.com
For book content technical questions or corrections.

corporate@oreilly.com
For educational, library, government, and corporate sales.

proposals@oreilly.com
To submit new book proposals to our editors and product managers.

international@oreilly.com
For information about our international distributors or translation queries. For a list of our distributors outside of North America check out:

international.oreilly.com/distributors.html

adoption@oreilly.com
For information about academic use of O'Reilly books, visit:

academic.oreilly.com